Joseph Fitzgerald Molloy

Court life below stairs

London under the last Georges, 1760-1830

Joseph Fitzgerald Molloy

Court life below stairs
London under the last Georges, 1760-1830

ISBN/EAN: 9783337108014

Printed in Europe, USA, Canada, Australia, Japan

Cover: Foto ©Suzi / pixelio.de

More available books at **www.hansebooks.com**

COURT LIFE BELOW STAIRS

OR

LONDON UNDER THE LAST GEORGES

1760—1830

BY

J. FITZGERALD MOLLOY

AUTHOR OF
'THE LIFE AND ADVENTURES OF PEG WOFFINGTON,' ETC.

A NEW EDITION

WITH PORTRAITS OF GEORGE III. AND GEORGE IV.

DOWNEY & CO. LIMITED
12 YORK STREET, COVENT GARDEN, LONDON
1897

PREFACE TO THE FIRST EDITION.

THE popularity of the first volumes of this work—practically proved by a demand which sent the book into a second edition in three weeks, and out of print in as many months—has induced me to continue the pictures of Court Life under the Georges.

The reigns of George III. and George IV. are no less interesting and instructive, to those who study the social history and manners of courts, than those of George I. and George II.; and, it is mournful to assert, are far more scandalous. George III., it is true, was from the day of his marriage a moral man; but the grossly voluptuous and glaringly corrupt example of his immediate predecessors yet affected the conduct of his courtiers and tainted them grievously. Concerning George IV. there can be no second opinion.

As in the former volumes, so in these, I have omitted as much as possible all reference to politics, save where they are responsible for the actions of Kings, Princes, and Courtiers. No statement is made without authority; and due care has been taken to paint faithful portraits of the various characters introduced. To give a vivid picture of the Court life, neither time nor labour has been spared. For this purpose, I have consulted upwards of five hundred volumes, principally autobiographies, biographies, correspondence, and diaries, likewise manuscripts, pamphlets, newspapers, and the ballad literature of the day.

J. FITZGERALD MOLLOY.

COURT LIFE BELOW STAIRS.

CHAPTER I.

The Child Born to be King—A Dull, Good Boy—'Uncommonly full of Princely Prejudices'—Death of Frederick, Prince of Wales—What the Princess said of the King—My Lord Bute and the Dowager—The New Prince of Wales—None Suffered to Approach Him—Her Highness of Wolfenbüttel and the King—The Story of Hannah Lightfoot—The King is Dead—A New Order of Things.

On the 4th of June, 1738, a male child was born to their Royal Highnesses Frederick and Augusta, Prince and Princess of Wales, who subsequently gained the reputation of being the dullest prince in Europe. It happened that this child born to be King first saw the light in Norfolk House, St. James's Square. Only a few months previously, His Sacred Majesty George II. had quarrelled with the heir-apparent, and driven him and his family from St. James's Palace.

A little while after this infant had come into the world, he gave such strong indications of his intentions of immediately quitting it, that it was deemed advisable to have him baptized at once, that he might depart a Christian. Dr. Secker, Lord Bishop of Oxford and Rector of St. James's parish, was therefore summoned in hot haste, and performed the ceremony; according to the manuscript entry in the register of births in St. James's parish, 'the name pronounced upon the occasion was George William Frederick.'

When this triple-named Prince arrived at the age of six years, his education commenced, and he and his brother Edward, afterwards Duke of York, were placed under the charge of Dr. Ayscough. This reverend gentleman had won the Prince of Wales's Mammon-loving heart by his management of the privy purse. Mr. Pelham remembered being told by a very worthy man that 'Dr. Ayscough was a great rogue.' He was certainly a man of parts, not adverse to his own advancement, nor bound by any narrow orthodox prejudices; he could flatter, mimic, and preach heterodoxical doctrines with equal ease, and indeed his various talents soon enabled him to become Bishop of Bristol.

Under this tutor, the Prince, who grew up a dull, good boy, made but little progress. He had indeed, without any direction from his reverend preceptor, learned several pages of hymns writ by one Dr. Doddridge, a Dissenting clergyman; but it was doubtful if he understood them. At the age of eleven years, the future King of Great Britain could not read the English language correctly; when the Princess of Wales was informed of this, and complained to Dr. Ayscough, he cheerfully replied that it mattered little, 'the Prince could make Latin verses.'

Later on, his preceptors were Dr. Thomas, Bishop o Peterborough, Dr. Hayter, Bishop of Norwich, and Mr. George Scott. Many years afterwards, when the Prince was King, he complained that 'most serious inconvenience had arisen from disagreements and intrigues amongst those who were entrusted with the care of his education.' The Lord Bishop of Norwich he considered 'an intriguing man, influenced in his conduct by the disappointment he met with in failing to get the Archbishopric of Canterbury,' and added, 'that his Lordship was the author of the gross and wicked calumny on George Scott, accusing him, a man of the purest mind and most innocent conduct, of having attempted to poison his wife.'

In 1751, Frederick, Prince of Wales, after a few days' illness, died in the arms of his favourite, Desnoyers, the French dancing-master, who had just been playing the fiddle to him, whilst the gay courtiers in the next room were diverting themselves with cards. From the date of his death, the eyes of the nation were turned on George William Frederick, then a lad of thirteen, who suddenly became heir to the throne. When the news was conveyed to him of his father's death, he turned pale and laid his hand on his breast. The courtly Ayscough asked him if he were unwell.

'I feel,' said the lad, 'something here, just as I did when I saw the two workmen fall from the scaffold at Kew.'

Ten days after the Prince's death, the King paid a visit to the Princess and her children, and exhibited unusual emotion, wept, embraced the young Princess Augusta, and told her brothers 'they must be brave boys, obedient to their mother, and thus deserve the fortune to which they were born.' A month later, George William Frederick was created Prince of Wales, and placed by the King under the governorship of Lord Harcourt. According to Horace Walpole, Harcourt was a civil and sheepish man, who thought 'that he discharged his trust conscientiously, if on no account he neglected to make the Prince turn out his toes.' His Royal Highness was a quiet youth, who, according to his grandsire, 'was good for nothing except to read the Bible to his mother.' That lady had not a very high opinion of her son: 'he was a very honest boy, but she wished he was a little more forward and less childish at his age, and she hoped his preceptors would improve him.' She furthermore volunteered the information that 'those about him knew no more [of him] than if they had never seen him.' Lord Waldegrave, who succeeded Lord Harcourt as governor to the Prince, says he found His Royal Highness 'uncommonly full of princely prejudices contracted in the nursery and improved by the bed-chamber women and pages of the back-stairs.' There can be no doubt that much of the narrow-mindedness and bigotry which afterwards distinguished George III. was due to his mother's early training, and to the strict influence she held over him. From his earliest years she strove to keep him apart from the nobility of his own age, and, as he grew up, her vigilance in this respect increased—a fact which one of George III.'s sons afterwards remarked was 'an unfortunate circumstance,' of which he 'saw evident marks almost daily.'

When spoken to on the subject of allowing the Prince to mix more freely with his future subjects, she declared she 'was highly sensible how necessary it was that the Prince should keep company with men, but such was the universal profligacy, such the character and conduct of the young people of distinction, that she was really afraid to have them near her children; she well knew that women could not inform him, for their behaviour was indecent, low, and much against their own interests by making themselves so very cheap.'

During her husband's lifetime, the Princess had carefully suppressed her inclinations to meddle in public affairs; but when he was removed, and her ambition of one day becoming a Queen frustrated, she determined that, if she could not govern personally, she would at least rule the kingdom through her son. She was, however, a clever woman, and adopted a politic course of action. On the morning of the Prince's death, she rose at eight o'clock, 'and burned, or said she burned,' as Horace Walpole writes, all her husband's papers. Her next step was to recommend herself and her children to His Majesty, whom she heartily detested.

'The King and she,' says Walpole, 'both took their parts at once; she of flinging herself entirely into his hands and studying nothing but his pleasure, but with winding what interest she got with him to the advantage of her own and the Prince's friends; the King of acting the tender grandfather; which he who had never acted the tender father grew so pleased with representing, that he soon became it in earnest.'

But, as she told Bubb Dodington in one of the confidential conversations which took place when they had dined and played at comet, she did not allow the King's kindness to the children, or his civility to herself, to impose on her. 'She wished the King was less civil, and that he put less of their money into his pocket; that he had got full £30,000 per annum by the poor Prince's death. If he would but have given them the Duchy of Cornwall to have paid his debts, it would have been something. Should resentments be carried beyond the grave? Should the innocent suffer? Was it becoming for so great a King to leave his son's debts unpaid?' Bubb Dodington said it was impossible to new-make people; the King could not now be altered. She said she could not bear it, nor help sometimes giving the King to understand her in the strongest and most disagreeable light. She had done it more than once, and she would tell how it happened the last time.

'You know,' continued she, 'that the Crown has a power of resumption of Carlton House and gardens for a certain sum. The King had not long since an inclination to see them, and he came to make me a visit there; we walked in the gardens, and he, seemingly mighty pleased with them, commended them much, and told me that he was extremely glad I had got so very pretty a place. I replied it was a very pretty place, but that the prettiness of a place was an objection to it, when one was not sure to keep it. The King said that there was indeed a power of resumption in the Crown for

£4,000, but surely I could not imagine that it could ever be made use of against me; how could such a thought come into my head? I answered no, it was not that which I was afraid of, but I was afraid there were those who had a better right to it than either the Crown or I. He said, "Oh! no, no, I do not understand that; that cannot be." I replied I did not pretend to understand these things, but I was afraid there were such people. He said, "Oh! I know nothing of that; I do not understand it," and immediately turned the discourse.'

So far did her good graces succeed in winning the King's regard that she was appointed Regent in case of His Majesty's death, to the exclusion of the King's only surviving son, William, Duke of Cumberland, commonly called Billy the Butcher, from the atrocities he had countenanced after the battle of Culloden. Between the Princess and the Duke a hearty hatred existed, which deepened to distrust on her side, and to jealousy on his, because of the power which this appointment might give her. She spoke of the Duke's discourtesy, and complained that, though she had been at Kew the whole summer, he had never vouchsafed her one visit; and, when she was ill and reported dying, he had never sent to make inquiries regarding her health. Dreading and disliking him, she took care to instil the same feelings into her son's mind, and to make him acquainted with what has been called 'the national antipathy' towards the man 'who loved blood.' So thoroughly did she impart this dread, which served not only then, but in the future, to destroy all influence which the Duke might otherwise have had over his nephew, that one day, when the Prince was alone with his uncle, the latter, to amuse him, having taken down a sword and drawn it, the boy turned pale with fright, believing he was about to be murdered.

The maternal influence over the Prince was blended and strengthened by that of John, Earl of Bute, who soon became a power in the royal household. Horace Walpole speaks of him as a 'Scotchman who, having no estate, had passed his youth in studying mathematics in his own little island, then simples in the hedges about Twickenham, and at five-and-thirty had fallen in love with his own figure, which he produced at masquerades in becoming dresses, and in plays which he acted in private companies with a set of his own relations.'

His love of masquerades and plays was sufficient to recommend him to Frederick, Prince of Wales, who was a thorough dilettante, and was never so happy as when surrounded by players and fiddlers and such children of the Muses. Lord Bute was soon made one of the lords of the bed-chamber, and after the Prince's death he continued the friend and counsellor of the Princess. So assiduous indeed were his attentions to her, that the public were not long in discovering they were prompted by a much warmer attachment than that of mere loyalty.

'He has a good person, fine legs, and a theatrical air of the greatest importance,' says Lord Waldegrave; who pleasantly adds: 'The late Prince of Wales, who was not over-nice in the choice of Ministers, used frequently to say that Bute was a fine showy man, who would make an excellent ambassador in a Court where there was no business. Such was His Royal Highness's opinion of his political abilities, but the sagacity of the Princess had discovered other accomplishments of which the Prince her husband may not perhaps have been the most competent judge.'

Whether the Princess was at Kew or Carlton House, my Lord Bute's visits continued with equal regularity.

'The eagerness of the pages of the back-stairs to let her know whenever Lord Bute arrived,' says Horace Walpole, 'and some other symptoms, contributed to dispel the ideas that had been conceived of the rigour of her widowhood. On the other hand, the favoured personage, naturally ostentatious of his person, and of haughty carriage, seemed by no means desirous of concealing his conquest. His bows grew more theatric, his graces contracted some meaning, and the beauty of his leg was constantly displayed in the eyes of the poor, captivated Princess. Indeed, the nice observers of the Court thermometer, who often foresee a change of weather before it actually happens, had long thought that Her Royal Highness was likely to choose younger Ministers than that formal piece of empty mystery, Cresset; or the matron-like decorum of Sir George Lee . . . . Her simple husband had forced an air of intrigue even on his wife. When he affected to retire into gloomy *allées* with Lady Middlesex, he used to bid the Princess walk with Lord Bute. As soon as the Prince was dead, they walked more and more, in honour of his memory.'

For reasons which had the object of forwarding his ambitious schemes, **Lord Bute** added his efforts to those of the Princess, in cutting the Prince off as much as possible from his grandfather's courtiers, and 'none but their immediate and lowest creatures were suffered to approach him. Except at his levées, where none are seen as they are, he saw nobody, and none saw him.'

'The Prince,' says one of the gossips of the time, 'lived shut up with his mother and Lord Bute, and must have thrown them under some difficulties: their connection was not easily reconcilable to the devotion which they had infused into the Prince; the Princess could not wish him always present, and yet dreaded his being out of her sight. His brother Edward, who received a thousand mortifications, was seldom suffered to be with him; and the Princess Augusta, now a woman, was, to facilitate some privacy for the Princess, dismissed from supping with her mother, and sent back to cheese-cakes and her little sister Elizabeth, on pretence that meat at night would fatten her too much.'

Their power over him was evinced on the occasion

of the King's proposing that he should marry; the Prince was only eighteen, but His Majesty was anxious to see him settled before his (George II.'s) death, lest afterwards the Princess might contrive an alliance for him with one of the Saxe-Gotha family, her relations, for whom His Majesty had no predilection. Accordingly, when at Hanover, he met the Princess of Wolfenbüttel, niece of Frederick II. of Prussia, with whose accomplishments and amiability he became so enamoured that he was desirous of making her his granddaughter, as he was too old to make her his wife. When, however, the Princess Dowager caught a rumour of this, she waxed exceeding wroth at the possible prospect of her power over her son being interfered with and perhaps overthrown. She threw off all pretence of subservient obedience to the King, and metaphorically shook her fist in his face. She should 'let him know how ill she took it; that she had eight other children to be provided for; that she hoped he would think of doing for them, and not leave her eldest son those young children to take care of before he had one of his own; that it was probable the Prince might have so many, that hers could not expect much provision.' Moreover, she disliked the proposed alliance. 'The young woman was said to be handsome, and have good qualities and abundance of wit, but if she took after her mother, the Duchess of Brunswick-Wolfenbüttel, who was the most intriguing, meddling, satirical, sarcastic person in the world, who made mischief wherever she went, she would certainly not do for George.'

Armed, therefore, with right womanly jealousy, she informed the Prince he was about being made a victim to gratify the King's private interests in the little Electorate of Hanover, and fearing lest the contemplation of such a sacrifice might not prove disagreeable to one possessing 'a vigorous, healthy constitution, to whom it might reasonably be supposed that a matrimonial companion would not be unacceptable,' Her Highness of Wolfenbüttel was represented as being hideous and hateful; indeed, a kind of female beast with whom Prince Beauty must not wed. The Prince therefore conceived a strong aversion to his proposed bride, and, to His Majesty's great chagrin, refused her hand, which so incensed the old man, then past his seventieth year, that he declared, if he were but twenty years younger, she should never have been refused by a Prince of Wales, for he should have made her Queen of England.

This act on the part of the Prince showed the King how much his grandson was governed by his mother, and he resolved, if possible, to remove him from her influence and from her residence at Leicester House. As he had now reached his eighteenth year, and was therefore legally of age, His Majesty sent a message to the Prince informing him that he would grant him an income of £40,000 a year and settle an establishment for him, and that he had already given orders that apartments in St. James's and in Kensington Palace should be fitted up for his use. The Princess, however, was not to be outwitted; she made her son write to accept the £40,000, but at the same time entreating His Majesty 'not to divide him from his mother, which would be a most sensible affliction to both.' It is worth noting that at the time he wrote this it was well known, as Bubb Dodington informs us, 'that he did not live with his mother either in town or country,' though the courtier carefully refrains from mentioning where or with whom the Prince resided.

To accept the annuity and decline a separate residence for the maintenance of which it was intended, was a possibility that the King had not anticipated; but it was now impossible for him to withdraw an allowance which had not been made conditional with the full acceptance of the offer, and so matters were allowed to rest for some time.

George William Frederick, though the dullest Prince in Europe, and perhaps the most carefully guarded, proved that he, like all common humanity, was susceptible to love's ways, by falling a victim to the tender passion on more occasions than one. Concerning what was probably the first of his amours, a tale hangs of which many versions have been given. So far, however, as the story can be cleared from its surrounding mystery, it runs as follows:—

Hannah Lightfoot, a young and beautiful girl, called 'the fair Quaker,' lived with her uncle, who kept a linen-draper's shop at the corner of St. James's Market, where the Prince frequently saw her as he passed from Leicester House, his mother's residence, to St. James's Palace. His heart was immediately touched by the passion which levels all ranks, and he began to sigh for the companionship of the fascinating Hannah. Pondering over the means by which his object could be accomplished without alarming the fair Quaker, he conceived the idea of engaging the services of one of those discreet friends who are ever ready to aid Princes in the pursuit of their desires.

His choice at once fell on Miss Chudleigh, a courtier with whom his father and grandfather had been in love while she was maid-of-honour to his mother, and who had varied the course of her romance by committing bigamy and making sad havoc of the decalogue generally. Such an office as the Prince trusted to her skill was naturally in accordance with her taste, and with that brilliant talent for intrigue which she had already exercised with so much personal success. Nor was she found wanting on this occasion; she soon discovered a convenient and private place for a rendezvous at the house of one Perryn at Knightsbridge, where the royal lover met the fair lady, and became yet more deeply enamoured of her charms.

A statement has been made in 'The Secret History of the Court of England, by the Right Honourable Lady Anne Hamilton, sister of his Grace the Duke of Hamilton and Brandon, and of the Countess of Dunmore,' published in

1832, that the Prince was secretly married to Hannah Lightfoot; and this assertion was repeated in a now forgotten pamphlet, entitled, 'The Appeal for Royalty,' by no less a personage than Lavinia Jannette Horton Ryves, 'calling herself Princess of Cumberland and Duchess of Lancaster.' Moreover, in the latter a copy of a supposed certificate of marriage between the Quaker and the Prince was given, signed by William Pitt as one of the witnesses. This certificate, however, at a late memorable trial, was pronounced 'a gross and rank forgery.'

The most probable story regarding the royal love-affair is that which is told in the *Monthly Magazine* for April, 1821, the year after the King's death, and subsequently authenticated by other statements from various writers. This narrative states that, the royal lover's relatives taking alarm at his passion for Hannah Lightfoot, Miss Chudleigh called on Isaac Axford, 'shopman to Barton the grocer on Ludgate Hill,' furthermore described as 'a poor-hearted fellow,' and proposed that he should marry Hannah, when a considerable sum of money would be given him; to which he consented, and immediately after the ceremony she was carried away by the Prince. This version of the royal intrigue is repeated with some minor details in a pamphlet entitled, 'An Historical Fragment.' A friend of the Lightfoot family, who received a letter on the subject of the marriage from a cousin of the fair Quaker's, sent a copy of the epistle to the *Monthly Magazine* of October, 1821. In this letter it is stated that Hannah 'eloped in 1754, and was married to Isaac Axford at Keith's Chapel, which my father discovered about three weeks after, and none of her family have seen her since, though her mother had a letter or two from her, but at last died of grief.' The person who encloses the communication adds, 'The general belief of her friends was, that she was taken into keeping by Prince George directly after her marriage to Axford, but never lived with him.'

That such a union actually took place is now beyond all doubt, the late Mr. John Jesse having discovered its entry in the registers of marriage celebrated by Alexander Keith in the books kept in his chapel, and removed in 1754 to St. George's Church, Hanover Square; the writer has obtained a certificate of the marriage, which was performed on December 11, 1753.*

Hannah—according to a writer in *Notes and Queries*, July, 1853, who had, when a lad, heard his mother speak of the fair Quaker, whose aunt, Anna Eleanor Lightfoot, was next-door neighbour to his grandfather—after her disappearance was advertised for by her friends; when some time had elapsed, they obtained information of her retreat, stating that she was well provided for, and her condition became known to them. 'A retreat was provided for her,' says this writer, 'in one of those large houses surrounded with a high wall and garden, in the district of Cat-and-Mutton Fields, on the east side of Hackney Road, leading from Mile-End Road, where she lived, and, it is said, died.'

* Mr. William J. Thoms, in his pamphlet entitled 'Hannah Lightfoot,' thoroughly discredits the story that the good young Prince ever had an intrigue with the fair Quaker. 'Whether the King' (George III.), he says in his preface, 'has or has not been made the scapegoat for his father, as has been suggested, or any of his brothers, is not the question which I undertake to investigate.' Frederick, Prince of Wales, however, died in March, 1751, two years before the Lightfoot marriage and subsequent scandal took place. Again Mr. Thoms says 'The first thing that strikes one as remarkable with regard to this piece of scandal is that no allusion to it is to be found (at least, as far as I am able to trace) in any historical, political, or satirical work published during the lifetime of George III.' But two months after the publication of this statement, he announces in the pages of *Notes and Queries* that his 'attention has been called to a printed allusion to this scandal as early as the year 1779,' which occurs in one of the works of William Combe.

Huish, in his 'Public and Private Life of his late Excellent and most Gracious Majesty George III.,' which is dedicated to that monarch's successor to the throne, refers to this amour. 'His affections became enchained,' he says, speaking of the Prince. 'He looked no more to Saxe-Gotha nor to Brunswick for an object on which to lavish his love; he found one in the secret recesses of Hampton, whither he often repaired, concealed by the protecting shades of night, and there he experienced, what seldom falls to the lot of princes, the bliss of the purest love. The object of his affections became a mother, and strengthened the bond between them. Being one day in the company of the late Duke of Chandos, who appears to have been honoured with his confidence, he expressed himself in the following terms: 'Ah, Chandos, you are a happy man; you are at liberty to live with the woman of your choice, whilst I, the future King of a great nation, shall perhaps, at some not very distant period, be obliged to take to my arms a woman whom I have never seen before, and whom perhaps I may never love."'

Hannah Lightfoot is said to have borne the Prince two sons, one of whom became mad, and, according to the authority last quoted from *Notes and Queries*, committed suicide. Another of them, named George Rex, went to the Cape of Good Hope; concerning him Mr. William Harrison, of Rockmount, Isle of Man, writes to *Notes and Queries*, February 9, 1861: 'With respect to the son born of this marriage' (the supposed legal union between the Prince and the Quaker), 'and said to be still living at the Cape of Good Hope, I think there must be some mistake. I was at the Cape in 1830, and spent some time at Mr. George Rex's hospitable residence at the Knysna. I understood from him that he had been about thirty-four years a resident in the colony, and I should suppose he was then about sixty-eight years of age, of a strong, robust appearance, and the exact resemblance in features to George III. This would bring him to about the time as stated when George III. married Hannah Lightfoot. On Mr. Rex's first arrival in the colony, he occupied a high situation in the colonial government, and received an extensive grant of land at the Knysna. He retired there, and made most extensive improvements. His eldest son was named John, at the time I was there, living with his father, and will now most probably be the representative of George Rex.' It is worth noting that, when the Duke of Edinburgh visited the Cape, he was entertained by a Mr. Rex, probably the Mr. John Rex just referred to.

On the morning of October 25, 1760, George II. died suddenly, and George William Frederick became King. The manner in which he received the intelligence of his grandfather's death was eminently characteristic of the new monarch, and gave proof of that dissimulation which he practised through life. He was riding from Kew to London, when he was overtaken by a man on horseback, who handed him a piece of coarse white-brown paper, on which was written one word, 'Schrieder.' This was simply the name of a German valet-de-chambre in the service of the late King, with whom the Prince had privately entered into an agreement that His Majesty's death should be communicated to him, immediately it took place, in this private manner.

He received the intelligence with all the hereditary stolidity of his race, briefly bade the messenger keep silent, and then, turning to his groom and informing him, by way of excuse for his return, that his horse was lame, rode back to Kew. When the man ventured to state that the horse was in good condition, George William Frederick made no reply until he was dismounted; then he remarked, with his usual calmness, 'I have said the horse is lame—I forbid you to say the contrary.' So he may be said to have ascended the throne with a lie upon his lips.

On Sunday, the next day after the death of his late Majesty of blessed memory, the new King was proclaimed; first before his residence, Saville House, where the officers of state, nobility, and privy counsellors were present with the officers of arms, all being on foot; then at Charing Cross; at Wood Street, in Cheapside; and finally at the Royal Exchange, the Archbishop of Canterbury, the Duke of Leeds, and Lord Falmouth attending the procession into the City. On Tuesday there was a levée held at Saville House.

'To-day,' writes Horace Walpole, 'England kissed hands, so did I, and it is more comfortable to kiss hands with all England than to have all England ask why one kisses hands. There is great dignity and grace in the King's manner. I don't say this, like my dear Madame de Sévigné, because he was civil to me, but the part is well acted. If they do as well behind the scenes as upon the stage, it will be a very complete reign.'

The opening of the new *régime* showed every sign of prosperity. Abroad, conquests had crowned the English arms with fortune and glory; at home, the factions which had disturbed the peace and threatened the dynasty of the two first Hanoverian monarchs had now become extinct, the fever and discontent of Jacobitism had gradually worked itself out, leaving the country in a more healthy state, and the new King had, without any merit of his, become popular with his subjects, on account of his youth, and of his being the first monarch of his line who was born a Briton. Moreover, the nation rejoiced in a state of prosperity, such as it had seldom experienced, whilst the administration was presided over by William Pitt, one of the most able and brilliant statesmen the country had ever known. Yet this fair prospect was gradually and totally changed by a proud and narrow-minded woman and an ambitious, inexperienced man.

Meanwhile all England generally, and London in particular, was moved by the great social event which had taken place. A monarch who had reached his seventy-seventh year, who had become blind and deaf, whose levée-room had grown to have 'an air of a lion's den,' was removed by death, and in his place an English-speaking King, just entering into manhood, ascended the throne. It was true his subjects had seen or heard little of him; as Lord Chesterfield said, 'He was like a new Sultan dragged out of the seraglio by the Princess and Lord Bute and placed upon the throne.' But their slight knowledge of him made them all the more curious to see this man who had been made their King by the grace of God. Accordingly courtiers and commoners rushed to be presented or to present addresses, and the drawing-rooms were filled with sufficient subjects to set up half a dozen petty Kings. Amongst others, the good Lord Mayor, with his aldermen all, came from the City, and, with as grave a face as he could assume, told His Most Gracious Majesty 'that as Almighty God had pleased to call to His mercy the late Sovereign Lord, King George II. of blessed memory, whose glorious reign and princely virtues must ever make his memory dear to a grateful people, he, the Lord Mayor of London City, begged leave to approach his gracious Sovereign's royal person, and to congratulate him on his accession to the Imperial Crown of these happy realms.'

The merchants of London likewise presented an address containing many expressions of loyalty, but this was far eclipsed by that of the archbishop, dean and chapter, archdeacon and clergy of the diocese of Canterbury, who, after condoling with His Sacred Majesty on the recent affliction caused him through the death of his grandfather, assured him of their sincerest joy on seeing the throne filled by one who was heir to his virtues as well as his dominions, one whose hereditary good dispositions had caused him to be received as a blessing to his people.

All the thoroughfares leading to Saville House were thronged with coaches and chairs, with lacqueys, soldiers, and idlers, who collected to see the courtiers making their way, or returning from seeing the new King; the ladies attired in mourning that consisted of 'black bombazine, plain muslin, or long-lawn linnen, with crape hoods and crape fans;' the men of quality also in black suits, 'without buttons on the sleeves and pockets, plain muslin or long-lawn cravats and wrappers, shamoy shoes and gloves, crape hat-bands, and black swords and buckles.'

On Sunday the King held a drawing-room at St. James's when he exhibited a mighty gracious air, and had a smile for all who approached him: he informed his stout old uncle, the Duke of Cumberland, he would introduce a new custom into his family—that of living in peace with all its members. Indeed, the new reign not only began with a prospect of domestic peace, but with a hearty denouncement of wickedness. Before he had been a week on the throne, the King issued a proclamation for the encouragement of piety and virtue, and the suppression of 'all vice, profaneness, debauchery, and immorality, which are so highly displeasing to God, so great a reproach to religion and government, and have so fatal a tendency to the corruption of many of our loving subjects;' furthermore, the proclamation prohibited all persons 'of what degree or quality soever from playing on the Lord's day at dice, cards, or any other game whatever, either in public or private houses, or other places whatsoever.'

All the ways and manners that had hitherto obtained in the godless Court of the late King were, it appeared, to be reversed; persons of piety and virtue (if such could be found) were to be distinguished by royal favour, the wicked to be punished. So alarmed did Miss Chudleigh become at such a turning of the tables, that this fair courtier, who had permitted old George II. to stroke her under the chin and kiss her at the drawing-rooms, assumed a virtue if she had it not, and, to mark her rigour, called for the council books of the subscription concert, and struck off the name of Mrs. Naylor, whose life was not, alas! surrounded with an odour of sanctity. Perhaps it is not wonderful that, owing to these pious changes, Dr. Secker, now Archbishop of Canterbury, whom the late King so detested that he had refused to hear him preach, should in the first days of the religious reign flatter himself with the idea of becoming First Minister.

'The Bishop,' writes Horace Walpole, 'who had been bred a Presbyterian and man mid-wife—which sect and profession he had dropped for a season, while he was president of a very free-thinking club—has been converted by Bishop Talbot, whose relation he married, and had his faith settled in a prebend of Durham.'

His spiritual lordship was unwearying in his attentions on the new King, having 'great hopes from the King's goodness that he should make something of him—that is, something bad.'

CHAPTER II.

Loyal Subjects—The King at the Playhouse—What His Majesty said to Lady Susan—The Princess Dowager's Alarm—In Search of a Queen—An Unknown Princess—Her Journey to England—The Marriage Ceremony—Loyal Addresses—The most Brilliant Drawing-room ever Known—Some Distinguished Courtiers—The Coronation Ceremony—What George Selwyn said—Charles Edward Stuart at the Coronation Banquet.

NOT only the courtiers but the people were ready to honour the King.

'It is not strange,' says Lord Macaulay, 'that the sentiment of loyalty—a sentiment which had lately seemed to be as much out of date as the belief in witches, or the practice of pilgrimage—should from the day of his accession have begun to revive.'

The first night he went to the play, a vast crowd assembled round the theatre; so great, indeed, was the crush, that the ladies could not get to their boxes where their servants sat keeping places for them. At His Majesty's entrance, the audience rose up and sang 'God save the King' in chorus; and towards the close of the second act the throng outside, whose numbers had increased every moment, forced open the doors, and crushed madly into the theatre. The play selected was 'The Minor,' and the Archbishop, from some expressions it contained, sought to have it changed. His Grace of Devonshire, in writing to David Garrick on the subject, says of Dr. Secker: 'He would have authorised me to have used his name to stop "The Minor," but I got off from it, and concluded with sending a recommendation by Mr. Pelham to the author, to alter those passages that are liable to objection; his Grace would not point them out.' His Grace was a wary man; had he made any alterations, Foote, the author of the play, said he would have advertised it as 'corrected and prepared for the press by his Grace the Archbishop of Canterbury.'

The town became as gay as in the palmy days of George II. The opera was crowded. Paganina, fat and forty, received an ovation wherever she sang, Philip Elisi, the primo tenore, was the idol of the hour, and David Garrick and Mistress Kitty Clive played to thronged houses at old Drury Lane. There were Drawing-rooms at the Court on Sundays and Thursdays, and there were vast assemblies given by the Duke of Cumberland, the Princess Amelia, the Duchesses of Norfolk and Northumberland, where all the fashionable world met, and gossipped, and danced, and gambled to their heart's content.

In the midst of the gaiety, the King fell in love: the object of his passion being on this occasion Lady Sarah Lennox, the great-granddaughter of the gracious, pleasure-loving Charles II., and daughter of Charles, second Duke of Richmond. Walpole, whose taste was fastidious, especially where female beauty was concerned, after seeing her acting in some amateur theatricals at Holland House, wrote of her to George Montagu: 'Lady Sarah was more beautiful than you can conceive: she was in white, with her hair about her ears and on the ground; no Magdalen by Correggio was ever half so lovely and expressive. This descendant of royalty was then at that most seductive period of life when girlhood blossoms into lovely womanhood, and was endowed with her full share of the hereditary beauty of her house. She was certainly the fairest ornament at the new Court, and the King quickly showed his appreciation of her graces by falling in love with her. Lady Sarah, highly flattered by the royal conquest she had made, gave him every opportunity of increasing his passion; she was frequently at the Drawing-rooms of St. James's, and in the mornings was to be seen attired in a fancy costume making hay in the meadows close by Holland House, the residence of her brother-in-law, Henry Fox, when the King was sure to pass that way for his customary ride.

That the young Monarch intended to place her on the throne, there can be little doubt. George Grenville says that Thomas Pitt told him how the King, at one of the royal Drawing-rooms, went up to Lady Susan Strangways, the companion and confidant of Lady Sarah, and asked her in a whisper if she did not think the coronation would be a much finer sight if there was a Queen. She said, 'Yes.' He then asked her if she did not know somebody who would grace that ceremony in the properest manner. At this she was much embarrassed, thinking he meant herself, but he went on and said, 'I mean your friend, Lady Sarah Lennox. Tell her so, and let me have her answer the next Drawing-room day.'

In a memoir of Henry Fox, preserved in the Holland House manuscripts, the following interesting details concerning this affair of the royal heart are set down :—

'On Thursday, Lady Susan (Strangways) was at Court with Lady Albemarle, Lady Sarah on the other side of the Room with Lady Caroline Fox. The King said to Lady Susan:

'"You are going into Somersetshire; when do you return?"

'Lady Susan—"Not before Winter, Sir, and I don't know how soon in Winter."

'King—"Is there nothing will bring you to town before Winter?"

'L. S.—" I don't know of anything."

'K.—" Would you not like to see a Coronation?"

'L. S.—" Yes, Sir, and I hope I should come to see that."

'K.—" I hear it's very popular, my having put it off."

'L. S.—[Nothing.]

'K.—" Won't it be a much finer sight when there is a Queen?"

'L. S.—" To be sure, Sir.

'K.—" I have had a great many applications from abroad, but I don't like them. I have had none at home—I should like that better." .

'L. S.—[Nothing—(frightened).]

K.—" What do you think of your Friend?—you know who I mean. Don't you think Her fittest?"

'L. S.—" Think, Sir?"

K.—" I think none so fit.'

He then went across the Room to Lady Sarah, bid Her ask Her Friend what He had been saying, and make Her tell Her, and tell Her all. She assur'd Him she would.

H. M. is not given to joke, and this would be a very bad joke, too. Is it serious? Strange if it is, and a strange way of going about it.

We are all impatient to know, and the next Sunday, or Sunday se'ennight, Lady Sarah go's to Court out of humour, and had been crying all the morning. The moment the King saw Her He goes to Her.

K.—" Have you seen your Friend lately?"

L. S.—" Yes."

K.— Has She told you what I said to Her?"

'L. S.—" Yes."

'K.—" All?"

'L. S.—" Yes."

'K.—" Do you approve?"

'L. S. made no Answer, but look'd as cross as she could look.

'H. M., affronted, left her, seem'd confus'd; and left the Drawing-Room.'

The second extract, which follows, taken also from the Holland House MSS., was sent by Henry Fox, afterwards Lord Holland, with a letter, to his wife, Lady Caroline. It is dated April 14, 1781. It bears reference to the King's marriage, and to an accident which the object of his admiration met whilst on her journey to Somersetshire.

'Tuesday.

To all whom it may concern.

'On Sunday I heard from good Authority that the Report of H. M.'s intended Marriage with a Princess of Brunswick was entirely without foundation. And that He was totally free and unengag'd.

'On Monday, therefore, which was yesterday, I went to Court. I saw the Marquis of Kildare and Conolly there, to whom I thought H. M. had spoke, and probably might not speak to me concerning Lady Sal. I determin'd, however, that He should, if I could bring it about. After a Loose Question or two, he in a 3rd supposes I am by this time settled at Holland House. (Now I have you.)

'"I never go there, Sir," says I; "there is nobody there."

'"Where is Lady Caroline?"

'"In Somersetshire with Lady Sarah."

'At that name His Voice and Countenance, gentle and gracious already, softened, and He colour'd a little.

'"I am very glad to hear She is so well."

'"As well as anybody can be with such an Accident, but the Pain was *terrible* from the Motion of the Coach till she got to Mr. Hoare's.'

'He drew up his Breath, wreath'd himself, and made a Countenance of one feeling Pain himself. (Thinks I, you shall hear of that again.) I added,

'" She is extremely chearfull now, and patient and good-humour'd to a degree."

'" Was She going down a Steep Hill when the Horse fell?"

'" I believe not, Sir; the Horse put his foot upon a Stone, which broke, and it was impossible He should not fall. Lady Sarah, I hear," says I, "proposes to ride to London upon the same Horse, to clear the Horse from all blame."

'" That shews," says He, "a good Spirit in Lady Sarah, but I trust there will be prudence in the Family to prevent it."

'" I fancy," says I, "Lady Caroline will dissuade it, but indeed the Horse was not to blame. In rising again, his Shoulder press'd Lady Sarah's leg upon the Stones of which that Road is full, and broke it."

'Then came the same Countenance and Expressions of Uneasiness, which I rather increas'd by talking again of the Pain the motion of the Coach gave; and then reliev'd by assuring him that she had nothing hard to bear now but the Confinement.

'" I fancy," says He, "that is not very easy to Lady Sarah."

'And then He left me for some conversation which neither gave him so much pain nor so much pleasure as mine had done.

'Don't tell Lady Sarah that I *am sure* He intends to marry her, for I am not *sure* of it. Whether Lady Sarah shall be told what I am sure of, I leave to the Reader's Judgment. I *am sure* that He loves Her better than N. (Lord Newbottle) do's.

'I have shortened, not exaggerated, a Word in this account, and I don't think it was prevention made me imagine something particular whenever he pronounced especially the last Lady Sarah'

Matters had arrived at this point when the Princess, ever jealous of her son, became alarmed; a future Queen, chosen by her, and, therefore, placed under a life-long obligation to her, might be held under the same influence as that which bound the King, and in this manner the Princess might still be enabled to govern the kingdom; but, if Lady Sarah were placed on the throne, all such ambitious hopes must come to a speedy end. There was, therefore, no time to be lost. The Princess privately despatched Colonel Graeme, as the 'Memoirs or the Reign of George III.' state, to visit various little Protestant Courts and make report of the qualifications of the several unmarried Princesses. Beauty, and still less talents, were not, it is likely, the first object of his instructions. On the testimony of this man, the golden apple was given to the Princess of Mecklenburg.

But, whilst Colonel Graeme was travelling on his private mission, the Princess was busy at home. She was determined to end the King's love-affair, and for this purpose called to her aid her cavalier, Lord Bute, and her eldest daughter, the Princess Augusta. A strict watch was placed on the King's movements; his mother informed him that Lady Sarah 'was a bad young woman,' and the Princess Augusta, with right royal manners, taunted her in the Drawing-room, laughed in her face, and strove to affront her moreover, Lady Bute had received private instructions to interrupt as far as possible all whisperings between the lovers.

Meanwhile, there were rumours abroad concerning the King's marriage. 'The private attachments of the King,' says Huish, speaking of this time, 'now became the subject of general conversation. The alarm was industriously spread throughout the country of the danger to which it was exposed from a spurious offspring of the Sovereign; the extent of his amours was investigated in the most inquisitorial manner; the circumstance of his being a father was bruited about as corroborative of the pressing necessity of an immediate union with some foreign Princess .... The pen of satire was employed to hold up to ridicule the amours of the Sovereign. The most scurrilous lampoons issued daily from the corrupted press, and the dexterity which distinguished their composition could only be equalled by the eagerness with which they were bought.'

On July 7, 1761, the King's messengers were suddenly despatched to all Privy Councillors in order to summon them to a meeting to be held at one o'clock next day at St. James's, the object of which, they were told, was urgent and important business. The business, however, consisted in announcing His Majesty's intended marriage with Charlotte, daughter of Charles Louis, Duke of Mirow, the second son of the Duke of Mecklenburg-Strelitz. This illustrious lady was quite unknown to those over whom she was destined to reign. 'Till that hour,' says Walpole, 'perhaps not six men in England knew such a Princess existed.'

The King, like his subjects, was kept in ignorance of the arrangements which were being made for his union for a considerable time, and up to the very day of its announcement had carried on his courtship with Lady Sarah, who only heard of the alliance when it was publicly declared. Neither His Majesty, the cabinet, nor the people looked favourably on this marriage with an insignificant Princess, and in the minds of the populace distrust was added to dislike by reason of the secret manner in which it was arranged. But the King was too weak, and had been too long under the control of his mother and Lord Bute, to oppose their wishes in any way; he therefore complacently, accepted the wife selected for him without a murmur, and Lord Harcourt was sent to demand the hand of this almost unheard-of Princess in marriage with the King of England.

'The handkerchief has been tossed a vast way,' writes Horace Walpole to Horace Mann; 'it is to a Charlotte, Princess of Mecklenburg. Lord Harcourt is to be at her father's Court—if he can find it—on August 1, and the coronation for both their Majesties is fixed for September 22.'

Matters were thus hurried on from various reasons, one of which was given by Lord Bute in writing to the Duke of Bedford: 'The numberless stories and insolent untruths,' says his intriguing lordship, 'propagated most artfully about this town have induced me to think that in accelerating the measure I was doing no unacceptable service to my King and country.' Whether the stories and untruths which this honourable patriot refers to were anent Hannah Lightfoot or were merely the more innocent gossip which introduced Lady Sarah Lennox's name it is impossible to say. Lady Sarah was disappointed, but not heart-broken, by the project of the royal marriage, as may be judged from a letter of hers to Lady Susan Strangways yet preserved in the Holland House MSS., which throws considerable light upon her feelings. This epistle bears the date, July 7, 1761, and runs as follows:—

'MY DEAREST SUSAN,

'. . . To begin to astonish you as much as I was, I must tell you that the King is going to be married to a Princess of Mecklenburg, and that I am sure of it. There is a Council to-morrow on purpose. The orders for it are *urgent* and *important* business; does not your Chollar rise at hearing this? But you think, I dare say, that I have been doing some terrible thing to deserve it, for you would [not] easily be brought to change so totally your opinion of any person, but I assure you I have not . . . I shall take care to show I am not mortified to anybody, but, if it is true that one can vex anybody with a reserved, cold manner, he shall have it, I promise him. Now as to what I think about it myself, excepting this little revenge, I have almost forgiven him; luckily for me I did not love him, and only liked, nor did the title weigh anything with me. So little, at least, that my disappointment did not *affect* my spirits above one hour or two, I believe; I did not cry, I assure you, which I believe you will, as I know you were more set upon it than I was. The thing I am most angry at is looking so like a fool, as I shall for having gone so often for nothing; but I don't much care. If he was to change his mind again (which can't be though), and not give a *very good* reason for his conduct, I would not have him; for if he is so weak as to be governed by everybody, I shall have but a bad time of it. Now I charge you, dear Lady Sue, not to mention this to anybody but Lord and Lady Ilchester, and desire them not to speak of it to any mortal, for it will be said we invent Storries, and he will hate us all anyway; for one generally hates people that one is in the wrong with, and that knows one has acted wrong, particularly if they speak of it, and it might do a great deal of harm to all the rest of the family and do me no good. So pray remember this, for a secret among many people is very bad, and I must tell it some . . .

'We are to act a play and have a little ball. I wish you were here to enjoy them; but they are forwarded for Ste, and to show that we are not so melancholy quite.'

'Lord Harcourt discovered the Court of Mecklenburg, and found England's future Queen enjoying an existence of rustic simplicity. She only dressed *en grande tenue* on Sundays, when, after service, she was allowed to put on her best gown, and then taken for an airing in a great, rumbling coach round her brother's principality. At the time when it was proposed she should become a Royal Sovereign, she had never 'dined at table.' But one morning her eldest brother came to her accompanied by his mother; he told her to put on her best clothes, for an ambassador from the King of England had come to visit them, and she should dine with them that day for the first time. The poor little Princess was delighted, and asked her mother if she should 'put on her blue tabby and her jewellery,' to which the elder lady made answer, '*Mon enfant, tu n'en as point.*' When she went down to the saloon, decked in her holiday finery, she saw it was more brilliantly lighted than usual, and noticed that at one end stood a table and two cushions, as if preparations had been made for a wedding. Her brother then gave her his hand, and said to the bewildered Princess, '*Allons, ne faites pas l'enfant—tu vas être Reine d'Angleterre,*' when the ceremony of marriage by proxy was gone through.

Rapid preparations were then made for her journey to England, and an outfit for the royal bride was prepared, to defray the expenses of which, according to Huish, five years' income of the little principality was required. This, it may be mentioned, the English nation was made to make amends for, and, moreover, the King soon granted his impoverished brother-in-law a pension, which was duly levied on the Irish establishment.

The new Queen was small and lean in person, pale and insignificant looking in appearance; her hair was dark brown, her nose flat, and her mouth extremely wide. Her manners in no way counterbalanced her want of personal attraction, and throughout her life she betrayed a selfish, avaricious disposition, incapable of generosity or consideration for others outside her family. Together with Lord Harcourt, the Duchesses of Ancaster and Hamilton had been sent to conduct her to England; 'but, as an earnest of the prison prepared for her,' says Walpole, 'and to keep her in that state of ignorance which was essential to the views of the Princess, they were forbidden to see her alone.'

The royal yacht despatched for her conveyance was, by way of delicate compliment to her re-named the *Charlotte*, and was furnished with a arpsichord, on which, during her journey to England, she played continually, accompanying herself as she sang some dreary Calvinistic hymns, which she had been wont to chant in her isolated home.

A quaint account of her arrival is given in a little pamphlet writ by one Joseph Taylor.

' At length,' says this good man and loyal, ' after different storms, and being often in sight of the English coast, and often in danger of being driven on that of Norway, the fleet, with Her Most Serene Highness on board, arrived at Harwich on September 6th. As it was night when the fleet arrived, Her Most Serene Highness slept on board, and continued there till three in the afternoon of the next day, during which time her route had been settled, and instructions received as to the manner of her proceeding to St. James's. At her landing she was received by the mayor and aldermen of Harwich with the usual formalities. About five o'clock she came to Colchester, and stopped at the house of Mr. Enew, where she was received and waited upon by Mrs. Enew and Mrs. Rebow; but Captain Best attended her with coffee, and Lieutenant John Seabear with tea. Being thus refreshed, she proceeded to Witham, where she arrived at a quarter-past seven, and stopped at Lord Abercorn's, and his Lordship provided as elegant an entertainment for her as time would permit.

' During the time of her supping, the door of her room was ordered to be wide open, that everybody might have the pleasure and satisfaction of seeing Her Majesty, and on each side of her chair stood the Lords Harcourt and Anson The fruits were choice melons, figs, pears, etc., and many other sorts, both in and out of season. She slept that night at his Lordship's house, and a little after twelve o'clock on Tuesday came to Romford, where she stopped at Mr.

Dutton's, wine merchant. The King's coach and servants met Her Majesty there, and she was by them served with coffee at this house. She stayed there till almost one o'clock, and then entered the King's coach. The attendants of Her Majesty were in three coaches; in the first were some ladies from Mecklenburg, and in the last was Her Majesty, who sat forward, and the Duchesses of Ancaster and Hamilton backward. Her Majesty was dressed entirely in the English taste; she wore a fly-cap, with rich lace lappets, a stomacher ornamented with diamonds, and a gold brocade suit of clothes with a white ground.

'They proceeded at a tolerable pace, attended by an incredible number of spectators, both on horse and foot, to Stratford-le-Bow and Mile-end turnpike, where they turned up Dog-Row, and prosecuted their journey to Hackney turnpike, then by Shoreditch Church and up Old Street to City Road, across Islington, along the New Road into Hyde Park, down Constitution Hill into St. James's Park, and then to the garden gate of the palace, where Her Majesty was handed out of her coach by the Duke of Devonshire (as Lord Chamberlain) to the gate, where she was received by His Royal Highness the Duke of York. As Her Majesty alighted from her coach, His Majesty descended the steps from the palace into the garden, and they met each other half-way; and, as Her Majesty was going to pay her obeisance, the King took hold of her hand, raised her up, saluted it, and then led her upstairs.'

At this meeting, Galt says, 'an involuntary expression of the King's countenance revealed what was passing within, but it was a passing cloud.'

All the town had been in a state of excitement and expectancy for three days previous to her arrival; messengers had reached London from Harwich announcing that she had arrived, meaning in the Harwich road, which was at once translated into landing. This news added fresh zest to the general bustle; the courtiers held discussions on precedence, and talked of nothing but processions, the City made great preparations for the entry, the bridesmaids, ten in number, were waiting with impatience, the guns were loaded, and the New Road and parks were filled with citizens anxious to catch sight of their future Queen.

At last her diminutive Majesty came, looking very plain and rather comical, arrayed in the finery of her fly-cap and lace lappets, and pale with fatigue and anxiety.

'Ah! my dear Duchess,' she said plaintively to her Grace of Hamilton, who had smiled when she saw that the little lady trembled, 'you may laugh, you have been married twice, but it is no joke to me.'

Then the cannon roared from St. James's and the Tower, and the mob cheered lustily, and in the City were vast rejoicings.

The King and his consort dined with all the royal family, and afterwards their gracious Majesties were so good as to show themselves in the gallery and other apartments fronting the Park to the people, who cheered them with great heartiness.

At nine o'clock the marriage procession began to move towards the chapel, the bride being conducted by the King's brothers, the Duke of York and Prince William, and preceded by one hundred and twenty ladies in extremely rich dresses. She was attired in a nuptial habit of white and silver; 'an endless mantle of violet-coloured velvet, lined with ermine, and attempted to be fastened on her shoulder by a huge bunch of large pearls, dragged itself and almost the rest of her clothes half-way down her waist,' says Horace Walpole, who was present at the brilliant ceremony. 'On her head was a beautiful little tiara of diamonds; a diamond necklace, and a stomacher of diamonds, worth three-score thousand pounds, which she is to wear at the coronation too.' Her bridesmaids were the daughters of six dukes, and her train was supported by the daughters of six earls.

The King's uncle, the Duke of Cumberland, gave the bride away, and the ceremony was performed by the Archbishop of Canterbury, at the conclusion of which the guns roared once more from St. James's and the Tower, as a signal to the people that their King was wed. Then these two who had been made one sat at the right side of the altar under a canopy, the bridesmaids grouped around the bride, 'all dressed alike in white lute-string with silver trimmings, with pearls, diamonds, etc.; a dress that attracted the eyes of everyone.' Opposite them sat the Princess Dowager of Wales in a chair of state, the rest of the royal family on stools, and 'the quality on benches, which consisted of all the foreign ministers, including Monsieur Bussy, all the peers and peeresses of the kingdom, together with the bishops.'

At night the cities of London and Westminster were brilliantly lighted; bands played right merrily; and vast crowds of people filled the streets. During the illuminations several persons, according to *Lloyd's Evening Post*, 'had their clothes very much burnt by having squibs and serpents put into their pockets, sleeves of their coats, etc.; particularly near Charing Cross, where a woman was so much burnt and terrified as to be carried away almost dead.'

Addresses, all more or less notable for their ponderous phrases, abject expressions, and flights of fancy when the royal personages were referred to, poured in on the Sovereign and his gracious spouse. The Lord Mayor, bluff aldermen, and Common Council of the City, the latter arrayed in all the finery of new mazarine lined with fur, and wearing full-bottomed wigs, majestic to behold, informed the King they 'adored the divine goodness that, as in all your Majesty's other conduct, so more particularly in a choice of the highest importance to your Majesty and your kingdoms, hath so visibly guided and inspired your royal breast.' These wise gentlemen referred to the Queen, of whom they knew nothing whatsoever, 'as a Princess of most exalted merit, a Princess who, by her descent from an illustrious lineage (respectable for their firm and constant zeal for the Protestant religion), was most worthy to engage your Majesty's esteem and affection, and to share the honours of the British crown.'

The most amusing of these stilted compositions was the humble address of the ladies of the borough of St. Albans to the Queen's most excellent Majesty. 'Formed by Nature,' said these daughters of Eve to their sovereign lady, 'and improved by the completest education, you were selected by the best of Kings to add the only happiness that was wanting in this world.'

What follows this eloquence is much more to the purpose, and shows that the ladies of the borough of St. Albans had homely wit.

'As subjects,' said these wise virgins, 'are greatly influenced by the example of their Sovereign, we have the strongest reason to hope that the matrimonial state will be duly honoured by your Majesty's dutiful subjects cheerfully following the royal example; an example too much wanted in this degenerate age, wherein that happy state is made the object of ridicule instead of respect by too many of vain, giddy, and dissipated minds. If the riches of a nation consist in its populousness, this happy country will in that respect *too soon* become poor, whilst the lawful means to continue posterity are either shackled by the restraint of mistaken laws, or despised by those who regard *none.*'

The day after the royal marriage, there was the most brilliant drawing-room held at St. James's 'ever known to the memory of man:' when the Spanish, Dutch, Tripolitan, and Moorish ambassadors attended in gorgeous apparel procured specially for the occasion. The great suite of apartments opening from one to another were crowded with men and women of the highest rank in the nation, all arrayed in the bravery of new clothes; the ladies bejewelled and be-wigged, with patches upon cheek and chin, enormous head-dresses piled high with false hair, decked with many ornaments, and surmounted with plumes of ostrich feathers; the men in square-cut velvet or satin coats of brilliant hues, the skirts distended with wire and buckram; with satin waistcoats, glittering with gold embroidery, deep of pocket and wide of gap; and high-drawn silk stockings, amber, crimson, or blue. Moreover, for their further adornment they wore rich point-lace cravats and ruffles, diamond-hilted swords, and carried lace-bordered, perfumed handerchiefs in hands that were radiant with jewels.

The sight of so much splendour awes Her Majesty, who stares at the goodly show that passes before her, waving its painted fans, fluttering its delicate ruffles, courtesying with inexpressible grace, smiling as if radiant with the happiness of heaven, whispering elaborately turned compliments, bandying phrases gemmed with sparkling wit, and detailing the latest scandal with an air of sweetness that would have become the utterance of a prayer. She speaks of none of these, for her knowledge of English is scant indeed, and her French but tolerable; but instead of words she gives her courtiers many smiles, which evidences of amiability are ridiculed by some of the worthy ladies, who declare 'her face is all mouth when she laughs,' and who titter behind their fans when she gives one of those sudden little ducks which do duty for a courtesy.

The King to-day has lost all traces of his habitual sullen aspect, his florid face beams with smiles, his round blue eyes are bright, his manner unusually unrestrained and agreeable. Near him stands Charles Lennox, third Duke of Richmond, who is young, singularly handsome, and as gallant as his fair admirers could desire; close by is another courtier, a rival of his Grace's, and, like him, descended from the Royal

Stuart line, Augustus Henry, the young Duke of Grafton, who is without the graceful bearing or comely looks of his more favoured kinsman. Lady Sarah Lennox is the most beautiful amongst that stately throng, and many eyes are critically turned from her to the colourless face of the Queen, whom one good courtier declares is possessed of 'an elegant plainness.' Old Lady Exeter stands near Her Majesty, and bluntly informs the King 'he is the handsomest man she ever saw,' upon which he laughs, being greatly pleased, and the Queen looks puzzled, until the flattering words are repeated to her in guttural German, when she indulges in one of those smiles that render her mouth like a cavern. The handsome Duchess of Hamilton and Argyll, once the penniless Maria Gunning, who was married with a bed-curtain ring, at half an hour after twelve at night, at Mayfair Chapel, and who became the wife of two Scotch dukes and the mother of four, is there laughing at a droll story which George Townshend tells her: for he has a reputation for wit, and is a mimic of uncommon ability, whose favourite butt is the old Duke of Cumberland.

Not far removed from her Grace is a man whom she detests, though she differs in this from many of her sex, to the injury of their good names; this is my Lord Talbot, who is now Lord Steward of the Household, a man of some parts, and of fashion, as may be inferred from the fact that a certain Duchess had been divorced for his sweet sake from her lawful lord and master. My Lord, who has the reputation of being a man who loves gold greatly, is a favourite with the King, who has been exceedingly gracious to him to-day—a fact which the Duchess of Bedford remarks to George Selwyn, courtier and wit. 'Yes,' replies Selwyn, 'His Majesty's condescension is so great, he takes notice of the meanest of his subjects.' Then he tells her Grace, with a slow and solemn air, as if he were imparting a State secret, that the brusque Lady Northumberland has been appointed one of the ladies of the bedchamber, because, as Her Majesty knew no English, her Ladyship had undertaken to teach her the *vulgar* tongue.

Two of the royal bridesmaids stand by the Queen, both young and beautiful, Lady Harriet Bentinck and Lady Caroline Russell, and by them my Lord Errol, whose stout person is dressed in tissue that makes him look like one of the giants in Guildhall new gilt. The old Duke of Newcastle, shrivelled looking and gouty and restless, hurries from one group to another, smiling on all; a man 'not without parts,' says Lord March, with a cynical smile. 'Certainly not,' answers one of the wits who overheard him, 'he has done without them for forty years. Amongst the vast throng is Lady Kildare, famous for her beauty, and the charming Lady Sutherland, and many other fair women and gallant men, loyal courtiers all.

But this Drawing-Room, the centre of so much splendour, did not pass without a ridiculous incident to mark it. The accident referred to happened to Bubb Dodington, a special friend of the Princess Dowager, an ambitious courtier, and a rare fop. He had come to the Drawing-Room, and approached to kiss Her Majesty's hand, as Cumberland says, 'decked in an embroidered suit of silk, with lilac waistcoat and breeches, the latter of which, in the act of kneeling down, forgot their duty, and broke loose from their moorings in a very indecorous and uncourtly manner.'

During the remainder of the week, my Lords Newcastle and Talbot and Mr. Pitt gave entertainments, as befitted loyal gentlemen rejoicing with their sovereign lord. One night in this gleeful time was devoted to the drama; the King and Queen went to Drury Lane play-house to see David Garrick perform in 'The Rehearsal,' which had been writ, in the days when the second Charles reigned as King, by the reckless, graceless George Villiers, Duke of Buckingham, a man of great parts and infinite wit. Their Majesties were carried in chairs, the King being preceded by the Duke of Devonshire, his Lord Chamberlain; and the Hon. Mr. Finch, Vice-Chamberlain; Her Majesty by her Lord Chamberlain, his Grace of Manchester; my Lord Cantalup, her Vice-Chamberlain; my Lord Harcourt, her Master of the Horse; and likewise by the Duchess of Ancaster and the Countess of Effingham. Then came the royal family in coaches, the ladies and gentlemen of the Court, attended by the Horse Guards, and a mighty fine procession it made. The people were all abroad to see it, and lined the streets from St. James's to Drury Lane, crushing, surging, and striving to catch a sight of the plain little woman, decked out in brocade and a vast number of diamonds, who sat quietly in her chair, and looked frighted at so great a crowd that doubled the number of her brother's subjects. Round the play-house the throng was prodigious; a few minutes after the doors were opened, every part of the theatre was full. Never was there so brilliant a house. In all the boxes were the ladies of the Court, dressed in the clothes and decked with the jewels they wore at the royal wedding, the gentlemen who accompanied them being likewise apparelled in much finery.

Outside was quite a different scene. The crowd increased every moment; thousands were disappointed at not being able to get inside the theatre, and all was bustle and excitement; several gentlewomen who attempted an entrance had their cloaks, caps, aprons, and handkerchiefs torn from them, and many gallants had the bags of their wigs, their swords, and money stolen. Some of the people were thrown down, the chairmen were hustled about, a girl was killed, and a man trampled upon.

However, all these sights and celebrations were but preliminaries to the grand ceremony of the coronation. Great preparations were made for the event; galleries were erected in Westminster Hall and in the Abbey, and a platform was erected from the upper end of the Hall, where the procession was to commence, and continued through New Palace Yard, Parliament Street, and Bridge Street, into King Street, and on to the west door of the Abbey and the choir, where the coronation was to take place.

About eleven o'clock, on September 22, the procession started, headed by the King's herb-woman, with her six maids, strewing the way with sweet herbs, followed by the Dean of Westminster's beadle, with a mighty staff in his hand, and the high constable of Westminster, his person arrayed in the great glory of a scarlet cloak. Then came fifes, drums, and trumpeters; six wise Clerks in Chancery, in gowns of black, and with silk loops and tufts upon the sleeves; the King's Chaplains, four abreast, all goodly men and meek; the two Sheriffs of London, the Recorder, thirteen Aldermen in their gowns, with caps in their hands; the King's Attorney, and his ancient sergeant, looking mighty grave; the gentlemen of the Privy Chamber, Barons of the Exchequer, Justices of both Benches in scarlet robes; the Chief Baron, with his great gold collar; the choristers of the Abbey in surplices; the sergeant of the vestry and sergeant porter in scarlet gowns, clad likewise with an air of vast importance; the children of the Chapel Royal in surplices, with scarlet mantles over them; the choir of Westminster, with their music-books; the organ-blower and groom of the vestry; gentlemen of the Chapel Royal in scarlet mantles; the Sub-Dean, in a scarlet gown turned up with black velvet; the Prebendaries of Westminster in surplices and capes, with their caps in their hands; the Master of the Jewel-house and his officers all; the Bath King-of-Arms, in the habit of his Order, carrying his coronet in his hand. Then came a vast throng of Baronesses, Barons, Bishops, Viscountesses, Viscounts, Countesses and Earls, Marchionesses and Marquesses, Duchesses and Dukes, all presenting a magnificent spectacle, arrayed in the gorgeous robes of State, and adorned with the magnificent badges of their various orders.

After them followed my Lord Chancellor, bearing the purse. and my Lord Archbishop of Canterbury in his rochet, attended by two gentlemen of the Privy Chamber in crimson velvet mantles lined with white silk, faced with miniver and trimmed with ermine; then the Queen's Chamberlain, and his Grace of Bolton, bearing her crown; and finally Her Majesty in proper person, in her royal robes, on her head a circlet of gold adorned with jewels, walking demurely under a canopy of cloth of gold, borne by sixteen Barons of the Cinque Ports, her train supported by Her Royal Highness the Princess Augusta, and at either side of her their Spiritual Lordships of London and Lincoln. Then came the King's regalia, the Lord Great Chamberlain of England bearing the white staff, the Duke of Cumberland, the Duke of York, and finally the King, under a great canopy of gold, his train supported by six eldest sons of peers.

Never was such a glorious sight seen before. In all the streets through which the brilliant procession moved, balconies had been erected on either side, which were hung with gay flags, brocaded cloths, and tapestry, and were filled with a vast concourse of people; banners waved, crowds cheered, and the sound of trumpets and drums, bravely discoursing processional music, was almost drowned by the jangle of bells that rang out from every steeple, tower, and turret.

Amongst those peers and peeresses, decked out in all the finery of pomp and State, were some men and women on whom the crowd looked down from balcony, window, and roof with interest and admiration. There was my Lord Errol—whose unhappy father, Lord Kilmarnock, had but a few years ago been condemned to the block in this hall, the scene of the coronation—figuring as the High Constable of

Scotland, and looking as loyal a man as any; and close by him my Lord Effingham, who had that morning owned to the King that the Earl Marshal's office had been neglected in some of the details of ceremony, but assured His Majesty he had taken such care for the future that the next coronation would be regulated in the most exact manner imaginable. My Lady Harrington was there, covered with all the diamonds she could borrow, hire, or seize, and looked extremely fine. She had complained a few days before that the herald had ordered her to walk with Lady Portsmouth, who would wear a wig and carry a stick. 'Pho!' said George Selwyn, to whom she had told her grievance, 'you will only look as if you were taken up by the constable.'

She was not, however, the only peeress who was dissatisfied with the partner assigned her for the procession. Lady Cowper proudly refused to walk with my Lady Macclesfield, because she was 'a common woman' (heaven help us!) whom her lord was mad enough to marry; but, when she was forced to obey the herald's orders, the haughty Countess set out at a round trot, and kept ahead of her companion all the way. The old Duchess of Queensberry, kind-hearted and mad—the friend of Gay and Swift, both of whom had now passed into silence and shadow-land—was in the procession, erect and with locks white as snow, feeling anxious to whisper to those around her, whenever opportunity offered, that her Grace of Bedford was so painted 'she looked like an orange-peach, half red, half yellow.' My Lady Suffolk, the mistress of George II., was likewise present, and old Lady Westmoreland, full of years and dignity; and so was my Lady Exeter, who was also venerable.

When the great coronation show had traversed the prescribed route, it returned to the Abbey, where, after some ceremonies, the Archbishop of Canterbury set the crown on His Majesty's head; on which the peers put on their coronets, the Dukes of Normandy and Aquitaine their hats, the bishops, Knights of the Bath, and judges their caps, and the Kings-of-Arms their crowns. Then the *Te Deum* was sung; the spiritual lords paid homage to the King, and the lords temporal likewise, each peer taking off his coronet, touching the King's crown, and kissing his cheek, and medals of their Sacred Majesties were thrown about by the Treasurer of the Household; so also was the Queen crowned, and there was much rejoicing.

After the coronation, their Majesties entered into the Court of Wards, until the great banquet in Westminster Hall was ready. This was not until evening, and when the King arrived, he found the place all in darkness, its illumination being reserved for his entry as a compliment.

'Conceive to yourself,' says a correspondent, writing of the banquet, 'if you can conceive, what I own I am at a loss to describe, so magnificent a building as that of Westminster Hall lighted up with near three thousand wax candles in most splendid branches, our crowned heads and almost the whole nobility, with the prime of our gentry, most superbly arrayed, and adorned with a profusion of the most brilliant jewels; the galleries on every side crowded with company, for the most part elegantly and richly dressed.'

When the first course had been served at the royal table, it was the duty of Earl Talbot, as Lord High Steward of the Household, to ride to the steps leading to where the King and Queen sat, and, after bowing to them, to retire. My lord was determined to make a fine figure on the occasion, and had trained his horse to back out of the hall when returning; but, alas for the vanity of human desires! to his great chagrin and the amusement of those assembled, when this bold Earl would have ridden into the presence of royalty face foremost, his horse was of another mind, and came into the hall and to the foot of the daïs with his tail turned to royalty. When this goodly show was over, in came the champion between the High Constable and Earl Marshal, followed by four pages and preceded by the herald, and out spake he:

'If any person, of what degree soever, high or low, shall deny or gainsay our sovereign lord, King George III., King of Great Britain, France, and Ireland, Defender of the Faith, grandson and next heir to our sovereign lord, King George II., the last King deceased, to be right heir to the Imperial Crown of the realm of Great Britain; or that he ought not to enjoy the same; here is his champion, who saith that he lyeth, and is a false traytor: being ready in person to combat with him, and in the quarrel will adventure his life against him, on what day soever he shall be appointed.'

Then the gauntlet was dashed down with proud defiance, and was ultimately picked up by one of the pages. A gilt bowl of wine, with a cover, was then brought to the King, when he drank deep to the champion brave, and subsequently sent it to him, that he might have the honour of drinking from it likewise.

After this the banquet continued, and all were merry, save perhaps those who looked on from the galleries, where they had sat for hours, and had, meanwhile, developed appetites.

'It was pleasant,' says James Heming, in a letter to the *Annual Register*, 'to see the various stratagems made use of in the galleries, to come in for a snack of the good things below. The ladies clubbed their handkerchiefs, to be tied together, to draw up a chicken or bottle of wine. Some had been so provident as to bring baskets with them, which were let down, like the prisoners' boxes at Ludgate or the Gate House, with a *pray remember the poor*.'

There, amongst these gay and hungry ladies, sat Charles Edward Stuart, whose legal right it was to sit upon the English throne. Lord Marschal told the historian Hume that the young Pretender, as he was called, was present at the scene.

'I asked my Lord the reason for this strange fact,' says Hume.

'Why,' says he, 'a gentleman told me who saw him there, and whispered in his ear, "Your Royal Highness is the last of all mortals whom I should expect to see here."

'"It was curiosity that led me," said the other. "But, I assure you," added he, "that the person who is the cause of all this pomp and magnificence is the man I envy the least."'

Before the day was done, an incident happened which was regarded with fear by those who believed in omens. The great diamond fell from the King's crown as he was returning to Westminster Hall. When, twenty-one years later, the North American colonies gained their independence, many persons remembered the accident which had befallen the regalia on the coronation day.

CHAPTER III.

'The Witch' and the Earl—How the new Reign was Disturbed—Pitt and Peace—Popular Feeling—The King ridiculed by the Mob—The Scotch Favourite—Public Demonstrations—What the Pamphlets and Ballads said—Caricatures of the Day—The Royal Prorogation—Wholesale Bribery—Triumph and Vengeance—The Toast to Wit, Beauty, Virtue, and Honour—Lord Bute Resigns.

At the beginning of this reign, the public looked forward with some apprehension to the power which the Princess Dowager of Wales—commonly known as 'the Witch'—and Lord Bute were well known to hold over the young monarch. 'What could be expected,' says Walpole, 'from a boy' (the King) 'locked up from the converse of mankind, governed by a mother still more retired, who was under the influence of a man that had passed his life in solitude, and was too haughty to admit to his familiarity but half a dozen silly authors and flatterers?'

Both the Princess and the Earl were, however, too wily to give any direct indication of their power within the first half year of the new reign. All things ministerial remained much as they had been through the last years of the reign of his late Majesty of blessed memory, a matter which occasioned some wonder.

'After all,' said Horace Walpole, raising his eyebrows to an expression of melancholy cynicism, 'there is nothing new under the sun.'

'No,' replied George Selwyn, the fine beau and excellent wit, 'nor under the grandson either.'

However, when the King had been proclaimed about six months, the Dowager and the Earl made their premier move upon the political chess-board, the result being that the Chancellor of the Exchequer, Legg, was suddenly dismissed, and Lord Holderness was ordered to give up the seals of Secretary of State, which were immediately delivered by the royal puppet to Lord Bute, the evil genius of his life. Legg had, in the late reign, refused to support a follower of the favourite at a Hampshire election, thereby proving himself worthy of all humiliation and punishment in the eyes of the young Sovereign. His downfall was not a surprise; Lord Holderness's dismissal, however, was unexpected.

These steps were taken without consulting Pitt, the great Minister, who, though naturally indignant, thought it best to take no notice of the slight for the present. Parliament was dissolved in March, 1761, and when it again assembled, Lord Bute, who had now become a Minister, gave some indications of his future course in a more open manner than he had yet ventured to adopt.

The Whigs, under the powerful leadership of Pitt, had become popular by a long war, which, crowned with success and fortune, had raised England to a pre-eminence over every other nation in Europe. France was, by repeated losses of her colonies, reduced to despair; in America she had been rifled of Quebec, in Africa her chief settlements fell, in the East Indies her power was abridged; her navy was almost annihilated, her commerce reduced to ruin, and she was therefore ready to grant whatever concessions this country might require. It was therefore plainly at the option of England to extend her victories and acquisitions still further. The country was in this situation when the King read his first speech to his Council, who were struck with astonishment to hear him refer to a war which had captivated the whole country as 'bloody and expensive,' and of his hopes 'of obtaining an honourable and lasting peace.'

Humiliated and indignant, Mr. Pitt, on the evening of its delivery, waited on Lord Bute, and, after a stormy argument which lasted for three hours, prevailed on him to alter the printed copy of the royal speech so that the objectionable phrase should be changed to ' an expensive but necessary war,' and that after the words 'honourable peace' should be inserted, 'in consort with our allies.' The inclination for peace which the King's speech indicated gave sudden and unexpected hopes to France; its Ministers, feeling the pulse of the Court, soon opened a negotiation with the Government, and, believing they could make easy terms with Bute, sued for peace. Pitt, however, demanded greater concessions than they seemed willing to make, and refused peace on any other terms than his own. It was subsequently proved that he was judicious in his demands, and that France, under a plea of negotiating for peace, was in reality secretly forming an alliance with Spain, in order to gain that country's assistance in her war with England. This treaty between these Powers was signed in August, 1761.

Pitt, having been secretly made aware of this treachery, and having also been informed of the preparations that were going on in Spain, proposed to recall the English ambassador from Madrid unless satisfactory explanations were given by the Spanish Government, and to issue an immediate declaration of war on that country; but he who had formerly led, now found his advice was rejected on the plea of temporizing; that his power in the Ministry had been undermined; and that factions which had been happily extinguished during the latter part of the late reign, in a desire for common weal, had now sprung to life again at the instigation of the King's favourite. He therefore declared he would not be responsible for measures not his own, and on October 16th resigned his office. This was exactly what Lord Bute desired.

'It is difficult to say which exulted most on the occasion, France, Spain, or Lord Bute; for Mr. Pitt was the common enemy of all three,' writes Horace Walpole.

The resignation of its favourite caused the whole nation a surprise which, after the first shock, quickly turned to indignation. The City of London proposed to address the King, in order to know why the Minister had been dismissed; but desisted on being told His Majesty would reply, Mr. Pitt had of his own will seceded from the cabinet. A general mourning was then proposed, but this extravagance was likewise abandoned. Meanwhile the Princess Dowager, who took an active part in all that was passing, but whose policy it was to be felt rather than seen, urged the King to press upon the statesman some reward for his past services, by the acceptance of which his popularity might, it was hoped, be at once blasted. His Majesty therefore offered him the Government of Canada, a peerage, or a large pension. He accepted a peerage for his wife, and a pension of three thousand a year for himself, a notice of which was immediately published in the *Gazette*.

This announcement was quickly followed by a series of attacks on the great statesman from Lord Bute and his faction. Newspapers, ballads, pamphlets, and caricatures were numerously distributed all over the town, in which Pitt was depicted, spoken, and sung of as the 'Demon of War,' who was anxious to embroil his country in a bloody struggle to gratify his love for carnage. Capital was of course made out of his acceptance of a pension. He had sold his country for gold, they said.

Incensed by the gross abuse so plentifully heaped upon him, Pitt wrote a letter to the people, explaining the cause of his resignation. This epistle, which was really an appeal to the City against the Court, had the effect of raising him still higher in popular estimation. The Common Council gave him a vote of thanks, and the City members were instructed to look to him as their recognised leader. Stirling, Exeter, York, Chester, and other towns and cities throughout England and Scotland, complimented him on his conduct; and the tide of censure with which his enemies had striven to overwhelm him was now turned back upon themselves, and threatened to ruin them.

Public wrath was excited, and was not to be appeased until it had given full expression to its sentiments. 'The City was all fire and flame.' Not only the Princess and Lord Bute were spoken of in the freest manner, but even the sacred person of the King was ridiculed. Once, when he was on his way to visit the Princess, the mob gathered round his chair, and asked him if he were going to imbibe refreshment at the maternal breast, using one brief and graphic word to express the operation; and on the walls of the Royal Exchange and Westminster Hall, notices were pasted, containing the words, 'No petticoat government. No Scotch favourite.'

But the King was heedless of such signs of the times, and regarded my Lord with almost as much affection as the Dowager did. Ample proofs remain of the Thane's great personal influence over His Majesty. The Countess Temple, in writing to her lord, in December, 1762, says:

'Mrs. Ryde was here yesterday. She is acquainted with a brother of one of the Yeomen of the Guard; and he tells her the King cannot live without my Lord Bute. If he goes out anywhere, he stops when he comes back, to ask of the Yeomen of the Guard if my Lord Bute is come in yet, and that his lords, or people that are with him, look as mad as can be at it. The mob have a good story of the Duke of Devonshire. That he went first to light the King, and the

King followed, leaning upon Lord Bute's shoulder, upon which the Duke turned about, and desired to know which he was waiting upon.'

Nor was Lord Bute without using the influence for his own benefit. The rangership of Richmond Park had been taken from the King's aunt, the Princess Amelia, that it might be given to him; and, in September, 1762, he had been, with great ceremony and splendour, invested with the Order of the Garter; on which occasion the famous John Wilkes wrote a ballad, that enjoyed an immense popularity, only three verses of which can be given.

THE THANE OF BUTE.
Installed Knight of the Garter, September, 1762.

'You may sing of Will Pitt or my Lord Albemarle,
You may toast your old friend or your favourite girl,
But my theme all your praises will equally suit,
And who should it be but John, Earl of Bute?
                Derry down.

'With manners unformed, and with language uncouth,
The rude north he deserted, to polish the south;
His loved bag-pipes he left, and began on his flute,
And a Princess soon yielded to John, Earl of Bute.
                Derry down.

    *   *   *   *   *   *

'The King gives but one, like his countryman, Chartres.
All England, to hang him, would part with both garters.
And, good lord! how the people would laugh and would hoot,
Could they once set a-swinging this John, Earl of Bute.
                Derry down.'

The 'Petticoat Government' of course referred to the Princess Dowager, who now came in for a very fair share of the public detestation which from this time continued to her death. When at this period of popular excitement she visited the theatre, she was greeted with a storm of hisses, and throughout the night vile inuendoes and open references to her Scotch lover were shouted from the galleries, which so exasperated her that she resolved never to venture within the walls of the play-house again. But the scandal which attended her name was by no means allowed to rest with the references of the unholy gods; the ballads, pamphlets, and prints of the day teemed with gross insinuations. One print, which gained a special popularity, represented her as reproving one of her maids-of-honour—Miss Chudleigh, to wit—for her erratic conduct, to which the gay young lady is made to reply, 'Madam, *chacun à son* —But?'

Those who regarded the dropping of the great diamond from the royal crown on the coronation day as an ill omen, now declared it was fulfilled in Pitt's loss to the government, and the following lines were freely circulated:

> 'When first portentous it was known
> Great George had jostled from his crown
>   The greatest diamond there;
>
> 'The omen-mongers one and all
> Foretold some mischief must befall,
>   Some loss beyond compare.
>
> 'Some fear this gem is Hanover,
> Whilst others wish to God it were;
>   Each strives the nail to hit.
>
> 'One guesses that, another this,
> All mighty wise, yet all amiss,
>   For, ah! who thought of Pitt?'

Other lines on the same subject, written by a gentleman in the country, appeared in the daily papers:

> 'The fatal omen is fulfilled too soon,
> See Pitt, the brightest pearl of the crown,
> The state's great bulwark and a nation's pride,
> Untimely severed from his Sovereign's side.
> O soon may Heaven the precious gem restore
> To shine unclouded and to fall no more.'

But the popular enthusiasm for the favourite and prejudice against Bute were more fully expressed on November 9th, at the annual state dinner at the Guildhall, to which the King and his consort and the Ministers were duly bidden, and of which a graphic account is given in the memoirs of the Marquis of Rockingham, and in those of his contemporaries. On the evening of the great banquet, the thoroughfares leading from the West End to the City were thronged by an anxious and turbulent mob, whose feelings were raised to a fever pitch of excitement. Lord Bute had some apprehensions for his safety, and, being wise in his generation, had taken care to hire a number of butchers and prizefighters, who had directions to follow his coach, and, in case of attack, to strike out and protect him from all violence. The fates, however, favoured him, and his coach passed through the vastly crowded streets unrecognised by the throng that impatiently awaited him, until he had almost reached the Guildhall. Then, when its prey had almost escaped it, the mob discovered him, and, rendered all the more furious because he had been suffered through mistake to pass in peace, set up a fierce howl of derision and hatred. Men, and women, ever the most demonstrative patriots, stormed round the coach, and amongst savage hisses, shouts, and yells, greeted my lord with such personal remarks as, 'We want no Scotch rogues!' 'Damn you, Bute!' 'Pitt for ever!' Mud was freely flung, not only on the coachman and footmen, but on the Earl and on Lord Barrington, who accompanied him. In vain the bruisers and butchers, who fought right boldly, strove to protect him; they were overpowered by numbers; the coach stood still, the servants trembled for their lives, but, just as the traces were cut in order to remove the horses, a force of constables bore down upon the mob, and after awhile succeeded in snatching the unpopular Earl from its grasp.

Scarcely was this scene over, when Pitt, accompanied by

Lord Temple, his brother-in-law, who had resigned at the same time as the favourite, drove up in a chariot and pair. His appearance was the signal for an outburst of enthusiasm; the crowd pressed forward and kissed the heads of the horses, cheered lustily, flung their hats in the air, and gave him every demonstration of their favour. Almost immediately after him came His Sacred Majesty, looking pale and anxious, his homely little Queen beside him, but the crowd had felt little loyalty to a King who allowed himself to be governed by two persons against whom the tide of popular hatred had set, and 'were quite exasperated,' as the Rev. William Robertson says, in courtly language, 'at the Queen not being handsome.' So their Majesties' subjects suffered them to pass almost without recognition, and scarce a cheer broke the silence that marked their reception. In the Guildhall, the King was received in like manner, hardly a murmur of applause running round the room at his appearance, whilst the great statesman had been welcomed with noisy acclamation.

These signs of public feeling, exhibited at the Guildhall dinner, were but the preliminary to a storm, which, gaining strength with time, burst in full force above the head of the favourite, and even threatened the safety of his Royal master. Three months after Pitt's resignation—a period of which Spain had availed herself to rally all her strength—the Government was obliged to declare war, notwithstanding the dislike which the King and Lord Bute had to such an act. Not long afterwards, the Duke of Newcastle, the nominal head of the Administration, having been frequently slighted by the King, His Majesty being anxious to get rid of him, resigned his office, which was on the same day filled by Lord Bute, who then became First Lord of the Treasury, and the most unpopular Minister who had ever directed the destinies of the English nation. He had at last reached the step which he had long coveted, and now resolved to use his power for the benefit of himself, his family, and his countrymen. His daughter and Lady Susan Stuart, daughter to the Earl of Galloway, had been already made ladies of the bedchamber to the King's eldest sister, the Princess Augusta. Lord Bute had also settled a royal pension of £400 a year on his sister, Lady Susan Ruren; but now he conferred the highest offices in Scotland on his brother, James MacKenzie, and obtained an English peerage for his son.

Dr. Nichol, one of the King's physicians, a very able man, was, without being guilty of any fault, removed to make room for Dr. Duncan, whose recommendation was, that he hailed from the 'land o' cakes.' When the King sat for his portrait, Sir Joshua Reynolds, then in the full enjoyment of his fame, was overlooked, and Ramsay, the son of the Edinburgh wig-maker and poet, selected as the artist.

So also, when a musician was required for the Queen, Dr. Arne's existence was ignored, and a Scotchman named Oswald, a retailer of second-hand music, who dwelt in the savoury district of St. Martin's Churchyard, received the appointment. Every place in the Court was, if possible, filled by the favourite with his countrymen and countrywomen. 'The Jacobites all flock to St. James's,' said George Selwyn, 'because there are so many Stuarts there.' Another wit, William Stanhope, my Lord Chesterfield's brother, said he was afraid of going to Court, fearing he might get the itch, and then he would have to go to the Princess Dowager to get some sulphur to cure him.

Since the rebellion in Scotland, in 1745, the Scotch, never in favour with the English, were in especially bad odour, and the patronage shown them was deeply resented. Pamphlets, caricatures, scurrilous and bitter ballads daily swarmed from the press, and passed from garret to drawing-room, from club to coffee-house, attacking the favourite and his friends in the plainest and, oftentimes, the coarsest language. One favourite verse was:

> 'Had paving London streets in taste
> Been left to me alone,
> On Scotchmen's heads we might have trod;
> And Bute's the corner-stone.'

Nor was my Lord left to suffer in single painfulness. The Princess Dowager's name continued to be infamously and frequently coupled with his. In one of the early numbers of the *North Briton*, a paper was published on the 'Loves of Queen Isabella and Mortimer,' which left not a shadow of doubt regarding the modern characters to which it pointed in most contemptuous language. The connection of the Princess and the favourite was, however, even more openly referred to when Mr. Calvert rose in the House of Commons, and drew a picture of a fictitious family in Surrey, whom he called the 'Steadys,' describing in language not to be mistaken the two old Steadys, and the young one; giving an account of young Steady's mother, and of her improper intimacy with a Scotch gardener, and concluding by expressing his hope that the true friends of young Steady would advise him to recall his old friends, and turn away the Scotch gardener.

The mob seized hold of what may be called the popular scandal, and one night a great concourse of people marched through the streets, carrying a miniature gallows, from which was suspended a Jack-boot (indicating John Bute), and a woman's petticoat, by way of representing the Princess Dowager, both of which articles they publicly burned amidst great rejoicing. Nor was the King spared in the general ridicule. In *The World as it Goes* the author describes a vision of a child in a cave, carefully guarded by the royal favourite. The bard says of His Majesty:

> 'Altho' a child, he like a man was dress'd
> In velvet mantle, and in ermin'd vest;
> His baby hand a golden sceptre bore,
> And on his brow a tott'ring crown he wore.

Changeful he seem'd, and languid, and cried by turns;
Now with sullen fits, and now with fury burns.
For other toys his watchful guardian teaz'd,
With the new bawbles for a moment pleas'd ;
Then threw them at his feet, and with disdain
Demands to leave the cave, and call his train—
When straight the stern Protector from his vest
Drew fourth a scourge, and thus the boy address'd :
" Behold this dreadful symbol of command,
To me entrusted by thy mother's hand !
Weav'd by her cunning art, and well design'd
To rule thy tetchy mood and stubborn mind."
Deep sunk the threats into the urchin's breast,
Who moan'd, and sobb'd, and cry'd himself to rest.'

The caricatures which were exposed in the windows of the print-sellers all over the town equalled the ballads and pamphlets in their open scurrility. One of these represented the high-roads from the north crowded with ragged, hungry-looking Scotchmen, forsaking their own country to find refuge in the south, whilst ship-loads sought the land of promise by sea; another, entitled 'The Royal Dupe,' shows the Princess Dowager seated on a sofa lulling the King to sleep, whilst Bute steals his sceptre, and Fox (Pitt's rival) picks his pocket. A third, entitled 'The Mountebank,' represents Bute as a quack-doctor standing on a stage, recommending his golden pills; Smollett, the paid Scotch advocate of Scotchmen, who conducted a paper called the *Briton*, which Bute had established in his own defence, is by his side dressed as a mountebank, whilst the Princess Dowager, dressed as a witch, looks on half-concealed by a curtain.

'By my saul, laddies,' Smollett is made to say, 'I tell ye truly I went round about, and I thank my geud stars I found a passage through Wales, which conducted me to a' the muckle places in the land, where I soon got relief, and straightway commenced to doctor for the benefit of mesel' and countrymen. See here, my bra' lads, in these bags are contained the gowden lozenges, a never-failing remedy that gives present ease, famous throughout the known world for their excellent quality. Now, as ye are a' my countrymen, and stand in most need of a cure, I will gi'e every mon o' ye twa or three thousand of these lozenges once a year to make ye hauld up your heads, and turn out muckle men.' Bute, as the quack-doctor, adds: 'Awa' wi' ye to the de'il, ye soothern loons; but a' ye bonny lads fra the north o' Tweed mak' haste and come to me; I am now in a capacity to gi'e ye a' relief. I ken fu' weel your distemper—I dinna mean that so peculiar to our country occasioned by the immoderate use of oatmeal. But it is the gowden itch wi' which ye are troubled (and, in truth, most folk are) that I learnt the art to cure. I mysel' was ne'er free frae this muckle itch while I lived in the north, but, having a geud staff to depend upon, I resolved to travel into the south to seek a cure.'

But the King, Lord Bute, and the Princess Dowager seemed to take little heed of the popular feeling, or, if they did, were at least determined that it should not prevent them from seeking the political ends they desired. The Princess imbued her son with the idea of exerting his royal prerogative, and rendering himself independent of either the Lords or the Commons, to whom he should dictate in all things. 'George, be a King—be a King!' was her cry; and the conduct of his life showed that her lesson had sunk into his heart, taken root there, and produced vile fruits.

'The instant his prerogative was concerned, or his bigotry interfered with, or his will thwarted,' says Lord Brougham, 'the most bitter animosity, the most calculating coldness of heart, took possession of his breast, and swayed it by turns.'

To exert the royal prerogative, as the King understood

the phrase, meant to strip the great houses of England of their hereditary influences; to reduce the powerful nobility to the condition of the petty, servile German nobles, in order that he might be able to exert his power over them with absolute sway. Church and State were to be governed, even to their minutest details, by his supreme will; the people were to have no voice, the Ministry no power, the King was to reign omnipotent in all things; his creatures alone were to rise to places of State, not by virtue of long lineage, splendid talents, or great deeds, but by reason of his royal favour, which would counterbalance the loss of all other qualities; whilst those who in any way differed from his opinions were to sink into the dark oblivion to which his displeasure would perpetually condemn them. All genius and talents were to be rewarded and gauged according to the dull level of his judgment, and all show of national independence was to be instantly crushed. Such was the dream of magnificent despotism which seized hold upon the little mind of the dull monarch.

He was now informed that the moment had come for him to exert his prerogative, and, backed by the Dowager's ambition, and Lord Bute's desire for power and distinction, George strove with all his might to be a ruler of his people. With the dogged obstinacy that ever distinguished his character, he determined to take the first steps towards such an end, by establishing a peace in spite of the opposition of the whole nation, and the prejudice it might entail to the country by giving up the most valuable of the English conquests for a cessation of hostilities, which might mean little more than a truce to his unprincipled allies.

The first movement made was to send the Duke of Bedford to Paris as ambassador, when he agreed with the French Government to a treaty of peace. As His Grace passed through London on his way to the French capital, he was jeered at and hissed by the populace, who had caught wind of his intended mission. This treatment so alarmed my Lord Bute, who had previously been heedless of the storm of vile epithets and ugly words showered on him, which, however, could break no bones, that from this time he never went out without an escort of prize-fighters, called in the language of the day 'mashers.' His sacred, though obstinate, Majesty showed greater wisdom yet, if less courage, by carefully staying at home, and his royal seclusion was shared by his mother.

The treaty of peace could not be ratified except by the sanction of Parliament. To obtain this was a herculean labour, which it was known could never be honestly accomplished. Yet Lord Bute did not despair of gaining it by fraud, with the sanction and approval of the King. It was a step of vast importance, not only so far as the Minister's own power and future career were concerned, but inasmuch as it would determine whether the King was to be ruled, or to rule. To succeed, therefore, no such trifles as honour, principle, or even personal dislike, were to be allowed to stand in the way. Bute, who had boasted that honesty should be the sign by which his administration should be known, now determined to resort to wholesale bribery and corruption. Henry Fox, Pitt's great rival, though thoroughly detested by His Majesty and the Princess, was called to their aid, and made leader of the House of Commons. To secure his services, the lucrative post of paymaster and a sinecure office were given him, and he was at once made a member of the Cabinet.

It was through him that the House of Commons must be bribed; and he set to work at his assigned task without a trace of false delicacy. Walpole says:

'He directly attacked the separate members of the House of Commons; and with so little decorum, on the part of either buyer or seller, that a shop was publicly opened at the Pay-office, whither the members flocked, and received the wages of their venality in bank-bills, even to so low a sum as two hundred pounds for their votes on the treaty. Twenty-five thousand pounds, as Martin, Secretary of the Treasury, afterwards owned, were issued in one morning; and in a single fortnight a vast majority was purchased to approve the peace ... The profusion which was exercised on this occasion, and which reduced the Court to stop even the payments of the King's bed-chamber, made men recall severely to mind the King's declaration on the choice of his Parliament, that he would not permit any money to be spent on elections.'

Years afterwards, Ross Mackay, who had been private secretary to Lord Bute, and was subsequently made Treasurer of the Ordnance, told Lord Besborough :

'With my own hand I secured above one hundred and twenty votes on that vital question to Ministers. Eighty thousand pounds were set apart for the purpose. Forty members of the House of Commons received from me a thousand pounds each. To eighty others I paid five hundred pounds a-piece.'

Having secured the interests of the House of Commons in this vile fashion, it was now imperative to gain that of the Lords. The first member of the upper House whose sentiments were gauged was the Duke of Devonshire— the Prince of Whigs, as the Princess Dowager derisively called him—but His Grace declined to support the Court scheme. A little while afterwards, when he went to pay his duty to the King, and sent a page to announce his attendance on His Majesty, royalty indignantly refused him the light of its countenance. 'I will not see him,' said the King. When the page hesitated, from amazement at such a message, he was ordered to go at once, and deliver the words as they had been spoken. The Duke, though astonished and indignant, had presence of mind left to send the page to ask what he should do with his key of office as Lord Chamberlain. A brief reply was returned: 'Orders will be given for that.' The Duke went hastily home, and, without waiting for the royal orders, took his key, and immediately carried it to the Secretary of State. Next morning, his brother, Lord George Cavendish, and his brother-in-law, Lord Besborough, resigned their respective places as Comptroller of the Household and Postmaster-General. Five days after, the Marquis of Rockingham resigned his place as one of the Lords of the bed-chamber. Lord Ashburnham, who held a similar post, did likewise, as did also my Lord Kinnoul. These vacancies were quickly filled up by those pledged to support the Government.

But the work was not yet complete. Lord Granby was daily expected on his return from the army, and messengers were stationed at various seaports to meet and bribe him with such offers as the Ordnance, and command of the army; the King, in order to make such an offer as the latter, completely set aside the claims of Marshal Ligonier, who had served with Marlborough, and had been invested with the insignia of the Bath by George II. on the field after the battle of Dettingen, where he had distinguished himself. Marshal Conway, who it was known would receive no bribe, was, to keep him out of the way, selected to conduct the army to England, and the Duke of York, the King's brother, who was not cautious in concealing his hatred for Bute and his measures, was sent to Italy.

On December 9th, 1762, the debate on the preliminaries took place in both Houses of Parliament. There was much excitement, though no one had any doubt as to the success of the Government scheme. In the Upper House, the Duke of Grafton, looking full at Lord Bute, openly accused him of bribery; in the Lower House, Pitt, who, though ill, had himself carried within the bar, from whence he had to be assisted to his seat, for three hours and a half denounced the peace as prejudicial to England's prosperity.

Then, exhausted, he left the scene as his rival, Fox, stood up to reply. In the House of Commons the preliminaries were approved of by a majority of three hundred and nineteen against sixty-five; in the Upper House there was no division. The Court clique had gained the day. Nothing could equal the exultation of its members. 'Now my son is a King,' exclaimed the Princess, in an outburst of triumph. 'Never more shall the Whig grandees be admitted to power,' exclaimed His Majesty, forgetful that but for the Whigs, over whose downfall be exulted, his great-grandfather had never left his little German Electorate to sit upon a throne. My Lord Bute, who was a lover of fine sentiments, satisfied himself on this occasion with an epigrammatic sentence; he trusted that a record of the share which he had in securing peace to his country might be inscribed on his tomb.

Thus a reign which had commenced under the unclouded auspices of domestic peace was suddenly turned to one of rancour; a united Government divided into factions, a contented nation stirred to its centre by animosities, by the united efforts of an unprincipled, dissembling woman, a dull, weak, narrow-minded King, and a designing, ambitious Scotchman.

The vengeance of the worthy trio during this crisis and after their victory is worth recording. His Gracious Majesty, at the first Cabinet Council held after the Duke of Devonshire's resignation, took a pen and crossed His Grace's name from the Council-book, a wanton and unmerited insult; moreover, the Dukes of Newcastle and Grafton and the Marquis of Rockingham were dismissed from the lieutenancies of their several counties, and a like affront was only saved the Duke of Devonshire by the interference of Fox. His Grace, however, resigned his lieutenancy after the dismissal of his friends. Mr. Wilkinson and Mr. Earle were dismissed from the Board of Ordnance on account of votes, and Thomas Townsend from the Green Cloth, without notification; Admiral Forbes, a younger son of the Earl of Granard, was removed from the Admiralty to make room for a friend of Fox, and Mr. Schutz, who had been for seven years a gentleman of the bed-chamber, was dismissed because he had no vote in Parliament, and could be of no use there. This mean vengeance went further yet, when the widow of Admiral Philip Cavendish was deprived of her post as housekeeper of one of the public offices, because her husband had been related to the Duke of Devonshire.

But the triumph was destined to be of but short duration. The expenses connected with the negotiations for peace were so heavy, that a sum of three millions and a half were borrowed in order to defray them, and with such improvidence as to leave a profit of £350,000 to the contractors; to pay this, it was resolved that a tax should be levied on cider, then a popular drink amongst the middle and lower classes. At this the indignation of the nation was raised once more, but with as little effect as when it had protested against peace. In the country, the farmers threatened to feed their pigs with apples, or cut down the apple-trees. Two protests were entered against the Bill on the journals of the House of Lords; the House of Commons likewise protested; the City sheriffs, without having asked leave, presented a petition to the King, praying him not to pass the Bill; but George was determined to be a King, and passed it next morning, the majority in both Houses being tools of Lord Bute's.

Nothing could now exceed the public hatred of Bute; his effigy was hung in public upon a gibbet, torn, and burned by the mob. He went abroad in disguise; once, taking alarm at some rumour of threatened vengeance by the crowd, he said, 'We shall have thirty thousand men come down to St. James's.' In the City, toasts were drunk to wit, beauty, virtue, and honour, these being the ironical designations of the King, Queen, Princess Dowager, and Lord Bute. The Duchess of Bedford set a dangerous example to her caste by refusing to visit the Drawing-rooms of the Dowager, and the press teemed with fresh abuse. The Princess was openly charged with having 'been so lost to all sense of honour and shame, and so abandoned in principle, as to sacrifice the peace, prosperity, and security of the English nation for the sum of five hundred thousand pounds, which she received from the Court of France;' and in one of the popular caricatures the King was represented as a donkey, on whose back the favourite rode triumphantly.

In the midst of this tumult, Lord Bute suddenly resigned. By character he was cautious; and terror of the public wrath had driven him from office, it was said; he, by way of accounting for his resignation, declared his health had begun to suffer from his attendance to public business.

'He was professedly the first or sole Minister very little more than ten months,' writes the author of the 'History of the Minority,' 'during which time he revived national animosities between the English and Scotch. He revived party distinctions among the English; he was the means of disgracing the best of our nobility, and of dismissing the ablest servants of the Crown; he stifled by his conduct the acclamations due from the people to their King; weakened the Crown by disposing of almost all the reversionary patents; turned out, with inhumanity, the innocent dependents of former Ministers; increased the peerage beyond the example of any of his predecessors; borrowed public money on exorbitant terms, and invented a new Excise.

Henry Fox retired at the same time as Lord Bute, and was raised to the peerage as Lord Holland.

CHAPTER IV.

Dark Pictures in the King's Life—Buckingham House—Birth of a Royal Heir—Seclusion of their Majesties—Edward, Duke of York—The Princess Augusta — A Gay and Gallant Soldier—Brunswick's Prince and his Popularity—The King's Insanity—Death of 'Billy the Butcher'—His Highness of Gloucester—Private Marriage—Romance of the Danish Court—The Queen and her Lover—Death of the Princess Dowager—Lord Bute's Wealth.

HISTORY holds no sadder or more painful pictures than those which the domestic life of George III. occasionally present during the long and eventful period which elapsed from his marriage, at the age of twenty-three, until the grave closed over him, in his eighty-first year. Yet they are not the less instructive because of their dark colours and sombre shadows, nor the less interesting from the absence, so far as the King was concerned, of the glaring colours of vice which made the reigns of the last two monarchs flagrant and revolting illustrations in the records of Courts.

Early in the King's reign, the Civil List was fixed at £800,000 a year, and after his marriage a gracious Parliament settled on his Queen the substantial sum of £10,000 per annum, with a dowry of £100,000, and Richmond Old Park and Somerset House, in case she became a widow. The King, however, not satisfied with these residences, purchased Buckingham House, which had been built by John Sheffield, Duke of Buckingham, for the sum of £21,000, and presented it to Her Majesty; and from this time it was usually called the Queen's House. In 1825, this red-brick mansion was pulled down, and the present hideous pile of buildings (known as Buckingham Palace) erected on its site. To this residence the King and his Consort, early in their married life, retired from the more lively quarters of St. James's, which Horace Walpole said was 'not a prison strait enough.'

The same seclusion which concealed his private life from his subjects before his marriage was now continued, the Dowager taking every precaution that none but her friends should have access to him.

'It will scarcely be believed,' says Sir Nathaniel Wraxall, 'but it is nevertheless true, that in order to prevent his conversing with any persons, or receiving any written intimations, anonymous or otherwise, between the drawing-room and the door of Carlton House (the Princess's residence), when he was returning from thence to St. James's, or to Buckingham House, after his evening visits to his mother, she never failed to accompany him till he got into his sedan-chair.'

Previous to the removal of the royal pair from a palace that had witnessed so many strange and eventful scenes, a child was born to them destined to bring them much tribulation. This happened on August 12, 1762, at half-past seven in the morning, the anniversary day of the succession of George Lewis Guelph, Elector of Hanover, to the English throne. My Lord Archbishop of Canterbury and the Lord Chancellor had sat up all night to be witnesses at the birth of the princely infant, whilst in an adjoining chamber, their Graces of Devonshire and Rutland, my Lords Hardwicke, Huntingdon, Talbot, Bute, Masham, and Cantalupe, with all the ladies of the bed-chamber and maids-of-honour, were in attendance. The 'person that waited on the King with the news of Her Majesty being delivered of a Prince, received a present of a £500 bank-bill;' whilst the intelligence was made known to the general public by the roaring of guns from the Tower, and the ringing of many bells from turrets and steeples.

The infant was baptized George Augustus Frederick, by the Archbishop of Canterbury, the sponsors being the Princess Dowager, the Duke of Cumberland, and the Duke of Mecklenburg-Strelitz. On this day, the Queen's bed, magnificently upholstered in crimson velvet, was removed to the great drawing-room.

'Though she is not to see company in form,' writes Horace Walpole, ' yet it looks as if they had intended people should have been there, as all who presented themselves were admitted, which were very few, for it had not been notified—I suppose, to prevent too great a crowd. All I have heard named besides those in waiting were the Duchess of Queensberry, Lady Dalkeith, Mrs. Grenville, and about four more ladies.'

A few days after the baptism, the royal heir was created Prince of Wales; 'for the eldest son of the British monarch,' as Hume says, 'does not possess that title by inheritance, but by creation.'

A short time subsequent to this event, their Majesties moved into the Queen's House, where they may be said to have set aside all signs of royalty, and lived in almost uninterrupted seclusion. To furnish this residence, the other palaces were more or less stripped of pictures and furniture, especially Hampton Court, a place which the King could not endure, from the fact that in this residence his grandfather had once, in a sudden fit of passion, struck him a blow. George III. never afterwards could pass through the room where the occurrence happened without betraying great repugnance. The King, influenced by the close habits of seclusion to which he had been subjected, as well as from a consciousness of his dulness, and from an intolerance in others of a brilliancy to which he could not lay claim, retired as much as possible from the nobility, and was scarcely to be seen or spoken to except on drawing-room days. His consort, on the other hand, excessively homely in appearance, without grace or polish of manner, or one intellectual trait to brighten her natural dulness, but steeped in an imperious, narrow-minded pride characteristic of her insignificant and stolid race, was as suitable a mate for him, as she was unfit to reign over courtiers whose sparkling wit and high-bred beauty were proverbial, whose grace and courtesy were fascinating, whose manners and conversation, studiously cultivated as an art, made their vices almost acceptable.

The royal pair sank to the dead level of domesticity on the very threshold of life, to the disappointment of the nobility, who had naturally looked forward to the reign of the young Monarch as a period of gaiety and brilliancy. The Queen's House came to be regarded by them as a place of imprisonment and gloom, and was not inaptly named Holyrood House. There were, it was true, two weekly drawing-rooms and two yearly balls, but they had nothing in common with those of former reigns. Gambling, the fashionable amusement of the age, was strictly forbidden in the royal palaces, and the drawing-rooms held on Sundays were abolished because it was considered a profanation of the Sabbath. The King had asked Lady Dorset as a favour not to hold assemblies at her house on that day.

'I am but a satellite, please your Majesty,' replied the lively Countess, 'moving in the orbit of a superior planet.'

'I understand your reproof,' said the King; 'the orbit of the planet shall be altered.'

'Then,' remarked her Ladyship, 'the satellite must follow.'

And so the royal drawing-rooms were held no more on the day of rest.

The King had, a few months before the birth of the Prince of Wales, a brief illness which was probably more serious than was generally supposed, as may be judged from a letter which Lord Chancellor Hardwicke wrote to Lord Royston in June, 1762. 'I fear,' said my Lord, 'His Majesty was very ill, for physicians do not deal so roughly with such patients without necessity. God grant him a speedy recovery.' Whatever the nature of his illness may have been, it certainly for some time left behind traces of mental depression of which he was unable to rid himself. In one of Dr. Birch's MS. letters written at this period, preserved in the British Museum, he remarks—'His Majesty is observed of late to have less cheerful spirits than usual, which even the Queen has taken notice of with some concern.' No doubt this indisposition was the shadow of the coming dreadful malady which soon clouded his life.

Under these circumstances, and with such patrons as their Majesties, it was not to be wondered at that the royal drawing-rooms missed the animation, splendour, and gaiety which had distinguished those of the last Monarch. The King looked grave as he received the homage of his courtiers; the Queen smiled, but could not venture to express herself in the language of her subjects. Some scrutiny was now observed as to the characters of the ladies admitted to the presence of the Queen; royal courtesans were no longer in request, and some show of decency was expected in the conversation that floated round the throne. The old order of things was thoroughly reversed in all its details; wit fell meaningless on the royal ears, grace found no favour in the royal eyes, and beauty was regarded with jealousy by the homely Queen as an incentive to wicked temptations that might waylay the virtuous King. Laughter was no longer heard, delicate morsels of scandal were whispered no more, fashions were wilfully neglected, and intrigues were foregone in the royal presence, where manners now became strictly decorous, but, alas! terribly dull.

Of Her Majesty, one of the lampoons of the age declared:

> 'She hates the manners of the times,
> And all our fashionable crimes;
> And fondly wishes to restore
> The golden age and days of yore,
> When silly, simple women thought
> A breach of chastity a fault;
> Esteem'd those modish things divorces,
> The very worst of human curses,
> And deem'd assemblies, cards, and dice
> The springs of every sort of vice.
> Romantic notions! All the fair
> At such absurdities must stare,
> And, spite of all her pains will still
> Love routs, adultery, and quadrille.'

Walpole gives an account of a ball which their Majesties gave shortly after their marriage, to which but six of the nobility not immediately connected with the Court were bidden. His Majesty danced with the Queen the whole time; and his sister, the Princess Augusta, with her four younger brothers. Some of the lords and ladies of the bed-chamber were present, and the maids-of-honour, but none were permitted to sit in the royal presence, save the Princess Dowager, the Duchess of Bedford, and Lady Bute. This lively entertainment commenced at half an hour after six, and at one o'clock the company were dismissed without supper.

It was scarcely to be wondered at that the brilliant and beautiful women, the wits and fine gentlemen, whose routs, masquerades, and divers amusements alone kept the town from a state of stagnation, gradually deserted the royal drawing-rooms, and were but on rare occasions, when their attendance was looked on as a necessary duty, seen within the walls of St. James's or Buckingham House.

According to Sir Nathaniel Wraxall, 'All the splendour of a Court was laid aside, or only exhibited for a few hours on a birthday. Rarely, during the first twenty years after his accession, did the King join in any scene of public amusement, if we except the diversion of the theatre. Still more rarely did he sit down at table with any of his courtiers or nobility. His repasts, private, short, and temperate, never led to the slightest excess.'

In private life, nothing could be more simple than the *régime* which the royal pair adopted. The Queen spent a great part of the morning with her tutor, Dr. Majendie, who strove to teach her English, but to the end of her life she never wrote or spoke the language with ease. When her lessons were over, her needlework commenced, and this employment was succeeded by exercise, when she walked or rode, accompanied by her royal companion, till dinner-time. In the evening, she played on the harpsichord and sang, then joined in a quiet game of cribbage, and so the day ended in monotonous dulness. When they adjourned to Richmond in the summer, their habits were unaltered. Their Majesties had, indeed, come to regard all public ceremonies as a tax imposed on royalty, of which they were ever anxious to rid themselves, and this increased their unpopularity amongst all classes.

'The Court,' writes Horace Walpole to my Lord Hertford, 'independent of politics, makes a strange figure. The recluse life led here at Richmond—which is carried to such an excess of privacy and economy, that the Queen's *friseur* waits on them at dinner, and four pounds only of beef are allowed for their soup—disgusts all sorts of people. The drawing-rooms are abandoned. Lady Buckingham was the only woman there on Sunday se'nnight. In short, one hears of nothing but dissatisfaction, which, in the city, rises almost to treason.'

With the exception of Edward, Duke of York, the King's brothers and sisters were yet retained in the seclusion which the King had once undergone, by the Princess Dowager. Prince Henry, a lively lad, was one day asked if he had been confined with the epidemic cold. 'Confined!' he answered; 'that I am, but without any cold.' On another occasion, the Princess asked him, when he had been long silent, if he were sulky. He replied, he was not; he was only thinking.

'And, pray,' said the Dowager, 'what are you thinking of?'

'I was thinking,' answered the boy, 'what I should feel, if I had a son as unhappy as you make me.'

In 1767, the eldest of the King's brothers, Edward, Duke of York, died. Gay, gallant, and free in his manners, he was a general favourite with all, save his mother and Lord Bute, whose schemes and favours towards his countrymen the Prince's lively tongue did not hesitate to ridicule. In appearance, he is described as having loose and perpetually rolling eyes, that were extremely short-sighted, heavy features, and hair so light that it resembled feathers. He had been sent into the Navy a few years before his grandfather's death, and, after a service lasting eleven months, was made captain of a frigate named the *Phœnix*. He was subsequently present at the capture of Cherbourg, sailing under Commander Howe, and likewise at St. Cas, where he behaved with great spirit.

Before he was eighteen, encouraged by his grandfather, he had managed to escape from the maternal influence, and freely mixed in the society of the day, to which his elder brother was then a stranger, and, with that easy gallantry proverbial to Princes, he felt little difficulty in making love to some of the fairest women whom fate cast in his way.

One of the first of these was my Lady Essex, then young and singularly beautiful, whose attractions, however, in a little while had to give way for those of the young wife of Charles, third Duke of Richmond, to whom he chattered a good deal of love and of the passion which he declared consumed him. His errant though Princely fancy again took wings, and this time settled on a charming widow, Lady Mary Coke, who was declared the envy of her sex, inasmuch as she was the happy possessor of youth, health, wit, wealth, beauty, and, better than all, liberty. But though Lady Mary always spoke of him as her betrothed, and mourned for his early death, the gay Prince was not constant to her, but sought fresh attraction in Lady Stanhope.

This charming woman vastly gratified the world by affording it some amusing scandal concerning her domestic feuds with her lord and master, Sir William Stanhope, brother to my Lord Chesterfield. The story is told of this happy pair that, returning from the Continent on one occasion, Sir William stopped the carriage at Blackheath, and, getting out, made his spouse the following vastly polite speech: 'Madam,' said he, 'I hope I shall never see your face again.' The lady was not behindhand in courtesy. 'Sir,' she replied, 'I will take all the care I can that you shall not.' And so they parted.

This was the lady to whom Edward, Duke of York, made love—a proceeding in which he was encouraged by her scampish brother, Sir Francis Delaval, who believed Sir William to be in a dying state, and who fondly hoped he might have a Royal Duke as his brother-in-law. But the fates decreed otherwise. The Prince was fond of the Continent, where he spent many a pleasant day, and had made friends with the foreign Courts he visited during his journeys. When, in 1762, on the passing of the Peace Bill, he had been sent out of England, that his too open expressions might not injure the policy of my Lord Bute, he willingly betook himself to the pleasant shores of the Mediterranean, where he enjoyed himself much to his satisfaction. When he was expected at Florence, Clement XIII., who then sat on the Papal throne, directed Cardinal Albani to inform Sir Horace Mann, the English Minister at that city, that, if His Royal Highness wished to visit Rome, he should be received there with all the honours due to his birth. Moreover, the Nuncio at the winter city was requested by his Holiness to wait on the Prince upon his arrival, and deliver him the same most civil message, which was received with pleasure. To Rome His Royal Highness went, where he was entertained by the Pope with graceful and dignified ceremonies.

Some rumours of his pleasures and extravagances reaching home, the pious Christians round the King complained of his brother's ways, and a popular preacher delivered a sermon for which he selected the text, 'The younger son gathered all together, and took his journey into a far country, and there wasted his substance with riotous living.' Alarmed by these reports, the King ordered his brother home, and took a peremptory means of securing obedience by stopping his remittances, which sensible scheme had not, however, the desired effect, for, though bereft of supplies, the Duke continued his riotous living in a far country.

It happened that he was in Paris, in 1767, when news reached him that a woman fair to see, who had once held his heart, was now at Genoa. This information at once made the Prince impatient to reach Italy and the object of his love. He therefore left Paris at once; on his way, he was entertained by the Duc de Villars at his villa, situated between Aix and Marseilles, where a ball 'was made for him,' at which he gaily danced all night, and then, impatient of delay, insisted on getting into his carriage, and proceeding on his journey. When he arrived at Marseilles, he was seized with sudden shuddering, but again determined to proceed on his way, and next day reached Monaco. Here he was obliged to be confined to bed, and, on the physicians being called, it was found a heavy fever had set in, under which he rallied for fourteen days, and then died, in the twenty-eighth year of his age.

A second child was born to the royal pair in August, 1763, who was baptized Frederick, was afterwards created Duke of York, and ultimately played an important part in the history of the country, of which more anon. At the close of the year which gave him birth, the dreary seclusion into which their Majesties had sunk was temporarily dissipated by the marriage of the King's eldest sister, the Princess Augusta. The Princess was not without some personal charms, though she had the heavy features and light hair hereditary to the house of Guelph. Her complexion was fair and soft, and her figure shapely; moreover, she had now reached the age of six-and-twenty, and it was considered desirable that a husband should be found for her. Her mother, the Dowager, had been brought to arrive at this conclusion from the fact that she discerned the Princess was inclined to meddle in the domestic politics of the Court. Like her brother Edward, and indeed most of her brothers and sisters, she had little affection for her mother, detested Bute, and, so far as in her lay, was apt to thwart his policy and unite her sympathies with those of the populace, in favour of William Pitt. That she might communicate this dangerous sentiment to the young Queen, became a dread to the Dowager; for Her Majesty might influence the weak-minded King, and allure him from the maternal allegiance to which he had hitherto blindly submitted.

The Dowager, however, could not hinder the Princess's visits to the Queen's House, but, to hinder the expression of any disloyal speech, she accompanied her there, and in this way prevented a freedom of conversation which she had come to fear. Meanwhile, she cast her eyes about for a husband who would remove the Princess to a sufficiently safe distance from the scene of English politics.

To accomplish this purpose, Charles William Ferdinand, hereditary Prince of Brunswick, was selected; for, though the rival house of Brunswick was hated by the Dowager, yet she deigned to honour it by alliance with one of her offspring, because it suited her purpose. The lady's dowry was, therefore, fixed at the handsome sum of £80,000, with an annuity of £8,000 a year, £5,000 of which was chargeable on the Irish revenue, and the remainder on Hanover. Such was the golden prize held out to the Prince, who was bidden to come and claim its possession. His Royal Highness was nephew to Frederick the Great of Prussia, and was, moreover, a gay and gallant soldier, who had fought well at the famous battle of Hastenbeck, and likewise at the siege of Crefeld. Not only was His Highness brave, but what is oftentimes more in women's eyes, he was handsome. A slight, tall, soldierly figure, and a bright, sun-tanned face added to his attractions. He was the beau ideal of a hero and a lover, and the people were all prepared to receive him as such, and give him a hearty welcome.

Accordingly, when he set foot on English ground at Harwich, he was met by a right loyal throng, who greeted him with shouts and demonstrations of joy, and at night they almost tore down the house at which he stayed, in order that they might see him again. A Chelmsford his reception was quite as enthusiastic. Here it was that an honest Quaker, forcing his way into the room where the Prince was resting, pulled off his hat, and said, 'Friend, my religion forbids me to fight, but I honour those that fight well. Thou art a valiant Prince, and art to be married to a lovely Princess; love her, make her a good husband, and the Lord bless you both!' Alas! His Highness did not know what the good man said, but he understood that some courteous speech was being made him, and, with the gracious instinct of a Prince and a soldier, grasped the Quaker by the hand in right friendly fashion.

If the friendly mood of the people prepared him for a like reception in the royal palace, he was doomed to disappointment. Though living far from the land of political strife, he had made himself intimately acquainted with the workings of the State machinery, and had openly, and in no measured terms, avowed his admiration for Pitt and his policy. This was an outrage which the King and the Dowager could not forgive, and they now determined to show him they had not forgotten his imprudent speeches. When he arrived in London, he at once called to pay his respects to their Majesties, who on this occasion were by no means gracious, the fourth question they put to him being, 'When do you go?' From the Queen's House he hied him to Leicester House, to wait on the Dowager, and see his future wife for the first time. He found his bride-elect gracious and pleasing, and he, who had already proved himself a gallant soldier, now showed he was likewise a polished courtier, for he delicately hinted he had intended to return unwed, if the Princess had not pleased him, but now he looked forward to the day of his marriage with delight.

It had previously been decided by His Majesty that the Prince's stay should be rendered as short and as disagreeable as possible, and this resolution was now put into effect. Somerset House was appointed as his residence previous to his marriage, but no guards were stationed there, and the Lord Steward of the Household was instructed to select the company who should dine with him. The marriage took place not in the Chapel Royal, but in the great Council Chamber, on Monday, January 16, 1764, when the servants of the King and Queen were forbidden to appear in new clothes, as was customary on such occasions, and the ceremony was curtailed as much as possible of all splendour.

The public were quick to notice the petty indignities shown to the Prince by the Court, and, aware of the cause which prompted them, soon resented these slights. The popularity of the King still more decreased, and that of the Prince rose rapidly. As he went one morning to St. James's, he saw in the crowd which surrounded him a soldier in the uniform of Elliot's Light Horse, a regiment with which he had once served in action, and gracefully kissed hands to the man; the crowd immediately turned to see who was the individual so favoured. 'What,' said they, 'does he know you?' 'Yes,' answered the soldier; 'he once led me into a scrape which nobody but himself could have brought me out of again.'

Horace Walpole, who relates the story, adds:

'You may guess how much this added to the Prince's popularity, which was at high-water mark before.'

An opportunity soon occurred of giving vent to this feeling publicly. On the Thursday after the marriage, it was known that the Prince and his bride, and the Court, were to attend a performance at Covent Garden, and the throng which gathered round the theatre was enormous.

'The crowd to see the Prince of Brunswick at the play exceeded all belief,' writes that worthy chronicler of gossip, Horace Walpole, to Horace Mann. 'Your brother James told me this morning that he went to Covent Garden at two in the afternoon, to wait till the doors of the play-house should be opened. He soon found himself in such a mob, that he could not even lift his hand to his head, and so remained for five hours, without getting in at last; and, though he had stood in the open piazza, he perspired so violently that, at his return, he was forced to change every thread he had on. The shouts, claps, and huzzas were immoderate.'

When the King and Queen entered the house, they were received with chilling silence, but on the appearance of the Prince and Princess the house rang with cheers. The gallery called for the hero of popular favour to come forward, and when he complied fresh applause filled the theatre, whilst His Majesty looked on in grave displeasure. In the middle of the play, the Prince went out, at which, according to the *Gentleman's Magazine*, 'the audience were agitated by various surmises. The fact was, His Serene Highness, as he did not well understand the language of the players, took that opportunity to pay his compliments to the Royal Society, of which he was elected a Fellow, and Lord Moreton, being in the chair, made him a very polite speech in the name of the society, which His Highness answered without hesitation.'

When he returned, the applause was renewed. On Saturday night, when the royal family attended the opera, the enthusiasm displayed was greater, if possible, than on the former night, and the crowd as large. So thronged indeed was the house, that three fair ladies, to wit, Her Grace of Leeds, Lady Denbigh, and Lady Scarborough, sat on chairs between the scenes. The doors of the front boxes were thrown open, and the passages filled; and women of fashion, arrayed in gorgeous silks and floating feathers, stood crushing against each other on the stairs during the performance.

On the next day, Sunday, the Prince more than ever offended the Court party by paying a visit to Pitt at his country house at Hayes, with whom he remained in conference for two hours; on another occasion he visited the Duke of Newcastle, who was as fully obnoxious to the King and Lord Bute, and arranged to meet the chiefs of the Opposition at the Duke's residence, which he did on a subsequent day. Nor was this all. He thrice dined with the Duke of Cumberland, who had not been to Court for a considerable time on account of a political disagreement with His Majesty. On one of the occasions on which the old Duke was his host, His Serene Highness, to show his resentment to his royal brother-in-law, was guilty of a breach of etiquette, which was not soon forgotten by the King. The incident is narrated by Walpole, who says, the first time the Prince dined with the Duke, he 'was appointed to be at St. James's at half an hour after seven to a concert. As the time drew near, De Feronce (his chief secretary) pulled out his watch. The Duke took the hint and said, "I am sorry to part with you, but I fear your time is come." He replied, "*N'importe*," and sat on drinking coffee, and it was half an hour after eight before he set out from Upper Grosvenor Street for St. James's.' On another occasion, when a ball was given for him at the Queen's House, the Prince did not put in an appearance until two hours after it had begun. At this assembly there were none of the nobility present, besides their Majesties' servants, but the Duchesses of Ancaster and Marlborough, and Lord Bute's two daughters; the usual royal economy was observed, and the guests were sent home supperless. The next day there was a subscription ball for him at Carlisle House, Soho, when a hundred and fifty men subscribed five guineas each, in return for which each received three tickets. This was chiefly got up by the Dukes of Grafton and Devonshire, whose very names were hateful to the royal ears. The Duke of Cumberland was present, and all the beauties of the town; the whole affair was brilliant and magnificent. The Prince was dressed in a rich suit of silver brocade that cost eleven guineas a yard, and so delighted was he with the entertainment that he danced till five o'clock in the morning. That day he and his bride reluctantly left town for Harwich, from whence they were to embark; on their way they were to pass through Witham, and rest the night there at Lord Abercorn's. My Lord stayed in town, and did not trouble to play the host. My Lady Strafford said to him, 'And so, my Lord, I hear your house is to be royally filled on Wednesday.' 'And serenely,' he answered, and closed his mouth for the remainder of the day.

Their departure had been originally fixed for the 26th, and they were now obliged to keep their agreement, though the Prince would willingly have tarried; however, a message was conveyed to him that a yacht was in readiness to convey them home, and he was obliged to take the hint. The day of their departure was by no means propitious; the weather was wild and threatening, and continued so on the following day when they set sail. A tempest overtook their yacht, and no news of them reached St. James's until the middle of February. Meanwhile a rumour arose that they had been driven away by the Court; the City was in an uproar, the town excited; reports were spread that the Princess's yacht was sunk on the coast of Holland, and their supposed deaths were said to have been caused by the King and the Dowager; even the basket-women in St. James's Market, according to Mrs. Carter, spoke their minds, and wished 'that those who sent the Prince and Princess away were in their places.' They arrived, however, in safety, after considerable danger, at Helvoetsluys. The daughter of this Prince and Princess afterwards became the unhappy wife of George IV.

Early in 1765, the King, then in the twenty-eighth year of his age, was afflicted by one of those mental attacks to which he afterwards became subject through life. To the public at large it was announced that His Majesty had caught cold and fever; but, this being considered an insufficient reason to give a gossiping and curious world for his confinement during three months, it was afterwards stated that a humour which should have appeared in his face had, by the neglect of his physicians, settled on his breast. The nation became anxious, but, so well was the secret kept by those allowed to see the King, that his Prime Minister was left in ignorance of the nature of his illness, and it was commonly whispered His Majesty had fallen into a consumption.

The sudden manner in which his madness first presented itself is recorded by Philip Withers, senior Page of the Presence, in a rare pamphlet called 'History of the Royal Malady.' The King and Queen were driving through Windsor Forest in a phaeton, when the King abruptly stopped the horses, and saying, 'There he is,' descended.

'His Majesty now approached a venerable oak,' says the author, who was in attendance at the time, 'that had enlivened the solitude of that quarter of the park upwards of a century and a half. At the distance of a few yards, he uncovered and advanced, bowing with the utmost respect, and then, seizing one of the lower branches, he shook it with the most apparent cordiality and regard, just as a man shakes his friend by the hand.

'The Queen turned pale with astonishment, the reins dropped from her hands. Never was I in such a consternation lest the horses in the carriage, finding themselves under no control, should run headlong to destruction. Nor did I dare call for assistance, lest the attendants should witness a scene that I desired to keep from their view. At last Her Majesty became attentive to her situation, and, as the reins were happily within reach, they were recovered, and the Queen commanded me to dismount, and to go and intimate, in a soothing voice and suppliant terms, that Her Majesty wished for his company. On my approach, I perceived the King was in earnest conversation, for His Majesty anticipated the answer from his royal friend, and then made a reply. It was the King of Prussia with whom His Majesty enjoyed this rural interview; continental politics were the subject. What I heard it would be unpardonable to divulge. I cannot, however, withhold a remark that must fill every loyal bosom with pleasure; His Majesty, though under a momentary dereliction of reason, evinced the most cordial attachment to freedom and the Protestant faith.

'I approached with reverence.

'"May it please your Majesty——"

'"Don't you see I am engaged?" answered the King.

'I bowed and withdrew.

'"Go again," said the Queen.

'I went.

'"May I presume to inform your Majesty that——"

'"What is the matter?" said the King, in great surprise.

'"Her Majesty is in the carriage, and I am commanded to intimate her desire of your Majesty's company."

'"Good lack-a-day," said the King, "that is true. Run on and inform Her Majesty I am hastening to her."'

This attack was, however, slight, and never rose to the height of frenzy; the principal symptoms which His Majesty showed were great restlessness and incessant chatter, which occasionally lasted for hours, and which was bereft of all coherency. In three months he was considered quite restored, and was not again afflicted with this dreadful malady until the year 1788.

During these three-and-twenty years, full of party warfare, national peril, and important political changes, the private life of the King was not without some interesting events. Children were born to him, alliances were made by his family, and death removed some of those nearest his heart. But amongst these latter, William, Duke of Cumberland, the King's uncle, who shuffled off the mortal coil in 1765, cannot be reckoned. This Prince, popularly known as 'Billy the Butcher,' was at one time the best hated man in England; but, retiring from public life, he outlived his unpopularity.

In youth he had been fierce and cruel, in the last years of his life hard-hearted and licentious. He had lost Fontenoy, a battle which cost the English nation ten thousand lives; had surrendered Hanover to Marshal d'Estrées; had been taunted by his father with having ruined him, and disgraced himself; had introduced the 'Bloody Mutiny Bill'; and had sneered at the death of his brother, Frederick, Prince of Wales. He had had a paralytic stroke, had undergone severe surgical operations for a wound in his leg which he had received at Dettingen, had suffered from gout, and had grown almost blind. He died suddenly on October 31, his last words being, 'It is all over.' His remains were conducted to Westminster Abbey with great pomp and state, and many external signs of a woe remarkable for its absence, and laid in the vault with his late Sacred Majesty. A few days after the funeral, the young King commanded that 'Much Ado about Nothing' should be played, when many wicked persons thought the title had a suggestive reference to a late solemn event.

In this year, William Henry, Duke of Gloucester, the favourite brother of the King, made a marriage which was regarded by His Majesty as a *mésalliance*. At this period the Duke had just arrived at his twenty-first year. As a youth, he had been notably dull; as a man, he was regarded as not being particularly bright, and was, moreover, wholly devoid even of that spare share of talents sufficient to render a Prince clever in the eyes of gracious courtiers. In character, however, he was staid, and far more respectable than his brothers of York or Cumberland, and it was noted that he had many traits in common with the King.

Before he had attained his majority, this susceptible Prince lost his heart to Maria, widow of James, second Earl of Waldegrave, one of the most beautiful and fascinating women of the day. This lady was one of the three daughters of Sir Edward Walpole and of Mrs. Clement, a milliner, on whose union the Church had never been asked to pronounce a nuptial benediction. The triple offspring were, however, fair to see, and married well, one becoming the spouse of the Hon. Frederick Keppel, afterwards the Right Rev. Bishop of Exeter; the second marrying Lionel, fifth Earl of Dysart; and the third, my Lord Waldegrave, who at the time of her marriage was old enough to be her father. My lord, however, considerately died whilst his lady was yet young and passing fair, leaving her three daughters and the mistress of considerable fortune. At an early period of her widowhood she attracted many suitors, the most favoured of whom was for the time the Duke of Portland; when, however, a Prince appeared upon the scene, the subject was dismissed, for my lady was ambitious, and a suitor of the blood royal must have no rivals. The Prince's frequent visits to her receptions became the talk of the town.

'The Duke of Gloucester has professed a passion for the Dowager Waldegrave,' writes Gilly Williams in 1764. 'He is never from her elbow. This flatters Horry Walpole not a little, though he pretends to dislike it.'

The fact was that Horace Walpole, her uncle, did dislike the attentions the Royal Duke openly paid her, and pointed out the improbabilities of his marrying her, or, if he were willing to do so, of his obtaining the King's consent. Lady Waldegrave was a woman of the world, and, seeing the wisdom of her uncle's advice, consented to copy a letter he wrote for her to the Duke, in which she begged to decline his further attentions, as she could not hope to be his wife, and could not deign to be his mistress. After this, the Duke's visits ceased for a fortnight; they then became more frequent and open than before; the fact was, he had married her at her own house, her chaplain, Dr. Norton, performing the ceremony. The Duke then made her promise not to own the marriage even to her father, upon any consideration in the world, without his permission. That permission was withheld six years.

My lady kept her word faithfully, refusing to satisfy her family as to her condition; but yet living on such open terms with the Duke, and in such a manner, that satisfied them of her marriage. The houses, or lodgings, which she took near the palaces in which he resided, were freely furnished from the royal wardrobe. She was covered with jewels; her liveries were changed to a compound between her late husband's and royalty. The Prince's gentlemen handed her to her chair in public; his coaches carried her home; and finally, their Majesties continued to receive her at Court, for reasons of their own.

'The King and Queen,' says Walpole, 'certainly intended it should be supposed Lady Waldegrave was the Duke's mistress. The world interpreted it in a contrary sense, in compliment to the Queen's virtue, who, on that occasion, wished her virtue might be thought more accommodating.'

Not satisfied with this, Lady Waldegrave became more anxious to show the world she was kin with royalty. She obtained apartments in the inner court at Hampton, and demanded permission of the Lord Chamberlain to drive her coach into it, an honour preserved to the royal family alone. My Lord Chamberlain, after some hesitation, spoke to the King, who peremptorily refused her the honour, on which she indignantly threw up her lodgings, and retired from Hampton.

The King and the Princess Dowager were indignant at the Duke's ambiguous conduct, but it was not until six years after his marriage, when his wife became pregnant, that the weak-minded Duke found courage to confess his union. As the Duke's heirs came within the line of succession to the throne, it was deemed advisable that the great officers of the State might be present at the birth. The Duke, therefore, wrote to the King, to notify his marriage and the condition of the Duchess, of which letter no notice was taken.

The King was surly and highly indignant; he would have been satisfied if the Duke had not decided on making his alliance public, and was yet, according to Lord Hertford, afraid of quarrelling with him. The Duchess said His Majesty 'seems not to have enough of courage to be angry with the Duke, but he will wound him in the dark, though he dare do no more.'

The Duke behaved with more firmness than was expected. He told Lord Rochford, the Secretary of State, that he would demand the attendance of the Privy Council, for the satisfaction of the nation.

'The King,' he added, 'may, if he pleases, forbid their coming; but I will summon them, and they shall answer it, at their peril, to the nation, if they refuse. I married like a boy, but I will defend my marriage like a man. Out of respect to the King, I concealed it; to satisfy him and the nation, I must now authenticate it; and if His Majesty does not forthwith take the necessary steps for verifying it, I myself will summon the House of Lords; will go there myself, and in person beseech the House to press the King for despatch.'

He then wrote to His Majesty a second time, when the King sent a message that his marriage would be inquired into after the birth of the child; on this the Duke begged that the examination might take place at once. Accordingly, the Lord Chancellor and two other lords were despatched to the Duke's residence, where they were received by the Duke and Duchess, the Lord Bishop of Exeter, and two men learned in the law, name Lee and Dunning. After various inquiries and attestations, the three wise lords retired; a council was afterwards held, and finally, His Majesty graciously inclined to countenance the marriage, and the officers of the State attended on the Duchess when she gave birth to the Princess Sophia Matilda.

Though the King acknowledged the marriage, he by no

means looked on the Duke or Duchess with favour. The latter he indeed regarded as a wily woman who had entrapped a Prince not over-wise into a union beneath his rank. He declared he never could think 'of placing her in a situation to answer her extreme pride and vanity;' nor could he receive her at Court 'without affronting all the sovereigns of Europe by countenancing a *mésalliance*.' His brother's conduct he stigmatised as disgraceful, and we find him writing to Lord North 'on the subject of this Duke, my heart was wounded.'

But, notwithstanding the tender condition of this organ, his economical Majesty refused later on to provide for his brother's children, but he finally behaved towards them with kindness and generosity. Though the Duke had risked much for the sake of his gracious lady, yet before his death he went the way of most princes, and loved another woman, Lady Almeria Carpenter, lady of the bed-chamber to his Duchess. Reference to this domestic scandal is made in one of Horace Walpole's letters. Sir Nathaniel Wraxall also, in his memoirs, says Lady Almeria, 'one of the most beautiful women of her time, but one to whom Nature had been sparing of intellectual attractions, reigned at Gloucester House. The Duchess remained its nominal mistress, but Lady Almeria constituted its ornament and its pride.' This siren caused the Duchess such annoyance, that a separation between husband and wife was agreed to in 1787. The Duke died in 1803.

Another marriage took place in the royal family in 1766, in the person of Caroline Matilda, the King's youngest sister. In the month of October in this year, when fifteen years old, this Princess became the wife of Christian VII., King of Denmark. ·She had been kept in her nursery, says the author of the 'Memoirs of the Reign of George III.,' 'till sent to Copenhagen; had had no company but servants, and could have seen nothing but an intimacy with

Lord Bute, which all the Princess's children spoke of with disgust; and could have heard nothing but passionate lamentations from the Princess on the impotence of power possessed by English Sovereigns—lessons that seem to have made but too deep impression on the inexperienced young Queen of Denmark when she came to have a lover, and be mistress of absolute power.'

This young Princess, whose union with the King of Denmark was arranged through State policy, was amiable, beautiful, and accomplished, whilst her husband was known to be a weak-minded, graceless libertine. All England looked forward to the marriage as one destined to bring but slight happiness to the Princess, whilst she herself, as the time drew near for her departure, became depressed and anxious. Her forebodings were soon destined to be realized, and the short chapter of her life and early death form one of the most interesting chapters in history.

The King was little more than sixteen at this period, but, though young in years, he was already far advanced in vice. In figure he was diminutive, in appearance he bore a strong resemblance to his grandfather, George II., whose complexion and white eyes he inherited. His Court was ruled by Juliana Maria, the Queen Dowager, whose desire it was to secure the throne for her son, Prince Frederick, and who subsequently became the prime cause of the young Queen's disgrace and misery. When Caroline Matilda arrived in Denmark, her bridegroom-cousin took an aversion to her which strengthened with time. After two years of married life, during which she was subjected to many gross humiliations through her husband's unconcealed amours, he left the kingdom in order to visit England and some other European countries. By the Court of St. James's he was received with some show of coldness, but by the nobility he was sumptuously entertained and studiously courted, notwithstanding that he spent his nights in drinking and dissipation, in the purlieus of St. Giles's, disguised as a sailor.

Indeed, he made no decent concealment of his lack of morals, as a crowded audience at Drury Lane noted on the occasion of his witnessing the play of the 'Provoked Husband.' In the comedy, the good old institution of marriage is continually ridiculed, and at every passage sneering at the ceremony, the little profligate clapped his royal hands in hearty approbation of such sentiments. A few nights later, a crowded house had the benefit of seeing him lying fast asleep in the royal box during the performance of 'Jane Shore.' Charming Mrs. Bellamy played Alicia, and, offended at this glaring instance of princely neglect, determined to rouse the sleeping King; she therefore, when opportunity permitted, approached the royal box, which was close to the stage, and in a tone so loud that it reached almost to a shriek, exclaimed, 'Oh! thou false lord:' whereon the King awoke in sudden alarm, and swore he would not have a woman with a voice like that as his wife for all the world could give.

His profligacy was, however, no drawback to his popularity, and he was enthusiastically received as the husband of an English Princess.

'The King of Denmark,' writes the Queen to Lord Harcourt, 'does amuse himself with plays, operas, balls, assemblies, and seeing the beauty of the country of England. This latter part, I must confess, I do envy him.'

Before leaving, the little King, in return for the great civility shown him, gave a masquerade ball held at the Opera House, at which two thousand five hundred persons were present; 'the greatest number of nobility and gentry ever assembled together upon any occasion of the like nature,' as the *Annual Register* remarks. The jewels worn at this entertainment were estimated to be worth two millions of money. The Opera House was most brilliantly illuminated; the various costumes of the guests magnificent, and the whole entertainment a vast success. The King and Queen sat in a box, looking gravely on at the immense parti-coloured throng moving in the wide area beneath, where His Danish Majesty danced with the charming Duchess of Ancaster, and where blacks and punchinellos, Moorish maidens and grim Turks, together with many heroes and heroines of all times and climes, made up a dazzling spectacle. Towards the close of the night, a noble Duke had the misfortune to lose a snuff-box in the crowd, on the lid of which was a portrait of the French King, set in diamonds; the finder of the valuable article was so pleased with it that it was never returned to its rightful owner, though a sum of 'fifty guineas, and no questions asked,' was offered for its restoration.

This magnificent ball was, however, surpassed by an entertainment given the King by the Prince de Condé at Chantilly, which, says the *Annual Register*, 'continued three days and three nights; during which there was an open house kept for all comers and goers, without exception. There was likewise a most grand hunt in the Forest of Chantilly by candle-light. After a wild boar had been chased for a good while, he was killed by a nobleman with a bow and arrow.

When Christian VII. returned to his Court, he was accompanied by a physician, named Struensee, whom he had met at Ahrensburg, adopted as a special favourite, and readily induced to accompany him to Denmark. Struensee was one of those brilliant adventurers who flash, meteor-like, through courtly spheres for a season, and whose career generally terminates in downfall and ignominy. Nature had given him a handsome person, brilliant talents, ready tact, and great grace of manner; and, with these good gifts, he now determined to win his way to rank and power. He was already high in favour with the King, and in a little while he succeeded in winning the confidence of the

Queen. In her husband's absence from the Court, she had commenced to interest herself in politics, to the annoyance of the Queen Dowager; and, on the return of the King, she was by no means desirous of laying aside the influence she had, meanwhile, gained. Struensee entered into her schemes with great readiness, and the King's physician and favourite was soon elevated to the rank of Prime Minister of Denmark.

Struensee, however, not only succeeded in gaining the young Queen's confidence, but in winning her love likewise; a fact which neither of them took much pains to conceal, and which soon became one of the scandals of the Court. Her conduct visibly changed; she became graciously indifferent to her husband's amours, surrounded herself with perpetual gaiety, and introduced a new costume to society, consisting of a slouched hat, black frock, and buckskin under-garments, in which she continually appeared in public, whether walking, driving, or riding. Sir Robert Murray Keith, the British Minister at Copenhagen, mentions in his memoirs that, during his stay in Denmark, he 'never saw the Queen in any other garb.'

Her open gallantries with her handsome physician and Prime Minister gave as much offence to the ladies of her Court, as the sudden elevation of the brilliant adventurer to position and power afforded the Danish nobles. The press denounced him, public opinion was inflamed, and the Dowager Queen saw that the moment was ripe for their downfall. With one stroke she might be able to rid the kingdom not only of Struensee, but the Queen; prove her children illegitimate; and see her beloved Prince Frederick once more heir to the crown. For the execution of this scheme, tact and boldness were necessary; nor were they found wanting when needed.

The night selected for the downfall of the Queen and her favourite was one on which a magnificent masked ball was held in the palace of Copenhagen. The King, Queen, and their attendants entered the ball-room at ten o'clock; the handsome, brilliant Struensee was there already, and Her Majesty danced with him through the greater part of the night. She then went to supper, where she remained until three o'clock in the morning with a gay and select circle of friends, at which hour both she and Struensee retired. The time had now arrived when those who had entered into the conspiracy of the Queen Dowager must act. Accordingly, one of her abettors, named Rantzau, went to the King's chamber, woke him, and told him, with much agitation, that there was a conspiracy on foot against his crown and life, at the head of which were the Queen and Struensee; he was, moreover, informed that his sole means of saving himself was by signing a warrant for their arrest, which was then produced. The King, startled from his sleep, was bewildered and shocked, but hesitated signing the order, upon which the Queen Dowager and Prince Frederick rushed into his room, and, repeating the same story, besought His Majesty to have the Queen and Prime Minister arrested. The King no longer deliberated, and Struensee was seized in bed and hurried to the citadel, from whence he was soon after conducted to the scaffold, after making a full confession of his intimacy with the Queen.

Meanwhile, Her Majesty was awakened by one of her female attendants to receive a mandate ordering her to quit the palace. In a moment she understood the situation in which she was placed, and conscious that, if she could but gain access to the King, she would overcome her enemies, she hastily rose, and, putting on only her petticoat and shoes, rushed towards His Majesty's apartments. In the ante-chamber, however, she encountered Rantzau, seated quietly in a chair, when, remembering her half-clad condition, she hastily ran back to her bed-room, and, putting on some clothes, once more made her way to her husband's chamber. Rantzau was not there; his place had been taken by an officer, who forbade her further approach. She at once seized him by the hair, and, demanding to see the King, pushed him aside and advanced to the door. Here two soldiers with crossed firelocks offered her further opposition. She commanded them to let her go by; they both fell on their knees and said, 'Our heads are answerable if we allow your Majesty to pass.'

The Queen, being a woman of determination and courage, without hesitation, jumped over their crossed muskets, and ran towards the corridor leading to the King's apartment, into which she finally forced her way, to find he had been removed by her enemies, who feared her intention, and had baffled its fulfilment. Exhausted and dejected, she returned to her rooms, where Struensee's white bear-skin cloak was found, and from whence, in the early dawn of a January morning, she was hurried to the Castle of Cronenburg, a fortress situated about twenty miles from the capital; and here, for the next four months, she remained, tortured by the uncertainty of the fate her enemies held in store for her.

In the last journals of Horace Walpole, a glimpse is given of Danish Court life.

'The Queen, Struensee, and Brandt (who aided and abetted Struensee, and shared his ignominious fate) had acted like mad people,' says the biographer. 'They certainly gave the King laudanum frequently; and yet, if he did not go to bed so soon after supper as they chose, Brandt used to kick him out of the room. Other instances appeared, on the trial, of similar indignity. Sir Robert Keith, after his return, owned to a person from whom I had it that the junto certainly had meant, by drugs, to hurt the King's understanding . . . . The Queen subsequently confessed her intrigue with Struensee, and signed that confession. When the counsellor who was to defend her went to receive her orders, she laughed, and told him the story was true.'

Meantime, the revolution and imprisonment of the Queen caused a vast sensation in England. In Denmark, articles were being framed against her for the purpose of proving her children illegitimate, and probably of bringing her to the block, when Sir Robert Keith was instructed to intervene, his interference, moreover, being backed up by the appearance of a powerful British squadron in the Baltic. These measures had the desired effect on the Court of Denmark. The Queen was at once liberated from the fortress, and, escorted by the British squadron, she sailed to Stade, in Hanover, from whence she was conducted to the Castle of Zell, the place where the ill-fated Sophia Dorothea, wife of George I., had spent thirty years of gloomy captivity. It was not, however, rendered a prison to Denmark's Queen; she was surrounded by a small Court, with whom she quickly became a favourite; saw her friends, and found time to enter into a conspiracy for her restoration to her throne. Death, however, frustrated this project, three years after her departure from Denmark, she died in the twenty-third year of her age.

When news of the revolution which displaced the Queen from her throne reached England, the Princess Dowager was fast approaching her last end. All her life she had been a woman of determination and courage, and now, when at death's door, these traits did not depart from her. For three months she had suffered from a cancer in her throat, but she refused to let anyone examine it, save a German page, who acted as surgeon, and the only medicine she would use was hemlock. Knowing that death was near, she had sent for her eldest daughter, the Princess of Brunswick; but neither to her, nor to any other member of her family, did she in any way allude to her approaching demise, or even acknowledge her danger. Scarcely able to speak from weakness, she received visitors, and once, a few days before her death, on reading in the newspapers a statement of her perilous condition, she at once ordered her coach, and drove through the streets, in order to disguise the real state of her health. That she was, at the same time, fully conscious of her approaching end there can be no doubt, from the fact that the Princess of Brunswick, on entering her mother's room suddenly, found her reading a book, which she hastily hid under her couch. When she afterwards left the apartment, the Princess looked at the work, and found it 'A Preparation for Death.' After hearing of her youngest daughter's imprisonment, she scarcely took any nourishment but cordials, and grew gradually weaker. Two days before her death, she had an interview that lasted a couple of hours with Lord Bute, who had continued her friend and adviser to the last; when he called next day, the King being there, she refused to see him.

Their Majesties had called to pay her their usual weekly visit an hour before their regular time; hearing they had arrived, she rose, dressed, and would have walked to meet them, but the Princess of Brunswick ran out and called in the King and Queen. They remained with her until ten o'clock, when she went to bed. A couple of women and her page sat with her during the night; at half-past six next morning, not hearing her breathe, the page softly drew the bed-curtains, and saw that the Princess was dead. This was on February 8, 1772.

For twenty years since the death of her husband, she had enjoyed a revenue of £64,000 a year, and though she lived in privacy, and with strict economy, she, to the surprise of all, left behind her but £27,000, which was found in one of her cabinets. It then obtained universal credence that she had given the vast sum she was previously supposed to have hoarded to Lord Bute; and this belief gained ground when it was remembered he had purchased an estate in Bedfordshire for £114,000, had built a house there, which he had furnished in a magnificent and costly manner, and furthermore erected a mansion in town, at a time when he had no visible source of wealth, or estate, and his wife's inheritance being so tied up that it was impossible for him to raise money on it.

Even His Majesty was not without having his suspicion as to the source of Lord Bute's wealth. Some years previously the Dowager had given him the library of her late husband, Frederick, Prince of Wales, to which she had no testamentary right. Lord Bute, however, had the books quietly removed before any knowledge of the affair came to His Majesty's ears. The King, when made aware of the gift, was justly incensed, and, though Lord Bute offered to restore it, declined on the ground that he 'should not be the first to proclaim to the world that his mother had done wrong.' When, however, the Bedfordshire estate was purchased, His Majesty, according to Huish, significantly said to his mother's favourite, 'Take care, my lord, that the people do not say you got your riches from the same quarter as you got your books.'

The Princess had been the best hated woman in her son's kingdom, and public rancour was kept up till the tomb closed over her remains. But a few days before her death a paragraph went the round of the papers which stated that 'fifty guineas were yesterday offered and refused to insure one hundred pounds on the life of a certain great lady in Pall Mall, for two months only; and five offered at the same time and refused to underwrite her for three days.' Nor was this all. As the funeral procession moved through the streets from Carlton House to Westminster Abbey, the mob huzzaed for delight, and forcibly stripped the black cloth from the platform at the Abbey, before half the procession had passed across. It is more extraordinary yet to record that the soldiers on guard, lest they should lose their share in the plunder, followed the felonious example of the crowd, and secured for themselves as much of the cloth as they could.

Her income went to the King, and her jewels, plate, and trinkets to her remaining children, who could not agree as to the adequate division of these precious mementoes, and therefore sent them down to Christie's in Pall Mall, where they were sold by public auction for the benefit of their joint owners.

CHAPTER V.

The King's Brother, Henry Frederick, Duke of Cumberland—Remarkable Intrigue—Lord Grosvenor's Courtship—The Royal Lover and his Amorous Letters—The Countess's Reply—Royal Marriage Bill—The King and Queen at Kew—The Prince and Perdita Robinson—The Meeting at Old Kew by Moonlight—The Duchess of Cumberland courts Popularity—Midnight Revelry at Lord Chesterfield's—Charles Fox—The Charming Duchess of Devonshire and the Westminster Election—Mrs. Crouch and Mrs. Bellington.

THE King's third brother, Henry Frederick, created Duke of Cumberland a short time after the demise of his granduncle, 'Billy the Butcher,' was destined to give his royal mother more trouble, and the nation more scandal, than either the Dukes of York or Gloucester. In appearance he had the advantage of his brothers; in intellect he did not surpass their dull level; in stature he was small; and in habits degraded. This is the Prince concerning whom a writer in the daily press declared he would not say any more just then; 'for to reproach a man with being an idiot is an insult to God,' said this religious scribe. From the strict confinement in which he had been kept until he had obtained his majority, he sallied forth to satiate himself with reckless vice, and bring ridicule and disgrace upon his name and family. The morals and manners of the age, and the proverbial frailty of Princes, would not perhaps have rendered his coarse amours in any way notorious, had he not engaged in an intrigue with the wife of the first Earl Grosvenor, then young and beautiful, witty and accomplished.

My Lord Grosvenor was a gay courtier, and a man of pleasure, who had married Henrietta, daughter of Henry Vernon, of Hilton, in the county of Stafford, Esquire. The circumstances under which they met were not without romance, and the manner of his brief wooing was certainly characteristic of the age. My Lord was walking one day in Kensington Gardens, whilst his coach waited for him at the gate, when, a sudden summer shower coming on, he took refuge in an alcove, where Miss Vernon and her sister likewise sought refuge. My Lord was gallant by nature, and addressed the ladies; they were most courteously inclined, and made reply, and their conversation ended by his Lordship requesting them to do him the honour of sharing his carriage, as the rain continued, which they, nothing loth, consented to do. In riding back to town, his Lordship became attentive to the elder of the ladies, and she, not to be behindhand in paying him a compliment, after the fashion of the day, said his Lordship's coach was the easiest she ever rode in, to which he replied he 'was vastly happy at its meeting with her approbation, and that she might be the mistress of it whenever she pleased.' The lady blushed, the Lord became more amorous of her beauty, and next day called on her parents and made proposals for her hand, when the pair were duly married. My lady bore my Lord four children; and all went well until Henry Frederick, Duke of Cumberland, came upon the domestic scene, and professed to admire her ladyship vastly.

Flattered by the passing admiration of a Prince of the royal blood, the Countess listened to his protestations of love, and was quickly lured to ruin and disgrace, which her husband—a worthless profligate—did not hesitate in exposing to the publicity of a divorce court. Their letters were produced at the trial, 'and never,' says Horace Walpole, 'was the public regaled with a collection of greater folly! Yet, to the lady's honour be it said, that bating a few oaths, which sounded more masculine than tender, the advantage in grammar, spelling, and style was all in her favour. His Royal Highness's diction and learning scarce exceeded that of a cabin boy!'

The records of this remarkable case have been preserved among the celebrated trials of the period, and throw no inconsiderable light on the Duke's character, as well as on the manners of the times.

The royal lover's remarkable epistles were addressed to ' My dear little Angel,' and ' My ever dearest Love.' Passing over some strong sentiments, the Countess is apostrophised in language that rises almost to the height of poesy, as, ' Thou dearest angel of my soul !' Then the Princely youth exclaims, ' O, that I could but bear your pain for you, I should be happy!' and adds, in language common to all lovers of other men's wives, then and now, ' What grieves me most ' (is) ' that they who ought to feel, don't know the inestimable prize, the treasure they have in you.' In another of these effusions, the amorous Duke tells my Lady, ' I got to supper about nine o'clock, but I could not eat, and so got to bed about ten. I then prayed for you, my dearest love, kissed your dearest little hair, and laid down and dreamt of you; had you on the dear little couch ten thousand times in my arms, kissing you, and telling you how much I loved and admired you, and you seemed pleased. But, alas ! when I woke, I found it all delusion ; nobody by me but myself—at sea . . . . O, my love, mad and happy beyond myself to tell you how I love you, and have thought of you ever since I have been separated from you.'

He then quotes some lines from Prior about amorous flames, beauteous eyes, the pangs of absence, and such-like subjects, which poets true, and lovers ardent, delight in discoursing, and finally closes the letter from which these extracts have been taken with the following rather incoherent, but remarkable expressions : ' God bless you ! I shan't forget you. God knows you have told me so before. I have your heart, and it is warm in my breast. I hope mine feels as easy to you, thou joy of my life. Adieu.'

These letters were written at a time when Lady Grosvenor was about to give birth to a child—a situation that did not, however, by any means prevent her replying to her lover. It happened that one day her lord met a servant going to post one of her pure love epistles, directed under cover to Mrs. Reda, a milliner, who made herself and her house useful in various delightful ways to lovers in distress. My Lord, who had become suspicious, opened the letter and read it. In the next effusion written by her ladyship to her royal lover, some reference is made to this unforeseen accident.

'He,' she commences, referring to her lawful lord and master, 'appears rather in better temper to-day, so I'm in great hopes he did not get enough of the Letter to make out much. He stayed out very late last night, which seems to have occasioned a *weezing* to-day. By means of my sisters, I think I can send and receive my letters very safe for the future. Carry,' continues the letter, ' is out of Town for a few days, so in the meantime I send them by another sister, who comes to see me every day, and she thinks it some business I have with Reda about some *Millenary* that I don't chuse he should know of; so, if she gets ever a Letter for me, she knows she is not to take it out of her pocket till we are alone. So it's all cleverly settled . . . I resume my pen to tell you to-day how sincerely I esteem you. He is still rather more come about again to-day. Yesterday he shook hands with me, and this morning he came and kissed me, and said he was going out of Town to

Walthamstow, to Dine with his Brother; perhaps he is gone to ask his advice, but I don't care; he may take what measures he pleases with me, if you will but love me. I had a note from Mrs. Reda this evening; she says she is certain he dares not say a word to her, but she wishes he would above all things, for that she knows very well how to answer him, for that she knows enough of his Intrigues for him to be afraid of saying anything to her, and she is sure he is not *assez Hardi* to say a word to her upon the subject . . . I hope I shall be in London when you come back; I dare say I shall. I fancy he had not a mind to part with me, let him have seen what he wou'd in ye Letter, for he asked me Yesterday when I should be able to go into Cheshire. I told him I coo'd not give the least guess, as it depended entirely upon how I was, and I think I'v laid a good scheme; for I've alreaddy complained I've got a pain in my side, and I intend to say it's much worse at the end of the month, and that I can't bear the motion of a carriage. It will, I really believe, be a very good plan, for, if I said I had a Feaver, or anything of that kind, a physician would know by my Pulse I had not, and might discover me to him. And, besides, this will be a more lasting complaint; so at the end of five or six weeks I'll grow very ill, and send for Fordyce the Apothecary, and make him send me a quantity of nasty draughts, which I'll throw out of the Window. Only think how wicked I am, for in reality I'm already as strong and as well as ever I was in my life . . . O my dearest soul, I'v just received Two the dearest letters in the World from you. How can I—I cannot express my feelings of gratitude and Love for you; your dear heart is so safe with me, and feels every motion mine does, with you. How sweet those verses are you sent me; they are heavenly sweet because they were remarked by you. I always liked Prior, but shall adore him because you like him. Your dear little heart is flurried, too, on reading ye dear letters; it has both laught and cry'd with Joy. It lies warm in my breast: I cherish it, and think of nothing else but to preserve it safe there and happy. My dearest soul, I send you ten thousand kisses; I wish I could give them.'

My lady finishes this amorous epistle by abandoning the colder English language for the more expressive French, and bursts out:

'*Amons tout Jour Tendrement, mon adorable ammi, mon tres chère ame.*'

Besides meeting Lady Grosvenor at many places of assignation in London, he followed her to Eaton Hall, and took up his residence at one of the nearest public-houses, that he might be near her. On these occasions he donned a disguise which was afterwards described in the evidence as consisting of 'a brownish wig which came low over his ears and down upon his forehead, with a handkerchief round his neck, a blue and white flannel waistcoat, and lightish drab coat.'

The Duke was known, whilst here, as 'the squire,' and was accompanied by two companions, one of whom was called Farmer Tush, the other simply John, as became one supposed to exercise the calling of a groom. It may be added that all three were mistaken for highwaymen by the mistress of the 'Toll House,' where they stayed, at Marford Hill, and also by her attendants. This opinion was likewise shared by those at the inn at Barnhill, which the Duke and his friends honoured by their presence, and was strengthened by the fact of one James Parker, servant at the latter-mentioned house of entertainment for man and beast, noticing that his disguised Royal Highness fell asleep at his breakfast, from which the shrewd fellow argued he had been awake all night.

At last my Lord Grosvenor's suspicions were, what the newspapers call, awakened, and his brother, together with John Stephens, Adjutant of the Cheshire Militia, were requested to watch the lady's movements. This they did to such good effect that the Duke and her Ladyship were discovered at the 'White Hart Inn,' at St. Albans. A divorce suit followed, and, notwithstanding that the Duke's not over-wise counsel pleaded—to the great amusement of the court—'that, however aggravating the circumstances were otherwise, they could not charge his Royal Highness with intriguing merely for the sake of intrigue, as the *incoherency* of his letters plainly proved him to be really a lover,' my Lord Grosvenor was awarded the sum of £10,000 damages, by way of healing the wounded honour of his house. This was an amount which the Royal Duke found it inconvenient to pay; and eight months after the trial, the King writes to the then Premier, Lord North :

'My brothers have this day applied about the means of paying the Duke of Cumberland's damages and costs, which, if not payed this day se'nnight, the proctors will certainly force the house; which, at this licentious time, will occasion reflections on the rest of the family. Whatever can be done, ought to be done.'

But, alas for the faith of princes! the divorce suit had scarcely commenced, when the gallant Duke, tired of his amour with his 'ever dearest little angel,' turned away from her, and commenced a new intrigue; whilst the ex-countess, some years afterwards, entered once more into the bonds of holy matrimony with General George Porter, who was Member of Parliament for Stockbridge.

The object of the Prince's fresh fancy was the wife of a city merchant, an extremely handsome woman, with a conveniently placid spouse. Indeed, Horace Walpole says, 'it was uncertain which was most proud of the honour, the husband or the wife.' His Royal Highness accompanied the lady to all places of public amusement, and showed her the most gracious courtesy; but quickly deserted her for Mrs. Horton, at whose shrine he now offered his passionate devotions. Mrs. Horton was the daughter of Lord Irnham, who afterwards became Earl of Carhampton; she had in early life married a wealthy husband, whom death untimely snatched from her. She was a lady of quality, worldly, ambitious, and pretty, with large, languishing eyes that dealt indiscriminate misery and happiness to her admirers, and bewitching manners that exerted universal fascination. Moreover, she was vastly accomplished; gave vent to wit and sarcasm with equal ease, and preserved her virtue intact. The result of the Duke's passion for her was that he offered to make her his wife, an honour she unhesitatingly accepted. They were, therefore, married at Mrs. Horton's residence, in Hertford Street, Mayfair, on October 2, 1771.

The next day, the Duke went to the King with a letter in his pocket, containing an avowal of his union, which he presented to His Majesty, after walking with him for some time in the garden. The King quietly slipped it into his pocket, saying:

'I suppose I need not read it now?'

'Yes, sir,' replied the Duke, 'you must read it directly.'

His Majesty then read it, and great was his royal wrath. 'You fool! You blockhead! You villain!' he broke out; and then followed some words of advice which the world would not call virtuous. Better, His Majesty inferred, that the Duke should multiply his late experiences a thousandfold than have married a subject.

'This woman,' he said, referring to the new-made Duchess, 'can be nothing—she never shall be anything.'

The Duke was frightened at this storm, and asked what was His Gracious Majesty's royal will.

'Go abroad,' said the King.

The Duke and his wife, therefore, immediately crossed to Calais.

His Majesty's indignation was terrible, but was exceeded by that of the Princess Dowager. The Duke's scandal with

Lady Grosvenor they could have forgiven, but a legal marriage with a subject was an offence rank, indeed, in the eyes of royalty, so much so that the Dowager declared she would never see him again, and never did, though this erring son waited on her a few days before her death. The King, to mark his anger, had word sent him that he was not to appear at Court. The Duke, happy in the thought that no further measures would be taken against him, led a merry life; gave some balls in Calais; travelled under a feigned name through France and Flanders, and finally returned to his London residence, Cumberland House.

His Majesty refused to see him, the guards were withdrawn, the Lord Chamberlain intimated that whoever visited the Duke or Duchess must not appear at Court, and the same message was given to the Foreign Ministers. The effect was that the bride and bridegroom found themselves deserted except by the Duchess's family, and the ambitious lady was, according to Horace Walpole, 'forced to bestow her hand to be kissed by her menial servants.' They soon retired to their residence in the Great Park at Windsor, and afterwards passed some years on the Continent. A little later on, this weak and licentious man used the cruellest possible means of revenging himself on the King for the indignities shown him, due record of which will be made.

So mortified was His Majesty by the marriages of his brothers to commoners that he resolved to prevent such an occurrence from taking place again in his family. He therefore speedily framed a message, which was delivered to both Houses of Parliament, informing them that, 'being desirous, from paternal affection to his own family, and anxious concern for the future welfare of his people, and the honour and dignity of his Crown, that the right of approving all marriages in the Royal Family (which ever has belonged to the kings of this realm as a matter of public concern) may be made effectual, recommends to both Houses of Parliament to take into their serious consideration whether it may not be wise and expedient to supply the defect of the laws now in being, and, by some new provision, more effectually to guard the descendants of his late Majesty King George II. (other than the issue of princesses who have married or may hereafter marry into foreign families) from marrying without the approbation of His Majesty, his heirs and successors, first had and obtained.'

Walpole says that the message was 'received with the utmost coldness and disgust by both Houses. It not only set out with a falsehood (the assertion of the King's power over such marriages), but contradicted itself by devising a remedy for the very deficiency of that power.' However, a marriage bill drawn up in accordance to the desire of the arbitrary royal message by Lord Mansfield, though powerfully attacked by Charles James Fox, Burke, and Wedderburn, passed on April 1, 1772.

Meanwhile the King's domestic life glided placidly by; it was only when dressed in the trappings of royalty that he assumed the regal character, which never sat easily on his shoulders, just as some poor player in velvet garb and tinsel crown, struts with an air majestic for a couple of hours before the footlights. When the affairs of state were laid aside, no one could be more simple in manners, more dull and decorous in habits, more exemplary as a husband and a father. Between the years 1762 and 1783, fifteen children were born to the royal pair, and Kew House was selected as the nursery for this too prolific progeny. Here the King and Queen led a life new to monarchs, the simple details of which are given in many memoirs of the day.

At six in the morning their Majesties rose, read, or walked about the grounds, sat down to breakfast at eight with the eldest of the children, at nine all the progeny were brought into the room for general inspection, when the elder members were sent to their daily tasks, and the younger to play in the gardens. Occasionally the King and Queen, attended by such of the family as were able to walk, marched two and two round the grounds in solemn and stately procession, after which the royal parents saw the little ones dine. Their Majesties' own dinner was of the plainest, the King living principally on vegetables, the Queen confining herself to a couple of dishes, both of them drinking but little wine. When a levée or council was to be held, the King rode into town on horseback, and returned as quickly as possible from the cares of state to the joys of domesticity. In the evenings he read selections from sermons or theological works to his consort, which Her Sacred Majesty listened to with reverent complacency, as she knitted or sewed, and took huge pinches of snuff; then the gay pair said their prayers and went to bed betimes, and so the day was done.

One of the wicked wags who lived and made ballads at this time celebrates the domestic felicity of their right homely and sacred Majesties in these verses—

> 'Cæsar the mighty King who sway'd
> The sceptre, was a sober blade;
> A leg of mutton and his wife
> Were the chief comforts of his life.
>
> 'The Queen, compos'd of different stuff,
> Above all things ador'd her snuff,
> Save gold, which, in her great opinion,
> Alone could rival snuff's dominion.'

At Kew the King was enabled to indulge his harmless craze for agriculture, which now exceeded his recent passion for the making of buttons; a species of regal industry and mechanism which filled the breast of his consort and the royal household with inexpressible wonder and admiration. 'Farmer George,' as he was called, superintended the tilling and sowing of his acres, and sent their produce into market with a careful eye to remuneration. At an early stage of their lives, he had trained his two eldest sons to till a small plot of land, and sow it with corn, which in good time they reaped, thrashed, saw ground to flour, and made into bread.

The second son, Frederick, created, after the death of his uncle, Duke of York, was, when six months old, made Bishop of Osnaburgh. The bishopric, which was a secular dignity with an ecclesiastical designation, had been held open for three years, in order that it might be bestowed on one of the King's sons. The revenue which this juvenile 'Right Reverend Father in God,'—as he was styled by an ordained and foolish sycophant who dedicated a book to him,—derived from his office was £2,000 a year until he arrived at the age of eighteen, when, his minorship being at an end, the amount of £25,000 per annum would become his by right divine.

At an early age, the Prince of Wales and the Bishop were taken from the nursery and placed under the charge of Lord Holderness, as governor; the Rev. Dr. Markham, head-master of Westminster School, as preceptor; and Cyril Jackson as sub-preceptor. Moreover, a royal chaplain was thrown in with the list, whose duty it was to read prayers to the Princes daily, and now their education commenced. Dr. Markham had, previous to undertaking his charge, asked His Majesty how he wished to have the future heir to the Crown treated, when the King made answer, 'Like the son of any private English gentleman; if he deserves it, let him be flogged, just as you used to do at Westminster.' The learned doctor, who had strong faith in the efficacy of corporeal punishment, smiled and bowed; and the privilege accorded him was freely made use of, as the royal back of his pupil could testify; for the Prince, even at the mature age of ten years, was not easily governed.

Their Royal Highnesses indeed became so refractory, that the governor and preceptors quickly resigned their posts.

This Prince of Wales would brook no authority, whilst the young scapegrace, the Bishop of Osnaburgh, ridiculed poor Lord Holderness to his face. In their places, the Duke of Montague, Bishop Hurd, and Mr. Arnold were named governor, preceptor, and sub-preceptor; but under this goodly trio matters seemed to make small improvement. Dr. Hurd, a pliant, easy-going man, who, 'though a scholar, was only a servile pedant, ignorant of mankind,' as Horace Walpole says, was inclined to let his pupils follow their own wills, and, so long as he continued in this frame of mind, his charge was not troublesome; but once, when he strove to imitate the discipline of Dr. Markham of flogging memory, the Princes rebelled, tore the rod from his right reverend hand, and laid the lash upon his episcopal back with hearty good-will.

His Majesty was shocked and grieved that his olive-branches had turned out firebrands. The traits of character they displayed thus early in life made him fearful of the future; and, as years went by, the conduct of the Princes was not calculated to lessen his fears. The strictest watch was kept upon them, even when they reached the years of manhood; newspapers were forbidden them; they were allowed no communication with youths of their own age; they were seldom set free even for a few hours from their household confinement, and spies were set to watch them. The result of this system was, as Horace Walpole states in his last journals, that, 'as soon as the King went to bed, the Prince and his brother, Prince Frederick, went to their mistresses.' It is further mentioned in the same page that the heir to the Crown, 'restricted from the society of women, had contracted a habit of private drinking,' one result of which was a humour that showed itself in blotches all over his face. 'Such,' says the author, 'were the fruits of his being locked up in this palace of piety.'

When he arrived at the ripe age of eighteen, the Prince

contracted his first liaison, the object of his love being charming Mary Robinson, famous alike for her beauty and talent. Mrs. Robinson was the daughter of respectable parents, and had been educated by the famous Hannah More. When only fifteen, she married an adventurer who passed himself off as the heir to large estates in South Wales, but who quickly proved himself to be a heartless scoundrel and confirmed profligate. Reduced by his extravagance to a dependent condition, with but a future prospect of debt and difficulties before her, she resolved to try her success as an actress, and mentioned her design to Brereton, a friend of hers, who was one of the *employés* at Drury Lane play-house. Brereton introduced her to Richard Brinsley Sheridan, who had just then purchased a share in the famous theatre. The author of 'The School for Scandal' in turn spoke of her to Garrick, then just retired from the stage, but who, on recognising the dawning talents of fair Mary Robinson, undertook to become her tutor and prepare her for the theatrical profession. After considerable trials and many rehearsals, it was finally decided that she should make her first bow to the public as Juliet. In her interesting memoirs, she has left a brief description of her premier appearance.

'The theatre,' she writes, 'was crowded with fashionable spectators; the green-room and orchestra (where Mr. Garrick sat during the night) were thronged with critics. My dress was a pale pink satin, trimmed with crape, richly spangled with silver; my head was ornamented with white feathers, and my monumental suit, for the last scene, was white satin and completely plain, except that I wore a veil of the most transparent gauze, which fell quite to my feet from the back of my head, and a string of beads round my waist, to which was suspended a cross appropriately fashioned. When I approached the side wing, my heart throbbed convulsively; I then began to fear my resolution would fail, and I leaned upon the nurse's arm almost fainting. Mr. Sheridan and several other friends encouraged me to proceed, and at length, with trembling limbs and fearful apprehension, I approached the audience.'

Her personation of the love-sick Juliet was a vast success; she had already published some volumes of very pretty verse, and she now appeared on the stage under the distinguished patronage of the brilliant Duchess of Devonshire and David Garrick. Accordingly, she soon became the fashion, and her society was sought after by 'ladies of quality' and men of all degrees.

'Were I to mention the names of those who held forth the temptations of fortune at this moment of public peril, I might create some reproaches in many families of the fashionable world,' she writes. 'Among others who offered most liberally to purchase my indiscretion was the late Duke of Rutland; a settlement of six hundred pounds per annum was proposed as the means of estranging me entirely from my husband. I refused the offer. I had still the consolation of an unsullied name.'

She was in her twenty-third year when the Prince of Wales first saw her at Drury Lane; on which occasion she personated Perdita in 'The Winter's Tale.' The play had been selected by their Gracious Majesties, and the royal family had come to witness the performance. Speaking of this hour, which was so fateful to her, Mary Robinson says:

'As I stood in the wing opposite the Prince's box, waiting to go on the stage, Mr. Ford, the manager's son, and now a respectable defender of the laws, presented a friend who accompanied him; this friend was Lord Viscount Malden, now Earl of Essex. We entered into conversation during a few minutes, the Prince of Wales all the time observing us, and frequently speaking to Colonel Lake and to the Hon. Mr. Legge, who was waiting on His Royal Highness. I hurried through the first scene, not without much embarrassment, owing to the fixed attention with which the Prince of Wales honoured me. Indeed, some flattering remarks which were made by His Royal Highness met my ear as I stood near his box, and I was overwhelmed with confusion.

'The Prince's particular attention was observed by everyone. On the last curtsey, the royal family condescendingly returned a bow to the performers; but, just as the curtain was falling, my eyes met those of the Prince of Wales, and, with a look that *I never shall forget*, he gently inclined his head a second time. I felt the compliment, and blushed my gratitude.'

The Prince was at this time handsome, well-made, and graceful in appearance; he has been described as 'one whose manners were resistless, and whose smile was victory.' He was evidently fascinated by the beautiful Perdita, and showed that he was no laggard in love. A couple of days afterwards Lord Essex waited on the lady, and presented her with a note expressive of ardent admiration, written by the royal hand, and signed 'Florizel,' to which the lady duly replied. This was followed by a correspondence amorous and confidential. Perdita, who had rejected the addresses of a Duke, was yet but a woman, and received the avowed adoration of a Prince. Before he had spoken a word to her, the heir to the realm sent the actress his portrait set in a case, within which she discovered a small heart (truly emblematic in size of his who had sent it), on one side of which was written, '*Je ne change qu'en mourant:*' on the other, in plain English, 'Unalterable to my Perdita through life.'

It now became the Prince's anxiety to arrange a meeting with this siren; but, on account of the strict watch placed on all his movements, this was by no means easy to accomplish. Once he proposed that she should visit him in his apartments disguised in male attire; but this she declined, on account of the danger of detection, and a mutual visit to Lord Essex's house was likewise objected to on the same grounds. At last it was determined they should meet at Kew, and the assignation was not devoid of some of the chief elements of romance; it took place by moonlight, and was attended by some danger of discovery. Perdita and Lord Essex waited one summer evening on the island between Kew and Brentford until a signal was given them by the Prince to cross over in a boat to the banks of the Thames, near the palace, where he was to receive them. Perdita declared that heaven could witness how many conflicts her agitated heart endured at that moment. At last a white handkerchief was seen to flutter in the dusky light of evening, and in a few minutes the trembling fair one and her conductor stood before the dark gates of old Kew Palace, where the Prince and his brother Frederick awaited them wrapped in great-coats, in order to disguise themselves.

The hour long sought and hoped for had come at last; the lovers met, but, alas! for but too brief a time; for, scarcely had they exchanged a few words expressive of their mutual delight, when a sudden noise of people approaching from the palace startled them all, and, after a few more phrases 'of an affectionate nature,' the royal youth hurried away, lest it should be discovered he was out at so late an hour. This was their first meeting, the memory of which remained fresh in the fair Perdita's heart long years afterwards.

'The graces of his person, the irresistible sweetness of his smile, the tenderness of his melodious, yet manly voice,' says the infatuated young woman, 'will be remembered by me till every vision of this changing scene shall be forgotten.'

Other meetings quickly followed. Perdita left the stage,

and became the acknowledged mistress of the heir-apparent, who gave her a bond, promising to pay her the sum of twenty thousand pounds when he came of age. Perdita, as she was now called, became the fashion; her carriage, as we learn from a paragraph devoted to details of London life in the *Ramblers' Magazine*, was the admiration of the town. 'The body is of carmelite and silver, ornamented with a French mantle, and the cypher in a wreath of flowers; the carriage scarlet and silver, the seat-cloth richly ornamented with silver fringe. Mrs. Robinson's livery is green faced with yellow, and richly trimmed with broad silver lace, the harness ornamented with stars of silver richly chased and elegantly finished. The inside of the carriage is lined with white silk, embellished with scarlet trimmings.' Perdita was luxurious.

When she went shopping or drove in the Park, she was surrounded by admiring crowds, and attended by worshipping gallants, whilst her poems were eagerly bought and read, and her pictures displayed in the windows of the print-shops. She was universally praised for her beauty, her talents, and her gifts, and her reign was right merry, though short. Long before the Prince came of age, he paid his devotions at the shrines of new goddesses, and his affection had become cold towards the fair Perdita, to whom he had promised eternal love and twenty thousand pounds. By degrees he deserted her in right princely fashion, when she appealed to him with tears and prayers not to forsake her. But these were all in vain; he would not even grant her an interview, until at last, afraid of her vehemence, he consented, when, to her great surprise, he appeared unchanged, and he repeatedly assured her he had never for a moment ceased to love her; only the next day, when she encountered His Royal Highness in Hyde Park, he passed her without the faintest recognition. Nor was this all: when she in due time presented her bond, he refused to pay it.

Though she had quitted her profession at his suggestion, he was quite unwilling to make her any compensation, and, when the matter came to the ears of the King, his virtuous Majesty agreed with the Prince's decision, and writes to Lord North that His Royal Highness sent Perdita 'letters and very foolish promises, which undoubtedly, by her conduct, she has cancelled.' A compromise was finally arrived at between the Prince and the actress, when his letters were bought for the sum of £5,000, and an annuity of £500 settled on her during life.

With this sum, Perdita went to Paris, where her fame had already preceded her, and where she was known as La Belle Anglaise; here she gained the notice of the ill-fated Marie Antoinette, who presented her with a purse worked by the hand of that daughter of the Cæsars. She afterwards returned to England, and devoted her talents to literature, which she, however, in common with others before and since, held as 'a destroying labour.' She gave the world several poems, whose very names, 'To a Swan,' 'Pity's Tear,' 'On a Kiss,' etc., will guarantee for their sentiment; wrote a tragedy, 'The Sicilian Lover,' and a couple of novels, 'Hubert de Sevrac,' and 'Vancenza; or, The Danger of Credulity,' all of which were more or less successful; later on, she undertook—wonderful to be told of those days—the poetical department of the *Morning Post*, and lived to the unromantic age of forty-three.

It was at this period of the social history of the Court that the Duke and Duchess of Cumberland came prominently forward once more. Her Grace had not been admitted to the royal drawing-rooms, and was ignored by her kingly brother-in-law, who, though he permitted the Duke to hold levées, forbade those who held any office at Court to attend the Duchess's assemblies. Her Grace, who was, however, a woman of the world, at once clever and wily, prepared to wage battle with royalty for her position, and to revenge herself on their Majesties when opportunity offered. This was not long in presenting itself in the person of the young Prince of Wales, then commencing a career of infamy, and of hostility to the King, which promised to become as vigorous as that which had notoriously distinguished the heirs to the throne of the first and second monarchs of his line.

The Duke of Cumberland, who resented what he regarded as the insults of the Court to his wife; who was dissatisfied with the King's treatment of himself; and who was, moreover, swayed by his spouse, readily agreed in using the Prince of Wales as a tool with which to punish His Majesty. Accordingly, the Duke professed a strong affection for his nephew, whom he familiarly designated Taffy, which a similarity in their dispositions soon cemented. Under the able guidance of the Duke, the Prince was led into scenes of the most degrading vice, introduced to money-lenders, taught to drink and gamble, and encouraged in his opposition to the King. His Majesty was indignant at this conduct, and complained to the Duke of Gloucester that his brother of Cumberland 'comes to the Queen's house fourteen times a week to my son the Prince, and passes by my door, but never comes in to me, and, if he meets me there, he only pulls off his hat and walks away.'

Meanwhile, the Duchess of Cumberland resolved to hold periodical drawing-rooms, but, fearing they might be deserted, as they had been shortly after her marriage, she had determined to court popularity; she therefore stooped to conquer. My Lord Shelburne being opportunely ill, she must call on my Lady to express her deep sympathies, and, having heard that Devonshire House had been re-furnished, she expressed to her Grace of Devonshire a strong desire to inspect it, and became enraptured with the exquisite taste displayed. Moreover, she called on the Duchess of Marlborough, invited herself to Lady Salisbury's house at Hatfield, returned the visits of Duchesses and Countesses paid her, would not suffer her hand to be kissed, and finally went to general assemblies. When this course had gained her sufficient popularity, she opened her drawing-rooms, which now became crowded.

Elated by so much success, the Duchess resolved on giving a ball on a magnificent scale to the Prince of Wales, but the King, strictly forbidding anyone connected with the Court to attend, this entertainment was changed to a dinner for the Prince's gentlemen and household. Alas! once more the royal mandate went forth prohibiting all good courtiers from sitting down to this feast, when the Duke became exasperated, and wrote his royal brother a wrathful letter, in which he declared that England was a country not fit for a gentleman to live in, and that he should go abroad. But this was merely a threat; the Duke stayed at home, and even went to the royal drawing-room, for if he absented himself, the Duchess sagaciously said, he might lose his influence over the Prince.

There was little fear, however, of such a possibility; the heir-apparent and his worthless uncle became faster friends than before. The Duke established a faro bank at Cumberland House, that the Prince might have a convenient opportunity of gambling, and, in consort with the Duchess, openly favoured His Royal Highness's new amour for Mrs. Armstead, afterwards the mistress and wife of Charles James Fox.

Whilst yet in his minority, the Prince steadily pursued a course of vulgar vice and degradation which the King seemed powerless to check. Speaking of him in May, 1781, Horace Walpole says, in his last journals:

'The conduct of the Prince of Wales began already to make the greatest noise, and proved how very bad his education had been, or rather, that he had had little or none, but had only been locked up and suffered to keep company with the lowest domestics; while the Duke of Montague and Hurd, Bishop of Lichfield, had thought of nothing but paying Court to the King and Queen and her German women. The Prince drank more publicly in the drawing-room, and talked there irreligiously and indecently in the openest manner (both which were the style of the Duchess of Cumberland). He passed the nights in the lowest debaucheries, at the same time bragging of intrigues with women of quality, whom he named publicly. Both the Prince and the Duke talked of the King in the grossest terms even in his hearing, as he told the Duke of Gloucester, who asked him why he did not forbid his son seeing his brother. The King replied that he feared his son would not obey him. The Duke of Cumberland dropped that he meant by this outrageous behaviour to force the King to yield to terms in favour of his Duchess, having gotten entire command over the Prince.' The King likewise complained that, when he hunted, 'neither my son nor my brother speak to me; and lately, when the chase ended at a little village where there was but a single post-chaise to be hired, my son and brother got into it and drove to London, leaving me to go home in a cart, if I could find one.' 'His Majesty added,' Walpole continues, 'that when at Windsor, where he always dines at three, and in town at four, if he asked the Prince to dine with him, he always came at four at Windsor, and in town at five, and all the servants saw the father waiting an hour for the son; that, since the Court was come to town, the Duke of Cumberland carried the Prince to the lowest places of debauchery, where they got dead drunk, and were often carried home in that condition.'

About this time, a royal carousal was held, a rumour of which got whispered about from drawing-room to club-room, until it was at last celebrated in verse in one of the public papers. It happened that one night, when the King had gone to bed, the Prince as usual stole out of Buckingham House, and, joined by his besotted uncle the Duke of Cumberland, and several boon companions, amongst whom were Charles Windham, St. Leger, and George Pitt, they immediately set out for Blackheath to sup with my Lord Chesterfield. This was the successor to the politest courtier and ugliest man of George II.'s reign; the wit and mimic who had amused and plagued Queen Caroline and her merry maids. The present Lord had some of the humour, but none of the elegant courtesy, of the late Earl, and had, moreover, the unpleasant reputation of having brought his tutor, Dr. Dodd, to justice and the scaffold, because the reverend man had forged his Lordship's name. However, he was one of the boon companions of the future King, and regarded by that august personage as one of his selected guides, philosophers, and friends.

Lord Chesterfield, though anxious to please his royal guest, refused, as a married man, to invite the company which the Prince very much desired; but this drawback to the amusement of the hour was speedily forgotten in the pleasures derived from the wine-bottle, and in a little while the whole of that goodly company were drunk. The Prince had filled his glass more frequently than his companions, and was at an early stage of the night's revelry conducted to his couch, whilst his friends continued to make merry. Suddenly one of them bethought him of drinking a toast which he had no doubt would be popular with his *confrères*, and, with glass in hand, rose up and proposed, '*A short reign to the King.*' The Prince had by this time sufficiently recovered to understand the purport of the words, and some sense of shame and remorse appealing to his confused senses, he roused himself, staggered to the table, and, filling a bumper, gave and drank the toast, '*Long live the King.*'

But this little *contretemps* was not allowed to interrupt the general harmony of the night, and presently one of the select company suggested that they should have a man-and-beast fight, which met with unanimous approval. My Lord Chesterfield was known to keep a fierce bulldog, and George Pitt, a muscular Christian with the reputation of a prize-fighter, declared he would tear the animal's tongue from its roots. The Prince and his friends were delighted at the prospect of such sport; the dog was accordingly let loose, and George Pitt strove in the royal presence to put his brutal boast into practice; but the animal, escaping from him in an agony, rushed at Charles Windham, whom he bit, and then at a servant's leg, which he tore and mangled. By the time this pastime ended, it was early morning; the Prince remembered he must get back, and my Lord Chesterfield insisted on lighting his guest to the door; but, alas, so drunk was the descendant of the polite letter-writer, that he mistook his way, and fell with a crash into the area, when it was thought his wit had gone out for ever. He was, however, spared to get drunk another day.

About this time the heir to the throne became acquainted with Charles James Fox, the second son of Henry Fox, first Lord Holland, one of the most distinguished, clever, and dissipated men of the day.

The favourite son of the statesman, he had been brought up in the most luxurious fashion, and treated with the most extravagant indulgence; and, whilst an Eton schoolboy yet under the age of fourteen, had been taken to Paris and Spa, where he first acquired that taste for gambling which ultimately became the bane of his life. Clever, handsome, and winning even as a lad, he gave promise of those brilliant attainments and powers of personal fascination which marked his early manhood and ripened with his later years.

Leaving Oxford whilst yet in his teens, with a thorough knowledge of classics, and a familiar acquaintance with the literature of his own country, he, in company with Lord

Carlisle, made the grand tour, and gained a polish which ever afterwards distinguished his manner, and a knowledge of the world such as is seldom attained by one of his years. Whilst yet abroad, he was, through his father's interest, elected as representative for Midhurst; this was in May, 1768, when he was in his nineteenth year. He returned to England in the following November a finished gentleman of the first water, a man with a future. His name, as the son of an ex-Cabinet Minister, had been a sufficient passport to the highest circles abroad, and the liberal allowance made him by his father had enabled him to maintain an extravagance of which eight servants was not the least item. He had mixed with the most accomplished society of which Europe could boast, had been graciously received at Courts, entertained by ambassadors, had played the fop at Turin, had gambled at Naples, had experienced the dissipations of Paris,

> 'Saw every Court, heard every King declare
> His royal sense of operas or the fair,'

had conversed with Voltaire at Ferney, and had received from the lips of the venerable cynic a list of his works such as would 'fortify him against religious prejudices.' After this interview, the French philosopher wrote to Lord Holland, 'Yr son is an English lad and j an old frenchman. He is healthy and j am sick. Yet j love him with all my heart, not only for his father, but for him self.'

Fox was not, however, spoiled by his experiences abroad; true, he for some time after his return to England wore the dress of a fop, but at heart 'he was a man made to be loved,' as Burke said, and his polished courtesy, scholarly lore, love of wit, reckless folly, unassuming manners, and genuine good-humour, gained him friends whose names were legion.

On account of his minority, he was unable to vote in the House of Commons, but, shortly after taking his seat, he spoke with great fluency in support of the expulsion of Wilkes. In the second year of his parliamentary career, he was made a Junior Lord of the Admiralty, an office he resigned two years later on account of his opposition to the Royal Marriage Bill, which first caused him to be regarded by the King with a dislike that afterwards deepened to hatred. He was soon after appointed one of the Lords of the Treasury, but was dismissed by the Premier, Lord North, whom he had defeated on a division. The political eminence he thus early acquired was fully equalled by the social distinction he gained; he was the friend of the beautiful Georgiana, Duchess of Devonshire, the companion of the distinguished Lord Carlisle, the intimate of that most excellent wit, George Selwyn; he was a member of Brooke's, White's, and Arthur's clubs, was sought after for his conviviality, copied in the cut of his coat, and flattered and loved by the most frail, brilliant, and pleasure-loving society of the period.

This was the man with whom the Prince of Wales was anxious to become acquainted, and with whom he shared many characteristics in common. The heir to the throne at this time bade fair to become popular; nor was this feeling towards him in the least prejudiced by the vices he exhibited in an age of general depravity. He possessed a certain grace seldom dissociated from youth; in his manner he betrayed an easy dignity, in his address an acquired polish, and in his character an appearance of generosity and open liberality which exerted a fascination over all those who approached him. In person he was remarkably well-made and handsome; he could boast of an education unusual in Princes, and his amours exhibited a gallantry which came as a relief to the disgusting coarseness that had distinguished those of his immediate ancestors. Moreover, he appreciated wit, loved good-fellowship, could make a pretty speech, return a compliment with exceeding suavity, and had a talent for acquiring friends.

His acquaintance with Charles James Fox rapidly led to a friendship which in turn soon glided into familiarity. His Royal Highness addresses the young statesman as his 'dear Charles' at a very early stage of their intimacy, and dined with him at his rooms in St. James's Street, where they both drank royally. Later on, but before the Prince had attained his majority, Horace Walpole speaks of him as having 'thrown himself into the arms of Charles Fox, and this in the most indecent and undisguised manner. Fox lodged in St. James's Street, and as soon as he rose, which was very late, had a levée of his followers, and of the members of the Gaming Club at Brookes', all his disciples. His bristly black person, rarely purified by any ablutions, was wrapped in a foul linen night-gown, and his bushy hair dishevelled. In these cynic weeds, and with epicurean good-humour, did he dictate his politics—and in this school did the heir of the Crown attend his lessons and imbibe them. Fox's followers, on whom he had never enjoined Pythagorean silence, were strangely licentious in their conversation about the King. At Brookes' they proposed wagers on the duration of his reign; and if they moderated their irreverent jests in the presence of the Prince, it was not extraordinary that the orgies at Brookes' might be reported to have passed at Fox's levées, or that the King should suspect that the same disloyal topics should be handled in the morning that he knew had been the themes of each preceding evening.'

His Majesty, therefore, looked upon the friendship between the Prince and Fox with fear and displeasure, feelings which troubled His Royal Highness but little; for he found Charles Fox as a friend to be one of the most delightful men in the kingdom, and as a politician he trusted he might prove one of the most useful to him in the Commons.

Early in 1783, Charles Fox came into power as one of the Secretaries of State in the new Government of which the Duke of Portland was First Lord of the Treasury, and in the August of the same year the Prince of Wales would attain his majority, when a revenue and settlement would be duly provided for him. The Prince looked forward with great expectations to the time when he should be free from all paternal control, and placed his faith and hope in Fox, that by his exertions he might be able to enjoy an income which would in no way curtail his Princely pleasures. Nor were these hopes misplaced. The new Ministry, at the instigation of Fox, proposed to allow His Royal Highness £100,000 a year, a sum just double that enjoyed by the last Prince of Wales long after he had a wife and children.

At this announcement the King was surprised and displeased; taking into consideration the heavy financial embarrassments under which the country then laboured, he declared £50,000 was a sufficient allowance for the Prince. On account of this disagreement, His Royal Highness 'had a fever with vexation,' and the Ministry was on the point of resigning, when Charles Fox went to his royal friend and begged of him to submit himself entirely to the King; which advice the Prince had sufficient sense to follow. No grant was therefore demanded from Parliament; the King, out of his own income, made the Prince an allowance of £50,000 a year, with the revenue of the Duchy of Cornwall, which amounted to £12,000 per annum. Parliament, however, gave £30,000 to pay the Prince's debts, and the same sum for the expenses of his new establishment.

The Prince now moved to Carlton House, which had not been occupied since the death of his grandmother, the well-abused Princess of Wales. The King's second and favourite son, Edward, Bishop of Osnaburgh, had a few months previously been created Duke of York and Albany, and had received command of the Coldstream Guards. He was now sent out of the country to a German university, in order that he might be free from the example and influence of the heir to the throne; for a similar reason His Majesty's third son, William Henry, was sent into the navy.

Having had his debts paid, and being now lord of himself, the recipient of a settled income, and master of a separate establishment which numbered his chosen friends, the Prince of Wales made Carlton House the central point of attraction, the scene of unchecked dissipation, and the general rallying-place for the Ministry, which was bitterly detested by the King. This Cabinet against which the royal wrath was directed was not destined to survive long. In this year, Fox introduced the famous Indian Bill, which passed through its various stages in the Commons by large majorities, but, meeting with the direct opposition of His Majesty, who declared he would consider those peers who voted for it as his enemies, it was rejected in the Upper House by a majority of nineteen.

This proved fatal to the Ministry, for, on the very evening of the day on which it had been thrown out, the King, glad of this opportunity of ridding himself of Ministers whom he hated, sent messages to Lord North and Charles Fox, stating he had no longer any necessity for their services, and requiring them to deliver up their seals of office as Secretaries of State. A new Cabinet was therefore formed, with Pitt as Premier, which had to contend with an Opposition, headed by Fox, more formidable in numerical force, as well as brilliant talent, than any which had appeared in Parliament since the days of Charles I. Pitt and his Cabinet were favoured by the King, Fox and his partisans by the Prince of Wales; and this feud between His Majesty and the heir to the Crown was widened by circumstances which quickly followed.

As supporters in the House of Lords, Fox could number the Dukes of Devonshire, Portland, Norfolk, Bedford, and Northumberland; the Earls of Derby, Cholmondeley, and Fitzwilliam; and Lords St. John, Ponsonby, Craven, and Southampton; whilst in the Lower House his party embraced some of the most influential commoners in the nation.

He was therefore determined that the Pitt Ministry should not stand, and, at an early sitting of the new Parliament, a motion was carried, declaring the new Ministers incompetent to conduct public business. The Premier, however, bore the sentence of condemnation calmly, and gave no indication of resigning. The King was subsequently addressed on three several occasions by the Commons to dismiss those in office, but to these requests His Sacred Majesty turned a deaf ear. Fox, however, was firm in his resolution to oust the Ministers from their places, and, with that courage which distinguished his career, moved a daring remonstrance to the King for persevering in opposition to the declared wishes of his faithful Commons. This was carried by a majority of one, and Parliament was dissolved.

Now came a time of trial and excitement for Fox and his friends, which will remain for ever memorable in the annals of electioneering warfare. Fox became candidate for the representation of Westminster, and no exertion or influence which the Court could use, or the Members of the late Government could bring into force, were spared to hinder him from representing a seat so conspicuous in Parliament, and which was now powerfully contested by men of interest and reputation—Lord Hood and Sir Cecil Wray—who had formed a coalition against him. On the other hand, Fox was supported by the influential interests of his noble friends, amongst whom was the heir to the throne. All minor details of the general struggle going on throughout the country were lost sight of in this powerful and exciting contention, on which the eyes of the whole nation were turned; whilst the city, during the forty-seven days which the poll was kept open, presented a continued scene of turmoil and bloodshed.

Matters were at this pitch, when one of the most brilliant women in England came forward as Fox's ally, and declared her determination of openly canvassing for him. This was the famous Georgiana, Duchess of Devonshire, whom Walpole has happily styled 'the empress of fashion.' 'Her hair,' says the gallant Sir Nathaniel Wraxall, 'was not without a tinge of red, and her face, though pleasing, yet, had it not been illuminated by her mind, might have been considered as an ordinary countenance.'

It was not, however, to her personal appearance that she owed her powers of attraction, but to the delicate grace of her manners, to the exquisite charm of her movements, and to the seeming unconsciousness of her gifts, all of which exercised an influence that amounted to fascination over those with whom she came in contact.

In a moment so critical for the candidature of Westminster, such a partisan could scarcely be sufficiently appreciated. Having been furnished with lists of voters in the outskirts of the town, the charming Duchess, accompanied by her sister, the Vicountess Duncannon, drove to their houses, where she exerted those powers which had hitherto always proved irresistible; neither entreaties, promises, nor, in some cases, kisses were spared, and she had frequently the triumph of conveying voters, whom her persuasions had won to her cause, in her own coach, to the hustings. It was during this canvass that an Irish labourer, whose interest she solicited, paid her a compliment which, coming voluntarily and unexpectedly, she was far prouder of than of the most courteous phrase from the lips of a polished courtier. 'Me lady,' said this gallant Hibernian, 'your eyes are so bright I could light me pipe at them.'

The result of her untiring exertion soon showed itself; before she had commenced her canvass, Sir Cecil Wray had surpassed Fox by a hundred votes, but at the close of the poll, Fox had outstripped him by more than double that number, and his victory was complete. He was now hailed as 'the man of the people.' The delight of his friends was unbounded, and the Duchess's praises were sung in a hundred ballads; one of which said,

> 'Array'd in matchless beauty, Devon's fair
> In Fox's favour takes a zealous part;
> But oh! where'er the pilferer comes beware,
> She supplicates a vote, and steals a heart.'

A procession in honour of this successful election took place at once, while the friends of the favoured candidate were yet in a fever of enthusiasm, and the mob half-mad with an excitement which reached its climax at this hour. First in this strange political demonstration came a gay cavalcade, one of the horsemen in which bore a floating banner with the inscription, in compliment to the Duchess of Devonshire, 'Sacred to Female Patriotism;' then followed the equipages of the Dukes of Devonshire and Portland, each drawn by six horses gaily caparisoned; then Fox's carriage, with his friends, the Hon. Colonel North, afterwards Earl of Guilford, and Mr. Adam, mounted on the traces; then amongst ringing cheers, followed by a vast crowd, came the hero of the hour, elevated in a chair hung with wreaths of laurel, having, as Sir Nathaniel Wraxall says, 'the ostrich plumes which transport us to the field of Cressy, and which, during more than four centuries, have constituted the crest of the successive heirs-apparent to the English throne, openly borne before him; an exhibition that inspired many beholders with sentiments such as were felt by numbers among the Roman people when Antony displayed the deities of Egypt, mingled with the eagles of the Republic,

> "Interque signa, turpe, militaria
> Sol adspicit canopeum"'

After traversing the principal streets at the west end of the town, the procession came to Carlton House, the gates of which were flung wide open to receive it, when it passed through the court in front, and then wound its way to Devonshire House, where the Prince of Wales, the Duke and Duchess of Devonshire, Lady Duncannon, Mrs. Crew, and a brilliant assembly were collected. Fox then addressed the immense crowd and dismissed them; but at night the populace gave further expression to its joy by an almost general illumination.

On the next day, May 18th, the Prince gave a fête to celebrate his friend's victory. This took the form of a breakfast, and at mid-day over six hundred guests, who included the rank, talent, and beauty of his adherents, assembled on the lawn in front of Carlton House. The day was bright and warm, and the scene one of unusual brilliancy. Scattered all over the smooth, grassy sward were groups of men and women—most of them attired in blue and yellow, the Republican colours adopted by Fox—whose sole business in life seemed the enjoyment of the present hour. Breakfast was laid under nine marquees, a band filled the air with music. At this hour His Majesty proceeded in state to open Parliament, and, separated from the lawn only by a low boundary wall, had the bitter mortification of seeing his political enemies being sumptuously entertained by his son. After breakfast the company rose to dance on a part of the sward shaded by a group of trees; the Prince and her Grace of Devonshire leading the way. Dancing continued until six in the evening, when the guests retired, to prepare themselves for a supper given by Mrs. Crew, wife of the member for the county of Cheshire, a woman of brilliant parts and a lively partisan of Fox's. At this entertainment all the guests, including the Prince of Wales, were dressed in blue and yellow. The supper, magnificent and costly, was enjoyed by all; at its close, His Royal Highness rose to give the toast of the evening, and, bowing to his hostess with that grace said to rival Louis XIV., the model of all gallantry, he drank to 'True Blue and Mrs. Crew.' This sample of wit and eloquence, coming from right royal lips, was received with a rapture befitting the occasion; the lady was overwhelmed by this honour, but was not to be outdone in courtesy; rising, she bowed low to the Prince, and raising her glass, cried out, 'True Blue and all of you.'

Nor was this all; a few days later a second fête was given by the heir to the Crown, which was intended to surpass in luxury and magnificence anything of the kind which had been yet attempted. It commenced on the noon of one day and ended on the morning of the next. The first of this series of alterations at Carlton House for which the Prince had a mania, and for which the nation dearly paid, had been completed a month previously, and now the various apartments opening on one another, the dining-room with its magnificent chandeliers, the gilded state-room, the spacious ball-room, and finally the orchestra, presented a superb sight. A banquet was served to the ladies, on whom, in a spirit of chivalry, the Prince and his male friends waited; and later on the ball-room became a scene of unequalled brilliancy.

By this time the Prince's amour with Mrs. Armstead had ended, and that lady had returned to the protection of Charles Fox, who regarded her change of feelings in a thoroughly unprejudiced, philosophic, and friendly light. The Prince's royal but fickle heart being once more free, he hastened to bestow it on the notorious Mrs. Billington, a second-rate public singer, who warbled at Covent Garden Theatre, behind the scenes of which he first met and became enamoured of her. The object of this tender passion was no beauty. In a manuscript letter in the collection of Richard Orlebar, Esq., of Henwick House, Bedfordshire, written in 1788 by Miss Orlebar, the actress is described as 'a pretty little figure, pale and seemingly consumptive, though a very cunning look in her eyes. When she exerts herself, you can absolutely see the bones in her poor, thin neck.' The writer concludes by mentioning she was the Duke of Cumberland's favourite. Moreover, this lady, whose attraction for the Prince must have been her previous reputation, was coarse in manner and avaricious; the result was that His Royal Highness soon left her for the greater charms of Mrs. Crouch, the daughter of Peregrine Phillips, an actress and singer of considerable merits. Mrs. Billington, it may be mentioned, afterwards became devoted to the Church, as represented in the person of a bishop, who acted as her friend not only in a sense spiritual, but temporal. Mrs. Crouch, as may be supposed, had had a husband and several lovers, some of whom were young, ardent, and poetic; many of the latter had written her execrable effusions, 'On Mrs. Crouch in the character of Æneas,' and 'On Mrs. Crouch on seeing her in the character of Venus,' and on beholding her clasping a rose, and engaged in various other occupations. One of these assured her,

> 'Clad like a modern courtly dame
> From Paphos' isle fair Venus came.'

She, of course, being the Venus; another gentleman, whose youth we may imagine was as tender as his heart, said of her,

'Methinks I see you in your iv'ry car,
Sparkling in gems, like the bright morning star;
In purple cloth'd, your head with roses crown'd,
And your moist hair with golden fillets bound.'

With the reckless extravagance which characterized him, the Prince lavished vast sums upon her; in one instance to the amount of £10,000, independently of a profusion of jewellery to the value of £5,000. Moreover, this generosity, for which the nation was destined to pay, was not limited to such sums, and he finally made a settlement on her of £1,200 a year for life, which, however, like the bond given to Perdita Robinson, he refused to pay shortly afterwards, as 'no valuable consideration had been given,' he said. Mrs. Crouch, whilst she enjoyed his favour, removed from her rooms in Pall Mall, and took a house in the more fashionable quarter of Berkeley Square, where she gave charming entertainments and concerts that were patronized by the Prince and his friends.

Meanwhile, whilst he devoted his nights to the society of various sirens, England's future King spent his days at cock-fights, dog-fights, and pugilistic encounters, in all of which he took great interest and delight. He also established a stud on a scale regardless of expense, ran his horses at all the celebrated courses, where he was to be seen backing his favourites with heavy stakes, and to hasten his descent of this road to ruin, on which he had set out with such speed, he gambled night and day, and lost immense sums.

'His nights which were not otherwise employed,' says Huish, in his memoirs of George IV., 'were spent at the raro-table, whither he was often taken in a state of almost helpless intoxication, to render him the greater dupe of those who were then fattening on the unhallowed spoil obtained by their villainy.'

The Prince's personal friend, Major Hanger, in his life, mentions an incident regarding one of His Royal Highness's carousals, which happened at a time when his coffers were empty. In company with such merry men as the Major afore-mentioned, Charles Fox, Sheridan, and Berkeley, the Prince sought adventure at the 'Staffordshire Arms' tavern, from whence he sent for further company agreeable to himself and his friends, who, presently joining them, created much diversion. The night was passed in a general carousal, and in the early hours of morning it was found there was not a sufficient sum amongst the united company to defray expenses. At this critical moment one of the party suggested that, as Sheridan was helplessly drunk, he should be left as a hostage for the debt, an idea at once acted on by the Prince and his other friends, who thus avoided payment of the reckoning. Poor, reckless, brilliant, spendthrift, good-hearted Sheridan! long years afterwards his corpse was arrested at the hands of the law for the sum of £500.

CHAPTER VI.

Richard Brinsley Sheridan and Miss Betsy Linley—Sheridan introduced to the Prince—Interview with a Child of Israel—The Royal Debts—Mrs. Fitzherbert—Flight to the Continent—The Prince's Tears and Despair—Letter from Charles Fox—Marriage of Mrs. Fitzherbert—Cowardice and Deception of the Prince—The King's Social Life—His Original Criticisms on Shakespeare—Her Majesty's Opinion of the 'Sorrows of Werter'—Mrs. Siddons at the Play and at Windsor—Signs of the King's Madness.

THIS new companion of His Royal Highness, Richard Brinsley Sheridan, was the son of old Tom Sheridan, the player, and Frances, his wife, a lady who wrote some excellent novels and clever plays, one of which—to wit, 'The Discovery'—Garrick declared to be one of the best comedies he had ever read. From her, Richard Brinsley no doubt inherited a share of that talent which afterwards so highly distinguished him. He was educated at Harrow, which he left, it may be here remarked, without being able to spell; and, when not long out of his teens, fell in love with Miss Betsy Linley, then in her sixteenth year, a public singer whose voice, according to the authorities of the day, rivalled the nightingale's, and whose beauty was simply angelic.

Miss Linley was not without admirers, one of whom was a gentleman named Long, whose suit, notwithstanding that his years numbered seventy, was looked upon with favour by a kindly, though practical parent, by reason of the suitor's wealth; another of these admirers was a gentle, romantic youth named Halhed, who informed Miss Betsy in a florid letter that, 'just as the Egyptian pharmacists were wont, in embalming a dead body, to draw the brain out through the ears with a crooked hook, this nightingale has drawn out through mine ears, not only my brain, but my heart also;' whilst a third lover, Captain Matthews, a coward and a scamp, gave more trouble than any of his rivals; his intentions, moreover, were dishonourable.

From these troublesome suitors she eloped with Richard Brinsley Sheridan to France, where they were married, to the great indignation of their unsympathetic parents. After marriage, Sheridan, who had not a penny in the world, was too dignified and too Irish to permit his wife to earn an honest income by her talents; yet they did not starve, as they had the interest of £3,000 which good-hearted Mr. Long had settled upon Miss Betsy when she had refused his suit. After awhile, being, alas! sorely pressed for money, Sheridan, who was naturally indolent, and seldom worked but when there was necessity for gold, wrote 'The Rivals,' which, owing chiefly to the bad acting of one of the performers, was a failure on the night of its first representation, but eventually proved a vast favourite with the public.

Its author now became a shareholder in the Drury Lane play-house, for which he paid down the sum of £10,000, to the great astonishment of all his friends, who failed to ascertain how he became possessed of such a sum. Sheridan, however, could keep a secret, and this one was so well guarded that his biographers have never been able to throw any light on the matter. He now wrote another play, 'A Trip to Scarborough,' and in 1777, when his years numbered six-and-twenty, gave the world that bright, clever comedy, 'The School for Scandal, which has become an English classic.

He was now at the meridian of his brilliant intellectual powers; his stories were repeated in all quarters of the town, his wit universally lauded, his society eagerly sought after. He soon made the acquaintance of Fox, who, delighted with his humour and the vivacious, easy flow of his conversation, introduced him to the Prince of Wales. His Royal Highness, impulsive and pleasure-loving, declared himself charmed with his conviviality; they soon became friends, and their friendship so quickly ripened into intimacy, that the Prince styled him his 'dear Sherry;' indeed, His Royal Highness found the player's son indispensable to his enjoyment, and in his company he drank, gambled, betted, and sought adventures of a certain class, for which they both had, alas! a common appetite and appreciation.

But such a career, without ample means to sustain it, soon reduced the reckless Sherry to many shifts, and brought him in contact with a large number of the children of Israel, whose threatened vengeance he not unfrequently turned aside by his wonderful force of persuasion, or his inimitable powers of acting. It was to one of these gentlemen, who rejoiced in the name of Moses Aaron, that Sheridan, on a memorable occasion, addressed himself on behalf of the Prince, who suffered at the time from a pressing pecuniary difficulty. The place of appointment was an ante-chamber in Carlton House, where the man of money was graciously saluted by Sheridan, who was alone in the apartment when the Jew entered.

'Ah! my friend Moses,' he said, with an air of great delight, 'how do you do?'

'I would do better, Mr. Sheridan,' replied the sagacious child of Israel, 'if I had my due.'

'Ah! my friend,' said Sherry, yet more blandly, 'if every man had that, many of them would have a halter.'

'It may be so, Mr. Sheridan,' remarked Moses, who knew his customer only too well. 'You, I know, are a most *conscientious* man, and I dare say you speak as you *feel.*'

'Well hit,' Sheridan said good-humouredly; 'but did you get that little bill done for me?'

'No, Mr. Sheridan,' said Moses firmly; 'it was not to be done,' and he rubbed his bony hands one over the other.

'Money must be devilish scarce,' replied Sheridan, with something like a sigh.

'Or there must be something the matter with the credit of the parties,' said the money-lender shrewdly, his under-lip curving as if about to smile.

'Ah! it's the times—the times,' remarked Sherry philosophically, as he watched the child of Israel.

'What security have you to offer?' asked the Jew, with an eye to business.

'My honour,' said the dramatist grandly, laying his hand upon his heart with a theatrical gesture.

'Won't do,' answered Moses, shaking his wise old head; 'it's quite threadbare long ago.'

'But if the Prince goes security?'

'Ah!' said the Jew, with a chuckle, 'that alters the case,' and he rubbed his dirty hands once more.

'Then,' said Sheridan, 'let us go in to the Prince,' and so saying he led the way to the next room.

From the introduction of Moses Aaron to the heir to the throne, the difficulties which soon beset the royal path, and quickly accumulated, may be said to have commenced. The loan required by Sheridan for the Prince was soon effected, and proved but the forerunner of many others which he, reckless in his expenditure, hurried on by his passions, and glad to find any temporary escape from his grievous difficulties, eagerly sought for and obtained on terms of usurious interest.

On one occasion Moses Aaron raised for him the sum of

£10,000, for a post-obit bond, payable on the death of the King. Of this money, he received in reality but £7,000, the remaining sum being made up, according to a practice known then and now, of various articles, the most useful of which were two hogsheads of French playing-cards, and three puncheons of French brandy, manufactured at a distillery in Whitechapel. There was also a diamond cross and a rosary, the diamonds being manufactured at Houndsditch, and two hundred tea-urns, which the Prince soon disposed of to another Jew at a quarter the price that honest Moses Aaron had charged him. It may be recorded in the history of these tea-urns, that in less than three months they found their way once more to Carlton House, under circumstances the same as those which first brought them within the precincts of that royal residence.

Notwithstanding his income of £62,000 a year, and the £60,000 which had been granted him by Parliament on his coming of age, his debts amounted in three years to £160,000. At this crisis in his affairs, the Prince resolved to consult Sir James Harris, afterwards Lord Malmesbury, who had been Secretary of the Embassy at the Court of Madrid, and Minister at the Court of Catherine II. at St. Petersburg. In his valuable diaries and correspondence, he has left us an account of the interviews he had with the Prince in 1785. The heir to the throne told him that, in the autumn of the previous year, he had written to the King, acquainting him with his embarrassed situation, and declaring his wish to live abroad, in order that he might retrench. This the King would not hear of, but gave the Prince to understand that, if he sent in an exact account of his debts, he would pay them. The Prince did so, *en gros*, but, when the statement had been kept four months, it was returned to him, saying it was not exact, as the articles were not specified. The Prince returned it once more, with every article minuted but one, a lump sum of £25,000, which he was not willing to account for. It was borrowed money, he told Lord Malmesbury, and he was in honour bound not to say from whence it came. The King insisted on knowing how this was incurred, and declared, if it was a debt the Prince was ashamed of, it was one which he, the King, ought not to pay. Here matters rested, His Royal Highness strongly expressing his determination of going abroad without His Majesty's permission.

At the second interview which Lord Malmesbury had with the coming King, that illustrious person announced that he had given up all idea of leaving England; a reason for which sudden change of opinion will afterwards be seen. Lord Malmesbury said, if the Prince would give him leave, he would propose to Mr. Pitt to increase his revenue to £100,000 a year, but to this His Royal Highness would not listen. The King, he said, hated him, and that he would turn Pitt out of office for entertaining such an idea; besides, he could not abandon Charles Fox and the Duke of Portland. His adviser, however, had wisely spoken to these politicians previously on the matter, and now told His Royal Highness they had informed him, they had no wish he, the Prince, should take any share in party concerns; he furthermore hinted that a reconciliation with the King would be wise. Once more the Prince repeated with warmth, and in the most forcible manner, that the King hated him, and added that, if Lord Malmesbury would not credit him, he would perhaps believe the King himself; saying which, he gave him the correspondence which had passed between them for the last six months.

'The Prince's letters,' said Lord Malmesbury, 'were full of respect and deference, written with great plainness of style and simplicity. Those of the King were also well written, but harsh and severe; constantly refusing every request the Prince made, and reprobating in each of them his extravagance and dissipated manner of living. They were void of every expression of parental kindness or affection; and, after both hearing them read and perusing them myself, I was compelled to subscribe to the Prince's opinion, and to confess there was very little appearance of making any impression on His Majesty in favour of His Royal Highness.'

Before the interview ended, Lord Malmesbury suggested the idea of the Prince marrying; but he declared with great vehemence he would never marry; that he had settled it with Frederick (his next brother), to whose children the Crown would descend.

The Prince had arrived at this conclusion as he at the time contemplated marriage with Mrs. Fitzherbert; a union which, according to the Royal Marriage Act, would prove illegal, and the children of which he knew would be regarded as illegitimate. That such a marriage took place, though long a matter of doubt, in consequence of its being repeatedly repudiated by the royal husband in the latter years of his life, is now an historical fact which has been conclusively established. Shortly after the death of George IV., and whilst Mrs. Fitzherbert lived, her friends considered it advisable that her union with his late Majesty should be rescued from all doubt, and placed on the high level of certainty; therefore the Duke of Wellington and Sir William Knighton, the executors of George IV., concurring with the Earl of Albemarle and Lord Stourton, Mrs. Fitzherbert's nominees, deposited, in a strong-box at Coutts' bank, in June, 1833, documents proving the marriage, amongst which were, according to a list attested by Lords Stourton and Albemarle, 'The certificate of the marriage, dated December 21, 1785; a letter from the late King, relating to the marriage, signed George IV.; a will written by the late King George IV.; and a memorandum written by Mrs. Fitzherbert, attached to a letter written by the clergyman who performed the marriage ceremony.' This box bore the superscription, 'The property of the Earl of Albemarle, not to be opened by him without apprising the Duke of Wellington.' Its seals, it is believed, are yet unbroken.

At the death of Mrs. Fitzherbert, her kinsman, Lord Stourton, wished to make use of these documents; she had written to him from Paris, December 7, 1833: 'I trust, whenever it pleases God to remove me from this world, that my conduct and character, in your hands, will not disgrace my family or my friends;' and, now that the period to which she referred had arrived, he considered it his duty, by the publication of these papers, to place her memory beyond reproach in the eyes of the world. However, before the necessary permission could be granted, he died; the desire was then repeated by his brother, the Hon. Charles Langdale, to the Hon. and Rev. Edward Keppel, Lord Albemarle's executor, who was by no means anxious to accede to Mr. Langdale's wishes. The documents, he wrote, 'would only prove the marriage of the Prince with Mrs. Fitzherbert, which is not questioned . . . the public might or might not be interested in the production of the papers, but the revival of the subject would only pander to the bad feelings or the curiosity of the great world without doing good.' This wise and reverent man withholding his consent, it was impossible for the Hon. Charles Langdale to get possession of the documents, and it therefore only remained for him to publish a narrative which Mrs. Fitzherbert had given his brother, and which was left by the latter to him; to this we are indebted for many of the following facts.

Mrs. Fitzherbert, whose subsequent life became the subject of a royal romance, was originally known as Mary Anne Smythe. She was the daughter of a baronet, and had been twice married and widowed when, in her twenty-sixth year, she was introduced to the Prince at her residence, Richmond Hill. Though not possessed of striking beauty, her personal appearance was pleasing, and her manners graceful, refined, and fascinating. For the Prince, to see her was to love her, and his passion, conceived at first sight, increased all the more that it met with but slight encouragement from its object. Her treatment of him was far different from that of any other woman who had crossed his royal path, and, the more determined she was to refuse him her affection, the more anxious he became to make any sacrifice which could win her love. Mrs. Fitzherbert, however, would not consent to become his mistress, and knew that, according to the provisions of the Royal Marriage Act, she could not become his wife. The Prince now grew desperate, and resorted to a highly dramatic stratagem, which he believed could not fail to succeed in obtaining him his desires.

One morning Keit, His Royal Highness's physician, Lord Onslow, Lord Southampton, and Mr. Edward Bouverie drove up, in hot haste, to Mrs. Fitzherbert's house in Park Street, and entered her drawing-room in a state of great consternation. The Prince, they said, had stabbed himself, his life was in imminent danger at that moment, and nothing on earth but her presence could save him. She was naturally much impressed and frightened on hearing this tale of woe, but, on consideration, declared nothing should induce her to enter Carlton House. These gallant men, however, continuing to assure her of the Prince's most critical condition, her alarm was thoroughly roused; and she consented to see him, if she was accompanied by her friend, the Duchess of Devonshire. To this they immediately consented, and calling at Devonshire House, they carried the charming Georgiana with them.

When Mrs. Fitzherbert entered the Prince's room, she found him lying pale, agitated, and covered with blood; the effect of this dramatic situation was so striking that she immediately fainted; but the tableau was not yet completed.

When the lady recovered consciousness, the Prince assured her in solemn tones that nothing would induce him to live, unless she promised to become his wife, and permitted him to put a ring on her finger. A ring was, therefore, taken from the Duchess of Devonshire, and this interesting scene ended. The audience and the fair heroine then adjourned to Devonshire House, where a deposition of what had occurred was drawn up, signed and sealed by each of the party, but she whom it chiefly concerned attached such little importance to it, that she left it behind her, and on considering over all that had passed, resolved quietly to quit the country; a resolution she carried into effect next day, having first written a letter to Lord Southampton protesting against what had taken place, as she was not then, she declared, a free agent. The Prince was now plunged in yet deeper despair, and, at this time, probably meant to follow her to the Continent.

With a taste and delicacy which require no comment, he rushed for consolation to his former mistress, Mrs. Armstead, who was then living comfortably with dear Charles Fox, at St. Anne's Hill, Chertsey. This lady afterwards told Lord Holland that the royal youth 'cried by the hour, that he testified the sincerity and violence of his passion and despair by the most extravagant expressions and actions; rolling on the floor, striking his forehead, tearing his hair, falling into hysterics, and swearing that he would abandon the country, forego the Crown, sell his jewels and plate, and scrape together a competence, to fly with the object of his affections to America.'

Mrs. Fitzherbert remained abroad for eighteen months, during which time couriers were continually sent to her, carrying her amorous letters and propositions from her royal lover. Lord Stourton saw one of these in the Prince's writing, which numbered thirty-seven pages, in which he stated the King would connive at their union.

At length, wearied by his entreaties, she returned to London, on the understanding that she should become his wife on conditions which would strictly satisfy her conscience, if not give her a legal claim to the throne. Rumours of her arrival soon spread about town, and the Prince's friends were at once alarmed at the consequences which might ensue. Fox, actuated by the great regard he held for his royal patron, wrote to him to say he had heard of Mrs. Fitzherbert's return, news which he would have learned with the most unfeigned joy, but that he was told at the same time that he, the Prince, was about to take a desperate step, and marry her. If such was really in his mind, he besought him, for God's sake, to consider the matter; for, in the first place, a marriage with a Catholic—the religion to which she belonged—threw the Prince contracting such out of succession of the Crown.

Charles then went on to say he had not heard of any public profession of change of religion on Mrs. Fitzherbert's part, and, if there should be a doubt of her conversion (which had never before, or after even, been hinted at), he prayed the Prince to consider how he should stand, 'the King not feeling for you as a father ought; the Duke of York professedly his favourite, and likely to be married agreeably to the King's wishes; the nation full of its old prejudices against Catholics, and justly dreading all disputes about succession.' He finished a long letter by declaring, if he were Mrs. Fitzherbert's father or brother, he would advise her not by any means to consent to a union which could not be considered other than a mock marriage, and 'to prefer any other species of connection with you, to one leading to so much misery and mischief.'

The Prince, on answering his dear Charles, gave a specimen of the duplicity that was a part of his character; he told his friend to make himself easy, and to believe him the world would soon be convinced 'that there not only is not, but never was, any ground for those reports which of late have been so malevolently circulated.' Eleven days after the date of the Prince's letter, on December 21, 1785, he was married to Mrs. Fitzherbert by a clergyman of the Church of England, though certain forms and circumstances were observed as were recognised and used by the Catholic Church in the celebration of the marriage service. The ceremony took place in the drawing-room of the bride's house, and was witnessed by her uncle, Harry Errington, and her brother, Jack Smythe. The marriage certificate was written in the Prince's handwriting, and was signed by him, as well as by the witnesses, but in a time of subsequent danger the names of the latter were cut off by Mrs. Fitzherbert, to save her relatives from the peril of the statute of *præmunire*, which, according to *Blackstone's Commentaries*, they incurred by 'assisting or being present' at an unauthorised marriage with a descendant of George II. This she afterwards regretted, she told Stourton; but a letter from the Prince, in which he thanked God that the witnesses of their union were still living, was preserved.

For a time the marriage was kept as a secret, but by degrees some rumours of it were whispered through the town, contradicted and repeated, doubted and re-asserted. In February, 1786, Horace Walpole writes to Sir Horace Mann:

'I am obliged to you for your accounts of the House of Albany; but that extinguishing family can make no sensation here, when we have other guess matter to talk of in a higher and more flourishing race; and yet were rumour —ay, much more than rumour, every voice in England—to be credited, the matter, somehow or other, reaches even from London to Rome. I know nothing but the buzz of the day, nor can say more upon it: if I send you a riddle, fame, or echo, from so many voices, will soon reach you and explain the enigma; though I hope it is essentially void of truth, and that appearances rise from a much more common cause.'

So important a matter as the marriage of the heir-apparent was not long confined to the whispering of gossips; the public was anxious to ascertain if there was any truth in the rumour, and accordingly, the first opportunity of bringing the subject forward in the House of Commons was eagerly seized on. This occurred when an appeal was made to increase the income of the Prince, who was now overwhelmed by debts and difficulties, the result of his determined extravagance, from which the King had wholly refused to extricate him. In April, 1786, Mr. Newenham, one of the members for the City of London, announced his intention to move an address to the throne, 'entreating His Majesty to inquire into the Prince's embarrassed situation, and to rescue him from it,' on which Rolle, the member for Devonshire, rose up, and, in covert language which was thoroughly understood by all, stated that the present situation of His Royal Highness directly affected the Constitution both in Church and State.

This note of alarm struck the Prince with dismay, for he saw the subject of his marriage must inevitably be referred to, and he dreaded the results. At such a moment this cowardly, selfish, and vicious man did not hesitate to blast the reputation of a woman he professed to love, and who he knew valued her virtue more than aught else in life; nor did he shrink from making his friend the innocent accomplice in a scheme of treachery and fraud. He sent for Charles Fox and Mr. Grey to Carlton House, and, referring to the rumour of his marriage, he, according to Lord Brougham, 'most solemnly denied the whole upon his sacred honour.'

Armed with this authority, Charles Fox, on the subject being resumed, attended the House of Commons, and assured a crowded and excited assembly that the report alluded to by Mr. Rolle was 'a mischievous calumny, a low, malicious falsehood, which had been propagated without doors, and made the wanton sport of the vulgar; a tale fit only to impose upon the lowest orders, a monstrous invention, a report of a fact which had not the smallest degree of foundation, actually impossible to have happened.' Rolle desired to be informed whether Fox had spoken from *direct authority*; a question to which he instantly replied that he had.

Though it was not doubted that he had the Prince's sanction to deny the marriage, yet the fact that no one believed the statement that His Royal Highness was not married to Mrs. Fitzherbert sufficiently indicates the regard in which the royal honour was held. But the princely duplicity was not yet complete. According to the Langdale Memoirs, he was the first to announce Fox's denial of their marriage to Mrs. Fitzherbert; for which purpose, he called on her early on the morning after the debate, when, going up to her, he took both her hands, and, caressing her in his usual affectionate manner, said,

'Only conceive, Maria, what Fox did yesterday. He went down to the House and denied that you and I were man and wife. Did you ever hear of such a thing?'

Mrs. Fitzherbert turned pale, and was too much overcome to make an immediate reply. The public, she told her relative, Lord Stourton, supported her by their conduct on this occasion; for at no period of her life were their visits so numerous as the day following the denial. The bell and the knocker of the door were never still, she said, during the day. Nor was Fox allowed to remain long ignorant of the gross deception which his royal friend had so successfully practised on him. In Lord John Russell's life of that statesman, he says: 'On the day after Mr. Fox's declaration, a gentleman of his acquaintance went up to him at Brookes's, and said, "I see by the papers, Mr. Fox, that you have denied the fact of the marriage of the Prince of Wales with Mrs. Fitzherbert. You have been misinformed. I was present at that marriage."'

It is stated that for twelve months afterwards Fox refused to see the Prince.

Meantime, Mrs. Fitzherbert, conscious of the cruel blow her reputation had received, and considering herself publicly compromised, determined to break off all connection with the Prince; but he assured her that he was quite blameless concerning what had passed, and now tried to heal, if possible, the wound which his perfidy had given to a sensitive and virtuous woman, whose sole misfortune was her love for him. He sent for Mr. (afterwards Earl) Grey, and pacing up and down the room in a hurried and shame-faced manner, declared that 'Charles had certainly gone too far;' and then, as Lord Grey mentions in a note to Fox's correspondence, he confessed his marriage, and finally asked his friend to explain the matter. Mr. Grey coolly and justly informed the Prince the mistake could only be rectified by His Royal Highness speaking to Mr. Fox, and setting him right on such matters as had been misunderstood between them. 'No other person,' he added, 'can be employed without questioning Mr. Fox's veracity; which nobody, I presume, is prepared to do.' Disappointed and chagrined by this unexpected reply, the Prince flung himself on a sofa, saying, 'Well, Sheridan must say something.' Accordingly, Sheridan took an early opportunity of paying a vague compliment in the House of Commons 'to female delicacy,' and declared that ignorance and folly could alone have persevered in attempting to injure the reputation of one whose character was open to no just reproach, and was entitled to the truest and most general respect. With these bland and meaningless compliments, which gave no contradiction to Fox's denial, the matter was allowed to rest. Mrs. Fitzherbert's friends assured her that, in the wide discrepancy between Fox's statements and those of the Prince, she was bound to accept her husband's word. Their connection was therefore once more resumed; but during her life she would never consent to see Charles Fox again.

It was now intimated to the Prince that if the original motion praying for an income were withdrawn, the King would strive to arrange his debts, which had by this time reached the round sum of £193,648. Accordingly, on His Royal Highness's gracious compliance, his liabilities were submitted to the inspection of Commissioners, appointed by His Majesty. The King finally sent a message to Parliament, declaring he had consented to a further sum of £10,000 being added to His Royal Highness's income, blandly stating that 'he had now to recur to the liberality and attachment of his faithful Commons for their assistance on an occasion so interesting (!) to His Majesty's feelings, and to the ease and honour of so distinguished a branch of his royal family.' His Majesty further observed that he 'could not expect or desire the assistance of the House but on a well-grounded expectation that the Prince will avoid contracting any debts in future.' The result of this most civil message was that His Royal Highness was voted £161,000 to pay his debts, and £20,000 on account of the unnecessary alterations being made at Carlton House.

After this, a sham peace was effected between the King and his heir, who attended a drawing-room at St. James's, and was paraded like a royal marionnette on the public terrace at Windsor, walking side by side with His Sacred Majesty, conversing freely, and behaving in the eyes of a vast concourse as a right loyal and truly model son.

We must now turn back to the domestic life of the King, which was so quiet and uneventful as to leave but little for the historiographer to narrate. For such glimpses as are obtainable, we are chiefly indebted to the very loyal and pleasant pens of Mrs. Delany and Fanny Burney. The former lady, when introduced to George III. and his family, had reached an advanced age, but still retained much of her mental vigour, and somewhat of that grace and beauty which, in her early days, had rendered her a toast for wits and a theme for poets. This charming and interesting gentlewoman was the widow of a man who had been an able scholar and eloquent preacher in his day. She was, moreover, related to the noble house of Lansdowne; had been maid-of-honour to Queen Anne of godly memory; had enjoyed the friendships of Swift and Pope, of Young, the gifted poet, and Horace Walpole, the accomplished gossip, and Lady Mary Wortley Montagu, the learned traveller, and a host of other individuals more or less distinguished.

Amongst the few friends of her earlier life who yet survived was Margaret, Duchess of Portland, whose praises had been sung by Swift and Prior, and whose beauty had rendered her a celebrity in her youth. Mrs. Delany and the Duchess, who, as Hannah More said, was 'of the noble and munificent style of the old nobility,' were fast friends, and it was whilst staying with her Grace at Bulstrode Park, in Buckinghamshire, that she had her first private view of their Gracious Majesties. The King and Queen, attended by Princes and Princesses, and escorted by their attendants, drove in an open chaise, on horseback, and in coaches, making what the dear old lady calls 'a splendid figure,' as they approached through the park and galloped into the court in front of the house. The day was as brilliant as even anyone so loyal as the narrator could desire, it being, by the way, the sixteenth birthday of the heir to the Throne; and there were the royal family in many coloured costumes, looking as gay as might be, 'the Queen in a hat and an Italian night-gown of purple lutestring trimmed with silver gauze,' quite graceful and genteel and dignified; the three Princesses all in frocks, the King in a uniform of blue and gold, very condescending, and in great good-humour. They all walked into the drawing-room, and through the great apartments, observing everything. Mrs. Delany did not follow in the courtly train, but remained in one of the drawing-rooms to rest; but, when she was missed, Majesty at once sent for her, and she hurried to its august presence as fast as she could travel, whereon the Queen said to her, 'Though I desired you to come, I did not desire you to run and fatigue yourself,' words which the good old soul to whom they were addressed repeated and treasured up in her courtier's heart as long as she lived.

'Then the King and all his royal children, and the rest of the train, chose to go to the gallery,' Mrs. Delany says, in all simplicity, 'where the well-furnished tables were set; one with tea, coffee, and chocolate, another with their proper accompaniments of eatables, rolls, cakes, etc.; another table with fruits and ices, in the utmost perfection, which, with a magical touch, had succeeded a cold repast.'

Indeed, it was all like a fairy tale to good Mrs. Delany; and to make it more so still, the Queen sat in the drawing-room, not eating bread and honey, but drinking a dish of tea served her by the Duchess. Presently the King and 'the young royals' returned, and His Gracious Majesty set a chair for poor, feeble old Mrs. Delany, who had been standing all the while in the sacred presence of the plain little Queen; at which act of courtesy she felt confused, but Her Majesty, turning to her, said, 'Mrs. Delany, sit down, sit down; it is not everybody that has a chair brought her by a King.'

The climax of the royal graciousness arrived when she was commanded, with the Duchess of Portland, to drink tea at Windsor on the following evening. When they arrived at the hour appointed, the two venerable ladies walked 'through a large room, with great bay windows, where were all the Princesses and youngest Princes, with their attendant ladies and gentlemen.' Then they passed on to the bed-chamber, where they found the Queen standing in the middle of the room. At eight o'clock, their Majesties, with eleven of the Princes and Princesses, walked out on the terrace in procession, to the sound of martial music, where the people were waiting to see the royal show, the Duchess of Portsmouth and her friend being left with the Bishop of Lichfield and Lady Weymouth.

'When they returned,' writes Mrs. Delany, 'we were summoned into the next room to tea, and the royals began a ball, and danced two country dances, to the music of French horns, bassoons, and hautboys, which were the same that played on the terrace. The King came up to the Prince of Wales, and said he was sure, when he considered how great an effort it must be to play that kind of music so long a time together, that he would not continue their dancing there, but that the Queen and the rest of the company were going to the Queen's house, and they should renew their dancing there and have proper music.' Then Mrs. Delany says she can say no more, for she 'cannot describe the gay and polished appearance of the Queen's house, furnished with English manufacture;' and so her narrative of this evening ends in what may be considered silent rapture.

Four months later, she gives another description of the honours she received from their Majesties at Windsor, on the Princess Royal's birthday, which is singularly quaint and not without interest. 'The Queen,' she writes to Miss Port of Ilam, who no doubt wished to be favoured with an account of the fashions indulged in by royalty, 'was dressed in an embroidered lutestring; Princess Royal in deep orange or scarlet—I could not by candle-light distinguish which—Princess Augusta in pink; Princess Elizabeth in blue. These were all in robes without aprons. Princess Mary—a most sweet child—was in cherry-coloured tabby, with silver leading-strings. She is about four years old. She could not remember my name, but, making me a very low curtsey, she said, "How do you do, Duchess of Portland's friend? And how does your little niece do? I wish you had brought her." The King carried about in his arms, by turns, Princess Sophia, and the last Prince, Octavius, so called being the eighth son.'

Mrs. Delany never saw more lovely children, or a more pleasing sight, after which admission, she goes on: 'The King brought in his arms the little Prince Octavius to me, who held out his hand to play with me, which, on my taking the liberty to kiss, His Majesty made him kiss my cheek.' Then there was a concert of vocal and instrumental music, but no supper; and their Majesties talked to her. Everything was pleasant; everyone was delightful; even the moon, which lit her on her way home through Windsor Great Park, was on that night found unusually brilliant and charming.

Such a favourite did Mrs. Delany become with royalty, that, six years later, in 1785, when she had lost her old and valued friend, the Duchess of Portsmouth, the King presented her with a house close to the royal residence at Windsor, which he furnished, and, furthermore, granted her an annuity of £300 out of the Privy Purse. This kindness was gladly accepted, and in the September of this year, she took up her residence in her new home, where it was that their Majesties first saw the famous Fanny Burney. The said Frances was daughter of Dr. Burney, a musical teacher, the reputation of whose works on subjects connected with his art, together with his talents and his happy temper, brought him much into the polite and literary society of the day. In turn, this polite and literary society graciously gathered beneath the doctor's roof, and unconsciously formed a study to a quiet, retiring child of the house, who, with open eyes and ears, closely noted all that passed before her. The result of this observation was that, in due time, she committed her impressions to paper, and produced a novel destined to be known to the world under the style and title of 'Evelina.' The manuscript was, with many hopes and fears, committed to Dodsley, the publisher, who rejected it, when it was sent to Lowndes, in Fleet Street.

The author gave the name of Grafton, and had her correspondence addressed to the Orange Coffee-house, Miss Burney considering it necessary that her incognita should be strictly preserved. Lowndes offered the delighted young authoress the sum of twenty pounds for her copyright, which was 'accepted with alacrity and boundless surprise at its magnificence;' six months after, the book appeared in all the glory of type in January, 1778. Then, in a little while, came the first burst of appreciation, which presently increased to a whirlwind of success. Reviewers became eulogistic, the public read it with avidity, Edmund Burke remained up all night to finish it, fine ladies wept over its pages, its merits were lauded in drawing-rooms, and its name grew familiar on the lips of all men.

By-and-by it became whispered that Fanny Burney was the authoress of 'Evelina,' and great was her social triumph; she now became what was called a person of distinction, and soon grew acquainted with and made the friendships of many worthy persons, amongst whom was Mrs. Delany; and it was whilst staying with this venerable lady at her house in Windsor, Fanny first came face to face with Majesty. Royalty was in the habit of visiting Mrs. Delany at all hours, and in the most unceremonious manner possible; and Miss Burney had on more than one occasion fled to her own room panic-stricken when the royal knock had thundered at her worthy hostess's door.

It happened, however, that one afternoon, when Mrs. Delany had retired for her after-dinner nap, Miss Burney was in the drawing-room teaching the old lady's little grand-niece a Christmas game, in which some friends who were present joined. They were all in right merry confusion, standing in the middle of the floor, when Mrs. Delany came in to inquire what was going forward. Frances was disentangling herself, when suddenly 'the door of the drawing-room was again opened, and a large man in deep mourning appeared at it, entering and shutting it himself without speaking.' A ghost, she says, could not have more scared her when she discovered, by the star on the large man's breast, that she stood in the sacred presence of royalty. Then Mrs. Delany's niece cried out, 'The King, aunt—the King.' Everyone scampered out of the way, whilst Mrs. Delany advanced to greet His Majesty. The child clung to Fanny, who rapidly retreated to the wall, on thoughts intent of gliding softly out of the room; but, even as she strove to put her purpose into execution, she, with fluttering heart, heard a loud whisper from the royal lips. 'Is that Miss Burney?' said the King. 'Yes, sir,' said Mrs. Delany. Then he bowed with what the authoress describes as 'a countenance of the most perfect good-humour,' whilst she curtseyed with reverence most profound. He then asked her, 'How long have you been back?' But her reply was so subdued and her tone so nervous, that, alas! it never reached the royal ears. The King now imparted to Mrs. Delany the important information that the Princess Elizabeth was using James's powders, that she had been blooded twelve times in the last fortnight, and had lost seventy-five ounces of blood, besides undergoing blistering and other discipline; the other children, he said, had whooping-cough, and he had rheumatism. He paid the strictest attention to simple diet, he added, for he 'preferred eating plain and little to growing diseased and infirm.'

When he had finished these interesting particulars, he told Mrs. Delany that Dr. Burney had repeated to him the whole history of the novel 'Evelina.' Then he went up abruptly to the trembling authoress, who, as she tells us, could never forget his face while she lived, and said, 'But what—what—how was it?'

'Sir!' cried she, not well understanding him.

'How came you—how happened it—what—what?' repeated His Majesty, with interest.

'I—I only wrote, sir, for my own amusement—only in some odd idle hours,' she replied.

'But your publishing—your printing—how was that?' asks the King incoherently.

'That was only, sir—only because——'

The *what* was then repeated with so earnest a look that, forced to say something, she, with ever-increasing confusion, stammeringly answered:

'I thought, sir, it would look very well in print.' Immediately she had spoken she felt that this was the silliest speech she had ever made in her life. He laughed very heartily, and walked away to enjoy it, crying out, 'Very fair indeed; that's being very fair and honest!' which made Fanny blush all the more.

Presently a violent thunder was made at the door, and a second afterwards the Queen herself entered the habitation of worthy Mrs. Delany.

'Oh, your Majesty is here!' she cried to the King, making him a curtsey when she set eyes on him.

'Yes,' he replied; 'I ran here without speaking to anybody.'

The Queen then spoke to Mrs. Delany, and Miss Burney instantly felt the royal eye on her face, and she, poor little woman, was about to sink with horrid uncertainty of what she was doing or what she should do; but the King came to her rescue, and she dropped a curtsey to the Queen, who returned it civilly enough, and entered into conversation with her. Then Her Majesty spoke of the drawing-room which she had held in town on the previous Thursday in the midst of a dense fog.

'I assure you, ma'am,' cried she to Mrs. Delany, 'it was so dark, there was no seeing anything, and no knowing anybody. And Lady Harcourt could be of no help to tell me who people were; for, when it was light, she can't see, and now it was dark, I could not see myself. So it was in vain for me to go on in that manner, without knowing which I had spoken to, and which was waiting for me; so I said to Lady Harcourt, "We had better stop, and stand quite still; for I don't know anybody, no more than you do. But, if we stand still, they will all come up in the end, and we must ask them who they are, and if I have spoken to them yet or not; for it is very odd to do it, but what else can we manage?" So there was standing by me a man that I could not see in the face, but I saw the twisting of his bow, and said to Lady Harcourt, "I am sure that must be nobody but the Duke of Dorset." "Dear," she says, "how can you tell that?" "Only ask," said I; and so it proved he.'

After more conversation of a like character, the King and Queen got into their royal coach, and were driven away to their royal castle, leaving the little groups in Mrs. Delany's drawing-room marvelling much at their mighty condescension, graciousness, and simplicity.

A few evenings after this, whilst Mrs. Delany, her niece, and Fanny Burney were sitting working in the drawing-room, the door opened, and who steps in once more but the King! They all started up, but he made his hostess resume her place, whilst he told her about the Princess Elizabeth and James's powders again. The conversation soon veered from this young lady, whom His Majesty, it appears, had left 'in a sweet sleep,' to Madame de Genlis and Voltaire, who was voted a monster by the King. Then followed a criticism on Shakespeare, startlingly original and refreshing. 'Was there ever,' cried the royal man, 'such stuff as great part of Shakespeare; only one must not say so. But what think you—what—— Is there not sad stuff—what—what?' Miss Burney ventured to hint that the stuff was mixed with certain excellencies, but was immediately interrupted. 'Oh,' said the King, 'I know it is not to be said, but it's true. Only it's Shakespeare, and nobody dare abuse him; but one should be stoned for saying so!'

Next morning Miss Burney had a conversation with the Queen, during which the royal lady gave her various opinions of several authors and their works. The authoress of 'Alphonsine,' she informed her new friend, had always sent her books to Her Majesty, even when she did not know there was such a lady as Madame de Genlis. She furthermore added that the 'Sorrows of Werter' was 'done by a bad man for revenge.' The Queen then went on to praise a book which she had picked up on an old book-stall. 'Oh, it is amazing what good books there are on stalls,' said her economical Majesty. 'I don't pick them up myself,' she explained, 'but I have a servant very clever; and, if they are not to be had at the booksellers', they are not for me any more than for another.' Her Majesty finished the discourse with a pinch of snuff and a snuffle.

"Mrs. Siddons, the actress,' as Miss Burney speaks of the famous tragedienne, was occasionally summoned to Windsor, to read before royalty. Not only their Gracious Majesties, but Fanny Burney (who had now become Her Gracious Majesty's dresser) patronized this wife of an ex-theatrical wig-maker.

'She is a woman of excellent character,' writes the aforementioned Frances, 'and therefore I am very glad she is thus patronized, since Mrs. Abingdon and so many fair, frail ones have been thus noticed by the great. She behaved with great propriety—very calm, modest, quiet, and unaffected. She has, however, a steadiness in her manner and deportment by no means engaging.'

The royal family went, in solemn state, to see her play Isabella in the 'Fatal Marriage,' in October, 1783. Their Majesties witnessed the performance in a box, having a rich canopy of crimson velvet and gold; that under which the Prince of Wales rested was adorned with blue velvet and silver, and the Princess's box was trimmed with blue satin and silver fringe. The dresses of the royal family were in keeping with such theatrical magnificence. His Gracious Majesty wore a suit of 'Quaker-coloured clothes, with gold buttons; the Queen, a white satin robe, with a head-dress which was ornamented by a great number of diamonds. The Princess Royal was dressed in a white and blue figured silk, and Princess Augusta in a rose-coloured and white silk, of the same pattern as her sister's, having both their head-dresses richly ornamented with diamonds; and His Royal Highness the Prince of Wales had a suit of dark blue Geneva velvet, richly trimmed with gold lace.' Mrs. Siddons on this occasion exerted her great genius to such a degree that she not only affected her audience, but also the actors who played with her. As for the King, he freely shed tears; her gracious, but more stolid Majesty, however, was less moved; she turned her back upon the stage, and declared the performance 'too disagreeable.'

Henceforth the King declared there was never any player in his time so excellent, 'not Garrick himself; I own it. What—what—what?' was the royal acknowledgment of her merit. The Queen proved her appreciation of Mrs. Siddons in another way, by appointing her preceptress in English reading to the Princesses, omitting, however, to grant a salary with the appointment; but in return for her services she was graciously permitted to hear Her Majesty's comments delivered in broken English, the actress standing in the royal presence the while, until she was ready to faint from fatigue.

Of one of her readings at Windsor Castle, Mrs. Delany gives a graphic description.

'Their Majesties,' writes the old lady, 'sat in the middle of the first row, with the Princesses on each hand, which filled it. The rest of the ladies were seated in the row behind them, and, as there was a space between that and the wall, the lords and gentlemen that were admitted stood there. Mrs. Siddons read standing, and had a desk with candles before her. She behaved with great propriety, and read two acts of "The Provoked Husband," which was abridged by leaving out Sir Francis and Lady Wronghead's parts. She also read Queen Catherine's last speech in "King Henry VIII." She was allowed three pauses, to go into the next room and refresh herself for half an hour each time. After she was dismissed, their Majesties detained the company for some time, to talk over what had passed, which was not the least agreeable part of the entertainment.'

Such are a few of the rare glimpses of the royal domestic life at this period which are afforded us.

. In the autumn of 1788, His Majesty's health became variable; his conversation grew more abrupt and rambling than before; a restless nervousness was noticeable in his manner; his moods became strangely changeable; his mind abstracted; and to those who watched him it was evident he was labouring under the first symptoms of an affliction which he in vain sought to overcome and conceal from those around him. This mental malady was preceded by a slight physical illness that gave some alarm to his family. 'He went out in the dew one morning just before his attack,' writes Lord Minto of His Majesty, 'and, instead of changing his shoes and stockings, came to town in them quite wet. After the levée, he returned to Kew, where the Queen wished him to take something cordial; but Georgy boy liked his own way best, and ate a pear and drank a glass of cold water. He was unwell all the evening, and went to bed at his usual hour. About one in the morning, he was seized with a cramp or some other violent thing in the stomach, which rendered him speechless, and, in a word, was *all but*. The Queen ran out in great alarm in her shift, or with very little clothes, among the pages, who, seeing her in that situation, were at first retiring out of respect, but the Queen stopped them, and sent them instantly for the apothecary at Richmond, who arrived in about forty minutes, during which time the King had continued in the fits and speechless. The apothecary tried to make him swallow something strong, but the King, who appeared not to have lost his senses, still liked a bit of his own way, and rejected by signs everything of that sort. They contrived, however, to cheat him, and got some cordial down in the shape of medicine, and the fit went off. He has been ill ever since, although he has been out and at Court.'

When he had recovered from this, signs of a more distressing malady quickly made their appearance.

On one occasion when Mrs. Siddons had been delighting the royal circle with a recitation, the King suddenly handed her a sheet of paper, which merely contained his signature; at another time, when he attended the weekly levée at St. James's, his disordered dress and vacant manner gave rise to many strange surmises. A little later on, a review at which he was to have been present was deferred, and the royal drawing-rooms were suspended. He complained of want of sleep and rest, and of physical weakness. Meanwhile, he was painfully conscious of his danger. One day he had been out riding, and had remained for hours unusually silent; on returning to Windsor he hastened through the passages, much agitated, but without looking to right or left, until he reached his own apartments, where, flinging himself down, he burst into tears, and cried out, in a pitiful voice, 'I am going to be mad, and I wish to God that I may die.' But the unhappy climax of this dread malady which had taken possession of the King had not yet arrived, and though vague rumours of his illness were rife in town, yet within the precincts of Windsor all was kept as secret as possible.

Miss Burney has left us a vivid picture of this distressing period. His strength seemed diminishing hourly; his countenance was altered strangely; his voice became so hoarse that he could scarcely be heard. 'You see me all at once an old man,' he said to Lady Effingham. 'God send him better,' writes kindly Fanny Burney. The gloom of an impending sorrow hung threateningly over royal Windsor in these early November days, and impressed itself painfully on all the household. The Queen, overpowered with secret terror, strove to maintain her calmness, but, when left alone, sought relief in violent bursts of tears; doctors passed noiselessly to and fro, looking sad and hopeless. The King was now kept in the greatest seclusion; the Prince of Wales drove up from Brighton, where he had been spending his days in scandalous dissipation; all music was forbidden, and the musicians ordered away; gentlemen of the household stood in silent groups in the chambers, thoughtful and gloomy, as if awaiting the announcement of death; and throughout the household an ominous atmosphere of depression reigned unbroken.

'Nobody stirred,' writes Miss Burney. 'Not a voice was heard, not a step, not a motion. I could do nothing but watch, without knowing for what. There seemed a strangeness in the house most extraordinary.'

At last the long-dreaded moment came. The royal family were dining in seclusion, when suddenly the King broke out in a frenzy, flew at the Prince of Wales, and, seizing him by the throat, thrust him against the wall. From that hour it was no longer a secret that the King was mad.

CHAPTER VII.

Old Wits in the New Reign—My Lord Chesterfield in his Last Days—Rehearsing his Funeral—His Courtesy Strong in Death—Remarkable Will—At Strawberry Hill—Walpole's Amiable and Polished Manner—Reads his Tragedy to a Bevy of Fine Ladies—His Contempt for Men of Letters—Chatterton writes to Him—Fight for Bread, and Death by Poison—At the First Academy Dinner—Kitty Clive at Strawberry Hill—The Misses Berry—Walpole's Last Days.

MANY of the distinguished men and women, whose wit and talent had served to render the social life during the last reign one of unusual brilliancy, had passed away before the third of the Georges ascended the throne. Little Mr. Pope was quietly sleeping in the aisle of Twickenham Church; 'Hervey the handsome,' cynic, courtier, and satirist, whom the poet detested and virulently abused, had gone where no bitter words could reach him; Sir Godfrey Kneller had laid down his brush for ever; poor Swift had ended his melancholy days in madness; Bolingbroke, politician and wit, was missing from many social boards; so also was Gay; and the beautiful Countess of Coventry, who had hastened her demise by smearing her face with paint, had closed her eyes on the vanities of this world ere the new King was proclaimed. But my Lord Chesterfield, Horace Walpole, and George Selwyn, three men of excellent wit, still happily survived; so also, but for a brief time, did my Lady Mary Wortley Montagu; and Lady Hervey, otherwise Molly

Lapell, the once charming maid of honour, now styled by Lord Carlisle 'the most impertinent old brimstone,' enlivened the not too melancholy days of her widowhood by giving charming little French dinners to the choicest spirits of the town.

My Lord Chesterfield, once loved for his wit and feared for his satire, now lived much retired; new men bore old names once familiar on his lips; unknown faces met his gaze in club and drawing-room, and manners had somewhat changed their form since his younger days. The 'lord amongst wits' lived chiefly in the magnificent mansion he had erected and named Chesterfield House, spending the greater part of his days in the seclusion of his library, which he boasted was the finest room in London. Rooms are more or less characteristic of those who dwell in them, and Lord Chesterfield's library was eminently a refined and stately apartment. 'The walls were covered half-way up with rich and classical stores of literature; above the cases were, in close series, the portraits of eminent authors, French and English, with most of whom he had conversed; over these, and immediately under the massive cornice, extended all round in foot-long capitals the Horatian lines:

> 'Nunc veterum libris, nunc somno et inertibus horis
> Ducere sollicitæ jucunda oblivia vitæ.'—*Sat.* ii. 6.

On the mantelpieces and cabinets stood busts of old orators, interspersed with voluptuous vases and bronzes, antique or Italian, and airy statuettes in marble or alabaster, of nude or semi-nude opera nymphs.

My Lord was now, as he said to his friend Dayrolles, in his grand climacteric, which he declared he would not live to complete.

'Fontenelle's last words at a hundred and three,' he wrote, 'were, "*Je souffre d'être;*" deaf and infirm as I am, I can with truth say the same thing at sixty-three. In my mind, it is only the strength of our passions and the weakness of our reason that make us so fond of life; but, when the former subside and give way to the latter, we grow weary of being, and willing to withdraw.'

Dayrolles, to whom these words were addressed, was one of those useful friends who always hang on to great men. He had spent many years of his life in the service of this illustrious Earl, who, when Lord-Lieutenant of Ireland, 'made him Black Rod, and gave the ingenious reason that he had a black face,' as Horace Walpole pleasantly writes.

Though Lord Chesterfield's manner was what has been described as 'exquisitely elegant' and polished to the highest degree, yet it failed oftentimes to give those he intended to impress most a belief in his sincerity. 'Garrick was pure gold, but beat out to thin leaf,' said Boswell, epigrammatically, 'but Chesterfield was tinsel,' with which opinion Dr. Johnson agreed, for the burly philosopher had ceased to hold him in esteem since the occurrence of their quarrel, the story of which forms one of the most interesting pages in the history of literature.

Johnson, before commencing his dictionary, dedicated the 'plan' of it to my Lord Chesterfield, who was then regarded as a distinguished patron of letters; the noble Earl highly approved of this, and made some useful suggestions which Johnson adopted. It was then the fashion for dedications to be paid for, and my Lord sent Johnson £10, after which he paid no further attention to the struggling man of letters. He had neglected Garrick, he ignored Sheridan, and behaved to Johnson 'in such a manner,' Boswell says, 'as to excite his contempt and indignation.' But there was probably a stronger reason to rouse these feelings in the great lexicographer than mere neglect. A story which gained general belief amongst Johnson's friends, and which was authenticated by Lord Lyttelton and Sir John Hawkins, stated that Johnson, on the occasion of a visit to the polite

Earl, was kept waiting in the antechamber a considerable time, the reason being assigned that his Lordship had company with him. At last the door opened, and out came old Colley Cibber, when Johnson, seeing for whom he had been excluded from his patron's presence, went away in a violent passion, vowing he would return no more.

'Cibber,' said Lord Lyttelton, 'who had been introduced familiarly by the back-stairs' (alas for the days of literary patronage!) 'had probably not been there more than ten minutes.'

Johnson denied the truth of this story, and declared stoutly 'his Lordship's continued neglect was the reason why he resolved to have no connection with him.' However, a reference in his letter to his 'waiting in his (Lord Chesterfield's) outer rooms,' would seem to imply there was some foundation for the anecdote. When the dictionary drew near its conclusion, the Earl, who flattered himself Johnson would dedicate his great work to him, wrote some letters to the *World*, in which, amongst other fine compliments, he declared the public in general, and the republic of letters in particular, were greatly obliged to Mr. Johnson for having undertaken and executed so great and desirable a work. 'And I hereby declare,' he said, with that touching humility which greatness can afford, 'that I make a total surrender of all my rights and privileges in the English language as a free-born British subject, to the said Mr. Johnson, during the term of his dictatorship.'

This praise failed to have the effect desired by the noble Earl of conciliating the said Mr. Johnson.

'When my dictionary was coming out,' said he, speaking of Lord Chesterfield, 'he fell a-scribbling in the *World* about it. Upon which I wrote him a letter.' This, for vigour, style, and expression of independence, is perhaps unequalled by any epistle in our language.

Some rumour of this letter and its contents got **abroad,**

and all men of independent spirit approved of Johnson's conduct. But Dodsley, the publisher, was not among these; he had a share in the dictionary, and believed the noble Earl's patronage might be of consequence. He told his friend, Dr. Adams, the Earl had shown him the letter.

'I should have imagined,' replied Dr. Adams, 'that Lord Chesterfield would have concealed it.'

'Pooh!' said the bookseller, with extreme contempt, 'do you think a letter from Johnson could hurt Lord Chesterfield? Not at all, sir. It lay upon his table, where anybody might see it. He read it to me; said, "This man has great powers," pointed out the severest passages, and observed how well they were expressed.'

In this manner, the noble Lord cleverly concealed the bitterness he felt, and to which he afterwards gave vent in portraying Johnson in the character of the 'respectable Hottentot.'

Dr. Adams expostulated with Johnson on his severity; his Lordship, he said, 'would have turned off the best servant he ever had, if he had known that he denied him to a man who would have been always more than welcome.'

'Sir,' said Johnson, 'that is not Lord Chesterfield; he is the proudest man this day existing.'

'No,' said Dr. Adams; 'there is one person at least as proud. I think, by your own account, you are the prouder man of the two.'

'But mine,' replied Johnson, 'was *defensive* pride.'

Though my Lord failed to gain the good graces of one whom he slighted as a literary hack, his politeness to the *beau monde* continued to the last. According to Walpole, the Earl 'took no less pains to be the phœnix of fine gentlemen than Tully did to qualify himself as an orator. Both succeeded,' says Horace, with a quiet sneer. 'Tully immortalized his name; Chesterfield's reign lasted a little longer than that of a fashionable beauty.'

A short time before the worthy Lord's days closed, Monsieur Suard expressed a desire to see *l'homme le plus aimable, le plus poli, et le plus spirituel des trois royaumes.* Alas! he found but a shattered old man. 'It is very sad to be deaf when one would so much enjoy listening,' said my Lord, courteous to the last. His visitor shortened his stay, fearful of fatiguing his most polite host. 'I do not detain you,' said the Earl cheerfully, 'for I must go and rehearse my funeral.' In this manner he referred to his daily drives. A short time before his death, being asked how a contemporary of his did, he said, 'To tell you the truth, we have both been dead this twelvemonth, but we do not own it.' Another proof that his old sense of wit had not departed from him at the close of his life may be mentioned. His sister, Lady Gertrude Hotham, who had become a strict Methodist, under the guidance of her friend, Lady Huntingdon, becoming anxious concerning the safety of his soul, conceived a scheme of luring him down to one of her seminaries in Wales. When she visited him, she, together with Lady Huntingdon, said nothing of their pious motives, but enlarged on the benefit he would derive from the air, and the general delight which the scenery would afford him, the views were so charming, the mountains so sublime. 'No, ladies,' said my Lord, with a knowing smile. 'I do not love such tremendous prospects. When the faith of your ladyships has removed the mountains, I will go to Wales with all my heart.' Later on his wife, Melusina—the daughter of George I. and the infamous old Duchess of Kendal—who had grown religious, sent for the Rev. Rowland Hill, but my Lord refused to see the good man, much to my Lady's distress, but she afterwards consoled herself by appointing the Rev. Rowland, whose eloquence she vastly admired, as her chaplain, when he preached to pious assemblies at Chesterfield House. When, in March, 1773, the Earl lay in the agonies of death, his old friend Dayrolles entered the room softly; but my Lord heard him, and, turning to his valet, gasped out the words, 'Give Dayrolles a chair.' The ruling trait of courtesy was strong in death.

My Lord made a remarkable will, in which he declared that, 'satiated with the pompous follies of this life, of which I have had an uncommon share, I would have no posthumous ones displayed at my funeral, and therefore desire to be buried in the next burying-place to the place where I shall die, and limit the whole expense of my funeral to £100.'

He bequeathed his property to his godson, Philip Stanhope, on whom he thought it necessary to place certain restraints.

'In case my said godson, Philip Stanhope,' he said, 'shall at any time hereinafter keep, or be concerned in keeping of, any race-horses or packs of hounds, or reside one night at Newmarket, that infamous seminary of iniquity and ill-manners, during the course of the races there, or shall resort to the said races, or shall lose in any one day, at any one game or bet whatsoever, the sum of £500, then, in any the cases aforesaid, it is my express will that he, my said godson, shall forfeit and pay, out of my estate, the sum of £5,000 to and for the use of the Dean and Chapter of Westminster.'

The Earl died satisfied with the belief that he could, as he said, 'trust to the want of lenity' of the Dean and Chapter of Westminster. But there was yet a better clause in his will. To his servants he left two years' wages. 'I consider them,' said my Lord, 'as unfortunate friends; my equals by nature, and my inferiors only in the difference of our fortunes. This was, perhaps, one of the most gracious sentences to which the noble courtier ever gave expression.

A friend and contemporary of Chesterfield's, Horace Walpole, survived him almost twenty years. This amiable cynic, to whose facile pen we owe such delightful glimpses of social life in the eighteenth century, now lived in elegant ease at Strawberry Hill, in the Gothic Castle, which had taken him twenty-three years to complete. He speaks of it as the prettiest bauble possible, 'set in enamelled meadows in filigree hedges.' To this court by the placid Thames, ruled over by one whose word was omnipotent in all things connected with art and literature, came a throng of noble lords and ladies fine, princes, poets, and players, authors and artists, philosophers, adventurers, literary hacks, wits, and even royalty itself. For each of these Horace had an appropriate word, a graceful bow, a pleasant smile, and delighted all of them with his gentle, affable manners.

'Not the smallest hauteur or consciousness of rank appeared in his familiar conferences,' says the editor of *Walpoliana*, 'and he was ever eager to dissipate any constraint that might occur, as imposing a constraint upon himself, and knowing that any such chain enfeebles and almost annihilates the mental powers. Endued with exquisite sensibility, his wit never gave the smallest wound, even to the grossest ignorance of the world, or the most morbid hypochondriac bashfulness.'

The owner of Strawberry Hill—which he called an inn, the sign of the Gothic Castle—was never so happy as when showing a batch of visitors through his wonderful rooms, which were stored with objects of art gathered from every quarter of the globe; his tall, lank figure bowing as he gave utterance to a finely-polished phrase, or received some pretty compliment on the justness of his taste; his dark, penetrating eyes lighting up the unhealthy pallor of his face. He was seldom without visitors eager to see his curiosities.

'I have given my assembly to show my Gallery, and it was glorious,' he writes, 'but, happening to pitch upon the feast of tabernacles, none of my Jews could come, though Mrs. Clive proposed to them to change their religion; so I am forced to exhibit once more. For the morning spectators, the crowd augments, instead of diminishing. It is really true that Lady Hertford called here t'other morning, and I was reduced to bring her by the back gate into the kitchen; the house was so full of company that came to see the Gallery, that I had nowhere else to carry her.'

With what pleasant pride he would point to Cavalini's wondrous shrine in mosaic, that had stood above the sepulchre of four holy martyrs in the church of St. Mary Maggiore in Rome; to Torregiano's famous bust of Henry VIII.; to the armour of Francis I., or to the famous collection of portraits in his gallery; and with what delight he would read some specially favoured visitors a page from his manuscripts, or a poem set up by his own hands, fresh from his press. Here one day he read his 'tragedy of the highest order,' to quote the author of 'Don Juan,' 'The Mysterious Mother,' to a trio of fair and favourite ladies, assembled for the purpose—to wit, Lady Aylesbury, Lady Lyttelton, and Miss Rich; what terms of graceful appreciation they must have uttered, what courtly compliments they must have paid him! all of which he accepted as his due, for he entertained no poor opinion of his work.

'I am not yet intoxicated enough with it,' he writes of the tragedy, 'to think it would do for the stage, though I wish to see it acted; but, as Mrs. Pritchard leaves the stage next month, I know nobody could play the Countess; nor am I disposed to expose myself to the impertinences of that jackanapes Garrick, who lets nothing appear but his own wretched stuff, or that of creatures still duller, who suffer him to alter their pieces as he pleases.'

Though 'the father of the first romance and of the last tragedy in our language,' as Lord Byron styles him, condescended to become an author by way of passing his elegant leisure, or diverting his friends, he regarded professional men of letters with a contempt which he did not care to disguise. 'I shun authors,' he wrote, 'and would never have been one myself, if it obliged me to keep such bad company. They are always in earnest, and think their profession serious, and dwell upon trifles, and reverence learning. I laugh at these things, and divert myself.'

Through his long life he never extended encouragement or help to one of the struggling herd, and his neglect of Chatterton must ever stand as a reproach to his memory.

In 1769, the marvellous boy wrote to the polite and learned Mr. Walpole, offering to furnish him with some account of eminent painters who had lived in Bristol, and enclosing some specimens of old poems, which he avowed he had discovered in an ancient chest in St. Mary Redcliffe Church, of which his uncle was sexton. This edifice was rebuilt in the reign of Edward IV. by one Thomas Canynge, merchant, who, with his friend, Thomas Rowley, a priest, Chatterton stated, had written the poems in question. The ingenious story was solely the fabrication of a highly imaginative boy, then in his seventeenth year, and the verses were the most extraordinary forgeries in the chronicles of literature. Chatterton also begged Walpole to help him to free himself from the drudgery of his employment as apprentice to a scrivener, a labour abhorrent to his temperament, and from which he longed to escape.

At first Horace believed the quaint poems, writ on strips of vellum, were the genuine productions of a past age, until his friends, Gray and Mason, poets both, laughed at his credulity, when, indignant at the deception sought to be practised upon him, he sent a cold, chiding letter to the boy-poet. Chatterton wrote demanding the poems, which Walpole had forgotten to enclose; they were then returned, but without a line. In a little while the young poet forced his way into the great wilderness of London, full of high hopes and great ambitions, anxious, with the ready impulse of youth, to commence that battle for literary fame which was so soon to end in despair and death.

'I get four guineas a month by one magazine,' he wrote, in the first flush of his hopes, to his poor mother in Bristol; 'shall engage to write a history of England and other pieces, which will more than double that sum. Occasional essays for the daily papers would more than support me. What a glorious prospect. . . . I am quite familiar at the Chapter Coffee-house, and know all the geniuses there. . . . Bristol's mercenary walls were never destined to hold me— there I was out of my element; now in it. London! Good God! how superior is London to that despicable place, Bristol!'

Poor boy, his fight for daily bread was vigorous, though brief. He got two shillings for a newspaper article, wrote sixteen songs for ten and sixpence, sent articles to magazines, and, whilst starving, wrote a burlesque burletta—think of the irony of such a fate. For four months he struggled before giving up all hope, living on a halfpenny roll or a penny tart a day, with perhaps an occasional sheep's tongue. Youth is strong, and hunger slow to kill, but at last the end came; he had remained for three days without food; on the morning of the fourth day he was discovered dead in a wretched garret of a house in a little street out of Holborn, with the cup which held the arsenic and water he had drunk clutched in his hand. He did not live to complete his eighteenth year.

The first intimation Walpole received of his death was whilst he was present at the first Academy dinner, surrounded by Sir Joshua Reynolds, Goldsmith, Johnson, Burke, and other luminaries. Goldsmith commenced to speak of the Rowley poems, and presently Walpole asked about Chatterton, when honest Oliver told him regretfully the lad had destroyed himself. He was startled, and perhaps conscience-stricken. 'The persons of honour and veracity who were present,' he wrote afterwards, 'will attest with what surprise and concern I thus first heard of his death.'

But no doubt he soon forgot this painful occurrence in an existence constantly busy with the small things of life and brightened by the society of so many remarkable friends; for not only were his visitors pleasant and distinguished, but so were his immediate neighbours. The Countess of Suffolk, the famous mistress of George II., spent her last days, which were included in the first decade of the new reign, in the seclusion of Marble Hill, which was later on occupied by Mrs. Fitzherbert, wife of George IV.; her eccentric Grace of Queensberry, the friend of Swift and patroness of Gay, was merely divided from him by the gentle waters of the Thames; that charming actress and fascinating woman, Mrs. Abingdon, dwelt at Twickenham, and the lively Kitty Clive, together with her brother, lived in a house on Walpole's property, which he was pleased to facetiously call Cliveden.

'I have quitted the stage, and Clive is preparing to leave it,' he wrote to George Montagu. 'We shall neither of us ever be grave; dowagers roost all round us, and you could never want cards or mirth.'

Mrs. Clive, indeed, wrote to her friend Colman that 'vexation and fretting in the theatre are the foundation of all Billou's complaints.' She declared she spoke 'by expeariance,' and that she was fretted by managers 'till my gaul overflow'd like the river Nile;' she therefore sought timely repose in Twickenham. Walpole thoroughly appreciated the society of Mistress Clive, who had, according to Goldsmith, more true humour than any actor or actress on the English stage.

'All the morning I play with my workmen or animals,' he writes, 'go regularly every morning to the meadows with Mrs. Clive, or sit with my Lady Suffolk, and at night I scribble.'

The actress's name often occurs in his letters, and ever in a pleasant and gracious manner. 'Strawberry is in perfection,' he writes to his friend, George Montagu; 'the verdure has all the bloom of spring, the orange-trees are loaded with blossoms, the Gallery all sun and gold, Mrs. Clive all sun and vermilion.'

In the year 1785, the merry-hearted actress quitted this world's stage for ever.

'My poor old friend is a great loss,' Walpole wrote. He had played cards with her but a few nights before; then she caught cold. 'On the Wednesday morning she rose to have her bed made, and whilst sitting on it, with her maid by her, sunk down at once, and died without a pang or a groan.'

Some time after her death, Cliveden had new tenants in the persons of Mr. Berry and his two daughters, gentle and amiable women, who in good time became his most valued friends. Mary's countenance he describes as pale, with dark eyes, and an interesting expression; she was 'an angel inside and out.' Agnes, the younger, was 'hardly to be called handsome, but almost,' and they dressed, he adds, 'within the bounds of fashion, but without the excrescences and balconies with which modern hoydens overwhelm and barricade their persons.' The elder understood Latin and spoke French fluently; the younger was an artist. It was not, however, on account of their accomplishments, so much as their quiet and graceful manners, that Horace Walpole became interested in them; there was, moreover, a story connected with their family that had a flavour of romance, which was in itself a rare charm to one whom knowledge of the world had made a cynic.

The grandfather of these ladies had an estate of £5,000 a year, but disinherited his son because he had married a penniless woman. She died after giving birth to two daughters, and the grandfather, desiring an heir male, pressed the widower to marry again. This he refused to do; he remained true to the memory of his first wife, and devoted his days to the education of his daughters. The property was therefore made over to the second son, who allowed his brother £800 a year, a sum that enabled him to take the two girls to the Continent, where they received an education which rendered them accomplished women.

To each of them Horace Walpole successively offered his hand, which neither of them accepted, though there was then a probability, which afterwards became a certainty, that such a marriage would raise his wife to the peerage; but their refusal did not prevent them from sharing the solitude of his later years, and he was seldom more happy than when in the society of his 'two Straw Berries,' as he named them.

For many years previous to his death, he suffered a martyrdom from gout and the ills of old age; yet, though his hands and feet were crippled, his spirits were always gay, and his wit retained all its old brilliancy. When able to hold a pen in his hand, he continued to correspond with his friends, a pastime that afforded him almost as much delight as it did those he favoured with his celebrated letters. He rose late, passed the forenoon in his gardens, or in reading; then dined sparingly off chicken, pheasant, or any light food, seldom drinking wine; his favourite beverage being ice-water, which stood in a decanter placed in a pail of ice under the table. After dinner he was assisted upstairs to the library by his valet; being now unable to enter a room 'in that style of affected delicacy' of which Miss Hawkins speaks, '*chapeau bras* between his hands, as if he wished to compress it—or under his arm—knees bent and feet on the tiptoe, as if afraid of a wet floor.'

In the library, enriched with rare and handsomely bound volumes, crowded with objects of art, and fragrant with caraway or orange-trees in bloom, coffee was served; and here Horace, lying on a couch, conversed with his charming neighbours, detailing, in his vivacious manner, some recent town gossip, or relating to them remarkable anecdotes of men and women of note whom he had known in former reigns. After dinner he touched no more food for the day; but 'the snuff-box of *tabac d'étrennes* from Fribourg's was not forgotten, and was replenished from a canister lodged in an ancient marble urn of great thickness, which stood in the window-seat, and served to secure its moisture and rich flavour.' He wore his age with dignity and cheerfulness; nay, he even jested at his weight of years.

'Since all my fingers are useless, and that I have only six hairs left, I am not very much grieved at not being able to comb my head,' he writes; and presently, when, by the death of his nephew, he became a peer of the realm, he supposed he would be styled Lord Methusalem. To be within convenient reach of his doctors, he left Strawberry Hill—the work of so many years, the realization of so many hopes, the subject of so much gossip, the scene where so many illustrious visitors had gathered—never to see it again. He moved to Berkeley Square, from where he wrote to the Countess of Ossory, a couple of months before his death:

'I scarce go out of my own house, and then only to two or three very private places, where I see nobody that really knows anything, and what I learn comes from newspapers that collect intelligence from coffee-houses; consequently what I neither believe nor report. At home I see only a few charitable elders, except about four-score nephews and nieces of various ages, who are each brought to me about once a year, to stare at me as the Methusalem of the family, and they can only speak of their own contemporaries, which interest me no more than if they talked of their dolls, or bats and balls.'

During the last weeks of his life, the wit which had enlivened two generations dwindled into darkness. He died on March 2, 1797, in the eightieth year of his age.

CHAPTER VIII.

George Selwyn, morbid and tender-hearted—Dr. Dodd—The Marchese Fagniani—Topham Beauclerk and Dr. Johnson—A Morning's Adventure—Lady Diana and her Spouse—Nancy Parsons and the Duke of Grafton—Further Adventures of Nancy—Lord Maynard—Mad Tom Hervey and his Letters—Elopement of Lady Susan Strangways with an Actor—Marriage of Lady Henrietta Wentworth and her Footman.

THOUGH Walpole hated many and liked few, he declared he 'really loved' George Selwyn, 'not only for his infinite wit, but for a thousand good qualities;' and this appreciation was shared by all who knew Selwyn. Witty, eccentric, at once a lover of horrors and of little children, a man about town, an exquisite beau, his various-sided character presented an anomaly which puzzled many. He was a courtier, a frequenter of all fashionable assemblies, and a member of many clubs. His friends, indeed, were legion, and his name was ever on their lips and in their letters; repeating a choice specimen of his wit or repartee, recounting some eccentric escapade, or dwelling on those traits of good fellowship which rendered him loved by all. His humour was not of that flagrant description destined to set a table in a roar, but rather vented itself in neat, pointed phrases, which were uttered with a quaintness and simplicity of facial expression that added considerably to their effect; a few examples selected from an abundant collection preserved by Walpole will suffice to show their general style.

One day when he, who 'had a passion for seeing coffins, corpses, and executions,' was asked why he had not been present to witness the death of Charles Fox, a malefactor who ended his evil days on the gallows, he calmly replied that he made a point of never going to rehearsals. He made another joke against his personal friend Fox when a public subscription was spoken of, for the purpose of paying his debts; some one speaking to Selwyn on the subject wondered 'how Fox would take it.' 'Take it!' replied George promptly, 'why, *quarterly*, of course.' The statesman, indeed, was often the subject of that ready wit, always sparkling, though never severe, which he did not the less appreciate for its being personal. Once at Brooks' Club, Fox was speaking of the successful peace he had made with France, and boasted that he had induced that country to give up the gum trade to England. 'That, Charles, I am not at all surprised at,' replied Selwyn; 'for, having drawn your teeth, they would be damned fools to trouble about your *gums*.'

One more saying of his regarding Sir Joshua Reynolds is worth repeating. When it was reported that the great painter was to stand for Plympton at the next election, the fine gentlemen laughed and made merry at the idea of an artist presuming to offer himself as a representative for Parliamentary honours. 'He is not to be laughed at, however,' said George, in his most solemn tone; 'he may very well succeed in being elected, for Sir Joshua is the ablest man I know on a canvas!'

White's Club was the chief rendezvous of Selwyn and his jovial friends, Charles Fox, Gilly Williams, Charles Townshend, Dick Edgecombe, Topham Beauclerk, and Rigby, 'an excellent *bon vivant*, having all the gibes and gambols and flashes of merriment which set the table in a roar.' Here in the last reign my Lord Chesterfield had gambled, Bubb Dodington had babbled of his intimacy with Frederick, Prince of Wales—who borrowed large sums from his dupe and then laughed at him—and old Colley Cibber, poet-laureate and player, 'feasted most sumptuously with Mr. Victor and his wife, and gave a trifle for his dinner;' and here in the present reign, wits, politicians, and beaux made ludicrous bets, drank deep, and half ruined themselves over dice and cards.

It was at White's that a waiter came up to Selwyn one day in a hurried manner, and whispered to him confidentially, 'Mr. Walpole's compliments, and he has got a housebreaker for you;' at which news the wit started up and hastened with all speed to his friend, who had such a rare treat in store for him. Selwyn's love of criminals was indeed well known, and he seldom lost an opportunity of visiting them in prison, or being present at their executions. His morbid love for these exhibitions carried him on one occasion so far as Paris, where he went to behold Damiens, who had attempted the assassination of Louis XV., torn with red-hot pincers, and finally rent in quarters by four horses. On the day of the execution, Selwyn, plainly dressed to avoid notice, mingled with the crowd, but managed to get close to the scaffold, when the executioner, noticing and recognising him, cried out, ' Make way for monsieur ; he is an English amateur.' The deaths of criminals in merry England were invariably witnessed by enormous numbers, for whom balconies and stands were erected; and these crowds were not only composed of the middle and lower classes, who regarded such sights as interesting tragedies provided by Providence for their better amusement, but by large contingents of fine gentlemen and ladies of high degree.

Such exhibitions were, however, occasionally rendered revolting by the general air of festivity with which they were accompanied. Sometimes the criminals on their way to execution exchanged jests and witticisms with the crowd, or decked themselves with ribbons and flowers, to indicate that they met their fate with a brave front. When Elizabeth Herring, in 1773, was sentenced to be strangled and burned for the murder of her husband, she was conveyed to Tyburn in a hurdle drawn by four horses gaily decked with streamers and ornamented with the boughs of trees and garlands of evergreens. Selwyn considered life worth living for the purpose of witnessing such tragedies, and, whenever one of them took place during his unavoidable absence from town, his friends were certain to write him a full account of the proceedings.

'Lord Harrington's porter,' who, by the way, rejoiced in the name of Whisket, 'was condemned yesterday,' writes Gilly Williams to the wit. 'Cadogan and I have already bespoken places at the Brazier's, and I hope Parson Digby will come time enough to be of the party. I presume we shall have your honour's company, if your stomach is not too squeamish for a single swing.' Subsequently the same writer adds, 'I give a breakfast on Wednesday next, the morning the porter makes his exit. If Parson Digby is in town, I shall send him a card; he is our Ordinary on all these great occasions.'

This criminal, whose exit was looked forward to with such evident relish, had robbed his master of £3,000, and his trial caused a considerable sensation in town. George Selwyn was in Paris at the time, but received a description of the tragedy from the Hon. Henry St. John, a beau whom his friends, in reference to his name, irreligiously called 'the Baptist.'

'I should not,' said this individual, 'have intruded on the gay moments you now pass your time in, had not my brother intimated to me your obliging request of hearing from me; and what served to encourage my writing was the curiosity which you expressed to hear of Whisket's execution, which my brother and I went to see, at the risk of breaking our necks by climbing up an old rotten scaffolding, which I feared would tumble before the cart drove off with the six malefactors. However, we escaped, and had a full view of Mr. Whisket, who went to the gallows with a white cockade in his hat, as an emblem of his innocence, and died with the same hardness as appeared through his whole trial. I hope you have had good sport at the *Place de Grève*' (the scene of criminal executions in Paris at that time) ' to make up for losing the sight of the execution of so notorious a villain as Lord Harrington's porter.'

Gilly Williams, who, with his friends, enjoyed himself on the occasion, wrote Selwyn a few minor particulars. 'The dog died game,' he says; 'went in the cart in a blue and gold frock, and, as an emblem of innocence, had a white cockade in his hat. He ate several oranges in his passage, inquired if his hearse was ready, and then, as old Rowe used to say, was launched into eternity.'

Another interesting execution which George Selwyn was prevented by absence from attending was that of Dr. Dodd, a graphic account of which, however, was duly forwarded him. Dr. Dodd was a celebrated and fashionable preacher, who married a woman who may be said to have had aristocratic connections; one of these, Lord Sandwich, was her professed lover; this little fact, however, was overlooked by the learned divine, who was not over-strict in his morals or prejudices, and who hoped by this alliance to gain my Lord's interest, and so forward his own ambitious views. The doctor had luxurious tastes, and was a man of pleasure and gallantry, whose eloquence in the pulpit was only equalled by his social and eminently fascinating qualities in society; moreover, he was the founder of a charity for discharging prisoners confined for debts, and the promoter of many others equally merciful. His numerous good traits rendered him an especial favourite with the fair sex, and his piety was accounted sufficiently exalted to gain him an appointment as one of the chaplains whose discourses were destined to edify royal ears. But his income, though aided by the contributions of pious matrons and others, whom his ministrations much comforted, was by no means sufficient to meet his expenses, which were considerable, or to satisfy his ambitions, which were great. He was, however, a man possessing so much ingenuity, that it ultimately led him not only into temptation, but to the gallows.

An instance of his peculiar talent occurred when there was a vacancy in the rectory of St. George's, Hanover Square; the nomination lay in the power of Lady Apsley, wife to the Lord Chancellor, to whom Dr. Dodd wrote anonymously, offering her the sum of £3,000 if he were appointed rector. This proposal, if made during the previous two reigns, would have been regarded as a fair piece of business, and the divine would have gained the post if no other reverend gentleman outbid him, but now it was quite different; matters ecclesiastical were dealt with in another way. Therefore, my Lady handed the letter to her lord, who in turn showed it to his King, whereon His Majesty, in great wrath, struck the name of this light of the Church, to whom the epistle was traced, off the list of his royal chaplains.

He survived the royal displeasure—unfortunately; and, indeed, so little heeded the warning which this indiscretion should have given him, that in an evil hour, whilst beset with debt and difficulties, he forged a draught for £4,200 on young Lord Chesterfield, whose tutor he had been; this was quickly found out, when he was arrested and brought to justice. The discovery may have been hastened by the fact that he had on a former occasion been mixed up with a little money matter by which he had striven to benefit himself; this was when my Lord Chesterfield gave him a bond of £1,000 for a lady whose society he no longer desired; the doctor obligingly cashed the bill, gave the fair one £100, and kept £900 for his trouble.

At his trial for forgery he fainted, confessed his guilt, expressed his love of life and his hope for pardon, and betrayed agonies of grief and fear. The Bishop of Bristol, who, it may be noted, was by no means so famous for his eloquence as the guilty doctor, declared, with episcopal mercy, he was sorry the wretched man should be hanged 'for the least crime he ever committed.'

The doctor's fair devotees were more humane; they set forth his charities, his learning, his courtesy, and his eloquence, which they had never been able to withstand; the Methodists, with whom he had been connected, also took up his cause with zeal; prayed for his safe deliverance, and, when their prayers had no avail with heaven, besought the throne to spare his life. However, on this occasion, the throne proved deaf to their address, and sentence of death was passed on Dr. Dodd. But the Methodists did not yet despair; again they begged the royal mercy in a petition signed by twenty-three thousand persons; the King remained unmoved, and justice took its unflinching way. Anthony Morris Storer forwarded the minute details of the execution to George Selwyn, and his letter gives an apt illustration of the period.

'I should be very inclinable to obey your commands which Lord March delivered me,' says this worthy correspondent, 'respecting the fate of the unfortunate divine, but though an eye-witness of his execution, as I never was at one before, I hardly know what to say respecting his behaviour. Upon the whole, the piece was not very full of events. The doctor, to all appearance, was rendered perfectly stupid from despair. His hat was flapped all round, and pulled over his eyes, which were never directed to any object around, nor even raised, except now and then lifted up in the course of his prayers. He came in a coach, and a very heavy shower of rain fell just upon his entering the cart, and another just at his putting on his night-cap.

'He was a very considerable time in praying, which some people standing about seemed rather tired with; they rather wished for some more interesting part of the tragedy. The wind, which was high, blew off his hat, which rather embarrassed him, and discovered to us his countenance, which we could scarcely see before. His hat, however, was soon restored to him, and he went on with his prayers. There were two clergymen attending him, one of whom seemed very much affected. The other, I suppose, was the Ordinary of Newgate, as he was perfectly indifferent and unfeeling in everything that he said and did. The executioner took both the hat and wig off at the same time. Why he put on his wig again, I do not know, but he did, and the doctor took off his wig a second time, and then tied on a night-cap, which did not fit him; but whether he stretched that, or took another, I could not perceive. He then put on his night-cap himself, and upon his taking it he certainly had a smile on his countenance, and very soon afterwards there was an end of all his hopes and fears on this side the grave. He never moved from the first place he took in the cart; seemed absorbed in despair, and utterly dejected, without any other signs of animation but in praying. A vast number of people were collected, as you may imagine.'

The love and tenderness which Selwyn betrayed for the children of his friends was a singular contrast to his delight in things morbid. His affection was especially shown to two children, one of whom was Anne, daughter of the Countess of Coventry, the once beautiful Maria Gunning. Little Lady Anne, whom Selwyn's friends in their correspondence refer to as 'your child,' was left motherless at the age of four, from which time Selwyn treated her with the greatest affection and care. Her spirit was 'much beyond her late mamma's,' as Gilly Williams writes to his friend.

Selwyn's second protégée was Maria Fagniani, known as Mie Mie. This latter was the daughter of an Italian nobleman, the Marchese Fagniani, and his wife, a handsome, artful woman, fond of intrigue and money; tastes which are often found together. George Selwyn considered himself the father of Mie Mie, and the same relationship was likewise claimed by the profligate Lord March, the pretensions of each being alternately, not only admitted, but encouraged by the frail and charming Marchioness, who, looking to the future, beheld a profitable result from this joint paternity. Selwyn was, however, the most favoured of the claimants, and Mie Mie was entrusted to his bachelor care when little more than an infant, the Marchioness and her spouse taking their way to the Continent. After a while, the child was claimed by her mother, simply because her husband's parents objected to their grandchild being left in England; besides, the arrangement, madame considered, might throw doubts on the sanctity of her reputation in the eyes of a vicious and sadly censorious world.

Nothing could exceed Selwyn's grief at the prospect of being parted from this little charge, on whom he lavished more than a parent's love.

'I am aware,' wrote the Marchioness, 'that the separation will cost you much; but prepare for it with courage, for there is no help for it.'

Selwyn hesitated to give up the child, and the mother wrote again:

'I have never doubted your good faith, and have given proof of this by leaving London without the child, contrary to the advice of everyone, and in opposition to the orders of my parents; indeed, your own countrymen assured me that you would never return me the child after I was gone.'

Later on, her language became stronger, and she characterized his conduct as 'devilish;' indeed, she and the Marchese were on the point of starting for England, to carry away Mie Mie, before George consented to part with her. He confided her to the care of his confidential man-servant, had a carriage specially built for her to travel in, and wrote out a list of the best hotels where he wished her to stay on her journey. His grief at her absence was vehement, and he received the genuine sympathy of his friends of both sexes on his loss

'I wish very much we were in town,' writes Lord Carlisle, 'because you think we could console you. Gregg writes me word that he has seen you, and makes me very unhappy by his account of you. He tells me you are dejected to the greatest degree, with several other circumstances that give me dreadful apprehensions of your health.'

Mie Mie, after a time, was restored to his care, and soon blossomed into a young woman, when she was duly presented at Court; a ceremony of which Storer writes to Lord Auckland:

'A great event has taken place in Selwyn's family. Mademoiselle Fagniani has been presented at Court. Of course Miss Fagniani—for she was presented as a subject of Great Britain—was very splendid; but George was most magnificent, and *new* in every article of dress.'

Amongst George Selwyn's friends were two men whose names constantly occur in the literature of the day; these were Frederick, Viscount Bolingbroke, and Topham Beauclerk. The former was a lord of the bed-chamber, and a man of fashion and gallantry; the latter was one of the great-grandsons of Charles II., who early in life earned for himself the reputation of a man who loved wit and learning, folly and intrigue. His manners had something of the courtliness of his royal progenitor, whom his appearance resembled, and his conversation sparkled with humour and satire.

'Everything comes from him so easily,' says Dr. Johnson, 'it appears to me I labour when I say a good thing.' The great man had met Beauclerk at Oxford, where, according to Boswell, the doctor became fascinated with him, and where 'the moral, pious Johnson, and the gay, dissipated Beauclerk were companions.' This singular friendship, formed between a young man of fashion and a philosopher in a scratch wig, afforded them mutual pleasure, and Beauclerk became one of the earliest members of Johnson's famous literary club. No one could take more liberty than Beauclerk with the learned doctor, who contradicted Boswell, chided Goldsmith, and spoke sharp words to Garrick, but who was unusually lenient to his young friend.

Knowing this, Beauclerk, on one occasion when he had supped at a tavern with his friend Bennet Langton, and remained up till three o'clock in the morning, bethought him of calling on the doctor, and inviting him to join them in a ramble. Accordingly they went, and soundly hammered at the door of the philosopher's chambers at this unseemly hour, until at last the gaunt figure of the doctor appeared at the window in his shirt, with a little black wig on the top of his head, and a poker in his hand, prepared to do fierce battle, if necessary, with disturbing thieves. When he saw his friends, he laid aside his weapon of defence, and listened calmly to their proposal. 'What, is it you, you dogs? I'll have a frisk with you,' he said, almost as merry as they; and presently, when he had dressed, the three sallied forth in search of adventure, all so gaily oh, before the break of day; they turned them into Covent Garden, where the fruiterers and greengrocers were arranging their hampers just arrived from the country, when the learned, but burly doctor made some attempts to help them. But, the honest marketmen eyeing him with grave suspicion, he and his friends soon thought it better to move on towards the brighter and better sphere of a neighbouring tavern, where Johnson made a bowl of bishop, a mixture of wines, oranges, and sugar, which he dearly loved, and over which he roared out some verses of Lord Lansdowne's famous drinking-song; after this, they took a boat and rowed to Billingsgate. Indeed, they were so pleased with their amusement that Johnson and

Beauclerk were resolved to spend the rest of the day, Boswell says, in dissipation; but Langton, pleading an engagement to breakfast with some young ladies, determined to leave them, at which conduct the doctor scolded him for deserting 'his social friends to go and sit with a set of wretched *un-idea'd* girls.'

But, though Johnson readily joined in such a harmless prank as this, he did not shut his eyes to his friend's faults. 'Thy body is all vice, and thy mind all virtue,' he once remarked to him, when Beauclerk not seeming exactly to appreciate the compliment, the doctor said:

'Nay, sir, Alexander the Great, marching in triumph into Babylon, could not have desired to have had more said to him.'

In making this remark, it is probable that Johnson referred to Beauclerk's well-known intrigue with Lady Diana Bolingbroke. Her Ladyship was the eldest daughter of Charles, second Duke of Marlborough, and was remarkable for her social brilliancy. She had married Viscount Bolingbroke in 1757, to whom she bore three children. After the birth of the last of these, she separated from her lord, vowing she would live with him no longer. Her friends declared he had behaved shamefully to her, and had used her very ill. On the other hand, my Lord writes to George Selwyn, claiming his sympathy.

'I intended to sup with you this evening,' he says, 'but I am so low, dejected, and miserable, that I cannot speak, I can only cry. The just parting with her whom I know (though she does not yet) I shall not see again this long while, quite overcomes me. I shall, therefore, go and lie out of town this evening.'

No doubt the condolence he sought was freely given him by Selwyn, who, a couple of days after the receipt of this letter, received an epistle from the Hon. Henry St. John, Lord Bolingbroke's brother, in which he says:

'My brother, whom you inquire so kindly after, is not sunk into such low spirits as you seem to have heard. I think, on the contrary, though he laments the loss of a home, he does not whimper and whine after the object that has been, these two years past, the cause of his melancholy, and, I fancy, he at least sees that object in its true light. From a desponding lover and husband, as we have seen him, he is determined to become more a man of the world, and not to sacrifice his pleasure and interest in life to the indulgence of a grief brought on by an accident originally, and afterwards continued by the foolish obstinacy of a woman, and promoted by the unfeeling behaviour and indolence of her brother.'

Lady Diana took a house in Charles Street, where she was visited continually by Topham Beauclerk, who became her lover. This did not apparently prevent her amiable husband from being on terms of politeness with her. When she was ill, he wrote to present his compliments, and trusted 'Lady Diana Beauclerk's condition was improved,' on which occasion, she, not to be outdone in courtesy, wrote to inform 'Lord Bolingbroke that Lady Diana Bolingbroke was in better health.' With the same sense of politeness and gracious desire for her welfare and his own, the Viscount sought a divorce a little later on, which was granted him, when her ladyship married Topham Beauclerk.

Domestic unhappiness was, in this loose and profligate age, if not quite the order of the day, at least frequently to be met with in polite society. Infidelities to the marriage vow were looked on with the most liberal leniency by husbands and wives, and generally spoken of with a charming frankness that scorned all secrecy. Indeed, an intrigue, full of pregnant details, was a morsel of news which the gossips of the club and drawing-room hailed as a boon, and dwelt on with an exceeding great relish; and it was, therefore, with no ordinary delight that the affairs of the young Duke of

Grafton's heart were discussed over cards and snuff, and the particulars of his amour whispered behind laced hats and wicked fans that screened no blushes.

This most famous scandal of the day connected the name of his Grace, Augustus Henry, third Duke of Grafton, with Nancy Parsons, described by Horace Walpole as 'one of the commonest creatures in London, once much liked, but out of date.' The said Nancy, beloved by a Duke, was the daughter of a Bond Street tailor, and had in early life given her too susceptible heart to a West Indian merchant, with whom she had gone to Jamaica; but, growing tired of that country and of her lover, she escaped from both by stratagem, returned to London, and hired rooms at a perfumer's in Brewer Street, where she met his gallant Grace of Grafton, who in a little while became so enamoured of her that he was willing to make any sacrifice for her sake. The Duke was not only 'a profligate by profession,' as Junius described him, but he was likewise First Lord of the Treasury under a sovereign who prided himself on his remarkable virtue. All the time he could spare from his official duties was devoted to this lovely Nancy; he drove her in the full glare of publicity to Ascot races, sat beside and made love to her at the opera-house, in presence of his wife and their Sacred Majesties, and placed her at the head of his table to entertain his guests.

'He brings everybody to dine with him,' writes Lady Temple; 'his female friend sits at the upper end of his table; some do like it, and some do not. She is very pious, a constant Churchwoman, and reproves his Grace for swearing and being angry, which he owns is very wrong, and, with great submission, begs her pardon for being so ill-bred before her. . Would he have done so to the Duchess of Grafton? But I am afraid she has lost him by her own fault, and is now very miserable.'

My Lady Temple, unfortunately for his Grace, was not

the only one who made this amour the subject of a letter; Junius, in one of those caustic epistles which have become a classic, publicly addressed him in bitter and trenchant language.

'The example of the English nobility,' says this famous writer, 'may, for aught I know, sufficiently justify the Duke of Grafton when he indulges his genius in all the fashionable excesses of the age; yet, considering his rank and station, I think it would do him more honour to be able to deny the fact than to defend it by such authority. But, if vice could be excused, there is a certain display of it, a certain outrage to decency and violation of public decorum, which, for the benefit of society, should never be forgiven. It is not that he kept a mistress at home, but that he constantly attended her abroad. It is not the private indulgence, but the public insult, of which I complain. The name of Miss Parsons would hardly have been known, if the First Lord of the Treasury had not led her in triumph through the opera-house even in the presence of the Queen.'

The wife of his profligate Grace separated from him, and a few years after, their marriage was dissolved by an Act of Parliament which received the royal assent. In the meanwhile, the Duke—as may be supposed of a man of his various tastes—got tired of Nancy and left her. 'His baseness to this woman,' says Junius, speaking of his desertion, 'is beyond description or belief.' But, no matter what his character was, there were many fair ones willing to be led by him to the hymeneal altar; his choice fell on one of the daughters of the Rev. Richard Wrottesley, who was quite ready to love, honour, and obey him in return for the advantages of becoming a Duchess. The ex-Duchess comforted herself and the Earl of Upper Ossory by entering into the holy bonds with him.

Nancy Parsons' romance, however was not at an end; the late intrigue had rendered her fashionable, and she had now many ardent admirers in her train. Having a natural taste for high life, she was resolved not to receive a lover of lower rank than his whose delight it once was to honour her; her choice therefore fell on the Duke of Dorset, who, it was whispered, had thoughts of marrying her; but perhaps Dukes are more fickle than other peers—at all events, the fair Nancy, whose charms were by this time on the wane, was once more deserted by the man of her choice. However, her perseverance equalled her stock of unlimited affection, and, having persuaded Lord Maynard to marry her, she finally succeeded in her efforts to become a peeress of Great Britain. This event took place in 1777, when his lordship was addressed, in 'A Letter to a Celebrated young Nobleman on His late Nuptials,' by one of those anonymous pamphleteers who were the terror of their age. This epistle is marked by a charming freedom of speech and frankness of comment that must have delighted the world for whose benefit it was written; a paragraph or two will be sufficient to show its racy style.

'You, my lord,' the writer says, 'in the opening of life were always to be found at Newmarket. We pitied you, indeed, and marked you down as one of those unfortunate young men whose ambition it is to degrade themselves to a level with their grooms; when on a sudden you were flown to France, that brilliant seat of every levity, and outdoing *petits maîtres* in insignificance. You will doubtless remember those amiable days when you were drawn gently along the Boulevards at Paris, reclining in the arms of an opera-dancer, who was supporting your pallid figure and comforting your affliction. The French all admired the affecting picture; they were in raptures at the sight of a young nobleman who showed such fondness for a woman somewhat advanced in life (indeed, you wanted the prudence of age), and who could generously pass over the former conduct of a woman distinguished chiefly for her irregularities. After having exhibited the goodness of your disposition through every street in Paris, you were kind enough to return to your own country to improve us by your example, and, still more bountiful, to bring over this amiable woman as a model for your countrywomen. To so engaging a partner, my lord, we were not surprised that you dedicated your time. If you were inquired after at Court, you were engaged; if you were asked for in the fashionable clubs, you were amusing yourself in a domestic *tête-à-tête* at home; and, if important business wanted your attention, you were detained by your mistress.

'From such a conduct we naturally imagined that Lord Maynard must at least be constant; when on a sudden we were alarmed with the indecent spectacle of her beating you in public for a supposed act of infidelity. You bore it like a brave man, for a woman is no antagonist. You patiently retired, and your lordship best knows the progress of reconciliation. It is probable you might consider it as a proof of love; and forgive the little effusion of passion in one whom, as a witty Lord observed, must be allowed to be a *striking beauty*. The blow, however, we imagine, made some impression, for soon after you were separated. In uniting yourself to a woman of known bad character, you perpetuate your follies, and rob yourself of those advantages a prudent union naturally bestows. . . . I will not on this occasion pay your lordship so bad a compliment as to enumerate Lady Maynard's charms; all the world knows them as well as yourself; her virtues you alone are acquainted with. Make your amiable wife as happy as she deserves, and, if any Christian duty can possibly result from such an union, let it be deferred no longer. All the world knows your wife has been—a great sinner; she cannot repent too soon. Continue, my Lord, to act as you have done, and "the joy of heaven over her will be complete."'

But perhaps the most amusing matrimonial squabble of

the reign was that which disturbed the domestic happiness of Thomas Hervey and his wife. This honourable gentleman was a son of the first Earl of Bristol, and consequently brother to the celebrated John Hervey, whom the Princess Caroline, daughter of the late King, loved not wisely, but too well, for her own happiness. Tom Hervey, as he was usually called, was fully as eccentric as his remarkable brother, and was, moreover, not only 'one of the genteelest men that ever lived,' according to Dr. Johnson, 'but also one of the most profligate;' his dissipation and wit rendered him a man of fashion, his conduct through life made him notorious. The first act of his which brought him prominently before the public was his elopement with the wife of Sir Thomas Hanmer; her ladyship, when subsequently departing from this sinful world, made a will in Tom Hervey's favour of certain estates of which Sir Thomas had a life-possession. In the course of time, Sir Thomas cut down some of the timber on the property, whereon Tom Hervey wrote him a letter of an extraordinary kind, which he had printed and widely distributed; and so pleased was he with this production and its results, that he several times afterwards had recourse to the same means of airing his public grievances. In his letter to Sir Thomas, he dwells with satisfaction on his amour with her late ladyship, whom he speaks of as 'our wife'—'For in heaven, whose wife shall she be?' he asks philosophically. 'At length,' he freely tells the good Sir Thomas, 'she conceived that passion for me which she has so fervently and so pathetically avowed. It was not her eyes and ears enthralled her, for, if she could have been captivated by words or forms, she might have been in love with you.' He then requests Sir Thomas, if he sells any more timber, to give him the refusal of it.

His second letter concerning his affairs domestic in general, and the wife of his bosom in particular, which was published for the benefit of the public at large, was addressed to Dr. Johnson. The goodly philosopher came to have his name mixed up in this disreputable affair in a very simple manner. The Herveys had been kind to Johnson in his early days of struggle, and he always remembered them with gratitude. 'If you call a dog Hervey, I shall love him,' he said.

'Tom Hervey had a great liking for Johnson,' Topham Beauclerk told Boswell, 'and in his will had left him a legacy of £50. One day he said to me, "Johnson may want this money now more than afterwards, and I have a mind to give it to him directly; will you be so good as to carry a fifty-pound note from me to him?" This I positively refused to do, as he might perhaps have knocked me down for insulting him, and have afterwards put the note in his pocket. But I said, if Hervey would write him a letter, and enclose a fifty-pound note, I should take care to deliver it. He accordingly did write him a letter, mentioning that he was only paying a legacy a little sooner. To this letter he added, "P.S.—I am going to part with my wife."'

Johnson wrote back, advising him against this step, when Hervey at once seized the opportunity of vilifying his wife in a letter addressed to his old friend, and published for the benefit of the public at large.

'I am persuaded that you are a very good man,' he wrote to Johnson, 'but you have thought fit to be an advocate for the most worthless woman that ever was on earth. Mrs. Hervey, as, to my eternal shame and sorrow, she is called, is a dishonour, not only to her sex, but to her kind.'

This is language devoid at least of all false delicacy, but what follows is more amusing:

'She has been near sixteen years in my house without ever having been invited to it. . . . She has constantly run out my fortune, being herself at the same time so arrant a beggar that she was going upon the stage at Dublin to get a livelihood. The maintaining of her mother, who likewise had not a single guinea of her own, was soon imposed upon me, and, to say true, she has near as good a title to be my pensioner as the daughter. In about a year or two after my last complaint, the house I had taken at Richmond (in Lord Edgcumbe's opinion, who succeeded me in it, the most agreeable in the town), was called a dog-hole, and my modest spouse importuned me for one of double the rent of the other; though I had objected, when I saw it, to the conditions, tenancy, and every other circumstance relative to it, you will be surprised, sir, when I tell you that the Prodigal, nevertheless, obtained it of me; yet what follows will surprise you more. Upon hearing she was sick there, and hoping to cheer her spirits by a visit, carrying with it in appearance some little remains of regard for her (though I most cordially hated her), I spent about ten days there, and, though this was the first and only time that I had ever obtruded my company upon her in either of her seats, something having ruffled her when I entered her chamber in order to wish her a good-night, she flew into a passion. Upon my asking her the cause of her disquiet, she replied, "How can it signify what it is? I am very ill. I had rather that you was not here; I want to be alone."

'I took my leave, you may be sure, and passed the night in a delirium, I suppose, as violent as ever was felt in Bedlam. . . . To tell you the truth, I had turned her off a dozen years ago, but, fatally, my poor heart relented, and I took the vagrant into my house again; but, believe me, I had done myself less injury, if I had set fire to it, though it had been the best in London. I have no material charge to bring against her in point of conduct; she has, notwithstanding, behaved herself in such a manner as to disgust and irritate me.'

The picture Hervey presents of his domestic life is not

complete without one scene, which he does not hesitate to give the public.

'In the last forcible entry she made into my chamber,' he says, 'she not only derided me and my sufferings (which, not long before, she had pretended to lament most pathetically in one of her penitent letters), but traduced my whole family. Upon which I spat in her face, and advised her to leave the room immediately, lest worst things happened to her; upon which she had prudence enough to withdraw.'

Some time after the appearance of these letters, which caused much amusement and gossip, the town was further diverted by two advertisements which appeared in the public papers from his pen, as follows:

'Whereas Mrs. Hervey has been three times from home last year, and at least as many the year before, without either my leave or privity; and likewise encouraged her son to persist in the same rebellious practices; I hereby declare that I neither am nor will be accountable for any future debts of hers whatsoever. She is now keeping forcible possession of my house, to which I never did invite, or even thought of inviting, her in all my life.

'THOMAS HERVEY.

'Bond Street.'

The second of these notices was still more remarkable and laughable:

'Having lately received another anonymous letter, containing an innuendo highly injurious to my reputation, I will so far befriend the contemptible author of it, as to advise him to remain for ever concealed, lest I should not allow him the accustomed means of defending himself against my just resentment. I declare, at the same time, to him and to all the world, upon the faith and honour of a gentleman, that I have not a single grief, either of mind, body, or fortune, though very sensibly suffering in all, but what I owe to the worthless subject of his remonstrance. Nobody living stood more in need of a friend than her good ladyship' (Lady Hanmer), 'and none had ever found a nobler. Should I, therefore, receive any further molestations from her' (his wife) 'weak advocates, who have been her greatest enemies, I shall publish her last penitential letter, for it is since that, many of the capital and most unpardonable of her transgressions have been committed. I think, however, that the conscience which would not serve her as a monitor, will in time be my avenger.

'THOMAS HERVEY.'

But there were other members of society whose affections were more happily, if not, according to the opinions of their friends, more judiciously placed; one of these was a lady, whose name has been already mentioned in these pages, and whose elopement caused one of the greatest sensations of the day.

This victim to love's toils was Lady Susan Strangways, eldest daughter of the first Lord Ilchester, and niece to Lord Holland, the lady who had once been the confidant of the King concerning his passion for Lady Sarah Lennox. Lady Susan's lover was William O'Brien, a handsome young actor, 'By nature formed to please,' as Churchill said of him, who fretted his hours upon the boards of Covent Garden and Drury Lane theatres Her ladyship and the actor, it appears, were wise in their generation, and were enabled to keep their mutual love a secret from the curious and gossiping world which surrounded them, for the space of a year and a half; during which time they carried on an uninterrupted correspondence, by reason of O'Brien's imitating the handwriting of Lady Sarah Lennox; so clever indeed was his imitation, that the unsuspecting Lord Ilchester often delivered the love letters to his daughter. Their place of meeting was usually at Miss Read's, 'the paintress,' where Lady Susan went to take lessons, and also sit for her portrait, and where William O'Brien repaired likewise. One day, however, Miss Read, probably fearful lest she might get into trouble, betrayed the trust placed in her by the youthful lovers; when Lord Cathcart called to see her, she eagerly said to him, 'My lord, there is a couple in the next room that, I am sure, ought not to be together; I wish,' added the discreet lady, 'your lordship would look in.' Lord Cathcart opened the door of the apartment in which Lady Susan was holding conversation with her lover, shut it again directly, and then proceeded to enlighten her father concerning her ladyship's amour.

Lord Ilchester was wrathful indeed, but clever Lady Susan was equal to the occasion; she flung herself on her knees at his feet, confessed her love, and vowed to break it off; but, as a last favour, besought permission to see her lover just once more, that she might bid him farewell for ever. Lord Ilchester, satisfied by her protestations, consented to the final interview, which took place early in the week. On the following Friday she came of age, and on Saturday morning she walked downstairs, and calling her footman, announced that she was going to breakfast with her friend Lady Sarah, but would call on her way at Miss Read's; when she was some distance from the house, she suddenly remembered a particular cap in which she wished to be painted, sent back the footman for it, and no sooner had he left her, than she whipped into a hackney-coach, and was carried to Covent Garden Church, where her lover already waited her, and where she was safely married.

'Poor Lord Ilchester is almost distracted,' writes Horace Walpole; and then the aristocratic cynic adds, with a sneer, 'Indeed, it is the completion of disgrace—even a footman were preferable.'

All the world wondered indeed how my lady could have married a poor player.

'She may, however,' says the authority just quoted, 'still keep good company, and say, *Nos numeri sumus*—Lady Mary Duncan, Lady Caroline Adair, Lady Betty Gallini —the shop-keepers of the next age will be mighty well born.'

It may be added that two of these ladies mentioned married respectively a surgeon and a medical doctor, the third wedded Sir John Gallini. Lady Susan's friends were indeed in sore distress at this act of hers; her husband being a Roman Catholic, it was of course impossible for him to get appointed to any office under Government.

Sir Francis Delaval being, as Walpole says, 'touched by her calamity, has made her a present—of what do you think?—of a rich gold stuff! The delightful charity! O'Brien comforts himself, and says it will make a shining passage in his little history.'

It was soon determined to send the actor and his wife out of the country, and this plan was speedily effected. They were married late in April, and in October Lord Holland wrote to George Grenville, then Prime Minister, of his endeavour 'to assuage the incurable wound given to my brother by his daughter. Mr. O'Brien,' he continues, 'is gone with her to New York, and the keeping him there in credit is all that can be done, whilst we, if possible, forget them here. I hear there is a complaint against Mr. Lambert Moore, who may probably, in consequence of it, be removed; in that case, I beg you to make Mr. O'Brien Comptroller of the Customs at New York in his room. I will be security that the public shall not suffer. His Majesty has shown so much compassion on this unhappy occasion that I flatter myself he will have no objection.'

This appointment was probably not given to O'Brien, who soon returned to town, though not to the stage, for which, however, he wrote a couple of comedies and a farce, which were more or less successful. Shortly after his arrival, he was appointed Receiver-General of the County of Dorset, and both he and Lady Susan, who never repented her marriage, lived to a good old age.

A few months after Lady Susan's elopement, another marriage took place yet more remarkable; the bridegroom was, according to Walpole's opinion, much more preferable than an actor, being a footman, one John Sturgeon, and the bride, the Marquis of Rockingham's youngest sister, Lady Henrietta Alice Wentworth. This alliance of her ladyship with a valet caused a commotion in all circles; bets were made in the clubs as to its truth, gossips waved their fans over the whispered details, and the lovers of scandal received it as a savoury morsel of which their palates did not easily tire. 'The girls,' writes Gilly Williams, 'talk of nothing but the match between Lord Rockingham's sister and her footman, John Sturgeon.'

About this marriage, however, there was no concealment or undue haste; indeed, according to some of the correspondents of the day, not sufficient haste. The lady was in her twenty-seventh year, and had a fortune completely at her own disposal, the arrangement of which, on such an occasion, proclaimed her a woman of no ordinary prudence. She settled the sum of one hundred a year for life upon her husband, entailed her whole fortune on such children as Providence might send her, failing which it went back to her own family. Indeed, she betrayed a wisdom too rarely met with before marriage in making provisions for any disturbances that might threaten her future state, by securing to her spouse his annuity, even in case they separated. All this, drawn up in her own hand, she sent to Lord Mansfield, whom she appointed as her trustee, who gave it as his learned opinion that 'she had not left one cranny of the law unstopped, and that the settlements were as binding as any lawyer could make them.'

'Considering how plain she is,' says Horace Walpole, 'she has not, I think, sweetened the draught too much for her lover.'

After the ceremony, she retired with the footman to his family in Ireland as plain Mrs. Henrietta Sturgeon.

CHAPTER IX

Amusements of the Town—Some Masquerades — Strange Costumes—Mrs. Cornely's Entertainments—Suppers and Breakfasts — Madame de Boufflers at Strawberry Hill—Her Visit to Dr. Johnson—Favourite Opera-singers—Lord March and the Rena—The Archbishop of Canterbury scandalizes Lady Huntingdon—Rage for Gambling and its Consequences—The Bucks and the Macaronies—Samuel Foote, 'the Celebrated Buffoon'—Fashionable Rogues—Some Strange Notices.

THOUGH the Court remained virtuously dull, the royal example, excellent in itself, was by no means followed by the town, where assemblies raged, masquerades obtained, and gambling was the order of the day. The fashionable world spent its days and nights in attending routs, balls, and operas; in gambling, intriguing, sinning, and dressing; satisfied with itself, if all these things were accomplished with good taste. Amongst the most brilliant members of this gay and pleasure-loving society were the young Duke and Duchess of Richmond, whose entertainments were usually magnificent, and always popular. One of these, a masquerade, given in the earlier part of this reign, in honour of the King's birthday, was especially noted for its splendour.

It was held in the wide gardens attached to Richmond House, which sloped down to the Thames, and were lit with coloured lamps; here, on a sultry June night, princes, peers, and courtiers, maidens fair, and stately dames, to the number of six hundred, arrayed in every imaginable costume, held revelry till early dawn. Here came the beautiful Duchess of Hamilton and Argyle, stately and graceful, arrayed as Night, in trailing robes, strewn with innumerable stars; and here also was her father, in the habit of a running footman, with the portrait of his other daughter, poor Lady Coventry, hung at his button-hole, like a Croix de St. Louis; then there was Lucy Southwell, 'that curtseys like a bear,' attended by that brilliant rake, Lord March, who was perpetually in love with the ladies of the opera, and George Townshend, who passed his time very agreeably to himself and his friends in mimicking the Duke of Cumberland. Augustus Hervey, another member of a family famous for its eccentricity, was present, and, being perfectly disguised, treated everybody whom he recognised to a piece of his mind concerning their respective private histories, not forgetting to level the choicest shafts of his sarcasms at the fair Miss Chudleigh, to whom he was then privately married.

Her Grace of Richmond, the hostess, shone in all the glory of her dazzling beauty, which was enhanced by the costume of a Persian Sultana; whilst the Duchess of Grafton, scarcely less handsome, was arrayed as Cleopatra. His Grace of Cumberland was present, keeping close to charming Mrs. Fitzroy, who, clad in a Turkish costume, looked sufficiently bewitching to cause the Margrave of Anspach to wish himself a Turk. Lady Pembroke looked divinely fair in the robes of a pilgrim, and Lady George Lennox and Lady Bolingbroke went as Greek girls. Then there were knights of every clime and century, not wanting in gallantry, and emperors whose sole ambition was to reign over hearts, and Punches who were at liberty to scream out secrets at the pitch of their wicked voices, and devils who led those who hearkened to them into temptation, and bards who were songless.

The lower apartments of Richmond House were brilliantly lit, and spread with many supper-tables; and presently there were fireworks let off from an encampment of barges stationed in the middle of the Thames, and decked with streamers, and by their light a vast crowd of heads was discovered at the windows and on the roofs of the neighbouring houses, looking at the gay scene.

Another great masquerade was given at 'Almack's Assembly Rooms,' where the balls were presided over by a committee of ladies of quality; and where was established a club 'for lords and ladies,' which had at first met at a tavern, but subsequently, to satisfy the scruples of Lady Pembroke, one of the foundresses, in a room at 'Almack's.' In this club the ladies nominated and elected gentlemen, and *vice versâ;* so that no lady could exclude a lady, or no gentleman black-ball a gentleman, no matter how much he or she desired it. Here, as Gilly Williams says, 'Almack's Scotch face, in a bag wig, waiting at supper, would divert you, as would his lady in a sack, making tea, and curtseying to the Duchesses.' The only admission to these balls was by vouchers of personal introduction. The great room set aside for dancing was handsomely decorated with gilt columns and pilasters, classic medallions, vast mirrors, and cut-glass lustres. The masquerade held here in 1773, was remarkable for its excellent music, its fine entertainment, and the number of elegant figures that attended it. Amongst others who composed this gay and motley throng, were my Lady Archer, dressed as a blue-coat boy, and my Lord Edgcumbe as an old washerwoman, in a linen bed-gown. There were also two charming Eves, accompanied by two handsome Adams, such dull fellows in good truth, that a wag went whispering all round the room he did not wonder his first mother was tempted by a serpent, if the companion of her blissful bowers was such a heavy fellow as these Adams. Four officers, dressed in the uniform of the Swiss Guards, made a fine show, dressed in blue with red neckclothes that made them look, 'twas said, like Norfolk turkeys with their throats cut; a chattering mungo who teased many, asked George Selwyn, who was present as a sage, what was his fate. 'Tyburn,' said the wit briefly; he had also something to say to Samuel Foote, who was in a handsome cavalier costume. 'Ah, Mr. Foote, if your comedies were as well-made as your clothes, what a genius you would be!'

Lord Minto speaks of another masquerade at Hammersmith, given by Mrs. Sturt, to which he went with Lady Palmerston and Mrs. Crew, Windham, and Tom Pelham, from which they did not return till six in the morning. There were a vast number there, amongst others Jack Payne, who was dressed as a young lady, and looked and acted so remarkably well that this assumed character, it was said, suited him infinitely better than his own. The gallant captain was chaperoned by Mrs. Fitzherbert. The three Princes were there likewise, all in Highland dresses, and looking very well.

'Their knees were bare,' Mrs. Crew told Lord Minto, 'and I saw the Prince of Wales make a lady feel his bare knee. She had asked him something about that part of the dress, and he said it was exactly right, and she should see it was. "There," said he, "you may squeeze it if you like," which she did accordingly. They had breeches, however, and only rolled up the breeches' knees,' added Mrs. Crew.

Decency, indeed, was not always preserved on such occasions, and we read of several strange 'figures' which attended the public masquerades given at Carlisle House in Soho Square by the famous Mrs. Cornely. This remarkable and enterprising lady, said to be Irish by birth, had once upon a time been a public singer, but, having taken Carlisle House, set about ministering to public pleasure in another form. Here she established assemblies and subscription balls, and presided over the diversions of the nobility; at first she had somewhat scandalized the public, but, the fame of her entertainments getting abroad, her gorgeous balls were soon crowded by the righteous, who were not satisfied to leave all amusement to the wicked. She had altered, rebuilt, and decorated Carlisle House at a vast cost, until it assumed the appearance, according to a writer of the period, of 'a fairy palace.' Even the underground apartments were magnificent; they consisted of seven rooms, 'which, from the vast variety and ornaments, the grandeur and magnificence of some, the elegant simplicity of others, together with the amazing beauty of the lights, one of the principal excellencies of the whole, form a view, on descending a perpendicular flight of stairs, most sumptuously and strikingly pleasing.'

Nothing could be more magnificent than the brilliancy of her masquerade balls, which usually commenced at nine and ended at six o'clock the following morning, and which were attended by the rank, wealth, and beauty of the town. Here came her patrons and patronesses, arrayed in every imaginable costume which taste or eccentricity could suggest, all of which were more or less costly, and which went to make up a scene of unequalled brilliancy. To one of these remarkable masquerades, which set the whole town a-talking for days, 'two great personages,' the King and Queen, were, according to the *London Chronicle,* 'complimented with two tickets, which they very politely returned;' but the refusal of their Majesties did not prevent the numerous attendance of their faithful subjects, and of some members of their royal family. Here was the Duke of Cumberland as Henry VIII., the Duke of Gloucester 'in an old English habit with a star on the cloak,' the Countess Waldegrave as Jane Shore, Lady Pomfret as a Greek sultana, Lady Stanhope as Melpomene, the Duchess of Bolton as the chaste Diana, Lady Edgecumbe as a nun, the Duchess of Buccleugh as the Witch of Endor, all in most costly garb. But their richness of apparel was surpassed by Miss Monckton, Lord Galway's daughter, who appeared in the character of an Indian sultana, 'in a robe of cloth of gold and a rich veil, the seams of her habit being embroidered with precious stones, and a magnificent cluster of stones on her head;' the jewels she wore were valued at £30,000.

In the midst of the blaze of magnificence which the scene presented, a figure entered which immediately attracted every eye, this being none other than Captain Watson of the Guards in the character of Adam, who had his dress fitted so close and painted so naturally that, on his first approach, the eager and curious crowd who surrounded him believed he was wholly unadorned.

Another figure was that of a Savoyard carrying a hurdy-gurdy and leading a bear; they had been stopped on their entrance, as the bear had only a half or lady's ticket, but were admitted on the Savoyard assuring the door-keeper that it was a female bear. But, if the aristocratic throng inside had their amusement, so also had the ignoble throng which gathered in vast numbers in the streets leading to Mrs. Cornely's fairy palace, and who, holding torches aloft, made the occupants of the various chairs and coaches let down the windows that they might be afforded a sight of their dresses; some of them went further still, and insisted in a good-humoured way on the masks shaking hands with as many of them as could reach their conveyances, a complacency which one lady had cause to regret, for no sooner had she placed her delicate palm in the hand of a friendly and dexterous thief than he slipped three valuable rings from her fingers into his safer keeping.

The presiding genius over this and kindred entertainments, the charming Mrs. Cornely, it is sad to narrate, was afterwards obliged to sell asses' milk at Kensington, disguising her individuality under the common but familiar name of Smith, and she finally ended her days in the Fleet prison.

Suppers were also much in vogue, and were usually held when the guests had returned from the opera or play-house; wit and wine flowed freely at these convivial repasts, repartee was exchanged, and scandal talked till the small hours. Walpole tells us he went to a supper one night at my Lord Edgecumbe's in Upper Grosvenor Street, after witnessing 'a very wretched comedy, Dr. Goldsmith's "She Stoops to Conquer."' When he was yet at supper, 'that macaroni rake, Lady Powis, who is just come to her estate and spending it,' called in with news of a fire in the Strand. It was then past one in the morning, but my Lady Hertford, Lady Powis, Mrs. Howe, and Horace must set off at once, and were 'within an inch of seeing the Adelphi Buildings burnt to the ground.'

Sir Francis Delaval, who was a gay soul, used to light up Lord Lexborough's house, and give suppers to gay assemblies of wits, macaronies, and opera-girls.

Breakfasts were by no means so fashionable as suppers; after the fatigues of nights spent in rounds of pleasure, men and women of fashion were too exhausted to exert their powers to please in the forenoon, or to give utterance to those flashes of wit and humour then invariably expected at all social gatherings, but which best harmonized with candle-light. Such entertainments were, however, occasionally given; the Duchess of Gloucester once entertained four hundred guests at breakfast at her house at Blackheath; and a record is left us of a yet more famous breakfast, at which Horace Walpole entertained La Comtesse de Boufflers, *sçavante galante,*' who was mistress of the Prince de Conti. When this lady arrived in town, she was, by reason of her interesting reputation and beauty, immediately lionized, and hurried about from one sight to another from morning till night, until she, 'never having stirred ten miles from

Paris, and having only rolled in an easy coach from one hotel to another on a gliding pavement,' was quite worn out. Walpole thought she was spoiled by her unrelaxed attention to applause. 'You would think,' he says, 'she was always sitting for her picture to her biographer.'

To the great breakfast which he made for her at Strawberry Hill, he invited some distinguished friends, amongst whom were the Duke and Duchess of Grafton, Lord Hertford, Lady Mary Coke, Duclos, the author of 'The History of Louis XI.' and several novels, Lord and Lady Holderness, and the famous Chevalier d'Eon, then secretary to the French ambassador, who, in the latter years of his life, was compelled to dress as a female.

Madame de Boufflers went thither 'with her eyes a foot deep in her head, her hands dangling, and scarcely able to support her knitting-bag.' The feast was spread in the big parlour, and the host had filled the great hall and cloisters by turns with French horns and clarionettes. Presently Horace conducted them to see his printing-press, where what should they find but half a dozen lines celebrating the inimitable graces of madame, already in type, and just waiting to be turned out, a gentilesse which pleased; then he carried them to another apartment which he called the cabinet, where the yellow glass at the top, having a charming sun for a foil, surmounted the indifference of all, and delighted her Grace of Grafton, who entered into the air of enchantment and fairyism of the place.

Madame la Comtesse, before she left town, paid a morning visit to another distinguished man, who did not, however, receive her with such state. Madame, who was the friend of Rousseau, was anxious to make the acquaintance of the English philosopher Dr. Johnson, and, having expressed her desire to Topham Beauclerk, that worthy man undertook the task of introducing her to his learned friend. Accordingly, they went to his chambers in the Temple, where madame was for some time entertained by his conversation; when her interview was over, she and her friend left, and had got so far as the Inner Temple Lane, when all at once they heard a voice like thunder, and looking round, saw Johnson, who, suddenly taking it into his head that he ought to have done the honours of his literary residence to a foreign lady of quality, hurried after them in violent agitation, and, brushing in between Beauclerk and the Countess, seized her hand, and conducted her to her coach. The philosopher's dress on the occasion was a rusty brown morning suit, a pair of old shoes by way of slippers, a little shrivelled wig on the top of his head, whilst the sleeves of his shirt and the knees of his breeches hung loose.

Private concerts were another form of entertainment which, at this period, when there was a general rage for music, were extremely fashionable; and the names of Riccarelli, Guadagni, Manzoli, Tondino, Zamparini, and Pacchierotti, whom pretty Mrs. Sheridan could not hear without tears, became household words. Almost every lady of quality had her weekly musical parties, where Italian singers and French fiddlers came dressed in velvet, lace, and embroidery, so as sometimes to be taken for foreign ambassadors. Dr. Burney avowed that Manzoli's voice was 'the most powerful and voluminous soprano,' and Gilly Williams writes to tell Selwyn, 'the knowing ones agree nothing like Manzoli has been imported into this country for ages.' This singer became such a public favourite that, at his benefit, his receipts were a thousand guineas, free of all charges.

'This,' says one of the newspapers of the day, 'added to the sum of fifteen hundred pounds which he has already saved, and the remaining profits of the season, is surely an undoubted proof of British generosity. One particular lady complimented the singer with a two hundred pound bill for a single ticket on that occasion.'

Walpole says of him, he 'is come a little late, or I think

he would have had as many diamond watches and snuff-boxes as Farinelli had.'

Guadagni, another singer of renown, was the cause of one of those pretty quarrels, concerning which party-spirit ran high, and which mightily diverted the town. The Hon. Mr. Hobart, Lord Buckingham's brother, who was manager of the operas at the Haymarket, grievously offended Guadagni by preferring the Zamperin, his mistress, to the singer's sister. Guadagni was a man of vast importance, who was accustomed to command, and who had held such sway in Vienna that, to pique a man of quality, he had named a Minister to fair Venice; he, therefore, could not brook any disregard to his desire, and left the Haymarket, when several of his great lady friends, amongst whom were the Duchess of Northumberland and Lady Harrington, espousing his cause, he opened an opera at Mrs. Cornely's. There Guadagni established his operas, which were wonderfully well attended by the fashionable portion of the town.

To avoid the licensing act, Mrs. Cornely announced the entertainments under the names of Harmonic Meetings, and took no money, but received subscriptions to provide coals for the poor, just as she had fitly described her masquerades as being for the benefit of commerce. The Haymarket opera-house began to thin; Mr. Hobart's coffers grew empty, and, in his rage, he informed the Bench of Justices regarding Mrs. Cornely's operas, when they were quashed, to the grief of the Guadagni's fair friends, one of whom, Lady Bingley, gave an annuity of £300 to this charming signor.

Another Italian singer was the Rena, for whom Lord March had a tender regard. When Horace Walpole entertained the Earl at Strawberry Hill, my Lord brought my Lady in his train, to which Walpole, with the freedom of his age, had not the slightest objection, but feared 'it would not raise his reputation in the neighbourhood.' The same liberality was, on another occasion, extended to the Earl and his operatic friend by the Baron d'Holbach, a man of parts and fortune, who was invited by George Selwyn to meet Lord March; it was intimated to him that the charming Rena would be present, but the gracious Baron declared he would consider himself honoured by the society of mademoiselle, 'for nothing prudish entered into his character.'

My Lord, however, was seldom constant to one amour for long, and in due time the Rena gave place in his capacious heart to another singer, likewise an Italian, 'the little Tondino,' who reigned mistress of his affections for some time. When taking her departure for France, Lord March wrote to Selwyn, who was then in Paris, concerning her, and his lines betray a deeper feeling than might have been expected from a man of his reputation.

'I am just preparing to conduct the poor little Tondino to Dover,' he says, 'and, as I shall hardly be able to write to you there, I shall endeavour to say two or three words to you while she is getting ready. I am sure you will be good to her, for I know you love me, and I can desire nothing of you that I shall feel so sensibly as your notice of her. . . . My heart is so full that I can neither think, speak, nor write. How I shall be able to part with her, or come back to the house, I do not know. The sound of her voice fills my eyes with fresh tears. My dear George, *j'ai le cœur si serré que je ne suis bon à present qu'a pleurer.* Farewell, I hear her coming, and this is perhaps the last time I shall see her here.'

In her absence, however, the fickle lord's heart was consumed by Zamparini, who was not only a singer of the first celebrity, but a dancer of such merit that the graceful movements of her light fantastic toe made sad havoc on the too susceptible hearts of those beaux who witnessed her performance, and completely captivated my Lord March. The Zamparini belonged 'to a rascally garlic tribe, whose very existence depends on her beauty,' from whose society my Lord had much difficulty in separating her.

'He looks miserable,' says Gilly Williams, 'and yet he takes the Zamparini off in her opera-dress every night in his chariot.'

Presently news came of the Rena's return to town from Paris, and he writes to tell Selwyn his violent fancy for the Zamparini has a little abated, and hopes it may be quite so before the Rena's return, 'else I fear it will interrupt our society.' He furthermore avows his friendship and affection for her, and, as one whom he loves very much, he hopes she 'will have some indulgence for my follies,' a contrary behaviour, he adds, 'would be quite ridiculous and affected.'

These various ladies, the history of whose amours lent them additional interest, were received with great courtesy by the noble dames at whose mansions they warbled operatic arias, for the benefit of ears polite, whilst the gossips of the day recounted in whispers what heroes of the horse and foot guards wore chicken-skin gloves, how much false hair her Grace of Manchester had recently bought, and the name of the famous face wash which was used by the Macaroni.

The town indeed was extremely lively.

'Every drawing-room,' says the *Westminster Gazette* of 1773, 'is as different in its manners and modes as it is in its company. One is celebrated for cards, another for wit, a third for beauties, a fourth for coxcombs, a fifth for old maids and scandal, a sixth for fashion, and a seventh for cotillions.'

Not only did routs, balls, and gambling obtain in the drawing-rooms of wicked worldlings, but such like sinful amusements found their way into the episcopal palace of Dr.

Cornwallis, Archbishop of Canterbury, to Lady Huntingdon's vast horror. Her Ladyship was a mighty pious woman, who was styled the 'Queen of the Methodists.' Whitfield had preached in her drawing-rooms to fashionable but heedless sinners, and had spoken of her as 'the lady elect'; but the prophet had come to shame, according to Walpole, who tells that the holy man one day asked my Lady Huntingdon for forty pounds for some distressed saint or other. Perhaps she considered that distress was the most proper condition for saints; at all events, she declared she had not so much money in the house, but was finally induced to give her watch and chain, which the preacher said were vanities, not worthless vanities, however.

'About a fortnight afterwards,' says Horace, 'going to his house, and being carried into his wife's chamber, among the paraphernalia of the latter, the Countess found her own offering. This has made a terrible schism.'

But her Ladyship was sufficiently a saint in her own right to regard diversions as Satan's harvest for lost souls, and hearing that routs were given at the episcopal palace, she sought an interview with their Majesties, in order to complain of Dr. Cornwallis.

'I have been told so many odd things of your Ladyship,' said the King, staring at her with his round blue eyes, 'that I am free to confess I felt a great degree of curiosity to see if you were at all like other women.'

After this courteous remark, Lady Huntingdon stated the object of her visit, when the Queen asked her many questions, and insisted that her Ladyship should take some refreshments before she departed, a most unusual piece of hospitality on the part of her economical Majesty, who had refused her maids of honour the nightly suppers which it had always been the habit of those who formerly held that post to enjoy. After refreshments had been partaken of, their Majesties grew so agreeable as to permit her Ladyship to kiss their royal hands, a piece of vast condescension for which she returned her most grateful thanks.

Soon after the interview, the King wrote indignantly to the good prelate, telling him of 'the grief and concern with which his breast was afflicted' at the news that routs had made their sinful way into his palace; declaring he held 'those levities and vain dissipations as utterly inexpedient, if not unlawful, to pass in a residence for many centuries devoted to divine studies, religious retirement, and the exclusive exercise of charity and benevolence.' He concluded by trusting he would have no occasion to show further marks of his displeasure, and signed himself his Lordship's 'gracious friend.'

But the principal vice of the age may be considered to have been gambling, which was limited neither to age nor sex.

'As the gambling and extravagance of the young men of quality has arrived now at a pitch never heard of, it is worth while to give some account of it,' writes Horace Walpole in his last journals (1772). 'They had a club at one Almack's in Pall Mall, where they played only for rouleaus of £50 each rouleau; and generally there was £10,000 in specie on the table. Lord Holland had paid above £20,000 for his two sons. Nor were the manners of the gamesters, or even their dresses for play, undeserving notice. They began by pulling off their embroidered clothes, and put on frieze great-coats, or turned their coats inside outwards for luck. They put on pieces of leather (such as is worn by footmen when they clean knives) to save their lace ruffles; and to guard their eyes from the light, and to prevent tumbling their hair, wore high-crowned straw hats with broad brims, and adorned with flowers and ribbons; masks to conceal their emotions when they played at quinze. Each gamester had a small neat stand by him, with a large rim to hold his tea, or a wooden bowl with an edge of ormolu, to hold his rouleaus. They borrowed great sums of the Jews at exorbitant premiums. Charles Fox called his outward room, where those Jews waited till he rose, the Jerusalem Chamber. His brother Stephen was enormously fat; George Selwyn said he was in the right to deal with Shylocks, as he could give them pounds of flesh.'

Gibbon the historian said Almack's 'was the only place which still invites the flower of English youth.' It was a common occurrence for young men of fashion to lose ten, fifteen, or twenty thousand pounds in one night. Lord Stavordale, whilst yet a minor, lost at this club on one evening eleven thousand pounds, but recovered it by one great hand at hazard; whereon his Lordship swore a great oath. 'Now, if I had been playing deep,' quoth he, 'I might have won millions.'

Certainly gambling was Charles Fox's ruling passion; night after night he was to be found at the faro-table of one of his clubs, where he lost enormous sums and ran himself hopelessly into debt, when he was often reduced to borrow a guinea from one of the club waiters, and was dunned by the chairmen whom he employed. In the early part of one night he won eight thousand pounds, but, alas! this was but a trifling sum, the greater part of which he paid away before standing up from the table; the remainder he staked again and lost. His father, Lord Holland, at his death left him £154,000 to pay his debts, but this amount did not cover his liabilities, and in a few years the gambler was obliged to sell all he possessed, including his library, for the benefit of his creditors.

'Charles tells me,' writes Lord Carlisle to George Selwyn, 'he has not now, nor has had for some time, one guinea, and is happier on that account.'

During the races at Newmarket, gambling was carried on to a vast extent, by way of counter excitement to the events of the day. In 1772, a correspondent of Lord Harcourt's writes to him:

'Play ran higher, if possible, at Newmarket this meeting than at any of the former; even rouleaus were despised, and nothing but bank notes seen on the table. They say a £10,000 was carried from London; even Lord Carmarthen, after all his sage resolutions not to game, was there drawn in to lose £1,200—a mere trifle in these days, but more than either he or the Duke of Leeds can afford to pay.'

The 'Cocoa-tree Club' was another resort of fashionable gamblers; here, after the play was over, and both Houses had risen, peers, politicians, counsellors, and men of fashion might be seen 'supping at little tables covered with a napkin, in the middle of a coffee-room, upon a bit of cold meat and a sandwich, and drinking a glass of punch,' after which they adjourned to the gambling-rooms, to play until next morning.

This diversion, which was the cause of so much anxiety, excitement, and ruin, was shared by women. Cards had obtained during the last two reigns, but faro-tables were now introduced into drawing-rooms, and guineas changed ownership with great rapidity.

'The women,' writes Lord Nuneham, 'play more than the men at "White's" did twelve years ago, and Miss Pelham on Sunday lost £400 at a sitting.'

Perhaps the first to set up a gambling-table in her saloons was Her Royal Highness the Duchess of Cumberland, who, with her sister, presided over it with great profit, if not edification, to themselves. The latter, Lady Elizabeth Luttrell, had the reputation of being dexterous, a fame of which she subsequently showed herself not unworthy. To better her fortune, Lady Elizabeth went to Germany, where her proverbial good luck at games of hazard followed her, until she was discovered cheating, when, as a punishment, she was made to draw a barrow, to which she was chained, through the streets; after this severe chastisement, she retired to another principality, where she was discovered at her old tricks, for which offence she was clapped into prison, where this sister-in-law of a Royal Duke ended her life by poison. Lady Essex was another woman of high degree who had a passion for gambling, and who kept the town alive by the splendour of her card-parties.

Play went high on some occasions amongst ladies of fashion, whose discretion was more limited than their fortunes. The *Court Miscellany* of 1765 makes a statement that 'the lady of a right hon. personage last night attempted to shoot herself, on account of some losses at play, which she did not choose should come to the ears of her husband. Happily, however, the pistol missed fire, but the snap alarming her woman, who was in the antechamber, she instantly came in, and prevented any second endeavour of executing the terrible purpose of her mistress.' Another magazine in the following year states that 'a lady at the west end of the town, lost one night last week, at a sitting, three thousand guineas at loo;' whilst the *London Chronicle* for August 13, 1775, states that on 'Wednesday evening, two ladies of distinction, having a dispute at a party of cards, repaired yesterday morning in their carriages to a field near Pancras, and fought a duel with pistols, when, one of them being shot in the left arm, the affair terminated.'

'A lady who ruins her family,' says Mr. Sergeant Circut in the 'Lame Lover,' a play satirising the follies of the age, 'by punctually paying her losses at play, and a gentleman who kills his best friend in a ridiculous quarrel, are your only tip-top people of honour.'

The beaux during this reign, and in the last, were divided into two classes; one of which was composed of robust scamps, and the other of effeminate noodles, called macaronies. Speaking of the former, the *Court Miscellany* ventilates its opinions in language not to be mistaken:

'There is a part of taste,' says this article, 'that seems at present extremely prevailing in these kingdoms, which deserves particular attention, that of imitating the dress of grooms, the walk or roul of common sharpers and pickpockets, the oaths of fishwomen, chairmen, draymen, and porters; with all the additional flowers of rhetoric and figures of speech extracted from Newgate itself. Where this refinement will end, it is not easy to guess, since it is already practised by almost all ranks, from the highest to the lowest, under the notable sanction of that senseless and despicable class of people called "bucks."'

Attending cock and dog fights in the morning, drinking at taverns and gambling at clubs in the evening, provoking a fight or beating a watchman at night, was the usual manner in which they passed their days; a mode seemingly much to their satisfaction. The Prince of Wales, who loved prize-fighting, attended one of these exhibitions with a group of his friends, when, so rare was the sport exhibited on this occasion patronized by royalty, that one of the combatants was crushed out of all semblance to humanity, and beaten to death. One of his friends, my Lord Lichfield, was more humane, as may be judged from the fact that he dismissed his French cook for flogging a pig three weeks old to death, in order that it might eat tender; monsieur the executioner thought himself ill-repaid for a labour which had taken him three hours, but my lord turned him out of the house with a legacy of oaths, and public feeling was so much against the cook that he had to repair to his native land.

Three other beaux of this class were Captains Scaurn and Crofts of the Light Dragoons, and Mr. Lyttelton, who ogled Mrs. Hartley, a mighty fine actress and a pleasant woman, when she was diverting herself at Ranelagh. This lady was sitting beside the Rev. Mr. Bates, who, like her, had come to take the air, and who was vastly affronted by the conduct of these fine gentlemen, who, in return for his frowns, made faces, not at him, but at each other. The reverend man volunteered the remark that they were 'dirty, impertinent puppies,' in reply to which information one of the gallant sons of Mars informed the parson he was 'indeed a tight good fellow,' and wished to know if he threatened him because he was a boxer. With most unclerical spirit, Mr. Bates declared, if he said three more words, he 'would ring his nose off his face;' when the captain, wishing to preserve his nose and his honour, asked for the parson's address; and at two o'clock the next morning the reverend man was waked by a message from Captain Crofts to say, if he would not appoint an hour and place for a fight, the gallant Captain aforenamed would 'pull Mr. Bates' nose, spit in his face, and drag the black coat off his back.'

The worthy parson sent word he would meet him at the Turk's Head Coffee-house in the Strand. Accompanied by two friends all ready for combat, Mr. Bates dined there, and, that pleasant meal being over, Captain Crofts and his second, the Hon. Mr. Lyttelton, entered on the scene. Dinner has a proverbially soothing effect, even to those who thirst for blood, and so, after many preliminaries, Captain Crofts said Mrs. Hartley was ungenteelly treated, and confessed Mr. Bates had acted with spirit and propriety in defending her; to which speech the parson replied, 'that being granted, he begged Captain Crofts' pardon for any unguarded expression which arose from a misunderstanding on both sides.' After these handsome speeches, healths were drunk and hands were clasped, and peace was restored between the worthy parson and the gallant captain.

In the early hours of morning the buck was at his best; then, emboldened by wine and an ample supper, he was ready to smash lamps, give false alarms, or make the watchmen measure their lengths upon the ground. Three of these young gentlemen, in crossing St. John's Square, Clerkenwell, one morning, fell upon one of those honest guardians of the peace, whom they seemed to regard as their natural enemies, and beat him unmercifully; the watch seized one of them by part of his waistcoat, and called out murder, when the valiant young bloods thought proper to take to their heels, leaving a part of the waistcoat behind, in the pocket of which the poor watch found three guineas and sixpence, an amount he considered sufficient compensation for the hard blows he had received.

The bucks patronized all the feats of strength and extraordinary exhibitions of the day, and were much delighted by 'The Original Female Sampson,' after whose performances 'some of the most wonderful phenomenons that ever were known' were shown. 'The Roman Boy stone-eater;' 'The Female Satyr, or Horned Woman, at the end of Piccadilly and Shrug Lane, Coventry Street, Haymarket, where she may be seen every day for one shilling;' 'Primrose, the celebrated Piebald Boy;' Miss P. Burte—otherwise the 'Norfolk Fairy, being in her fifteenth year, and measuring thirty-nine inches,' who humbly solicited 'the attention of the nobility and gentry at her rooms in Jermyn Street, St. James's,' were all favourites of the buck. But a special protégé of theirs was Johnson, the Irish equestrian, who at Astley's rode one hundred yards standing on his head in the saddle, or galloped round the ring on three horses, feats which until then were almost unknown. Dr. Johnson has, by a ponderous sentence, rendered his acrobatic namesake famous. 'Sir,' said the lexicographer, 'such a man should be encouraged; for his performances show the extent of the human powers in one instance, and thus tend to raise our opinion of the faculties of man.'

The second class of beaux, known as macaronies, were the petted darlings of society, who wore long curls and spying glasses, and who for the most part had travelled and brought back with them not only the fashions of the countries they had visited, but likewise their worst vices.

Their heads were compared by one of the publications of the day to a poet's garret, 'interiorly, very poorly furnished, but exteriorly plastered, painted, and otherwise finely ornamented.' They dressed in the extreme of the fashion, and were gorgeous in coloured velvets, brilliant satins, and rich laces, which were all usually imported from Paris; they carried long canes, from which gold and silver tassels were suspended, and held gilt essence-bottles in their daintily gloved hands; moreover, they simpered blandly, ogled women through their gold-mounted spying glasses, waved their fans or perfumed handkerchiefs with grace, and walked on their toes with the elasticity of a French dancing-master. When one of these men of fashion, young or old—for, as Walpole said, the old fools will hobble after the young—went abroad, the correspondence of their friends contained repeated requests for patterns of spotted velvets or satins for suits, for embroidered waistcoats, worked stockings, and such like articles of attire.

The Rev. Dr. Warner writes to George Selwyn that he sends him 'the prettiest work-bag in the world;' and Lord March, writing to the wit, tells him, 'Lady Townshend has sent me a fan for you, which I will send by the first opportunity;' and in return his Lordship is sent a muff. 'The muff you sent me by the Duke of Richmond I like prodigiously; vastly better than if it had been *tigré* or any glaring colour,' says the Earl, and he adds, 'Several are making after it.'

'The men imitate the women in almost everything,' says the *Westminster Gazette* for 1773; 'perfumes, paint, and effeminate baubles engross most of their time, and learning is now looked on as unworthy attainment.'

The conversations of the macaronies were usually inane, and very freely interlarded with what Bob Acres calls the 'curst French lingo'; their idea of love was intrigue, and to wrap up indecencies in the thinnest and most graceful covering was an art which, according to their opinions, showed excellent parts. These pretty gentlemen lounged about town in the mornings; met in Betty's fruit-shop in St. James's Street, a popular resort; were carried in their chairs to the houses of ladies of quality; or went to see Mr. Samuel Foote, the son of a Cornish gentleman and member of Parliament, whom Walpole disdainfully speaks of as 'the celebrated buffoon,' who vastly entertained the town with caricatures of living persons, which he introduced into his comedies with a faithfulness it was impossible to ignore. Davies said there was hardly a public man in England who had not entered Mr. Foote's theatre with an aching heart, under the apprehension of seeing himself laughed at. Foote was no bad judge of human nature. 'Demolish a conspicuous character,' he said, 'sink him below our level, then we are pleased, then we chuckle and grin, and toss the halfcrown on the counter.' To demolish conspicuous characters became the object of his performances, and gold flowed freely into his coffers in return.

Once he intimated his intention of personating the great Dr. Johnson, whose gruff voice, rolling eyes, brusque manner, and untidy dress offered unusual capabilities for reproduction with comic effect. Now Johnson, all through his life, despised actors.

'Players, sir!' he once said; 'I look upon them as no better than creatures set upon tables and joint stools, to make faces and produce laughter, like dancing dogs.'

'But, sir, you will allow some players are better than others.'

'Yes, sir, as some dogs dance better than others.'

Moreover, perhaps, of all players, he disliked Foote most; his mimicry, he said, was not a talent, but a vice, from which others abstained; and his conversation a mixture of wit and buffoonery. Hearing that Foote was about to hold him up to ridicule, he was indeed wroth, and gave the mimic to understand that, if he attempted the like, he would chastise him before the whole audience; whereon Foote abandoned his idea.

'Sir, he knew I would have broken his bones,' said Dr. Johnson.

But a greater favourite with the macaronies was Mademoiselle Heinel, a celebrated dancer, at whose appearance the poetry of motion, according to Dr. Burney, first gained the ascendant over music. This lady, a Fleming by birth, was tall, shapely, and very handsome, and had copied her attitudes from classic models.

'She moves as gracefully slow as Pygmalion's statue when it was coming into life,' writes Walpole, 'and moves her leg round as imperceptibly as if she was dancing in the Zodiac.'

To this lady's performances the whole town crowded, but she was the especial admiration of the macaronies; who, besides the six hundred pounds salary allowed her by the Hon. Mr. Hobart, the manager of the opera, complimented her with a *regallo* of six hundred more from their club.

Robberies were extremely rife in this age, and the cool manner in which they were perpetrated, as well as the easy light in which they were regarded, cannot but astonish us. The newspaper press of the day furnishes us with some extraordinary histories of felons and felony.

'Friday, between five and six o'clock in the evening,' says one of these reports, 'as a gentleman was passing by the end of Fleet Bridge, near a china-shop, a fellow came up to him, and, seizing him by the collar and throat, forced him a few yards down towards Bridewell, whilst another took a white-silk purse out of his pocket containing twelve guineas, and attempted his watch, but, having a button-hole at the fob, the chain broke, and they were disappointed; they then threw him over the rails into a ditch, and made off. The gentleman received no manner of hurt, but, having fell on one side, that part was entirely covered with mud; and, as soon as he recovered from his surprise, he called out for help, which a man hearing, that was watering the horses at the coach-stand, went with proper assistance, and drew him up with a rope.'

Another paragraph tells that, at two o'clock in the morning, a person in woman's clothes, well-mounted upon a bay gelding, robbed a gentleman upon Barnes Common of his watch and almost eight pounds in money. This genteelly-attired robber had a servant in livery awaiting him, who, whilst his master filched the money, coolly took that opportunity of girting his saddle tighter.

When entertainments were advertised to take place at Vauxhall or Ranelagh, it was usually announced that 'twelve lusty fellows would patrol the way,' and afford a guard against the knights of the road. But it was not only the suburbs and roads, but the streets and squares likewise, which were beset by these vagabonds, who were wholly unawed by the sight of the pestilential corpses of those who had in life sinned likewise, and which now swung from the gibbets in the Edgware Road and other public places as a dreadful warning.

On one occasion, a gang of nine thieves were arrested, and after being examined by the Sitting Justices, at the 'Angel and Crown,' Whitechapel, were by order walked, hand-cuffed and fettered, through the city, and marched back in the same manner, in order that people who had lately been robbed might have a view of them, and discover if any of these had been the delinquents; most of them were under the age of eighteen.

When John Wilkes had his coach drawn by the mob through the streets, a number of people lost their purses, and some of them complained to the Lord Mayor.

'I suppose,' said his lordship, 'some of Mr. Wilkes' coach horses have picked your pockets.'

In 1773, a batch of those malefactors, whose conduct had been a scourge to all peaceable citizens, were captured, and when sentence had been passed on them, were marched from Newgate to the Docks, from whence they were to embark for the plantations; they were preceded by fifes and drums, playing the lively air, 'Through the wood, laddie,' in which they joined, shouting the song right merrily. 'You are a joyful lot,' said a respectable spectator. 'Joyful!' answered one of the black sheep; 'you only come with us, and you will find yourself *transported*.' They were a bad lot, no doubt, past praying for, as the Rev. Robert Temple discovered when he went to administer consolation to five of them who were about to be executed, but who savagely turned round and beat the good man soundly.

They cared indeed neither for the living nor the dead : one of the journals of the day complains that 'some irregularities' (mark the gentle expression) 'were committed on Saturday night last at Kensington, during the interment of the late Earl of Godolphin, by the crowd assembled on the occasion, some of whom tore the escutcheons off the hearse before the corpse was taken out, and one man took away an escutcheon from the side of the desk when the clergyman was reading the service.'

Here is the account of a droll robbery taken from the *Monthly Chronicle*:

'Tuesday night, about twelve o'clock, a young man, happening to listen to the pleadings of a good-natured nymph in the Strand, a fellow came up to him and demanded what he had to do with his wife, and throwing at the same time a paper of snuff into his eyes, ran off with his hat and wig; the woman slipped away long before he could recover the use of his sight, proving pretty clearly that it was a preconceived scheme.'

But thieving, like all other crimes, was not confined to the lower classes, and was, according to the press, occasionally practised by persons of quality. 'A woman of no inconsiderable consequence,' says the paper just quoted, ' was last Wednesday evening handed out of a very elegant company for mistaking a gold snuff-box, and supposing it to be her own property at the same time, though she knew it belonged to another lady in the company.'

Another gentle offender was 'on Wednesday turned out of a polite assembly at the west end of the town for making rather too free with a purse of guineas belonging to a lady who was his antagonist ;' whilst 'a genteel young gentleman was brought before Sir John Fielding on a suspicion of robbing his master of fifty pounds. He was just going off in a post-chaise with a well-known courtezan of Covent Garden.' A second genteel young fellow named James Sampson, ' dressed in blue and gold, with a servant to attend him,' was also brought before the same worthy justice on a charge of forgery.

Even at the Court, gentility was found appropriating its neighbour's goods ; for at one of the Queen's drawing-rooms held in 1777, Cumberland, who was present, narrates : 'Sir George Warren had his order snatched off his ribbon, encircled with diamonds to the value of £700. Foote was there, and lays it upon the parsons, having secured, as he says, his gold snuff-box in his waistcoat pocket upon seeing so many black-gowns in the room.'

CHAPTER X.

News of the King's Madness—Public Anxiety—The Prince's Conduct—What Captain Jack Payne wrote to Sheridan—Removal of His Majesty to Kew—Cruel Treatment of the King—A German Page—The Prince of Wales and Duke of York—Political Factions—The Plan of Regency—Dr. Willis and the King—Miss Burney pursued by His Majesty—What Willis said to the Chancellor—Recovery and Rejoicings — Thanksgiving at St. Paul's — The Bishop of Llandaff and the Queen—The Duke of York's Duel—The Queen smiles upon Colonel Lennox.

MEANWHILE, the news of the King's madness spread throughout the kingdom, and the consternation and excitement which followed were intense. Vague reports, not only of the violence and hopelessness of his malady, but of his death, were whispered daily, and added to the agitation which possessed all classes alike. The Stocks fell two per cent.; petitions for His Majesty's restoration were offered up by all religious sects, and in the Jewish synagogues, before the Privy Council had framed a form of prayer to be used in the Church of England; and men of all shades of political opinions hurried to town, anxious, and embarrassed that both Houses of Parliament stood prorogued to November 20, beyond which date no power existing in the State could postpone the meeting. Above all, a strong feeling pervaded the public mind that the King's death would bode no good to the country.

His Majesty's most bitter affliction seemed indeed to suddenly stir a sense of loyalty in the hearts of the people. Sir Lucas Pepys, one of the royal physicians, told Miss Burney that none of his colleagues' lives would be safe if the King did not recover, and that they all received threatening letters daily. Sir George Baker, another of the medical attendants, had his carriage stopped by the mob, who asked him how the King did, and, on his replying that his case was a bad one, they shouted out, 'The more shame for you.'

But, if there was gloom and consternation abroad, there was fear and depression under the royal roof. The Prince of Wales took possession of Windsor, when all order was banished from the household; and here he remained until the King's removal to Kew, believing he might at any moment be called upon to occupy the throne. The Queen, stunned and miserable, lived entirely in two apartments, interfering in no way, and seeing only her daughters and a few of the ladies of her household. She was already slighted as if her reign were a thing of the past, scarce consulted in any of the arrangements concerning the King, and humiliated to find herself ignored by the physicians; who, after leaving His Majesty, proceeded to make their reports to the Prince, whom they regarded as the rising sun, and with whom they hoped in this way to gain favour. Left almost friendless and hopeless, her sense of desolation and grief were extreme; her cry, as Miss Burney tells us, '" What will become of me? What will become of me?" uttered with the most piercing lamentation, struck deep and hard into all our hearts.'

The Duke of York, the King's second and favourite son, who had returned to England, and had been received with every demonstration of affection by the King a short time before his illness, now joined his brother in his control over the royal household, and became a partner in the disgraceful and unfeeling conduct of the heir to the Crown. In the presence of the Queen, they spoke of their father's malady in a brusque and heartless manner; and, at a time when the King's malady was sought to be kept secret, the Prince of Wales introduced his friend Lord Lothian into His Majesty's room when it was darkened, that he might hear his ravings at a time when they were at their worst; later on, he overhauled His Majesty's private cabinet, when he came upon some secret papers and a 'vast hoard' of jewels and money. When this latter fact became known to Her Majesty, she, as the Prince afterwards wrote in complaint to his father, 'condescended to a species and warmth of reproaches, into which nothing could have surprised or betrayed Her Majesty, but a degree of passion which I have never witnessed, nor believed to exist, in Her Majesty before.'

The Prince was attended at Windsor by his personal and disreputable friend and private secretary, Captain, or as he was more generally and familiarly termed, Jack Payne, who had recently been refused admittance into Brooks' Club. This worthy gentleman had as little delicacy in speaking of the King's affliction as if it were a subject for amusement, or, indeed, as the Prince himself; and, as he considered 'all secrecy with regard to His Majesty's situation any longer almost inadvisable,' wrote full details of its various stages to his friends, Richard Brinsley Sheridan and Lord Loughborough; moreover, these letters, in which he 'spoke his mind freely,' scarcely conceal a desire, not limited to the captain, for the King's demise.

To Lord Loughborough he writes that His Majesty's 'dissolution is almost the best that can be hoped;' and two days afterwards he says, 'From what I can understand from the *best* authority, the *last* stroke to this unhappy affair cannot be far off. It is what every person in a situation to see is obliged to wish, as the happiest possible termination to the present melancholy scene.' To Sheridan, who was to have been Prime Minister under the new King's reign, the captain says : 'The Duke of York, who is looking over me, and is just come out of the King's room, bids me add that His Majesty's situation is every moment becoming worse. His pulse is weaker and weaker; and the doctors say it is impossible to survive it long .. Since this letter was begun, all articulation even seems to be at an end.' In his next epistle to the same friend, he writes that the King woke at night from a profound sleep, 'with all the gestures and ravings of the most confirmed maniac, and a new noise in imitation of the howling of a dog . . . his theme has been all this day on the subject of religion, and of his being inspired;' and again he speaks of an effort the King made to fling himself from a window.

But days passed, and though His Majesty in no way gave signs of recovering his reason, his physical health improved. It was then deemed advisable that he should be removed to Kew, which would be more convenient to the physicians, as being nearer London, and they declared it likewise best for their patient, on account of the garden, as in Windsor there was none but what was public to the spectators from the terrace or tops of the houses.

The Queen's knowledge of the King's strong aversion to Kew made her consent to the change with great reluctance; the Prince, however, was in favour of his removal, and the physicians gave it as their unanimous opinion that such a step was now not only advisable, but necessary; accordingly, a Privy Council was held at Windsor with the Prince of Wales, when the Chancellor, Mr. Pitt, and all the officers of State, were summoned to sign permission for His Majesty's removal. The only difficulty remaining was that of removing him quietly from his favourite Windsor. If they attempted force, Sir Lucas Pepys said, they had not a doubt but his smallest resistance would call up the whole country to his fancied rescue; yet how at such a time prevail by persuasion? The date fixed for his departure was November 29, a day of unusual depression to the Queen and her household; her mind, she said, 'quite misgave her about Kew; the King's dislike was terrible to think of, and she could not foresee in what it might end. She would have resisted the measure herself, but that she had determined not to have upon her own mind any opposition to the opinion of the physicians.'

It was settled between the Prince and the doctors that the Queen, with the Princesses, should quietly depart for Kew, when the King should be informed they had left, and permitted to go through their rooms to assure himself of the fact; he was then to be allured to Kew on the promise of seeing them. On the morning of the 29th, the royal household was in a state of confusion, packing and preparing for the removal; physicians and pages whispering and plotting, the Prince anxious, the Princesses weeping, with a chill foreboding at heart of impending misery. About ten o'clock the Queen departed; 'drowned in tears, she glided along the passage, and got softly into her carriage, with two weeping Princesses and Lady Courtown. Then followed the third Princess, with Lady Charlotte Finch. They went off without any state or parade, and in a more melancholy condition than can be imagined. There was not a dry eye in the house. The footmen, the housemaids, the porter, the sentinels—all cried, even bitterly, as they looked on.'

The Prince had, some days previously, driven to Kew, in order to make arrangements there according to his desires for the reception of the King, Queen, and Princesses. Accordingly, when Her Majesty arrived, she found the names of those who were to occupy the various apartments written on the doors in chalk; the house was in a miserable condition; no fires were lighted, the rooms needed washing; the wind blew through the ill-fitting windows and doors of the palace, which had never been intended for a winter residence; there were no carpets in the Princesses' apartments, and everywhere, on this bleak November day, an air of chill discomfort pervaded.

Towards evening, the King with great difficulty was persuaded to quit Windsor; he was accompanied by only three of his gentlemen, but almost all the inhabitants of the town gathered round the railings to see him enter his carriage, many of whom believed they would never set eyes on him again. On passing through the gates of the park, he covered his face with his hands, and cried; but, recovering presently, he spoke of the pleasure he would have in meeting his wife and daughters, a satisfaction cruelly denied him. The Right Hon. William Massey, who derived the private information furnished in his 'History of England during the reign of George III.' from the diary of Lady Elizabeth Harcourt— Lady of the Bedchamber to the Queen, and sister-in-law to General Harcourt, one of the King's favourite equerries— states that when His Majesty arrived at the palace, he found himself a prisoner.

'Proceeding,' the historian writes, 'towards the apartments he usually occupied, he was stopped, and conducted into a large room, where he found the pages who were to be his keepers waiting to receive him. The equerries, among whom was his faithful and valued servant, General Harcourt, according to the orders they had received, withdrew. The physician also, who had accompanied the royal patient from Windsor, having consigned him to the charge of the pages, also thought proper to retire, and actually returned to London the same night. The King then impatiently demanded to see his family; and the promise under which he had been induced to leave his palace of Windsor was, in cruel mockery, fulfilled. The Princesses were brought before the window; the King, on seeing them, rushed forward to lift the sash, but it was screwed down. A paroxysm was the immediate consequence of this cruel restraint; the Princesses were hastily removed, and the King was dragged from the window, entreating to be allowed to speak to his children.'

Next morning, Miss Burney says she—by the desire of Her Majesty, who had passed a wretched night—went through the cold, dark passages to procure speech of one of the pages, when she learned 'the night had been the most violently bad of any yet passed—and no wonder.'

In the seclusion of Kew Palace, the King's physicians, little understanding his malady and its treatment, no longer dealt with him as if he were a human being; cruelty was indeed considered by the eminent medical faculty of the day the shortest method of restoring reason to the unfortunate victims they undertook to cure of insanity, and such was not spared the King. From Massey's excellent history we learn that the King's body was enclosed in a machine which left him no liberty of action; he was sometimes chained to a staple, frequently beaten and starved, and kept in subjection by menacing and violent language. All this was persisted in, though he was seldom violent, unless when provoked. His malady betrayed itself chiefly in ravings, that sometimes continued uninterruptedly for a whole day, and, in one instance, for nineteen hours without intermission. His wife and daughters were not permitted to see him, and he was now chiefly entrusted to a German page named Ernst, whom royal patronage had lifted from an obscure position. This creature used to strike the helpless maniac, and on one occasion, when he wished to prolong his walk in the garden, Ernst seized him in his arms, carried him into his apartments, and, throwing him violently on a sofa, exclaimed to the attendants, 'There is your King for you.' This incident was remembered by His Majesty after his recovery, and was repeated by him to Lady Harcourt. It made such an impression on him that he also mentioned it to Miss Burney.

'He gave me,' she writes, 'a history of his pages, animating almost into a rage as he related his subjects of displeasure with them, particularly with Mr. Ernst, who, he told me, had been brought up by himself.'

The Prince of Wales and the Duke of York were now seldom seen at Kew, but occupied themselves with schemes for the future, when the former should be proclaimed either King or Regent. His faction was headed by Richard Brinsley Sheridan, in the absence of Charles Fox, who was, at the period when the King's illness was first discovered, travelling through France and Italy with Mrs. Armstead; the Prince had despatched a courier for him, his advice and assistance being sorely needed at this crisis by his friends, who looked for his coming 'as the Jews look out for their Messiah.' The whole town was divided into factions that raged with great vigour; the general voice being in favour of the King and Pitt, against the Prince, whose reign they dreaded, and his dissipated followers. These latter, urged on by the royal example, sought every means of ridiculing the King and turning his affliction to heartless merriment.

Massey gives it as an authentic fact that 'the Prince of Wales, who had a talent for mimicry, and indeed possessed the social qualities suited to the witty and profligate men and women with whom he lived, was in the habit of amusing his companions by *taking off*, as the phrase was, the gestures and actions of his insane father. That which he did himself, he suffered his friends to do; and the standing topic in the Prince's circle was ridicule of the King and Queen. The Duke of York vied with his brother in defamation of his parents; but he was wholly destitute of the lively talent which sometimes carries off the grosser parts of the most ribald discourse; and the brutality of the stupid sot disgusted even the most profligate of his associates.'

Captain Jack Payne must, of course, follow the royal example, and, according to Lady Harcourt, when he had 'one day uttered some ribaldry about the Queen in the presence of the Duchess of Gordon, "You little, insignificant, good-for-nothing, upstart, pert, chattering puppy," said her Grace, "how dare you name your royal master's royal mother in that style?"' a hearty rebuke by which the gallant man scarcely profited, as may be judged from a letter, preserved in the Auckland Correspondence, from Miss Sayer, whose information was derived from the said Duchess of Gordon, a staunch supporter of the King and Pitt.

'A few days ago,' says Miss Sayer, 'Mrs. Richard Walpole gave a supper to the two Princes, Mrs. Fitzherbert, Colonel Fullarton, Jack Payne—who is such a favourite he is to be a Lord of the Admiralty, and leans on the Prince as he walks, not the Prince on him—Miss Vanneck and a few others. The Duchess of Gordon the only Pittite. The Prince says, "What a fine fellow my brother York is! He never forsakes me. The other day, when we went to look for the King's money, jewels, etc., at Kew, as we opened the drawers, my mother looked very uneasy and grew angry. Says York to her, "Madame, I believe you are as much deranged as the King." Then says Jack Payne, after a great many invectives against Mr. Pitt, calling him William the Fourth, William the Conqueror, etc., "Mr. Pitt's chastity will protect the Queen," which was received by all present as a very good thing. The Duchess of Gordon—for which you will like her, though a Scotchwoman—declared, if they began to abuse the Queen, she would leave the room.'

But at Brooks' Club indecent abuse of the King, Queen, and Pitt was indulged in without reserve; and a cant phrase used at the whist-table was, 'I play the lunatic' (the King).

The contest between the two political factions increased daily. The ladies who espoused the Prince's cause wore Regency caps, badges, and ribbons emblematic of their party; whilst their more loyal sisters refused to attend their private entertainments or visit them.

Parliament assembled on November 20, but was again adjourned till December 4, in consequence of the King's condition; when it met on that date, both parties agreed to appoint a select committee to examine the King's physicians regarding the probable time which his madness might last. Six days later, the reports of the committee which declared His Majesty to be incapable of meeting Parliament, or transacting any business, were laid upon the table of the House of Commons, when Pitt brought in a 'plan of Regency,' according to which the management of the King, and of the royal household and all appointments concerning it, should be vested in the Queen; the royal authority being exercised by the Prince of Wales under certain restrictions. These were that the Prince was not to dispose of the King's real or personal property, nor grant any pensions, nor any office in reversion, nor create any peers. Such restrictions were exactly those which the Prince and his friends dreaded, and which they were now determined to oppose by might and main. Accordingly, Charles Fox rose to his feet, and, in an excited speech, declared the Prince of Wales had 'as clear a right to assume the reins of Government, and fully exercise the powers of sovereignty, as if His Majesty had undergone a perfect and natural demise.'

Pitt listened, with a smile of satisfaction, to these bold expressions, which, he felt convinced, were far more damning to the Prince's party than any argument of which he could make use; leaning across to the Treasury bench, he whispered to a friend, 'I'll un-whig that gentleman for the rest of his life.' No sooner had Fox sat down, than his opponent rose. The doctrine, he said, they had just listened to was little less than treason to the Constitution. He 'met the claim of right preferred on behalf of the heir-apparent with a positive contradiction, and denied that, under the circumstances, the Prince of Wales had any more right to assume the Government than any other person in the kingdom. It was the province of Parliament, and of Parliament alone, to make provision for the government of the country, whenever any interruption of the royal authority took place.'

Whilst the Regency Bill was before Parliament, the Prince lost no time in seeking friends to support his cause, an effort in which he was of course seconded by his brother; the latter held a meeting in his own house, to confer with the Opposition, as the Prince's political followers were styled, and made a speech, remarkable for neither eloquence nor intelligibleness, in favour of granting full powers to the Regent. Indeed, the Prince now caused the report to be spread that he would not accept the Regency under any restrictions; furthermore, both he and his friends declared the King's madness was hopelessly incurable.

The conduct of the royal brothers now became, if possible, more reckless and dissipated than before; hopeful of the success of their plans, they enjoyed themselves without restraint; dined publicly with their friends, and were seen at night continually at Brooks', where they gambled and got drunk.

'The behaviour of the two Princes,' Mr. Granville writes to the Marquis of Buckingham, 'is such as to shock every man's feelings .... If we were together, I could tell you some particulars of the Prince of Wales's behaviour towards the King and Queen within these few days that would make your blood run cold.'

Lord Bulkeley adds his testimony.

'The Princes,' he says, 'go on in their usual style, both keeping open houses, and employing every means in their power to gain proselytes; attending the Beefsteak Club, Freemason's meetings, etc. .... The Duke of York never misses a night at Brooks', where the hawks pluck his feathers unmercifully, and have reduced him to the vowels I O U.'

It may be mentioned here that, eighteen months after the

Duke's return from Germany, he was indebted to his creditors for the sum of £60,000.

So assured was the Prince that his hour of triumph was at hand, that he already named some of his Ministers of State; the Duke of York was to be appointed Commander-in-Chief; Sheridan, Treasurer of the Navy; Fox, one of the Secretaries of State; Earl Spencer, Lord-Lieutenant of Ireland; Jack Payne was to be made an admiral at once; and my Lord Loughborough, Lord Chancellor. Concerning this latter appointment, an amusing incident occurred, which is given in the Auckland Correspondence, on the authority of the Archbishop of Canterbury.

'On Friday night an odd thing happened,' writes his Grace, 'at a great assembly and ball at Devonshire House, given for all the world. When it was very full, the doors flew open, and "Lord Chancellor" was announced; when lo! Lord Loughborough walked in. The servant probably considered him, and had been used to call him so, three weeks ago.'

The Prince not only intended awarding his followers high offices of State, but his liberality went further, and he selected three of them as the future husbands of the three marriageable Princesses; however, this intended generosity on his part was principally contemplated by way of countenancing his own union with a subject.

The party spirit which divided the town was not long in reaching the royal physicians. A short time after the King's removal to Kew, a fresh medical adviser, in the person of the Rev. Francis Willis, was added to their staff, which was yet further increased a little later on by the addition of his son, Dr. John Willis. The elder was a Lincolnshire clergyman, who had for some years made madness his special study, and who kept a private asylum, where he had given practical proofs of the success of his treatment. Dr. Willis was an honest, simple-minded man, who, happily for his patient, understood more about his case than those who had been, and yet remained, in attendance on him. From their harsh treatment of him, the King regarded them all with an abhorrence which he was ready to extend to his new attendant. When Willis was introduced to him, His Majesty looked at him quietly, and then asked why he had given up his sacred calling for a profession which brought him more worldly profit.

'Sir,' answered Willis, 'our Saviour went about healing the sick.'

'Yes,' said the King sagely, 'but He did not get seven hundred a year for it.'

His Majesty, however, soon perceived that this new doctor was of a different type from his colleagues; his mild, firm, and humane treatment worked a beneficial effect on his patient, over whom he quickly gained a strong influence. Even at his second interview the King opened his mind to him, complained of the insolence to which he was subjected by the pages; of not being permitted to see his wife or daughters, of not being allowed the use of a knife, or fork, or razor, fearing he might cut his throat, at which he was most indignant. Dr. Willis soothed him, and promised him all that he required.

'Your Majesty is too good a Christian, and has too much sense of what you owe your people, to commit such an act,' he said, handing him a razor, with which the King quietly shaved himself. He likewise allowed him the use of a knife and fork at table, adding that, with His Majesty's leave, he would have the pleasure of dining with him. Once, when he was walking in the garden, he looked up wistfully at the windows of the apartments occupied by the Princesses; but, seeing no friendly face there, the poor prisoner complained very heavily that his daughters would not show themselves to him. 'In consequence,' Dr. Willis said, in his examination before the Commons' Committee, 'the next day I did desire that they should appear, and myself stood at the window with two of the Princesses when His Majesty was coming by; and His Majesty showed extravagant joy at the sight of them, though he said his eyes did not suffer him to see the Princess Amelia as well as he could wish.'

But yet the greatest privilege granted him was permission to see the Queen, and their meeting was most affecting. He held her hand during the half-hour's interview allowed him, kissed it repeatedly, and took the young Princess Amelia on his knee; to add to his kindness, Dr. Willis had the German page, Ernst, dismissed.

The improvement which the King made under the care of the Willises was by no means agreeable to the other physicians, headed by Dr. Warren, who from the first asserted that His Majesty was a confirmed lunatic; and, having once committed himself to such an opinion, he stoutly maintained it, even to within a few days of the King's perfect restoration, on which occasion he, in the presence of the Prince, quarrelled with Sir Lucas Pepys for expressing a doubt regarding the infallibility of his decision.

On the other hand, Dr. Willis held it that the royal patient's recovery was but a question of time; he even went further, and boldly asserted that, had the King been in a private station, a few weeks would have sufficed to restore his intellect. Dr. Willis was, therefore, looked up to, and lauded by those who ardently hoped for the King's recovery; whilst Dr. Warren, whose words had greatly influenced the conduct of the Princes and their friends, was believed in and relied on by them. As may be supposed, Warren was continually finding fault with Willis's treatment of the King, and, during one of the inquiries as to His Majesty's health by the Commons' Committee, the former complained that he had one day found His Majesty reading 'King Lear,' and, when he had asked who it was that gave it to him, the King had stated it was Dr. Willis. This Willis denied, not that he was really guilty of falsehood, but because the shrewdness of his patient deceived him.

His Majesty had urgently requested Willis to let him read this play, in which he fancied he saw a parallel between the sad old king and himself; but this the doctor, though indulgent in many ways, at once refused. The King pressed him no further, but, after a while, begged that he might be allowed a copy of Coleman's works, in which he was aware 'King Lear,' as altered and 'corrected'! by Coleman, was included. Dr. Willis was ignorant of this, and granted the request.

When, some time after, the King's daughters came to visit him, he spoke much to them of ' King Lear.'

'The play is very beautiful, very affecting, very awful,' he said sadly. 'I am like poor Lear,' he added; 'but, thank God, I have no Regan, no Goneril, but three Cordelias.'

Meanwhile, the Regency Bill was before Parliament. The second examination of the doctors took place in January; Warren declared, if there was any change in the King, it was for the worse; Willis expressed himself of a contrary opinion, and was severely cross-examined by the Prince's friends who sat on the Committee, and occasionally censured him. It was even insinuated that he was acting in collusion with the Queen, in order to misrepresent His Majesty's condition, and so defeat the Prince's claims. The Bill, however, passed the Commons, and was carried to the Lords on February 12.

The Opposition, having exhausted their efforts to gain better terms for the Regent, were now anxious the Bill should pass as quickly as possible, in order that they might come into power without further delay. But, before it could receive the sanction of the Lords, a sudden and favourable change was reported in the King, and Willis announced his patient convalescent.

When Willis pronounced him cured, Warren jealously refused to agree with him, and the other doctors maintained a cautious reserve. Willis, therefore, boldly came forward, and declared to the Lord Chancellor that the King's state was such that the Regency Bill ought not to be proceeded with. Thurlow informed him he did not believe it; when Willis said he would publish the King's restoration, and threatened the Lord Chancellor with impeachment if he dared to act on the assumption of His Majesty's incapacity. The result of this was, the Chancellor had an interview with His Majesty, lasting two hours, which satisfied him that Willis was right, and the Bill was therefore abandoned. On February 23, 1789, the King wrote to Pitt announcing his recovery; and three days later the last bulletin was issued declaring 'the entire cessation of His Majesty's illness,' and was signed by Dr. Willis, Sir George Barker, and Sir Lucas Pepys.

This sudden convalescence gave a turn to political affairs which neither the Prince nor his supporters expected, and great was their discomfort thereat; at first they refused to believe it, but when it could be no longer denied, they were plunged into deep confusion. Edmund Burke, one of His Royal Highness's most enthusiastic supporters, became almost mad from disappointment; Charles Fox, who had been ailing for some time, grew seriously ill; and the Princes, according to Lord Bulkeley, were 'quite desperate, and endeavoured to drown their cares, disappointments, and internal chagrin in wine and dissipation.' The Duke of York, he adds, 'plays much at tennis, and has a score with all the blacklegs; and in the public court tells them they shall be paid as soon as his father can settle with him some Osnaburgh money which he owes him.'

When the King's recovery was fully established, the Princes became anxious to see him, in order that they might, if possible, disabuse his mind of all prejudice which their conduct was calculated to cause; accordingly, they intimated a desire to visit their father, who agreed to receive them, and, as he wrote to Pitt after the interview, 'chose the meeting should be in the Queen's apartments, that all parties might have that caution which at the present hour could but be judicious.' The hour appointed by the King for their meeting was one o'clock, but their Royal Highnesses, having been rioting and drunk at a masquerade the previous night, did not arrive at Kew before half-past two. The King embraced them both, and shed tears; the visit lasted but half an hour, and care was taken, as the King said, 'that the conversation should be general and cordial. They seemed satisfied,' he added.

Lord Bulkeley writes, 'Lord Winchelsea, who was at Kew the whole time, told me that, when they came out, they told Colonel Digby that they were delighted with the King's being so well, and remarked that two things in the half-hour's conference which they had with him had struck them very forcibly; that he had observed to them how much better he played at piquet than Mr. Charles Hawkins, and that, since he had been ill, he had rubbed up all his Latin; and these facts, which are facts, I expect to hear magnified by the Carlton House runners into instances of insanity.'

The day after the Princes' visit, Mr. Grenville writes to Lord Buckingham: 'The two Princes were at Kew yesterday, and saw the King in the Queen's apartments. She was present the whole time, a precaution for which, God knows, there was too much reason. They kept him waiting a considerable time before they arrived; and, after they left him, drove immediately to Mrs. Armstead's, in Park Street, in hopes of finding Fox there, to give him an account of what had passed. He not being in town, they amused themselves yesterday evening with spreading about a report that the King was still out of his mind, and in quoting phrases of his, to which they gave that turn. It is certainly a decent and becoming thing that, when all the King's physicians, all his attendants, and his two principal Ministers agree in pronouncing him well, his two sons should deny it. And the reflection that the Prince of Wales was to have had the government, and the Duke of York the command of the army during his illness, makes the representation of his actual state, when coming from them, more peculiarly proper and edifying. I bless God that it is yet some time before these matured and ripened virtues will be visited upon us in the form of a government.'

The Prince's friends, as usual, took their cue from him; when the King's name was mentioned, they shook their heads, admitted with some hesitation His Majesty was better, but were generally inclined to assert, with Lord Rawdon, that, though the King was tranquil on ordinary subjects, 'there were certain strings which will, whenever they are touched, produce false music again.'

On March 9, the royal physicians left Kew, and on the evening of the following day, there was a general illumination on a magnificent scale of the streets, squares, and suburbs of London. Signs of the people's joy and satisfaction at the King's recovery, or more strictly speaking, at being delivered from the reign of the Regent, were universal. The whole city was one blaze of light from end to end, literally extending from Hampstead and Highgate to Clapham, from Greenwich to Kensington; there was no house that did not bear some decoration, no window that was not lighted; even the cobblers' stalls in the streets exhibited rows of farthing candles. The thoroughfares were thronged with crowds; in the midst of which the Queen and her daughters drove, gratified by the scenes that everywhere met their gaze.

On this night, the Prince and Duke of York, having dined heartily, were on their way to the opera in His Royal Highness's carriage, which, in some of the narrow streets, got blocked up amongst other coaches. The mob, soon recognising the Princes, called out, 'God save the King;' when the Prince let down the glass of his coach, and joined in the cry. Then one sturdy fellow asked him to call out, 'Pitt for ever! God bless Pitt!' which the Prince refused, but shouted out, 'Fox for ever! God bless Fox!' The mob, incensed at this, insisted on him crying, 'Pitt for ever!' but the Prince angrily said, 'Damn Pitt. Fox for ever!' This was too much for the crowd, then in a state of great excitement. One man sought to pull the coach-door open, on which the Prince, now much frightened, endeavoured to jump out and escape, but the Duke of York held him back, hit the man a blow on the head, and called to the coachman to drive on, which he was now enabled to do at a great pace, the door of the carriage flapping about as they went.

When the opera was over, the Prince, who had met some of his friends, and was in excellent spirits, declared he would walk through the crowd to Carlton House; and when he arrived there, he insisted on walking through the streets to see the illuminations. After some time, his friends first persuaded him to call at Brooks', when they pushed their way, in a right merry fashion, through Pall Mall. At St. James's, he fell in with a gang of butchers, with marrowbones and cleavers, who began to play before him, and clear the way for him, shouting and performing all the way up St. James's Street, and giving him three cheers when he reached his destination, in return for which civility he gave them ten guineas. He then tarried some time at the club, from where he was persuaded by his friends to drive home; a piece of advice with which he was obliged to comply.

A few days after this general rejoicing, the King and his family returned to Windsor, and he then announced his intention of celebrating his recovery by a public thanksgiving. Many of his friends sought to dissuade him from this design, fearing the excitement might produce an ill effect on his mind; amongst whom was his Grace of Canterbury.

'My Lord Archbishop,' answered the King, 'I have thrice read over the evidence of the physicians on my case, and, if I can stand that, I can stand anything.'

The ceremony was therefore fixed for April 23, on which day the King, accompanied by the Queen and Princesses, his brothers, the Dukes of Cumberland and Gloucester, and his sons, the Prince of Wales, Duke of York, and Prince William, and attended by the Lords and Commons, and great officers of the State, went to St. Paul's. The procession set out at eight o'clock in the morning, headed by the Members of the House of Commons in their coaches, who were followed by the Masters of Chancery, judges, and peers, such of the latter as were knights wearing the collars of their respective orders; finally, came the royal family, attended by the Horse Guards, the King's coach being drawn by eight cream-coloured horses. The streets through which the stately procession passed were lined by the Foot Guards as far as Temple Bar, and by the Artillery Company and City Militia from thence to St. Paul's. Dense and anxious crowds pressed forward to see and greet the King; balconies were erected along the way, and decorated with coloured cloths; the church-steeples were hung with flags and streamers; bells rang incessantly, and cannon thundered from the Tower and St. James's.

At Temple Bar the King was met by the Lord Mayor in a crimson velvet gown, accompanied by the Sheriffs in scarlet gowns, and by a deputation from the Aldermen and Common Council, being all on horseback; the Lord Mayor surrendered the City sword to His Majesty, who returned it to his good keeping, when his Lordship carried it bareheaded before his Sovereign to St. Paul's. The King looked tranquil and well, though somewhat thinner than before his illness, and was much affected by the demonstration of joy which greeted him. He was dressed in the Windsor uniform, the Queen and Princesses being arrayed in blue silks trimmed with white, and bandeaux inscribed, 'God save the King.'

As the procession moved slowly through Pall Mall, His Majesty was received with but slight applause, but the Prince of Wales, who had stationed his partisans there for the purpose, was loudly cheered, as he was likewise in parts of the Strand, where he had also posted his friends and dependents; but from Cockspur Street to St. Paul's the huzzas which met the King were hearty and continual, which caused His Royal Highness to lose his temper completely, and he never recovered it afterwards, 'for at St. Paul's,' says Lord Bulkeley, 'he was in the worst humour possible, and did everything he could to expose himself in the face of an amazing concourse of persons, and of all the foreign ministers.'

Arrived at the great cathedral, the King was met at the west door by the Bishops of London and Lincoln, between whom he walked, preceded by the Marquis of Stafford carrying the sword of state. Scarcely had he entered when the pure fresh voices of five thousand children burst in a loud thanksgiving chorus on his ears; for a moment the King's feelings were stirred to their depths, he covered his face with his hands and silently wept. He, however, soon recovered himself. 'Now,' he whispered to the Bishop of Lincoln, 'I feel that I have been ill.' He took his seat by the Queen under a canopy of state near the west end, opposite the altar. There, in the presence of the peers and peeresses of the realm, the foreign ministers, officers of state, and Members of the House of Commons, he returned humble thanksgiving for his recovery; but during these solemn moments, when the Queen and Princesses and many present could not restrain their tears, the Prince of Wales his brothers, and his uncles, in the face of that vast concourse, 'talked to each other the whole time of the service,' as Lord Bulkeley writes, 'and behaved in such an indecent manner that was quite shocking.' Nor was this all. When the service was concluded, the Prince, without waiting for the King, rushed to his carriage, and, attended by a number of the mob, drove off, leaving the remainder of the procession to accompany His Majesty.

The town now became for a while the scene of vast gaiety: crowds thronged to St. James's to offer their congratulations to the King, and amongst others came some of the followers of the Prince of Wales. One of the King's friends, looking one day at a group of these in the royal drawing-room, said quietly:

'*Tempora mutantur et nos mutamur in illis.*'

'Yes,' said a friend, who overheard him, ' *the King's recovered, thanks to Doctor Willis.*'

The Queen gave a magnificent ball, which was succeeded by superb entertainments by the Spanish and French ambassadors. At that given by the latter, Her Majesty, the Princesses, the Prince of Wales and his two brothers were present, but these gentlemen would 'neither dance nor stay to supper, lest they should have the appearance of paying the smallest attention to Her Majesty.' White's Club, frequented by Pitt and his supporters, was not behindhand in doing honour to the occasion, and resolved to give a fête at the Pantheon to celebrate the double event of the King's birthday and recovery. The Queen and Princesses signified their intention of being present, and the entertainment was to be given on a scale of great splendour; in order to render it as select as possible, the price of the tickets was fixed at three guineas and a half each. The ladies who were to attend determined to show their loyalty, and resolved to dress all in white, and wear on the fronts of their headdresses the motto, 'God save the King,' in letters of gold.

Whilst all these preparations were being made, the Prince

used every exertion to keep his friends away from the fête, and sent round to canvass the non-attendance of everyone of his party; when tickets were forwarded to him and the Duke of York, they accepted them, but sent them immediately to Hookham's Library in Bond Street, to be sold to anyone who would buy them. The club committee, hearing of this indignity, adopted a regulation that every member who presented tickets should sign them, in order to keep the company amongst which the Queen and her daughters were to mix select; but, their Royal Highnesses hearing of this, the Duke of York instantly sent for the tickets, and wrote his name on the backs of them when they were sold. On the same night that this fête in honour of his father was held, the officers of the Guards got up a ball expressly for this gracious youth, the female guests at which were noted courtesans.

The conduct of both the Princes, indeed, sorely grieved their parents, to whom, under the mask of attention, they showed every possible insult. The behaviour of the Prince of Wales did not surprise his father, who had ample proof of it before his illness; but that his favourite son, the Duke of York, should follow so closely in his brother's infamous ways was a bitter pang. 'It kills me—it goes to my soul; I know not how to bear it,' was His Majesty's expression when speaking of the Duke's open contempt for him. The Queen publicly resented their insults, as might be expected, and looked coldly on those who had sided with them during the King's madness. Amongst such was included Dr. Watson, Bishop of Llandaff. When this Right Reverend Father in God believed the King's recovery was impossible, he stood up in the House of Lords and delivered himself of a learned speech, declaring the full powers of His Majesty should be vested without restraint in the disreputable Regent.

It may be mentioned that at the time the holy man was inspired with these sentiments, the snug See of St. Asaph had just become vacant; which would be in the Prince's power to bestow when he came into full authority. Not in the least ashamed of his late action, so objectionable to Her Majesty, the Bishop made his episcopal appearance at an early drawing-room after the recovery, to offer her his congratulations. He had, indeed, in the meantime, in conjunction with his clergy, presented addresses to their Majesties, expressive of his gratitude to God for the restoration to health which had been so mercifully vouchsafed to his gracious Sovereign, and of his admiration for Her Majesty's 'amiableness and purity as a Queen, as a wife, and as a mother.'

So much eloquence had not, however, the effect of soothing the royal lady's wrath, and she received the holy man, as he tells us, 'with a degree of coldness which would have appeared to herself ridiculous and ill-placed, could she have imagined how little a mind such as mine regarded, in its honourable proceedings, the displeasure of a woman, though that woman happened to be a Queen.'

The Prince of Wales was standing by on this occasion, and knowing Her Majesty's reasons for slighting the Bishop, went forward, spoke to him in a manner more than usually friendly, and invited him to dinner. But his Grace, though flattered by such extreme courtesy, hesitated before consenting to step within the threshold of such a disreputable mansion as Carlton House; when His Royal Highness turned to Sir Thomas Dundas and desired him to give a dinner at his residence, which the good Bishop duly attended, and where he had the pleasure of meeting His Royal Highness of York, and several of his boon companions, and of being spoken of by the Prince as a man whose talents should never be lost to the public. 'And mind who it is that tells you so,' said His Highness, in the excess of his after-dinner friendship and condescension.

But this was by no means the only slight which Her

Majesty administered to those who had supported the Opposition; none such were invited to her parties at Buckingham House, a discourtesy which on one occasion at least was extended to her sons, to whom she wrote that they would be welcome to her concert, but that the entertainment to follow was intended for those who had supported the King on a late occasion. The Princes in return abused their gracious mother in round terms, and, according to Lady Harcourt's diary, slandered the Princesses in a manner too gross to be repeated in these pages. The ill-feeling between the royal mother and her sons was strengthened on the occasion of the duel fought between the Duke of York and Colonel Lennox of the Coldstream Guards, nephew and successor of Charles, Duke of Richmond.

The royal Duke had, at a public masquerade, said that 'language had been used at D'Aubigny's Club towards Colonel Lennox to which no gentleman ought to submit.' This imputation of cowardice was 'made to a masque,' upon the supposition that it covered the person of Colonel Lennox. Next day, May 15, being a field-day of the Coldstream Guards, Colonel Lennox stepped up to the Duke, and asked him for an explanation of his words. In answer, His Royal Highness, who was his superior officer, briefly ordered him to return to his post. After parade, he summoned Colonel Lennox, and, in the orderly-room, before the officers, asked him to state his complaint; upon this the Colonel demanded an explanation, which the Duke refused. Colonel Lennox then wrote to every member of the club, desiring each of them to let him know if he could recollect any expression to have been used in his presence which could bear the construction put upon it by the Duke. No member remembering to have heard such, Colonel Lennox once more demanded either an explanation or satisfaction. His Royal Highness being unable to give the former, was—

unless he wished to brand himself as a coward—compelled to give the latter.

A duel was therefore arranged to take place on Wimbledon Common. Lord Rawdon, the Prince of Wales's friend, acted as the Duke's second, and the Earl of Winchelsea, one of the Lords of the King's Bedchamber, attended Colonel Lennox. The Duke did not discharge his pistol, but a ball from his adversary's grazed a curl at the side of his royal head. After this narrow escape, Lord Winchelsea strove to induce the Duke to give Colonel Lennox an explanation of his words; but this he doggedly refused, and even declined to repeat the usual phrase, that he believed his antagonist to be a man of honour and courage. He had not fired, he said, nor was it his intention to fire; but the Colonel might repeat his fire, if he chose. This was, of course, out of the question. They therefore left the common, and this duel, which ended in this unsatisfactory manner, had the effect of lowering the Royal Duke in the eyes of his friends and the people generally.

When the duel was over, the gallant Duke returned to Carlton House, where he found the Prince walking about the yard in great agitation, impatiently waiting news of the result. 'It is all over,' the Duke said, coming up to him coolly, 'and all is quite well; but I have not time to tell you the particulars, for I must go to the tennis-court.' The Prince expressed his desire that the tennis-court might go to regions uncomfortably warm, and wished to hear the full details. When he received these, he set off for Kew, where the King was, and sent up a message to say he wished to see His Majesty alone. 'Very well, very well,' said the monarch; 'but I want just to go up to the Queen first.'

When he received the Prince, not only Her Majesty, but the Princesses, were present. The Prince said he had something particular to say, and begged that the Princesses might retire. He then fully related the occurrence which had led to the duel, and turning to the Queen, said, 'Madame, you know I acquainted you with these circumstances a week ago ;' which he had, in order that the duel might be stopped by authority. The King said, 'Ah, indeed! I never heard a word of it before.' When he described the Duke's escape, she calmly, and without the slightest discomposure, looked out of the window.

The affair soon got spoken of, and caused much sensation in town ; but neither Colonel Lennox nor his second received any censure from the Court. Lord Winchelsea was continued in his place as Lord of the Bedchamber, and Colonel Lennox was received by the Queen next day 'with every mark of graciousness and favour.' To further indicate her approbation of his conduct, she invited him, soon after the duel, to a Court ball, where she publicly showed him marked attention, and 'kissed her fan to him two or three times, though half the length of the room lay between them.' This had the effect on the Princes which was desired ; so indignant did the Prince of Wales become, that he made it a subject of complaint to the King.

'Your Majesty is my witness,' he wrote, 'that during the whole relation the Queen did not utter a syllable either of alarm at the imminent danger which had threatened the life of my brother but an hour before, of joy and satisfaction at his safety, or of general tenderness and affection towards him, which might appear natural in moments thus afflicting. Nor were these the only testimonies of indifference that I was obliged to observe. For your Majesty must well remember that the first word the Queen pronounced, and the whole tenor of the only conversation she afterwards held, was a defence of Mr. Lennox's conduct, strongly implying a censure on that of my brother.'

CHAPTER XI.

The Royal Princes—The Duke of Clarence—Mrs. Jordan at Richmond—The Wicked Duke of Queensberry—Colonel FitzClarence and the Lieutenant—The Duke of York and his Duchess—Trial before the House of Commons—The Duchess of York and her Dogs—The Duke of Sussex and Lady Augusta Murray—The Duke of Cumberland—The Sellis Scandal—The Duke and Lady Graves—The Duke's Marriage—The Queen and the New Duchess.

WITHIN the next few years, some of the Royal Princes came into prominent notice. Amongst them was the King's third son, William, created Duke of Clarence in 1789, who afterwards came to the throne as William IV. When he had finished his education in Germany, he had been sent into the navy, and made commander of the *Pegase;* but during his father's illness, believing that he would be soon rid of all further governance, he suddenly returned to town.

Shortly after his creation as Duke of Clarence he resided at Richmond, not far from Walpole, who describes the residence as 'a house in the middle of a village with nothing but a green short apron to the river, a situation only fit for an old gentlewoman who has put out her knee-pans and loves cards.' Here he entertained a gay and gallant company, amongst whom were the Prince of Wales and Duke of York, Captain Jack Payne, the millionnaire Duke of Queensberry, and Mrs. Jordan. This lady, afterwards famous as the mistress of the Duke of Clarence, was of Irish nationality, having first seen the light of the world in

Waterford, a city which also gave birth to Charles Kean. At this period, when she occasionally joined the Duke's guests, she was playing at Drury Lane, where her attractions, if not her talents, bade fair to rival those of the great Siddons.

In the year 1791, Mrs. Jordan, who had already been the mistress of Ford, proprietor of Drury Lane Theatre, and the mother of his four children, left him to become the *protegée* of the Duke, who promised to allow her a thousand a year, at which piece of generosity the King was much incensed.

'What, what—you keep an actress?' said His Majesty to the Duke. 'Yes, sir,' he answered, readily enough.

'How much do you allow her? What—what?'

'A thousand a year.' 'A thousand a year!' said His Gracious Majesty, in astonishment. 'What—what? that's too much. Give her five hundred. What—what—what?' It happened, however, that the actress derived no pecuniary benefit from her royal lover's promise; her professional earnings amounted to no less than £5,000 a year, to which she added an annuity of £1,000, settled on her by a relative of her mother's. Soon after she had formed a connection with the Duke, it was noticed that, when she drove to the treasury door of the theatre to receive her salary, she was invariably accompanied by this scion of royalty, whom public gossip plainly said appropriated her earnings; nay, it was even proved after her death that her nightly salaries at Drury Lane were constantly paid in advance, and the sums received by a messenger, who hurried with them to a gambling-house in Pall Mall, where the Duke played for high stakes. It was well known that before her intimacy with him commenced, she had saved a handsome fortune, and it is a fact in her biographical history that she died abroad in neglect, and, if not in poverty, at least in debt. Though continually suffering from public slights in consequence of her relationship with the Duke, that worthy did not think well of allowing the mother of his children to withdraw into the seclusion of private life, whilst her labours brought such a profitable return to the royal coffers.

Mrs. Jordan bore the Duke ten children, the eldest of whom was raised to the peerage as Earl of Munster, and to the others were granted 'the title and precedency of the younger issue of a Marquess.'

This illegitimate progeny became in after years extremely tenacious of their rank, and singularly haughty in their manners; but occasionally these characteristics were severely checked. A story is told of the second son, Colonel Fitz-Clarence, who, dining one day as the guest of some brother officers, noted a young lieutenant carving fowls in a particularly awkward manner. The Colonel looked on with ill-concealed disgust for some time, and then remarked sneeringly, 'My father frequently said that to carve well was one of the signs of a gentleman.' The young lieutenant laid down his knife and fork for a minute, and looking the speaker full in the face, coolly asked, 'And pray, Colonel FitzClarence, what did your mother say?' Profound silence followed the question.

The Duke, after some years, grew tired of the mother of his ten children, and coolly discarded her.

'You have probably heard,' writes Fremantle to the Duke of Buckingham, 'all the history of the Duke of Clarence. Before he went to Ramsgate, he wrote to Lady Catherine Long to propose, who wrote him a very proper letter in answer, declining the honour in the most decided terms. After his arrival, he proposed three or four times more, and upon his return to town, sent her an abstract of the Royal Marriage Act altered, as he said it had been agreed to by the Prince of Wales, whom he had consulted, and also conveyed the Queen's best wishes and regards—to neither of whom had he said one single word on the subject. Upon finding she had accepted Pole, he wrote to Lord Keith to propose for Miss Elphinstone, who, in her most decided and peremptory terms, rejected him; he is, notwithstanding, gone to his house. During all this, when he returned to town, he wrote to Mrs. Jordan at Bushey to say she might have half the children, viz., five, and he would allow her £800 per annum. She is most stout in rejecting all compromise till he has paid her what he owes her; she stating that during the twenty years she has lived with him, he has constantly received and spent all her earnings by acting; and that she is now a beggar by living with, and at times supporting, him. This she repeats to all the neighbourhood of Bushey, where she remains, and is determined to continue. While all his gallantry was going forward at Ramsgate, the Duke of Cumberland (who must interfere in everything) apprised Mrs. Jordan of what he was doing. Mrs. Jordan then writes him a most furious letter, and another to the Duke of Cumberland, to thank him for the information, and by mistake directs them wrong; in consequence of which, there has been, of course, a scene between the brothers. Altogether, the conduct of these illustrious personages is a most melancholy and alarming feature in the difficulties which every hour increase upon us; and it is not without great forbearance one can impute it to any other ground but an affection of the same nature as that under which the King labours.'

Later on, the Royal Duke, who was still anxious to bestow the honour of his hand in marriage, proposed to Miss Wykeham, and the same correspondent, writing on the subject, says:

'There is a grand emotion in the royal family, and with some reason. The Duke of Clarence has thought proper to propose to Miss Wykeham, who has accepted him. The Prince, accompanied by the Duchess of Gloucester, went to Windsor on Tuesday to inform the Queen of this happy event, who was of course outrageous. The Council have sat twice upon the business, and it is determined, as I understand, to oppose it. My own private belief is that the Prince has been encouraging the Duke of Clarence to it at Brighton, and now turns short round upon him, as is usual, finding it so highly objectionable.'

The Duke was finally persuaded to break off the match; he was, therefore, once more available in the matrimonial market, and was finally accepted by a Princess of Saxe-Meiningen, who had no objection to the Jordan scandal and ten illegitimate children.

In September, 1791, the Duke of York was married at Berlin to the Princess Frederica, eldest daughter of Frederick William II., King of Prussia, and was subsequently re-married, in the Queen's drawing-room at Buckingham House, by the Archbishop of Canterbury in November. Even so good and gracious a courtier as Lord Malmesbury could not help admitting that the new Duchess 'was far from handsome;' but in return for such admission, it was avowed that she was 'lively, sensible, tractable, and formed to confer happiness on her husband.'

The Duke and the Prince of Wales had been forgiven by their parents, and had been taken once more into their Majesties' favour. The bridegroom, therefore, to prove his submission to the Queen, had left to her selection the nomination of the ladies of his future household:

'This,' said the wily Lord Malmesbury, who had suggested the act to His Royal Highness, 'will relieve the Duke from the embarrassment of applications, and particularly such as might be suggested to the Prince to make, which it would be difficult for him to refuse, and from the complexion of the Prince's society, it might be by no means advisable for him to grant, as it is of the last consequence that the Duchess should begin well, and under the most respectable impressions possible.'

The royal bride had a dowry of £30,000, and her father, moreover, paid the debts of her profligate husband, which had amounted to £20,000. A grateful nation had also voted the Prince, whose subsequent conduct proved a disgrace to his country, £18,000 per annum, which, added to the sum of £12,000 a year already granted him, and £7,000 a year levied on the Irish Establishment, gave him a yearly income of £37,000, all of which soon proved insufficient for his wants. For a while the Duke and Duchess lived in harmony; she made herself a favourite not only with the royal family, but with all who came in contact with her; she detested ceremony; sought retirement, and loved her husband until his glaring vices repelled her. He was not long in accomplishing this. Soon after marriage he resumed his connection, as the Duchess of Brunswick told Lord Malmesbury, with a former mistress, a fact which his spouse was graciously inclined to overlook; but his repeated infidelities, and the grossly open manner with which they were conducted, gradually alienated all her affections from him, and in six years after their union they separated, though in the latter years of their lives they lived beneath the same roof.

In 1793 he was placed in command of the English troops which were destined to aid the army under the Prince of Saxe-Coburg in Holland, where he fought with some show of spirit. In the following year he again embarked for the Continent, to fight the French army under General Pichegru, who forced him to cross the Meuse, and to retreat beyond the Waal. So unsuccessful did his generalship prove, and such a disaster did it cause his country, that Pitt was obliged, in consequence, as he said, of the want of confidence felt by the army in 'his general management,' to insist upon the King recalling this gallant son of Mars from a post for which he proved himself so eminently unsuited.

His Majesty did so with great reluctance, but soothed the Royal Duke's feelings by creating him, three weeks after his return, Field-marshal and Commander-in-Chief of His

Majesty's land forces; posts which the death of Lord Amherst, a veteran of four-score, had opportunely left vacant for a man his junior by half a century. How the Duke was compelled to quit these high offices remains to be told. In 1799 he again commenced a campaign against the French in Holland, heading an army of 35,000 men, including Russians; but here, owing to his blunders and want of generalship, the greatest disasters befell his troops, and he was compelled to enter into a convention with the French General, by which it was stipulated, that in consideration of the surviving portion of the Duke's army being permitted to evacuate Holland, several thousand seamen, then prisoners of war in England, should be given up to the French Government.

At home and abroad popular feeling was now excited against him, and his name became a word of reproach; through his fault, it was said, the country had suffered a defeat which lowered her in the eyes of Europe and covered her with disgrace and debt. But public indignation arrived at its climax when the Royal Duke was charged in the House of Commons, by Colonel Guillym Lloyd Wardle, with allowing Mrs. Clarke, his mistress, to sell military commissions and other posts, in the large profits of which His Royal Highness ignominiously shared.

Mrs. Anna Maria Clarke, the daughter of a compositor, was born in an alley; in due time she married a bricklayer, from whom she, after a few years spent in conjugal discord, separated; after many adventures, amorous and otherwise, she became the mistress of Sir James Brudenell, and subsequently of Sir Charles Milner, a coxcomb of the first water. Her intrigues became the public scandal of the day, and attracted the attention of the Duke of York, who immediately became enamoured of her and made her his mistress, promising her £1,000 a year and a retiring pension of £400 per annum, a sum he subsequently refused to pay her.

In person she was elegant and handsome, her complexion being singularly fair, her eyes large and blue; her conversational powers vivacious, and her manners fascinating. In a short time her ascendancy over the Duke became almost unbounded, and at the trial it was proved beyond a shadow of doubt that at her dictation he had awarded military promotions, granted commissions, and effected exchanges, being well aware she received large sums from those whom she recommended. 'Nothing,' Earl Temple writes to Lord Buckingham, 'can wipe off from the public mind the first impression of connivance, at least, which the bad character of the woman only tends to strengthen and confirm. I see plainly that the Duke is lost in public estimation.' According to Mrs. Clarke's statement before the House of Commons, His Royal Highness had hinted to her that a handsome income might be derived from the sales of commissions. 'The Duke,' she said, 'about half a year after I went to Gloucester Place, on my being very much distressed and pressing him for relief, told me *that I had more interest than the Queen*, and that if I was *clever*, I need never trouble him for money.' She at once acted on the hint given her, and henceforth nothing could equal the splendour in which she lived; she was clad in purple and fine linen, dined off services of solid silver, drove in equipages whose appointments rivalled those of royalty itself, and lived in a mansion furnished with superb taste and costly magnificence. From the gross and open insult of the woman's presence, the Duchess of York had retired to Oatlands; but Mrs. Clarke, desiring a country residence, took a house close to the neighbourhood of the Duchess, and on Sundays attended the same church, where her devotion was remarkable.

The excitement, indignation, and triumph which the general public felt at these gross charges, the truth of which had been long suspected, was intense, and scarce abated during the two months that the parliamentary inquiry lasted.

Day after day the House of Commons was crowded; members old and young flocked to hear the extraordinary charges made; to see the fashionable courtesan whose name was on all men's lips stand at the bar of Parliament to implicate her royal lover; to listen to the gross scandal which the witnesses examined coolly disclosed; and to laugh over every *double entendre* which fell from their lips. Never had there been such an exposure of scenes of profligacy and folly as those which took place between His Royal Highness and his mistress. During the hearing of the case, all signs of dignity and morality seemed set aside in the House of Commons, and the trial was regarded as a sensational drama which was the more interesting from the fame of those it concerned.

Colonel Wardle had undertaken to substantiate his charges, and the facts which the trial elicited proved he had not boasted in vain. He disclaimed all animosity against the Commander-in-Chief, and declared no other motive than a sense of public duty prompted him to bring forward the charge.

'It was necessary,' he continued, 'in the first instance, to put the House in possession of the true purposes for which the disposal of commissions in the army was placed in the hands of the Commander-in-Chief. It was for the purpose of defraying the charges of the half-pay list, for the support of veteran officers, and increasing the Compassionate Fund for the aid of the widows and orphans of officers; and therefore any commissions which fell by deaths or promotions the Commander-in-Chief had no right to sell or dispose of for his own private emolument, nor to appropriate for the like purpose any differences arising from the change or reduction of officers from full to half-pay.'

In the course of the investigation it was proved amongst other transactions that Mrs. Clarke engaged to get her favourite footman appointed to a commission in the army, had received £200 from Colonel Brookes on his exchange being gazetted, and had caused Major Tonyn of the 48th Regiment to be appointed major two years after receiving his commission as captain for the sum of £500. Through her aid, Major Shaw, whom the Duke disliked, had been appointed Deputy Barrack-Master-General at the Cape of Good Hope on promising to pay her £1,000; the worthy major forwarded her half that sum, and then betrayed an inclination to let her memory fade from his heart; but she was not a woman to allow her friends to forget her, and sent him word of what she considered his just debts, and, on his refusing to pay her, she complained to the Duke, who immediately placed the major on the half-pay list. Another gallant son of Mars with whom she found an opportunity of transacting a little business was Colonel French, of the Horse Guards, who was appointed to a commission for raising new levies. This officer was introduced to her by Captain Huxley Sandon, and it was arranged between them that she was to have a certain sum out of the bounty for every recruit raised, and a portion of patronage in the nomination of officers.

As the levy went on, she received various amounts; for a majority £900, for a captaincy £700, for a lieutenancy £400, and for an ensigncy £200. Nor did she always expect those who purchased commissions from her to serve; Mr. Malling, a clerk of Greenwood, the army agent, was appointed, through her favour, an ensign, lieutenant, and captain in the Royal African Corps in the space of three years, during which time he never left his desk.

So successful were her friends in the army in gaining rapid promotion, that the Church likewise sought her favour, and she ultimately opened an office in the City where army commissions, and places in various departments of the Church and State, were offered at reduced prices, her clerks making no concealment of the fact that they were employed by the favourite mistress of the Duke of York. Not only were such truths brought to light, but a parcel of documents and papers in connection with these transactions were seized and submitted to the inspection of a select committee.

'The report' (of these) 'is not yet made,' writes Earl Temple in the 'Courts and Cabinets of George III.,' 'but Leach, the chairman, has told me that the scene of infamy they open is dreadful, and that all that has passed is a trifle when compared with them. A complete system of traffic of every sort, for votes in the House upon particular questions, for every sort of military appointment, is laid open—a statement of particular facts which could only have come to her knowledge from the Duke of York; repeated directions to Sandon to call at the office, where he will find such and such official letters for him. A complaint on the part of the Duke that she has not been dealt fairly by, in consequence of a person for whom she has interested herself having made interest elsewhere; all this, and much more, is exposed in these cursed papers.'

'Every day, and every hour,' writes Mr. Fremantle, 'adds to the evidence against the Duke of York, and it is quite impossible but that he must sink under it.'

Mrs. Clarke, elegant, gracious, and unruffled, went to the House to give her evidence, attired 'in a light blue silk gown and coat, edged with white fur, and a fur muff;' and in her answers betrayed wit, cleverness, and playful repartee, qualities which went a far way towards fascinating at least the younger members. During a severe cross-examination, which lasted three hours, she completely foiled Gibbs, a lawyer who defended His Royal Highness. Indeed, she occasionally undertook to divert the House, with a cool impertinence which challenged admiration. Once, when asked who delivered her letters to the Duke, she replied the Morocco ambassador, which she subsequently condescended to explain was Mr. Taylor, a Bond Street shoemaker, who owed his wealth to princely patronage.

The letters just referred to were of course made public property, and were found to be such remarkable specimens of eloquence as had not interested and charmed the world since the appearance of those of the Duke of Cumberland to Lady Grosvenor. In one of these, his enamoured Highness addresses his mistress as 'Lovely charmer of my soul.' After easing his foolish heart by giving vent to such expressions as, 'Oh my angel, how you are beloved ; how I long to return to my love,' he rapidly proceeds to business.

'General Clavering, my love, is mistaken,' he writes. 'There are no new regiments to be raised ; they are only second battalions that are to be formed ; so that his business cannot be done, and tell him so.'

Another of his epistles is written in a far finer style, and betrays more lofty sentiments.

'MY DEAR LITTLE ANGEL,' it commences, 'How can I sufficiently express to my sweetest darling love the delight which your dear, dear, pretty letter gave me, or how do justice to the emotions it excited! Millions, millions of thanks for it, my angel, and be assured that my heart is wholly fixed on your affection. I am quite hurt, my love, that you did not go to the Lewes races. It was kind of you to think of me on the occasion. News, my angel, you cannot expect from me from hence, for the life I lead here is in the family, and I am hurrying them to leave this, that I may the sooner return to clasp my angel in my arms. Dr. O'Meara gave me your letter. He wishes to preach before royalty, and I shall endeavour to procure him the occasion. What a long time it is, my darling, since we parted ! I shall long for Wednesday se'nnight, that I may return to my love's arms. Adieu.

'Yours, and yours alone,

'FREDERICK.'

DUKE AND DARLING.

The town dwelt on this scandal with delight; pamphlets and ballads ridiculing the Royal Duke issued in numbers from the press; caricatures filled the shop windows, and the joke among the people was, when they tossed up half-pence, not to cry heads and tails, but duke and darling.

'It was established beyond the possibility of doubt,' says Sir Samuel Romilly, in the 'Diary of his Parliamentary Life,' 'that the Duke had permitted Mrs. Clarke, his mistress, to interfere in military promotions; that he had given commissions at her rcommendation, and that she had taken money for the recommendations. That the Duke knew that she took money, or that he knew that the establishment which he had set on foot for her was partly supported with the money thus illegally procured by her, did not appear otherwise than from her evidence. She, however, asserted the fact directly and positively; and her evidence was supported in many other particulars which seemed the most incredible, by such strong corroborations, that her immortal character, her resentment, and her contradictions were not sufficient to render her evidence altogether incredible.'

Towards the close of the trial, the Duke wrote a letter to the Speaker of the House of Commons, in which he declared he 'must ever regret and lament that a connection should have existed which has thus exposed my character to animadversion;' he furthermore, on his 'honour as a Prince,' asserted his innocence. At the mention of his honour, the Prince of Wales openly sneered, but the Duke said its consciousness led him 'confidentially to hope that the House of Commons will not, upon such evidence as they have heard, adopt any proceedings prejudicial to my honour and character;' he also resigned his appointment as Commander-in-Chief, when the following motion was carried, 'That the Duke of York, having resigned the command of the army, the House does not think it necessary to proceed any further in the consideration of the minutes of the evidence, so far as they relate to His Royal Highness.'

Three years subsequently, when the Prince of Wales was Regent, the Duke of York was reinstated in the office of Commander-in-Chief, on which occasion Lord Milton moved a resolution in the House to the effect that 'it has been highly improper and indecorous in the advisers of the Prince Regent to have recommended to His Royal Highness the reappointment of the Duke of York to the office of Commander-in-Chief;' the motion was, however, defeated by a majority who wished to keep well with the Regent.

Meanwhile the Duchess lived in retirement at Oatlands Park, Weybridge, a residence that had the reputation of being 'the worst managed establishment in England.' Her Royal Highness had become singularly eccentric, and one of her crazes was to surround herself with parrots, monkeys, and dogs in vast numbers; she also kept a menagerie on a small scale, where kangaroos, ostriches, and other birds and animals received royal attentions. The Duchess seldom went to bed, but took a few hours' sleep, sitting dressed on a couch or chair, now in one apartment, now in another, and delighted in taking solitary walks at dead of night, or in the small hours of the morning. At three o'clock she breakfasted and dressed, when, surrounded by all her dogs, which never numbered less than forty, she went into the park or village. When any of these animals died, they were decently interred in a spot set aside for the purpose, close by the fish-pond, their resting-places being marked by small marble headstones bearing their names, and occasionally touching inscriptions in verse recording their eminent virtues.

The Duke, with some friends, usually visited her every Saturday, when they stayed till the following Monday morning; the guests were allowed to amuse themselves as they pleased, without the least ceremony being observed; they went to church, if so inclined, or, if not, played with the dogs and monkeys, ate fruit in the garden, or shot at marks with pistols.

Another of the Royal Princes, Augustus, Duke of Sussex, came prominently before the public in 1793. He had, with his brothers Ernest and Adolphus, been sent to the University of Göttingen, in order that he might be free from the evil example of the elder members of his family; and from thence, being delicate, he had gone to travel in Italy. In Rome he met Lady Augusta Murray, daughter of the Earl of Dunmore, with whom he soon became deeply enamoured. He was, at the time, one-and-twenty, whilst the young lady whom he was pleased to style 'his soul,' and 'his treasure, without whom he would pass the days in one constant melancholy, wishing them soon to conclude, and finding every one longer than the other,' was fourteen years his senior.

The Royal Marriage Act, which pronounced the union of a Prince and a subject null and void without the consent of Parliament, was an obstacle that threatened their happiness; but this the love-stricken Prince determined to set aside, and drew up a paper in which he declared that—

'On my knees before God our Creator, I, Augustus Frederick, promise thee, Augusta Murray, and swear upon the Bible, as I hope for salvation in the world to come, that I will take thee, Augusta Murray, for my wife . . . and may God forget me if ever I forget thee. The Lord's name be praised! So bless me, so bless me, O God!'

After some difficulties, they were married in Rome by a clergyman of the Church of England, on April 4, and subsequently, on their return to England, the ceremony was repeated in St. George's Church, Hanover Square, on December 5, in the presence of a coal-merchant, named Jones, and his wife. The banns had been duly published (the names of the bride and bridegroom being given as Augustus Frederick and Augusta Murray), but neither the rector nor anyone else had the least suspicion of their rank or position.

Shortly after the last ceremony, the lady gave birth to a boy—afterwards Sir Augustus Frederick d'Este—and rumours of the union became gradually noised about town; when the Prince, fearing his royal father's wrath, thought it prudent to quit England. When the news reached the King's ears, his virtuous Majesty gave orders that proceedings should at once be taken to prove the marriage null and void, according to the infamous and despotic Act he had framed. It remains to be added that, though Augustus Frederick had prayed so fervently that God might forget him if he forgot Augusta Murray, yet in a few years he took advantage of the vile sentence which had pronounced this union void, to utterly and heartlessly desert her; and Lady Augusta was obliged to petition the Court of Chancery that, out of the £12,000 per annum which the grateful nation allowed her husband, she might receive a sum sufficient to maintain herself and his two children. After her death, the Duke married again, his selection being once more the daughter of an Earl, Lady Cecilia Underwood.

Ernest Augustus, Duke of Cumberland (fifth son of George III.), was the most unpopular member of the royal family. In appearance, he was a tall, powerful man, with what Stockmar describes as 'a hideous face,' rendered all the more repulsive from the fact that 'one of the eyes turned quite out of its place.' His disposition was repellent, and his severities over the regiments he commanded showed him to have been cruel and sanguinary. When twelve years old, he was created Duke of Cumberland and Teviotdale, and Earl of Armagh, and obtained a Parliamentary grant of £12,000, which in a few years was increased to £18,000, and finally to £21,000. Colonel Willis describes his conversation as 'of a nature as to coarseness that would have disgraced one of his grooms.'

'There never,' said his brother, George IV., to the Duke of Wellington, speaking of His Royal Highness, 'was a father well with his son, or husband with his wife, or lover with his mistress, or friend with his friend, that he did not try to make mischief between them.'

In 1810 an event happened to the Duke which startled the public, and caused the most infamous scandals to be freely circulated.

On the morning of May 31, it was announced that an attempt had been made on the Duke's life, whilst he was in bed in his apartments in St. James's Palace, by his valet, a Corsican named Sellis. His bed-room was large, and was faintly lighted by a lamp, which it was his habit to keep burning all night. About half-past two, the Duke asserted, he was awakened by a blow; this could not have been severe, as he states his first impression was that a bat had got into the room, and was beating about his head.

Left by the dim light of the lamp, he soon discerned the flash of a steel weapon; he then raised his hand towards the bell-rope, in order to give alarm, but could not find it, on which he jumped from bed and rushed towards the door of an apartment communicating with his own, where a page named Neale slept, pursued by his assailant, who cut him on the thigh, and inflicted some other injuries on him. The man who had, in this strange and singularly clumsy manner, attempted the life of the Royal Duke, then made his escape without hindrance; whilst His Royal Highness cried out to his page, 'I am murdered—I am murdered.'

When Neale, more heroic than his royal master, rushed towards the bedroom, the Duke, with a trait of humanity new to his character, held him back; the murderers, he said—for it now seemed to him his assailants had increased in numbers—were in that room, and would surely kill him; but Neale accidentally treading on a weapon, which, singularly enough, proved to be a favourite sabre of the Duke's, which he always kept in his bedroom, the royal nerves were somewhat quieted.

The household was now aroused, but Sellis, for whom the Duke particularly asked, was wanting. Meanwhile a surgeon was sent for, who immediately pronounced that His Royal Highness's wounds were by no means fatal, and his subsequent recovery fortunately proved extremely rapid. Sellis not appearing, Neale the page went in search of him, but found his bedroom door locked; it was then remembered that there was another entrance to his apartment, by a door that opened on the principal staircase; no sooner was access gained by this than Sellis was discovered sitting in a semi-erect position in bed, with his head almost severed from the body, life being, of course, quite extinct. A razor lay beside him; marks of blood were discovered on his coat, which was carefully folded and laid at some little distance from his bed, and a basin containing water tinged with blood was also noticed. It was now, of course, quite clear to the meanest comprehension that he had striven in the strangest fashion to murder the Duke with a remarkably awkward weapon, and that His Royal Highness providentially saved his life only by flying from this would-be assassin, who, it may be remarked, was much inferior to the Duke in strength and stature; and finally, that, fearing detection, the unhappy Sellis had, before the slightest suspicion could rest on him, put an end to his wretched existence. It only remained for a jury to be summoned, who, after four hours' mature deliberation, returned a verdict that Sellis had committed suicide; when his body was buried without ceremony in the high road.

This tragedy caused the wildest sensation in town; it became fashionable to visit the Duke's apartments in the absence of His Royal Highness—whose injuries were not so severe as to prevent his removal to Carlton House—the rooms having been left in the same condition as found on the morning of the occurrence for several days, for the benefit of public curiosity.

In a little while, when the public had recovered from the surprise caused by the horrible occurrence, it began to speculate as to the reason which had actuated Sellis to perpetrate this desperate deed; it was then whispered by the Duke's friends that Sellis had been jealous of his royal master, who had paid some attentions to his valet's wife, and it was timely remembered that the Duke had stood godfather to Sellis's child; it was also said that the valet had been slightly mad, and there were those who now remembered several signs of the dread malady in his manner, though they had been culpably negligent in not remarking this to His Royal Highness, thereby exposing his valuable life, as it afterwards proved, to the most imminent risk. Others, again, had no doubt Sellis, who was a Catholic, merely revenged himself on his royal master because of the constant gross and violent abuse of that religion which the Royal Duke, with his customary signs of good-breeding, was in the habit of addressing to his servant.

Of course, such an opportunity as this afforded was seized on to circulate the grossest scandals, which, strange to say, gained wide credence. It was openly and plainly stated that the Duke had murdered Sellis, and inflicted some slight wounds upon his own person, in order to give colour to his story of having been attacked in bed; moreover, it was vilely asserted that the coroner's jury who had held the inquest on the body had been packed and improperly influenced; and that the motive of getting rid of Sellis was, the Duke feared lest he should reveal a secret of which he had become accidentally possessed, which inculpated his royal master in a penal crime. Singular to say, two circumstances favoured these most atrocious reports. It was well-known that Sellis was a left-handed man, but one of the physicians who saw the body declared, if he had inflicted the wound, it must have been with his right hand; another of the medical faculty went further still, and actually had the audacity to state that, having carefully examined Sellis's wounds, he was certain that the cuts on the back of the neck could not possibly have been inflicted by the deceased; moreover, he had the monstrous hardihood to make the subject the basis of a lecture to his pupils, in the course of which he said that, if Sellis died by his own hand, he did not cut and wound the back of his neck.

'Sellis,' he declared, 'had not one, but several wounds on the back of his neck. If Sellis had meant his own decollation, he must have begun behind his neck—but, labour with the razor as he might, it would only hack and hew his flesh; for no physical strength would be sufficient to terminate the existence of an individual by beheading himself.'

The Duke was sufficiently forbearing to overlook these statements, and many of the gross assertions concerning his character in general, and this tragedy in particular, which continually appeared in the press, until the publication, so late as 1832, of a book entitled 'The Authentic Records of the Court of England for the last Seventy Years, written by Lady Anne Hamilton.' In this work, the tragedy concerning Sellis was gone into with great minuteness, and in summing up the various circumstances of the case, it concluded with the words:

'Had it been the case of a poor man, he must have been hung, and his body given for dissection, merely upon circumstantial evidence; but the son of a reigning monarch had, by circumstantial evidence alone, been acquitted.'

The publisher of this wicked libel was one Josiah Phillips, who dwelt in the Strand. He was prosecuted and punished. Many years after Sellis's death, the Duke's name was unfortunately mixed up with another suicide in a most unpleasant manner. The Duke, it was well known, though at this time a married man, had an intrigue with Lady Graves, whose husband was so sensitive to the injury inflicted on his honour, that he ended his life by his own hand. The Duke, who had become used to such tragedies, was too philosophical to let this affair prey upon his royal mind, and, immediately after the funeral of the unhappy man, was seen day after day driving about in public with the widowed Lady Graves.

In 1814 he contracted a marriage with his cousin, Frederica Caroline Sophia, daughter of the Duke of Mecklenburg-Strelitz, Queen Charlotte's brother. This lady possessed a temperament usually designated as gay; she had thrice entered the holy bonds of matrimony, and been once divorced. The Queen, unaware of this latter little circumstance in the life of her future daughter-in-law, wrote to the Duke of Mecklenburg to say she would endeavour to render the residence of her niece as pleasant as circumstances would permit, 'considering,' says Her Majesty, 'that my sedentary life prevents me contributing much to the amusement of the Princesses, and that the greater part of my time is passed in the country, where our society is very limited, and our life uniform.'

She then requested her brother to inform his daughter of certain usages of English society.

'It is not the fashion here,' said royalty, 'to receive morning visits from gentlemen, to which she will be exposed, by reason of the Duke being colonel of a regiment, unless he himself introduces them to her: she should also be very circumspect in the choice of ladies with whom she shall associate, which will be so much the more necessary, as the Duke has acquaintances amongst our sex who, though not actually of bad conduct, might, however, become injurious to her in point of policy.'

Her Gracious Majesty finally informed the Grand-Duke of Mecklenburg-Strelitz that she sent him, by the courier who conveyed her letter, 'six pounds of tea and two cheeses. Eat the latter,' she added, 'to my health, and, in drinking the tea, remember a sister whose attachment to you will not cease but with death.' His Serene Highness the Grand-Duke of Mecklenburg-Strelitz gratefully accepted the cheeses and the six pounds of tea from his royal sister—presents worthy of so great a Queen.

When the Royal Duke brought his bride to England, her aunt, who had meanwhile heard various little items of her history, more entertaining than edifying, refused to receive her at Court, or hold any communication with her; the universal detestation which was felt towards the Duke was at the same time expressed by the refusal of Parliament to grant him an addition of £6,000 per annum, as had been the custom to bestow on the Royal Dukes when they married.

The Dukes of Kent and Cambridge were by far the most estimable of the King's sons; their public careers were not brilliant, but their private lives were respectable, and they have fortunately left behind them no disreputable histories.

CHAPTER XII.

The Prince of Wales and his Difficulties—His Proposed Marriage—Lord Malmesbury at the Court of Brunswick—The Bride-elect—Her Journey to England and Reception by the Prince—Marriage and Honeymoon—The Evil Genius of her Life—The Story of the Lost Letters—The Prince's Debts—Disloyalty of the People—The Cry of 'No King!'—The King's Life Attempted—Birth of a Young Princess—The Prince's Separation from his Wife—The Lord Chancellor's Opinion of his Sanity—Mrs. Fitzherbert Communicates with Rome.

MEANWHILE the Prince of Wales sank lower and lower in the morass of debt and dissipation which now threatened to swamp him; the outlay on the whimsical, unnecessary alterations of Carlton House reached the enormous figure of £56,950; his stud cost him, he admitted, £30,000 a year; and the sums he squandered on any woman who chanced to please his amorous fancy were prodigious. He had signed bills and bonds in numbers, heedless of the consequences of the future if he could relieve the necessities of the present; and had, in conjunction with the Dukes of York and Clarence, whose respective incomes of £18,000 and £12,000 a year were insufficient for their expensive tastes, raised large sums on their bonds through the respectable agency of the Prince's German cook, Weltjie.

Nor was this all; the heir to the throne offered £10,000 and an Irish peerage (which must have weighed but little in his estimation), after the King's death, for every £5,000 which was given him in the present. But, finding that even on these terms there were few who were ready to swallow the bait and trust him, he resolved on a yet more desperate proceeding; this was to raise £350,000 on the Duchy of Cornwall and the Bishopric of Osnaburgh, with payments by drawings and a sinking-fund, the whole to be paid off in twenty-five years; this transaction coming to the King's knowledge, much trouble followed, covering the royal brothers with dishonour.

The Prince was now, as the Duke of Portland lamented to Lord Malmesbury, but little respected, so little, indeed, that his creditors frequently stopped him in the streets to demand their just debts from him, after seeking every other mode for payment in vain; the workmen at Carlton House petitioned the Prime Minister for their wages; and several executions had been levied in the royal residence. Notwithstanding that his annual income amounted to £73,000 per annum, his debts now reached the round sum of £600,000, an amount he had squandered in reckless prodigality, and he resolved to bring his difficulties once more before the eyes of an indulgent nation, which he had no doubt would again assert its benevolence in removing from his royal shoulders the inconveniences which he suffered. In an interview which he had at this time with Lord Malmesbury, he again used the threat of going abroad, and living in a retired manner. He did not, he said, stand so well with the King, but was better than ever with the Queen, whose favourite he had always been; her wily Majesty had advised him, he said, to press the King, through the Chancellor, to propose that Pitt should bring the consideration of an increase of his income before Parliament, and she had promised to give this scheme her earnest support. On this occasion the Prince talked coldly of the Duke and Duchess of York, because the latter had refused to treat Mrs. Fitzherbert *en belle sœur*, and of the Duke of Clarence slightingly, and was, indeed, inclined to be in ill-humour with the world at large.

On an appeal being made to the King for an increase of income for the Prince, and for the payment of his debts, His Majesty gave it to be understood that the sole terms on which such advantages could be obtained were the marriage of the heir to the Crown, who was then in his thirty-third year; a step which, it was hoped, might have some restraining effect on his career of unbridled excesses, and secure the prosperity of the nation. To this proposal the Prince did not lend such an unwilling ear as might have been expected. He had long since proved faithless to Mrs. Fitzherbert, now openly styled in a pamphlet by Horne Tooke, 'Both legally, really, worthily, and happily for the country, Her Royal Highness the Princess of Wales;' and almost as freely spoken of by the members of the royal family, according to the Harcourt diary, as his lawful wife.

Not to mention others, his connection became notorious with Lady Jersey, a bold and beautiful woman, whose husband was appointed Master of the Horse to the Prince, in reward for her ladyship's infamy. Already an open adulterer, His Royal Highness did not hesitate to commit bigamy when, by that crime—urged on him by the virtuous King, who was certainly cognisant of his marriage with Mrs. Fitzherbert—he had the prospect of ridding himself from the humiliation of debt, and of receiving from the nation a larger income, which would afford him greater facilities for the indulgence of his base passions.

'Others, with whom he lived upon the most intimate terms,' says Lord Brougham, 'are supposed to have interposed fresh obstacles to this scheme; but these were overcome by an understanding that the new wife should enjoy only the name—that systematic neglect and insult of every kind heaped upon her should attest how little concern the heart had with this honourable arrangement, and how entirely the husband should continue devoted to the wedded wives of other men. Everything was settled to the satisfaction of all parties; the old spouse was discarded—the old mistresses were cherished, fondled, and appeased.'

Accordingly, he resolved to enter into the holy bonds of matrimony, but was perfectly indifferent as to who his future bride should be; the King, however, undertook to spare him this trouble, and selected as the future Princess of Wales, Caroline of Brunswick, the daughter of His Majesty's eldest sister, His Royal Highness agreeing to this choice with a complacency that savoured but too strongly of indifference. His Gracious Majesty wrote to the Prime Minister that he had an interview with the Prince of Wales, who had 'acquainted me with his having broken off all connection with Mrs. Fitzherbert, and his desire of entering into a more creditable line of life by marrying.' As to his niece, the King declared, 'undoubtedly she is the person who naturally must be most agreeable to me .... provided his plan was to lead a life that would make him appear respectable, and, consequently, render the Princess happy.' His Majesty, with an eye to the financial result of this union, sagely added, that he informed the Prince 'that, till Parliament assembled, no arrangement could be taken.'

In good time, Lord Malmesbury, a clever diplomatist and able courtier, was despatched to the little Court of Brunswick, to negotiate a marriage with the Princess Caroline, a lady whom neither the King nor the Prince had ever seen, and who was now in her twenty-seventh year. My lord received his instructions personally from the King, who was most eager for the marriage, and who gave him no discretionary powers, to give either advice or information to His Majesty or the Prince regarding the object of his mission: though he subsequently took heed of many things of which he did not approve, in the manners and ways of the lady, whom he terms his 'eccentric charge,' he, believing his opinions were not required at St. James's, wisely, or unwisely, held his diplomatic tongue.

He was received at Brunswick with all the honours befitting the importance of his mission. When his arrival was made known, no less a personage than the high and mighty Grand Marschal Munchausen called upon him, to offer him the use of a palace during his stay, with servants, a carriage, a valet-de-chambre, a concierge, three footmen, and two sentinels; moreover, he was honoured by an invitation to dine, from the Duchess of Brunswick, mother to the bride-elect.

Here he met the Princess Caroline, who was much embarrassed at seeing him, and his first impressions of that ill-fated woman were not very favourable; her face, he said, was pretty, but not expressive of softness; she had fine eyes, he admitted, 'tolerable teeth, but going, fair hair and light eyebrows, good bust, short, with what the French call *des poitrines.*' Mrs. Harcourt, when she arrived at the Brunswick Court to accompany the Princess to England, remarked that in her appearance there was 'some resemblance in miniature to what Mrs. Fitzherbert was when young;' whilst the courtiers of St. James's subsequently spoke of the resemblance she bore His Gracious Majesty, 'especially in the upper lip, which protrudes.'

Lord Malmesbury tarried a month at the Court, when Major Hislop arrived from England in hot haste, bearing the Prince's portrait, and, strange to say, a letter from that illustrious person, vehemently urging the diplomatist to set out with the Princess Caroline immediately. A ceremony of marriage, at which Lord Malmesbury stood proxy for the Prince, was then gone through with due solemnity, after which stately compliments and gracious felicitations were expressed; then came a heavy dinner, followed by whist, at which the new-made Princess of Wales, as she was now entitled to be called, took a hand, and played an excellent game; the celebrations of the day closing with a sumptuous supper, at which the whole Court assisted.

The morality practised in the bride's home was distinguished by all the looseness which marked the petty German courts of the period. The Duchess of Brunswick mentioned to Lord Malmesbury, not at 'all by way of compliment, but incidentally, in the course of one of their conversations, that her husband, at the time he came to England to marry her, was in love with three ladies of rank, and enjoyed the friendship of an Italian girl likewise. Mademoiselle de Hertzfeldt was now his acknowledged mistress; this lady dressed with all the elegant *appareil* of her situation, and had her acknowledged place in all Court ceremonies. The Duke, a man of the easiest morals, had written out in German a code of conduct for his daughter to pursue in England, amongst which he specially advised her never to show any jealousy of her husband, and 'that, if he had any *goûts*, not to notice them.' For all that, he dreaded, he said, the Prince's habits, the fame of which had spread through Europe, and was gravely apprehensive of the future. His daughter could not help feeling likewise concerned, and her fears were strengthened by some anonymous letters which both she and her parents received, warning them of His Royal Highness's character, and the fate she might expect. Another letter which reached the Court also filled her with some alarm, this was written not by an anonymous, but by the royal hand of George III., who expressed his hopes to the Duchess that his niece 'would not indulge in too much vivacity, but would lead a sedentary and retired life.'

Now, when the irrevocable steps had been taken, the new Princess strove to make the best of her position, and to appear gay and cheerful; but at times her eyes filled with tears, and now and again she ventured to express her thoughts. She declared she was fearful of her future mother-in-law, who she was sure would be jealous of her, and do her harm; she also asked about Lady Jersey, whom she considered an *intriguante*, said she knew the Prince was *léger*, but she was already prepared on that point, and determined never to appear jealous; that her sole wish was to become popular, and to gain the love of the people.

At this avowal, my Lord Malmesbury pricked up his courtly ears and told her, in severe tones, that 'popularity was never gained by familiarity; that it could only belong to respect, and was to be acquired by a just mixture of dignity and affability.' The diplomatist then referred to his gracious Queen as a model, and informed her gravely 'that the sentiment of being loved by the people is a mistaken one—that sentiment can only be given to a few, that a nation at large can only respect and honour a great Princess, and that its love can be procured, not by pleasant openness and free communication, but by strict attention to appearances—by never going below the high rank in which a Princess is placed.' Over these autocratic words the poor bride pondered long in silence, but she was positively startled when, *àpropos* of intrigues, my lord thought well to inform her that 'it was death to presume to approach a Princess of Wales.' She asked him if he were in earnest; he answered it was the English law 'that anybody who presumed to approach her was guilty of high treason, and punished with death, if she was weak enough to listen to him; so also would *she* be.

Mrs. Harcourt now arrived at Brunswick, and took a more hopeful view of the bride's future; she, poor lady, said, in courtly words, she was sure the Prince would adore his bride; and she added that the Princess 'was prepared and disposed to adore him, and do her duty by him.' It may be argued, in favour of her sincerity, that she had not been in England for a considerable time. Meanwhile, the bride set out for London; nothing could be more propitious than the weather; the wind was fair, the sea smooth as glass; there never had been, it was said, so happy a voyage. The Princess was full of good humour, affable in manners, sweet in temper, and delighted at her future prospects.

'It does one's heart good to see anybody so happy,' writes Mrs. Harcourt. 'All the officers of the ship declare they should have had more trouble with any London lady than Her Royal Highness has given.'

On Sunday, April 5, 1795, the Princess landed at Greenwich Hospital, when she was received by the governor, Sir Hugh Palisser, and his officers all; and here it was that she first met Lady Jersey, the woman destined to have so evil an influence on her fate. The Prince's mistress had been appointed by him as first Lady of the Bedchamber to the Princess; a gross and wanton insult, which he did not hesitate to inflict on his bride, and regarding which the Queen did not interfere. In this capacity, it was her ladyship's duty to have awaited the Princess's landing; she did not, however, put herself to any inconvenience in the matter, and only arrived at Greenwich an hour after the Princess had arrived. At their first meeting, she ventured to make some uncomplimentary remarks regarding the bride's dress, and behaved in such a manner that Lord Malmesbury was obliged to speak 'rather sharply to her.' She then produced a suit she had brought from London at the Queen's request, in which the Princess was to travel to town; this consisted of 'a mantle of green-sattin, trimmed with gold, with loops and tassels à la Brandenburg,' which remarkable costume was completed by a beaver hat.

When Her Royal Highness's toilette was finished, she got into one of the King's coaches, drawn by six horses, which awaited her. Here again Lady Jersey's behaviour called for the interference of Lord Malmesbury. The mistress refused to sit backwards in the coach, but desired to sit side by side with the bride-elect; my Lord, however, declined to allow such a breach of etiquette; my Lady declared she would have a headache; when he informed her she should never have accepted her situation as Lady of the Bedchamber, who never ought to sit forward; and, if she was likely to be sick, she could share the carriage allotted to him and Lord Claremount; an offer she promptly refused.

When the Princess was driven to St. James's, she was ushered into the apartments overlooking Cleveland Row, where, if this stranger in a strange land expected her bridegroom would be courteous enough to receive her, she was destined to bitter disappointment; but the people strove to make up by their enthusiasm for this lack of respect on the part of the Prince. They had lined the streets through which she had driven, and cheered her heartily, and now assembled in vast numbers outside St. James's, where they huzzaed until, according to that most courtly chronicle the *St. James's Gazette*, 'in a voice replete with melody and delicacy of tone, she thus addressed them from her palace window, "Believe me, I feel very happy and delighted to see the good and brave English people, the best nation upon earth;"' which parrot-like phrases, evidently delivered with the assistance of a prompter, were received with exceeding great joy by the mob, who were afterwards to be her best friends.

After a while, the tardy bridegroom came from Carlton House, close by, to greet his bride; but appeared much embarrassed, ill at ease, and perhaps conscience-stricken at the wrong which his bigamous marriage was about to inflict upon this helpless woman. He was introduced to her by Lord Malmesbury, no other person being in the apartment, when the Princess, according to the required etiquette, attempted to kneel; but the Prince raised her up, saluted her, and, uttering but one word, turned round abruptly, walked to a distant corner o. the apartment, and, calling Lord Malmesbury to him, demanded a glass of brandy. The diplomatist had probably certain reasons for replying,

'Sir, had you not better have a glass of water?' upon which he replied with a round oath, 'No; I will go directly to the Queen,' and, without another word, he left the room.

Amazed at such conduct from one whom she had heard called the first gentleman in Europe, the bride, trembling and frightened, cried out, 'My God! is the Prince always like that?' to which question the excellent courtier answered, His Royal Highness 'was naturally a good deal affected and flurried at this first interview.'

At five o'clock the Prince and Princess dined, she appearing in the wonderful head-dress in which she was painted in the picture sent to her bridegroom; whilst he was dressed in the hussar uniform of his regiment, as in the portrait painted by Conway and sent to his bride. At this dinner, all who had attended the Princess from Greenwich assisted —Lady Jersey of course included—whilst Lord Stopford, as Vice-Chamberlain, did the honours. At the conclusion, the Prince and Princess paid a visit to their Majesties at Buckingham House, when the Queen betrayed the uttermost dislike to this member of a rival house which she hated, asked her a few questions, and then remained silent during the interview; the King, on the contrary, was kind and good-natured. According to the loyal, but highly inflated language of tne *Oracle*, he, 'on first seeing his lovely relation, discovered the most amiable sensibility. Tears of joy bedewed his cheeks on receiving the hand of his favourite sister's daughter.' The Prince had by this time somewhat recovered himself, paid her some attentions, and strove to express his hopes for their mutual happiness. At eleven o'clock the Princess retired, when she was attended by her Lady of the Bedchamber, the crafty, jealous, and vicious Countess of Jersey.

'Lady Jersey,' says Huish in his 'Memoirs of George IV.,' 'who had appeared displeased by the attentions which the Prince of Wales had paid to his destined wife, now also retired, determined to avail herself of the period which would elapse prior to a second interview between the illustrious personages to represent to the Prince, in false and unmerited language, the character of her royal mistress. To Lady Jersey, the Princess of Brunswick had certainly most incautiously and unwarily stated her attachment to a German Prince, and Lady Jersey stated that the Princess said, " She was persuaded that she loved one little finger of that individual far better than she should love the whole person of the Prince of Wales." The accuracy of this statement to its full extent was subsequently denied by the Princess of Brunswick, but still she admitted that she had imprudently referred to a former attachment. Lady Jersey, on the succeeding day, apprised the Prince of Wales of that attachment, assured him that his intended consort had made the above declaration, found fault with her person, ridiculed the coarseness of her manners, predicted that the marriage, if consummated, would be unfortunate, and inveighed against the King for promoting the intended union. A great part of this statement was subsequently admitted by Lady Jersey, and what was not so admitted was stated by the Princess on the highest authority to have taken place.'

It was arranged that the marriage should be celebrated on the following Wednesday evening, when many preparations were made. Thrones for the King and Queen were erected in St. James's Chapel, the walls of which were newly covered with 'fresh paper, so as to imitate crimson velvet;' stalls were placed in the royal apartments, through which the bridal procession would pass, for the courtiers to witness the sight; the town was made ready for illuminations; long-winded addresses were prepared, and the muses put their nine heads together to compose some of the most wonderfully nonsensical rhapsody ever conceived for the occasion. Amongst many others, these goddesses of song inspired the gentle lay of Miss Churchill, of Queen Street, Chelsea an enthusiastic young lady much given to the use of notes of admiration, whose verses gained her some notoriety. 'She comes,' Miss Churchill somewhat unnecessarily announces, in reference to the Princess—

> 'She comes ! the lovely Caroline appears !
> Loud acclamations filled the vaulted air !
> While tott'ring age the information cheers,
> And old and young congratulate the fair !'

On Wednesday evening, the first act in the painful tragedy in the life of Caroline, Princess of Wales, was enacted, when the royal marriage was solemnized in St. James's Chapel. At half-past eight o'clock, the Queen's ladies, her Lord Chamberlain, and her Master of the Horse were summoned into Her Majesty's bedchamber, where the royal family were assembled. Then came the bridal procession, headed by trumpets and drums, heralds and ushers, and a goodly array of courtiers, preceding the bride, who was led by the Duke of Clarence, passed through the Queen's bedchamber on their way to the Chapel Royal. The Princess was pale and nervous, and was clad in a nuptial habit of silver-tissue, ornamented with many jewels, and a robe of crimson velvet, lined and bordered with ermine, which hung loose from her shoulders, and was borne by the daughters of two Dukes and two Earls. Then came the bridegroom, corpulent of person and red of face, wearing his Collar of the Order of the Garter, supported, in more senses than one, by the Dukes of Bedford and Roxburgh, the procession closing with their Gracious Majesties, attended by the officers of the household in full state.

Lord Malmesbury admits that, on this occasion, the Prince 'had recourse to wine or spirits ;' but Lady Harcourt goes further.

'The Duke of Gloucester,' she says, 'assured me the Prince was quite drunk ; and that, after dinner, he went out and drank twelve glasses of maraschino.'

Her description of the ceremony is worth recording:

'The Princess,' she says, 'looked dignified and composed; but the Prince, agitated to the greatest degree; he was like a man in despair, half crazy. He held so fast by the Queen's hand, she could not remove it. When the Archbishop called on those to come forward who knew any impediment, his manner of doing it shook the Prince, and made me shudder.'

So intoxicated was the bridegroom, that in the middle of the service he rose up. The Archbishop suddenly ceased, and a dead pause ensued; when, before all the assembly, the King stepped down from the *haut pas*, whispered in the Prince's ear, and, taking him by the arm, forced him into a kneeling position, where he remained until the solemn nuptial benediction was pronounced. After the ceremony, a drawing-room was held, followed by a supper to the Royal Family at Buckingham House, on the conclusion of which the Prince and Princess retired to their home, Carlton House.

During the succeeding weeks, there were balls given by their Majesties and the Foreign Ministers, and the Princess made her début to the public by a state visit to Covent Garden Theatre, when, by command of their Majesties, a new and not over-decent comedy, entitled 'Life's Vagaries,' was acted, to which was added the new drama, 'Windsor Castle,' and the 'Masque of Peleus and Thetis;' a full programme. A state box for the use of their Royal Highnesses was fitted up for the occasion, opposite their Majesties' box. This was gorgeously upholstered in crimson velvet, lined with white satin, surmounted by the royal plume, and otherwise adorned with gold foil in theatrical abundance.

The account given of the Princess's visit in the *Oracle* is worthy of being preserved:

With her happy consort,' says this credulous journal,

'she entered the house fully a quarter of an hour before their Majesties with five of the Princesses arrived. They were received with applause, which made the whole theatre *tremble;* and the polite acknowledgment on the part of Her Royal Highness redoubled the peals of loyal admiration. Upon the entry of their Majesties, with the usual ceremonies, the songs were called for, and sung by the whole pit, which had a very singular effect; and, indeed, a more exhilarating sight never appealed to hearts susceptible to family delights, and joying in the *loveliest* bond of nature.

'The Princess was very brilliantly dressed, and her deportment was in the most finished style of dignified elegance. The ease of the Prince is not now to be praised; but we never before saw his countenance sparkle with so much content. The whole *suite* of Carlton House attended; and the *ensemble* bespoke truly a royal box.'

Even in the first few weeks of her married life the Princess was destined to meet with but little happiness. Earl Minto, in his interesting 'Life and Letters,' throws some light on the manner in which the honeymoon of this unhappy woman was spent. He dined at Blackheath with the Princess, and was afterwards shown the correspondence which passed between her and the Prince, Lord Malmesbury, Lady Elgin, and others.

'It appears,' he writes of their Royal Highnesses, 'that they lived together two or three weeks at first, but not at all afterwards as man and wife. They went to Windsor two days after the marriage, and, after a few days' residence there, they went to Kempshot, where there was no woman but Lady Jersey, and the men very blackguard companions of the Prince's, who were constantly drunk and filthy, sleeping and snoring in boots on the sofa; and, in other respects, the scene was more like the Prince of Wales at Eastcheap, than like any notions she had acquired before of a gentleman. Still, appearances were maintained, and the bride and bride groom were seen walking on the terrace at Windsor, the former in a dress of plain white muslin, a plain black bonnet with a single black feather, a very deep black veil, and a black cloak with broad lace.'

Lady Jersey, who was in the Princess's society at all hours of the day, found a thousand ways of insulting the wife of her royal paramour, for whom she did not care to conceal her aversion, and from whom she did not seek to hide her infamy. Driven at last to resent this woman's conduct, the Princess appealed to her husband to protect her from the insults she had no longer patience to endure, and hence arose their first quarrel. The first gentleman in Europe coldly informed his wife he required her to treat Lady Jersey 'as his friend;' this she passionately refused, and declared she would never sit at the same table with her unless he was present. He persisted that she should; bitter, vehement upbraidings followed, which ended by the injured wife demanding the dismissal of the mistress; but this the Prince refused, and quitted Carlton House overwhelmed with passion.

The Princess used frequently to repeat, years afterwards, that the King told her his brother, the Duke of Gloucester, informed him 'an arrangement was made with Lord Carlisle to give up Lady Jersey to the Prince—that this was agreed to at Rochester, when Lady Jersey first set out to meet the Princess of Wales, and that there was an understanding that she should be always the object of his affections.' The Princess now resolved to appeal, not to the pious Queen, who received her eldest son's mistress in her drawing-room, and permitted her to play cards with the Princesses, but to the King, her uncle, beseeching his interference, when His Majesty, after an interview with the Prince, arranged that Lady Jersey should no more come into waiting; an engagement which was but in part fulfilled

The Princess had not been married many months, when an opportunity occurred which enabled the malignant Countess to injure her in the estimation of the Queen, who from the first had regarded her daughter-in-law with marked coldness and dislike. The Princess, rendered miserable by the life opening before her, sought relief by expressing her feelings to her parents, and some of her friends in Germany, in letters she wrote them; unfortunately, she likewise passed rather free comments on her gracious but snuff-taking Majesty, by no means complimentary. These epistles were entrusted for delivery to the Rev. Dr. Randolph, then meditating a journey to Brunswick. It happened, however, that the reverend man was prevented from going abroad by the illness of his spouse; he, therefore, forwarded the package of letters to the Princess, directing them under cover to Lady Jersey, and sending them by the Brighton post-coach from town, as he was told at Carlton House this was the usual mode of conveying the Princess's papers and packets.

The letters never reached the Princess, though she caused every inquiry to be made concerning them. No doubt was, however, left on her mind as to their fate, for not only did Her Gracious Majesty's manner become more chilling to her daughter-in-law, but she was pleased to let fall from her royal lips several expressions which the unfortunate epistles contained, and which she likewise repeated to her friends. The Princess then accused Lady Jersey of having forwarded her letters secretly to the Queen, who, of course, made no scruple of opening them; and, the matter getting whispered about, the press took up the subject, and charged the Countess with treachery, embezzlement, and deceit. In order to clear her immaculate character, she wrote Dr. Randolph a letter, which was printed in the *Pall Mall*, in which she entreated him to publish the account of the transaction in any of the newspapers he might think fit. To this the reverend doctor made no reply, when her much-abused ladyship wrote to him once more, saying she should consider his silence as countenancing that calumny which false representations had so shamefully drawn down upon her. To this he made answer that he had sent a friend to London to trace the missing package, when, if his efforts did not prove successful, he should return to town and pursue the discovery himself, but repeated he had forwarded the letters by the Brighton coach. Whereon my Lord Jersey, mindful of his wife's honour, made pretence to the world at large of quarrelling with Dr. Randolph, a line of conduct which the Princess, in common with many others, regarded as a manœuvre to exonerate her ladyship and the reverend man from the charge in which she believed both were concerned.

In the meantime, the consideration of the Prince's debts came before the House of Commons. The King, in his message, informed those in Parliament assembled that he relied on the liberality and affection of his faithful Commons, and on the cordial interest which they had manifested in the Prince's marriage, to grant him an establishment. His Majesty also declared that, with 'the deepest regret,' he pointed out the necessity of freeing the Prince from 'the encumbrances to a large amount to which he is now subject,' as it was delicately put. Moreover, His Gracious Majesty avowed he had no idea of proposing to his Parliament to make any provision, otherwise than by an application of part of the income which might be settled on His Royal Highness to the payment of his debts.

The message, which had been listened to in unbroken silence, was, at the conclusion, received with a universal murmur of indignation and surprise. Pitt then moved that the message be referred to a committee of the whole House, on which Colonel Stanley begged that the King's message delivered to the House eight years ago, on the occasion of the Prince's debts coming before Parliament, should be read, when the following passage was listened to with keen attention :

'His Majesty could not expect, or desire, the assistance of the House, but on the well-grounded expectation that the Prince will avoid contracting any new debts in the future.'

Colonel Stanley then moved for a call of the House on the day when the Prince's debts were to be considered. Pitt trusted the honourable gentleman would not press for a call; but, the House being now excited, the Prime Minister was obliged to give way. Mr. Grey, the man whom the Prince had formerly asked to refute Fox's statement concerning Mrs. Fitzherbert, then stood up, and in a brief but forcible speech gave expression to the general feeling of the House. It would make no difference to the public ultimately, he said, and it would be more eligible at once to pay the debts of His Royal Highness, and to create a tax specifically for that purpose. He wanted the matter to b plainly, fairly, and distinctly done, that the public might clearly see what burdens they were to bear for His Royal Highness. When the cries of the starving poor were assailing them on all sides, the House would not be doing its duty by granting establishments to Princes with a profusion unparalleled. He had heard much of the dignity of His Royal Highness, but he was of opinion that the dignity of the Prince of Wales would be best maintained by his showing a feeling heart for the poor, and an unwillingness to add to their distresses.

Long and stormy debates followed the consideration of the Prince's debts, when His Royal Highness was accused of breaking the promise he had previously made the House of incurring no further debts; and many bitter and personal allusions were made to His Royal Highness which his friends were pleased to consider derogatory to his high station.

During the discussion of the subject in the House of Lords, the Duke of Clarence, with an exquisite and characteristic delicacy, stated that the Prince's 'marriage was part of a bargain, the price being the payment of his debts.'

The Prince of Wales finally submitted to the decision of Parliament; the result being that he was allowed an income of £125,000 a year, exclusive of his revenue of the Duchy of Cornwall, which amounted to £13,000 per annum; the Princess's jointure was fixed at £50,000, and the important sums of £26,000 for the furnishing of Carlton House and £20,000 for jewels were also granted him; however, out of this revenue a yearly deduction was made, in order that his debts might be gradually discharged.

At the period when the vast extravagance of the heir to the Crown was day after day exciting the attention of the nation, a growing dissatisfaction, which required but little to raise it to the rank of a revolution, was gradually gaining strength in the minds of the people, in consequence of the disastrous and ruinous war with France. The taxes levied on the country were enormous; the public debt increased, provisions became scarce, and famine was anticipated. Throughout the nation a turbulent spirit everywhere manifested itself; seditious ballads were circulated, demonstrations held, and petitions forwarded to the King, praying for peace with the French Republic.

The strong voice of popular indignation at last found vent in October, 1795, when the King proceeded in state to open Parliament. Dense and sullen crowds, to the number of 200,000, from whom ominous murmurs were heard, had collected, and lined the way from Buckingham House to Westminster, and when the carriage of the Duke of Gloucester appeared, it was greeted by a storm of hisses. Presently there were fresh signs of subdued excitement in the mob, and then the great lumbering state coach containing the King and two of his officers of state entered the park; this was the signal for a cry that suddenly and appealingly rose from the vast assemblage.

'Bread—give us bread! Peace, peace!' and then came an echo, 'No King, no King!' followed by hisses and groans. When the royal carriage reached the Ordnance Office, a bullet pierced the glass window of the coach on one side, and passed out at the other. One of the Lords became alarmed, but the King remained calm. 'Sit still, my Lord; we must not betray fear, whatever happens,' he whispered. When he entered the House of Lords, the first person he met was the Lord Chancellor, to whom he said, 'My Lord, I have been shot at.'

On His Majesty's return from Westminster, the attitude of the mob was still more offensive; when he entered St. James's Park, words of abuse and sedition assailed his ears; mud, filth, and stones were flung at the royal coach, some of which struck the King, who was now much agitated, and motioned to the Horse Guards at either side to keep off the people, whose shrill, threatening cry rose again and again, 'Bread! bread! peace! No King, no King!' Still pressed by the mob, the coach drove rapidly out of the park, and round by the stable-yard into St. James's Palace. When the King was about to alight, a fresh tumult took place, on which one of the horses became frightened, and a groom was dashed to the ground, in the midst of which excitement the King escaped into the palace; the mob then attacked the state coach, and did it great injury, before the Guards were enabled to disperse them. Shortly afterwards the King entered a private carriage and proceeded to Buckingham House; but he was again pursued by the populace, who threatened to pull him out of the carriage, and would probably have done so, but for his rapid driving and the timely arrival of the Life Guards.

Nor did this feeling of disloyalty quickly subside; four months later, when their Majesties were returning from

Drury Lane, a stone was flung at the royal carriage which smashed one of the windows and struck Her Majesty in the cheek; a thousand pounds was offered as a reward for the discovery of the perpetrator of this act, but to no purpose. It is no wonder that, considering the state of popular feeling at the period, and the character of his successor, His Majesty felt assured, as he told Lord Eldon, that he should be the last King of England.

Early in January, 1796, the Princess of Wales gave birth to a daughter; the royal babe was baptized Charlotte, and a few months after its birth its unhappy parents separated for ever. The Prince, as usual, absented himself from Carlton House; hints were given the Princess that she should seek for a separation, which not being taken, Lord Cholmondeley informed her the Prince did not mean to live with her any longer; she replied that such an intention should be conveyed to her directly from her husband in writing, and that, should a separation take place, their intercourse should never, under any circumstances, be resumed. Nothing loth, the Prince wrote to her at once. Commencing by styling her 'madam,' he goes on to say:

'Our inclinations are not in our power, nor should either of us be held responsible to the other because Nature has not made us suitable to each other. Tranquil and comfortable society is, however, in our power; let our intercourse, therefore, be restricted to that, and I will distinctly subscribe to the condition which you required through Lord Cholmondeley, that, even in the event of any accident happening to my daughter, which,' adds this virtuous Prince, 'I trust Providence in its mercy will avert, I shall not infringe the terms of the restriction by proposing at any period a connection of a more particular nature.'

The Princess was of course obliged to acquiesce in this fate without complaint. In her reply, she said his avowal merely confirmed what he had tacitly insinuated for twelve months; that she should not answer his letter, if it had not been conceived in terms which made it doubtful whether this arrangement proceeded from her or from him; 'and you are aware,' she adds, 'that the credit of it belongs to you alone.' As she had no protector but His Majesty, she referred herself solely to him, she said, on the subject, and then adds:

'I retain every sentiment of gratitude for the situation in which I find myself as Princess of Wales; enabled, by your means, to indulge in the free exercise of a virtue dear to my heart—I mean charity. It will be my duty, likewise, to act upon another motive, that of giving an example of patience and resignation under every trial. Do me the justice to believe that I shall never cease to pray for your happiness, and to be your much devoted

'CAROLINE.'

When the Princess sought advice from the King, he suggested that an attempt at reconciliation should be made, and that she should show the Prince some anxiety for his return. It was hard for an outraged woman to assume such a tone towards a man who had so grossly wronged her, but she was told it was her duty. She complied, and accordingly wrote to her truant husband:

'I look forward with infinite pleasure to the moment that will bring you to Carlton House, and that will for ever terminate a misunderstanding which on my side, I assure you, will never be thought of again. If you do me the honour of seeking my society in future, I will do everything to make it agreeable to you. If I should displease you, you must be generous enough to forgive me, and count upon my gratitude, which I shall feel to the end of my life. I may look for this, as mother of your daughter, and as one who is ever yours.'

To this humble appeal the profligate proved unmoved, and

the Princess retired to Charlton Villa, Blackheath, where she lived in the most unceremonious manner possible.

Thurlow, the Lord Chancellor, according to the Duke of Leeds' 'Memoranda,' came to the conclusion 'that the Prince's strange conduct could only be imputed to madness;' and, years after, Charles Greville makes reference to this hereditary disease.

'I am persuaded,' he says, 'that the King' (George IV.) 'is subject to occasional impressions which produce effects like insanity; that, if they continue to increase, he will end by being decidedly mad.'

Lady Jersey had, by this time, fallen into disgrace with her royal lover, and was consequently dismissed, when the Prince betrayed a desire to return to Mrs. Fitzherbert, who had separated from him on his marriage with the Princess; but this wish of his was not acceded to with that readiness which he flattered himself it deserved. Mrs. Fitzherbert had, during the period of their interrupted intimacy, continued to maintain her magnificent establishment in Park Lane, which was supported by an allowance of £10,000 a year, made her by the Prince, and had continued to entertain society. Her guests included not only the most distinguished members of the nobility, but even royalty itself, as represented in the persons of the Dukes of the blood royal. There was not one of the royal family, she assured Lord Stourton, who had not acted with kindness to her, and as for the King, 'from the time she set footing in England, till he ceased to reign, had he been her own father, he could not have acted towards her with greater tenderness and affection.' But, of all the family, the Duke of York constituted himself her special friend, and was generally the organ of communication between her and royalty; knowing that she had been so wronged, and had borne her injuries with such patience, they strove to make her all the compensation they could.

When, therefore, the Prince urged his desire of renewing his connection with her, she was much beset with difficulties and doubts as to whether she could do so with satisfaction to her own conscience; and, whilst she hesitated, many members of this royal, but remarkable family, not only male, but female, urged a reconciliation, 'even upon a pretext of duty.' Mrs. Fitzherbert's scruples, indeed, went so far as to carry her to the highest authorities of her Church, and Father Nassau, a priest belonging to one of the ambassador's chapels in Warwick Street, was despatched to Rome to lay the intricate case before the Pope. His Holiness decided that, as her marriage with the Prince was perfectly legitimate, she was justified in resuming her connection with her husband. The Prince was delighted that his desires were thus acceded to, and urged her to allow him to take up his residence with her in a private manner; but this she declined, and resolved that their reconciliation should be made as public as possible; for which purpose she gave a splendid breakfast, when not only the Prince and his royal brothers attended, but all fashionable London.

For the next eight years they dwelt together, the Prince living in comparative retirement, in order to retrench his expenses. They were extremely poor, but as merry as crickets; 'and, as a proof of their poverty, she told me,' says Lord Stourton, 'that once, on their returning to Brighton from London, they mustered their common means, and could not raise five pounds between them. Upon this or some other occasion, she related to me that an old and faithful servant endeavoured to force them to accept £60, which he said he had accumulated in the service of the best of masters and mistresses.' Their separation was due to the Prince having formed a connection with Lady Hertford, and the subsequent humiliating slights which Mrs. Fitzherbert received. This time their parting was final.

CHAPTER XIII.

Attempts on the King's Life—Margaret Nicholson and His Majesty—The Queen Seized with a Consternation—The Madman at Drury Lane—Despard's Conspiracy—The Prince of Wales once more in Debt—Signs of the King's Malady—His Majesty's Fear of a Regency—Speaks of Resigning the Crown—His Visit to the Princess of Wales—The Queen Plays a New Part—The Town Divided into Factions.

DURING his reign three attempts were made on the life of the King, and, strange to say, two of the would-be regicides suffered from the affliction to which His Majesty was periodically subject. The first of these attacks was made by a woman, Margaret Nicholson, who, at the moment he was stepping from his carriage, in order to enter St. James's, suddenly broke from the crowd and presented him with a paper. The King stretched forward to take it, when, with a rapid movement, she aimed a blow at his heart with a knife. His Majesty stepped back, and the demented Margaret made a second blow, but so thin-bladed, old, and worn was the weapon which she wielded in this tragic manner that, though it struck with full force against the royal waistcoat, it bent without penetrating. Those around now rushed in alarm on the woman, the knife was wrenched from her hands, and she was immediately secured. His Majesty, judging from the absurd manner with which she had attempted his life, declared her a lunatic. 'The poor creature is mad,' he said, with evident fellow-feeling; 'don't hurt her; she has not hurt me.'

The news of the attack was of course immediately exaggerated, seriously spoken of as a diabolical plot, and caused the greatest sensation. The Queen, on first hearing from the King's lips that an attempt had been made on his life, was 'seized with a consternation,' as Miss Burney duly records, whilst a painful silence was only interrupted by the sobs of the Princesses, and not a dry eye was to be found in the Royal household except His Majesty's, who, being aware that he had been in no possible danger, took a more sensible view of the occurrence than those loyal ones around him. In due time Margaret Nicholson had the honour of being twice examined before the Privy Council, where she explained her claims to the British throne, which were, however, not admitted, and stated her belief that it was only by the King's removal that she could come into her own. She was accordingly removed to Bedlam.

The later attempts on the King's life were of a more dangerous character. In the spring of 1800 His Majesty held a review in Hyde Park, when a musket-ball struck one of the clerks in the Navy-office, who was standing within a few yards of the King, pierced through the fleshy part of his thigh, passed through the coat of a Frenchman, and finally this remarkable ball spent itself on the breast of a boy without doing him the least harm It was impossible to trace from which direction it had come, or by whom it had been fired, as the Grenadier Guards were discharging a volley at the same instant. The King remained unmoved, and evinced not the slightest sign of fear. Within a few hours later, a third attack was made, with, fortunately, as little effect as on the former occasions. The place selected for the design was Drury Lane Theatre, where the King had commanded the performance of Colley Cibber's comedy,

'She Would, and She Would Not,' in which his son's mistress, Mrs. Jordan, was to appear.

Scarcely had the King entered the royal box, when he was seen by the audience, who applauded as usual, and, on his coming forward to bow his acknowledgments, a man in the front seat of the pit levelled a horse-pistol at him, and fired. His Majesty retired a step or two at the report, but, almost immediately recollecting himself, came forward, coolly took up his opera-glass, and surveyed the house as if nothing had happened to disturb him. Lord Salisbury, his Lord Chamberlain, far more agitated, urged him to retire, when he hastily turned round, and said, 'Sir, you discompose yourself as well as me. I shall not stir one step.'

The intended assassin was immediately seized and roughly dragged over the spikes of the orchestra into the music-room at the back of the stage. He was found to be a lunatic named James Hadfield, who had formerly been a soldier in the 15th Light Dragoons, and who declared, with the air of a philosopher, he was tired of life, but had not the resolution to commit suicide. His pistol had contained two balls, one of which struck the wainscot a couple of feet above the King's head, and the other passed through a curtain some inches higher.

Meanwhile, the theatre was in a complete uproar from pit to gallery, cheers and cries of 'God save the King' filling the house. His Majesty was indeed the person who appeared most free from agitation on the occasion. When the Queen presently arrived, he spoke to her in German, to calm her.

'There was a squib,' quoth he.

'A squib!' said she. 'I heard the word pistol, and the report.'

'Squib or pistol, the danger is now over, and you may come forward and make your bow,' replied the royal spouse.

He then ordered the curtain to go up, and the play to begin as usual, and so strong was his inherent trait of imperturbability, that, between the comedy and the afterpiece, he was noticed to take a sound doze, as was usual with him whenever he attended the play.

Three years later, his life was supposed to be in danger through Despard's conspiracy. Despard had been a brave soldier, who had fought at San Juan with Nelson, and more than once hazarded his life for his country's glory. Unjustly discharged from a post which he had held in Honduras, refused a hearing, and indignant at a long confinement in Coldbath Fields' prison, his loyalty turned to hate, and it was believed he resolved to overthrow the Government and destroy the King's life. At his trial, Lord Nelson came forward to give evidence of his heroism and loyalty in the past; he said:

'We went on the Spanish Main together. We spent many nights together in our clothes upon the ground. We have measured the height of the enemy's wall together. In all that period of time, no man could have shown more zealous attachment to his sovereign and his country than Colonel Despard did.'

But even such testimony did not rescue him from death, and in February, 1803, Colonel Edward Marcus Despard, with six confederates, stood condemned to die. Their execution, which took place at Horsemonger Lane Gaol, was attended by a crowd numbering over 20,000 people, all in a state of suppressed excitement. Colonel Despard appeared calm and resolute; he addressed the crowd as 'fellow-citizens,' and told them that, after serving his country faithfully, honourably, and, he trusted, usefully, for thirty years, he was about to suffer death upon a scaffold for a crime of which he was not guilty.

'But, fellow-citizens,' he said, 'I trust and hope, notwithstanding my fate, and perhaps the fate of many others who may follow me, that still the principles of liberty, justice, and humanity will triumph over falsehood, despotism, and delusion, and everything else hostile to the interests of the human race.'

At the conclusion of this speech, ringing cheers burst from the vast crowd; then came the terrible moment when this man's soul was launched into eternity. After the execution, his head was severed from his body, when the headsman held it up to the crowd, exclaiming, 'This is the head of the traitor, Edward Marcus Despard,' at which the crowd hooted and hissed, and otherwise expressed feelings of disloyalty.

It may be mentioned here that, two days after Despard's execution, the Prince of Wales's debts were again brought before the nation, when a fresh appeal was daringly and shamelessly made for him. It was understood he wished to restore his establishment, but even the courtly Lord Malmesbury said that any fresh sums granted him would 'evidently be squandered away in the same way he has hitherto lived in, without his assuming any one single exterior mark of royalty or splendour—to prove that he and his hangers-on do not consider it a farce.' However, through the influence of Fox and the new Premier, 'the milk-and-water Addington,' who was anxious to secure the favour of his future King, the country was once more heavily burdened, and a sum of £60,000 a year, for three years and a half, was bestowed upon this spendthrift Prince.

Early in the year 1801, there were rumours abroad that the Roman Catholics had summoned up sufficient audacity to seek for an equality of those civil rights enjoyed by the rest of their fellow-subjects. Lord Castlereagh, it was known, had been for several weeks in London striving to negotiate for the measure with the Government. Such a movement as this was looked on by the King, whose narrow-minded bigotry in his best moments strongly savoured of insanity, with positive horror, and he resolved that his opinions on the subject should be quickly known. Accordingly, when holding one of his ordinary levées in the latter part of January, he addressed Mr. Dundas, the only Cabinet Minister present. 'What—what—what,' said his Sacred Majesty, abruptly, 'what is it that this young Lord has brought over that they are going to throw at my head? The most Jacobinical thing I ever heard of. I shall reckon,' he added, in a still more flurried manner, ' any man my personal enemy who proposes any such measure. What—what —what?'

Dundas, nothing abashed by this Royal speech, replied calmly, 'Your Majesty will find among those who are friendly to that measure, some whom you never supposed to be your enemies.'

His hurried manner and flushed appearance were then little noticed, though it was afterwards remarked as probably the first indication of his old malady.

Shortly after this Pitt wrote to the King, stating it as his opinion, and that of the majority of the Cabinet, that the admission of Catholics and Dissenters to Parliament would, under certain conditions, serve to traquillize Ireland, backing this statement with many strong arguments, and concluding by stating that his continuance in office must depend on His Majesty's consent to the proposed measures. The King wrathfully replied that his coronation oath prevented him from entertaining such a proposal, whereon Pitt sent in his resignation.

The King's mind was now far from tranquil; he read the coronation oath repeatedly to himself, then to his family, and asked them if they understood it. ' If I violate it, I am no longer Sovereign of the country,' he said. He next read it to General Garth, informing that military man 'he had rather beg his bread from door to door than consent to any measure which gave his Catholic subjects religious equality,' and finally he asked the Lord Chancellor's opinion on the question, having little doubt that it would fully agree with his own. But the Lord Chancellor held 'that His Majesty was not in any degree fettered by his coronation oath in giving the Royal assent to a measure which should have the previous approbation of both Houses of Parliament;' a conviction with which the King was highly indignant, as it suddenly bereft him of all hypocritical excuses for his gross illiberality.

A few days after Pitt's resignation, it was announced that the King suffered from a heavy cold. A little later, His Majesty wrote to the new Prime Minister, Addington, lauding James's powders, a medicine for which he entertained a special affection; still no suspicions of his madness were entertained. He was now staying at Buckingham House, and when Lord Chatham called there to see him, His Majesty said to him, with an air of great gravity, 'As for my cold, it is well; but what else I have, I owe to your brother' (Pitt). After some other of his friends had conversed with him, and noted the turn of his conversations, they were not unprepared to hear it announced that he was in a high fever; for the treatment of which, strange enough, a medical man who made lunacy his special study, to wit, Dr. Willis, was called in. None were now admitted to Buckingham House, except the physicians; and, as on previous occasions, all details of the King's illness were kept as private as possible, yet the truth gradually leaked out that the Ruler of Great Britain and Ireland was mad once more.

George Rose met Lord Essex, early in February, under the piazza of St. James's, when his Lordship informed him that the King was entirely deranged. Entering the levée-room, they found Lord Chesterfield, who spoke with great concern of the King, but said he knew of no particulars of his exact state, as no bulletins were issued. All through his illness, the scheme for Catholic emancipation preyed upon his mind; for a whole day he remained without uttering a word or taking anything, after which he persistingly exclaimed, 'But I will remain true to the Church—I will remain true to the Church—I will remain true to the Church,' a statement which he duly followed up by mentioning the names of Pitt, Dundas, and Greville—Ministers favourable to the measure—with hearty and horrible imprecations. He was then placed under restraint; but he declared he was not mad. His detestation and jealousy of the heir to the Crown now came to the surface, unrestrained by any conventional pretence of paternal regard. Lord Brougham says that he hated the Prince 'with a hatred scarcely consistent with the supposition of a sound mind;' but, now that his brain was diseased, this detestation became intensified; and he besought them not to send for the elder Dr. Willis, for there would be a Regency, in which case he would never again resume his functions as Sovereign.

During his attack, it was necessary to get his signature for the repeal of the Brown Bread Act, when a singular farce was gone through. The Chancellor took the commission for the Bill to Buckingham House, but was told he could not see the King; however, Dr. Willis, who had always great influence over His Majesty, undertook to obtain the royal signature, to which his lordship agreed. Willis then informed the King that it was necessary he should sign his name to the paper. 'Then,' said the King, readily enough, 'I will sign my best George R.'

The merciful Duke of Cumberland subsequently told the Prince of Wales that, for such conduct, the Lord Chancellor deserved a rope and a hatchet. At last the King's illness became so serious that, for a brief while, his life was despaired of, during which time the Prince was amusing himself about town as usual; and, at an evening concert given by Lady Hamilton, he asked the ex-French minister, '*Savez vous, Monsieur de Calone, que mon père est aussi fou que jamais ?*'

The Prince indeed really knew little of how the King did; for, when he called at Buckingham House, he was not permitted to see him, and was never communicated with as to the increase or decrease of his malady. But this attack of insanity, at least in its bad form, did not last long; early in March, on the night succeeding one of his most critical days, the King fell into a profound sleep, and awoke almost well.

On his recovery, he made some inquiries as to those who had asked for him, and regarding what had passed in the House of Commons, when he was told that one man had moved for an inquiry into the state of His Majesty's health. He asked who that was, and being informed it was Mr. Rich, 'Ah,' he replied, 'he was always an odd man.' His oddness at having dared to desire such an inquiry should be made was now glaringly perceptible. The King then bade Dr. Willis write to Lord Eldon, Addington, and Pitt of his recovery; and, speaking of the latter, he said,

'Tell him I am now quite well—quite recovered from my illness; but what has he not to answer for who is the cause of my having been ill at all?'

When Pitt heard this, he informed His Majesty that he would never during his reign bring forward the question of Catholic emancipation; on hearing which, the King delightedly said, 'Now my mind will be at ease.'

He was, however, far from being in the possession of his senses, and at the end of the month was unable to attend the drawing-room, at which both the Queen and Prince were present, when the latter, before a large number of courtiers, behaved with great rudeness to Her Majesty. A little later on the King expressed an idea to the Prince of Wales, which had floated through his mind during his former madness, to the effect that he would resign the crown. On hearing such a delightful piece of intelligence, the Prince sent in hot haste for Lord Eldon, the Lord Chancellor, and, as the

Hon. George Rose mentions in his diaries, informed him that His Majesty was anxious to devolve the government on him (the Prince); 'that he wished, therefore, the Chancellor would consider the proper mode of that being carried into effect, and that it was the King's intention to retire to Hanover or to America.' The Prince also visited Lord Rosslyn on the subject, but neither of their lordships seem to have given the matter serious consideration; the Prince then informed them it was the wishes of the Queen and of his brothers to take measures for confining His Majesty, and that he, the Prince, much objected to the attendance of the Willises; but the Lord Chancellor informed him they were placed about the King's person from 'notorious necessity.'

In May the King and the royal family retired to Kew, and in this month he was thought sufficiently well to preside at a Privy Council. No sooner was he allowed to ride alone than he paid a visit to the Princess of Wales, whose unhappy situation had given him much uneasiness during his madness.

'The first time he rode out after his illness,' writes Lord Minto, 'he rode over Westminster Bridge to Blackheath, never telling anyone where he was going till he turned up to the Princess's door. She was not up, but jumped out of bed, and went to receive him in her bedgown and nightcap. He told Lord Uxbridge that the Princess had run in his head during his illness perpetually, and he had made a resolution to go and see her the first time he went out, without telling anybody.'

Though he continued for ten years subsequently to wield the sceptre of the most important nation in Europe, it is doubtful if he ever recovered his senses. Three years later, in 1804, he was ill again, when the Prince of Wales had an interview with him, an account of which he at once communicated to Charles Fox, who, speaking of this visit, says:

'There was no cordiality or pretended affection, but common talk on weather, scandal, etc.—a great deal of the latter—and as the Prince thought very idle and foolish in this manner, and running wildly from topic to topic, though not absolutely incoherent.'

At this unhappy period, the Queen, always heretofore his friend and comforter, now shrank from him, fearing some outbreak of his dreaded frenzy. This conduct on her part grieved him intensely. Lord Colchester, in his diaries, says: 'The Queen lives upon ill terms with the King. They never sleep or dine together; she persists in living entirely separate;' a statement to which Lord Malmesbury adds his testimony.

'The Queen,' says his Lordship, 'will never receive the King without one of the Princesses being present; never says in reply a word. Piques herself on this discreet silence, and, when in London, locks the doors of her white-room—her boudoir—against him.'

After many fluctuations of sanity and insanity, the King became so violent that he had to be subjected to the strait-waistcoat; he also at this time suffered considerably from gout, when his legs swelled to a vast size, and his general health became so bad that his life was considered in imminent danger. Once more the Prince of Wales's hopes rose; the King's madness, he confidently assured Pitt, must last for several months; a Regency was again in contemplation, when His Majesty once more rapidly grew better, and was taken out in a carriage by the Queen, and driven through the principal streets to show his subjects how far he had recovered.

During his illness, the town had been, as usual, divided in its allegiance towards the King and the Prince; the former announced that his Majesty was perfectly well, whilst the latter hinted at dark things regarding their Sovereign's health. Lady Malmesbury, indignant that the new doctors who attended the King issued bulletins contrary to her desires, loudly proclaimed them merely 'signing physicians,' who set their names to what others reported; whilst one of the royal maids of honour wished them, 'As the Spaniards say, with Mahomet.' But, in the midst of this party warfare, 'Everybody,' says Lord Minto, 'goes to see "Valentine and Orson," and weep over the death of a bear.'

CHAPTER XIV.

The Princess of Wales in Retirement—The Young Princess and her Mother—The Douglas Scandal and its Consequences—The Secret Commission—The Princess Triumphs—Her Popularity Increased—The Real Lord Byron—The Princess's Indiscretions and Eccentricities—The Prince's Amour with Lady Hertford—The Regency Commences—The Princess's Visit to Windsor—Fresh Insults—The Feelings of the People.

DURING the early years of her separation, the Princess of Wales lived at Blackheath in comparative retirement, taking little part in the State ceremonies; holding no Court, but receiving her friends, whom she delighted to entertain with pleasant dinners and *petit soupers*, which were all the merrier from the hostess's hatred of ceremony. Her guests, at this time, numbered some of the most brilliant members of the nobility, and many of the most distinguished foreigners of the day; amongst the latter were the Comte d'Artois, afterwards Charles X., the Duc de Barri, Prince de Condé, and Duc de Bourbon. In private, her life was solaced by the company of her little daughter, then a most promising and vivacious child, who bade fair to become an interesting and clever woman. Lord Minto, who became the Princess's friend and adviser, gives us a pleasant picture of a few hours he spent at Blackheath in 1798.

'Our dinner,' he writes, 'consisted of Lady Jane Dundas, Lady Charlotte Grenville, and Lady Mary Bentinck. Some men, among whom was Tom Grenville, disappointed her.

Princess Charlotte was in the room till dinner, and is really one of the finest and pleasantest children I ever saw. The Princess of Wales romped with her about the carpet on her knees. Princess Charlotte, though very lively, and excessively fond of romps and play, is remarkably good and governable. One day she had been a little naughty, however, and they were reprimanding her. Amongst the rest, Miss Garth said to her,

'"You have been so very naughty, I don't know what we must do with you."

'The little girl answered, crying, and quite penitently,

'"You must *soot* me;" meaning shoot her; but they let her off rather cheaper. Our dinner was pleasant as could be.'

But the keen delight which the society of her child afforded the Princess was not long permitted her; and, under the plea that her surroundings were not suitable to the education of the heiress-apparent to the Throne, the Prince desired to take her under his own care; but here the King, fortunately, stepped in, and seeing the malignity which prompted this act, as well as fearing the pernicious influence of Carlton House, he insisted on the equal right of the unhappy mother to instruct her child, and claimed for himself the duty and responsibility of her education. The Prince, who had not looked for interference in this quarter, angrily remonstrated, declared this was a direct insult offered him, refused to relinquish his paternal rights, and avowed that nothing but 'strong, particular reasons' could justify His Majesty in his conduct. The King promptly admitted that he was influenced by 'strong, particular reasons,' and that necessity, as well as law, precedent, and the wishes of the mother, required he should become the guardian of his grandchild. To this the Prince, after much fume and fury, acting on the advice of Mrs. Fitzherbert and his ex-mistress, now Mrs. Charles Fox, **submitted.** The Princess Charlotte was then removed to a house in the vicinity of Blackheath, where she was placed under the charge of Lady Elgin ; and the intercourse between mother and daughter was limited to a weekly visit.

The maternal feelings of the Princess, being thwarted in this way, found vent in adopting children, and placing them out under care in the village, where she constantly visited them ; but, not satisfied with this, she subsequently had one of them, an infant of a few months old, named William Austin, removed to her own house, where she tended him with the greatest care and affection, an indiscretion she soon had cause to bitterly repent. Her interest in children, indeed, prompted her to form the acquaintance of a woman who subsequently almost effected her ruin. Hearing that her neighbour, Lady Douglas, had been confined of a remarkably fine infant, she, with that want of discretion and thought so characteristic of her, without making any inquiries as to her ladyship, called on her, and an acquaintance so commenced soon ripened into intimacy. Lady Douglas was the daughter of a soldier who rose to the rank of colonel ; being a handsome and vivacious woman, she succeeded in marrying Sir John Douglas, a warrior of some renown.

Soon after the Princess made her acquaintance, Sir Sidney Smith, an old naval friend of Sir John's, returned to England, and became almost a part of the Douglas family. Sir Sidney in due course became known to the Princess, and visited her frequently, a circumstance of which Lady Douglas, whose reputation, it may be mentioned, was not above reproach, by no means approved, and at which she could not conceal her resentment. The friendship between her and the Princess lasted two years, when the Douglases went to Devonshire. In their absence, the Princess came to hear of some remarks her ladyship had made concerning her, and she then for the first time made inquiries into Lady Douglas's character, which had not a satisfactory result ; accordingly, when, on my lady's return to Blackheath, she called on the

Princess, Her Royal Highness refused to see her, and directed one of her ladies to write and request Lady Douglas not to visit her again.

This woman so scorned became a dangerous thing, and she resolved to have her revenge. Soon after, she declared, she received by the twopenny post a very coarse drawing, which was accompanied by an anonymous letter, charging her with intriguing with Sir Sidney Smith, and other indiscretions; this she affirmed to be written 'by that mischievous person, the Princess of Wales;' and the language it contained, she added, 'would have disgraced a housemaid.' Hearing of the accusation, the Princess sent for the Duke of Kent, and brought him to defend her from the charge; accordingly, he had an interview with Sir John Douglas and Sir Sidney Smith, when the matter was allowed to drop.

But this arrangement by no means suited Lady Douglas's plans, and she now freely circulated not only the story of the letter, but, by an afterthought, several scandalous charges against the Princess, some of which soon reached the Duke of Sussex's ears, who promptly demanded an interview with her. To him she made the most infamous statements, cleverly calculated to completely ruin the honour of the friendless woman who had slighted her. The Princess, she informed the Royal Duke, was not only a coarse, but a vicious woman; that she had acknowledged to her some time since she was about to become a mother; that her person had even evidence of pregnancy; and that to baffle suspicion, she had pretended to adopt a child who was in reality her own.

The Duke of Sussex immediately rushed, not to the slandered woman for explanation or denial, but to the Prince of Wales, who hailed this chance of ridding himself of the woman he so unjustly hated with signs of rejoicing; these base charges were accordingly taken down in full detail and submitted to Lord Thurlow and Sir Samuel Romilly The former declared at once he did not believe Lady Douglas's incoherent statements, that they 'did not hang together,' and had no dates. The princely husband was, however, by no means rejoiced at such an opinion of his wife's virtue, and a commission was therefore formed to take the evidence of witnesses to whom the immaculate Lady Douglas referred. Over five months were expended in striving to get up a case as damning as possible, which should be sufficient to blast the Princess's reputation for ever The light of publicity was withheld from the sittings of the commission, and neither the accused nor her representative counsel were permitted to attend; moreover, the witnesses, after examination, were enjoined to secrecy, and no cross-examination was allowed.

The principal witnesses against Her Royal Highness were her own servants, who had been appointed to her household by the Prince, and whom she was humiliatingly forced to take back again into her service. One of these, John Cole, whom she had recently insisted on discharging, bore testimony that criminal intercourse had taken place between the Princess and Captain Manby and Sir Sydney Smith; whilst another of them, Bidgood, who had been seen in serious converse with Lady Douglas, accused the Princess of like conduct with Captain Hood and Lawrence, the painter. Sir John and Lady Douglas also made their charges of her having been delivered of a child; but, notwithstanding the manner, in every way prejudicial to the Princess, in which the commission was conducted, the evidence was completely rebutted by her medical attendant, as well as by other trustworthy witnesses; whilst the crowning blow was dealt her slanderers by the positive proof given that the boy Austin was the son of a shoemaker, born in Brownlow Street Hospital. The whole testimony was now laid before the King, who, though satisfied of her innocence, yet allowed nine weeks of cruel suspense to pass without communicating with her; at the end of that time the Princess addressed a letter to him, begging that he would hasten his judgment on the matter, and grant her relief, for this unhappy delay caused her to sink in the regard of his subjects, and gave an unfair and temporary triumph to her enemies.

No notice was taken of this appeal, when letters came from the unfortunate Princess's parents imploring that a decision might be given; but yet over two months were allowed to elapse since the Princess had written before His Gracious Majesty deigned to reply. The facts of the case, he said, did not warrant any further steps to be taken by the Government, excepting such as his law servants might think fit to recommend for the prosecution of Lady Douglas; that there was no longer a necessity for him to decline receiving the Princess into his royal presence; that he had seen with satisfaction the decided proofs of the falsehood of the accusation of her pregnancy and delivery; but that there were other evidences against her which he regarded with serious concern. These circumstances were her easy condescension and ready familiarity, which often amounted to indiscretion, in her bearing to those around her, and which were most deadly sins in the eyes of his sacred and ceremonial-loving Majesty.

Upon receiving this letter, she wrote, requesting permission to wait on the King at Windsor—a favour denied her since her accusation—to which he replied he would prefer seeing her in town some day during the week, of which he would duly apprise her. A short time after this, a second note came from His Majesty, which caused her some alarm. Lest she might be led to expect, from his former letter, that he would name a day for her reception, His Majesty thought it right to acquaint her that the Prince, 'on receiving the documents concerning her investigation, made a formal statement to him of his intention to put them into the hands of his lawyers, and prayed that His Majesty would suspend any further steps in the matter until the Prince should be able to submit to him the statement he proposed to make.' The King, therefore, deferred naming a day for seeing her for the present.

To this she replied that she had already been banished seven months from the royal family, pending an inquiry affecting both her life and honour; that at the termination of the inquiry, it was the opinion of his sworn servants, there was no longer any reason why His Majesty should decline to receive her. She declared this renewed application, made by the Prince of Wales for a fresh trial, was a severe infliction, one which she hoped His Majesty would avert. Finally she besought his permission to pay her duty to him. The King made no answer, when she wrote once more to express her disappointment, and to acquaint him that, unless the justice was done her of being received by him, she felt herself bound to take a step which he might regret.

The step to which she referred was the publication of her case, in the shape of an appeal to the nation for the justice denied her by the Court. It was prepared by Spencer Percival, afterwards Premier, who was assisted by a member of Parliament, and printed by Edwards, of Crane Court, Fleet Street. The most profound secrecy was observed regarding it. Five thousand copies of the work were got ready for circulation, but at the last moment were not distributed, owing to the fact that the existing Ministry, which was hostile to the Princess, was turned out of office, and was duly replaced by one, the members of which were her friends, Mr. Percival being First Lord of the Treasury and Chancellor of the Exchequer. A few copies of this appeal, known as 'The Book,' which escaped being delivered to Mr. Percival, were subsequently purchased by Government for the respective and respectable sums of £1,500, £1,000, £750, and £500. The new Cabinet quickly informed the King that, in its opinion, it was 'essentially necessary, in justice to Her Royal Highness, that she should be admitted with as little delay as possible to His Majesty's presence, and that she should be received in a manner due to her rank and station in His Majesty's Court and family.' Nor was this all: His Majesty's confidential servants thought it due to her to request that some apartments might be allotted to her in one of the royal residences for her more convenient attendance at Court; she was therefore allowed the use of rooms at Kensington Palace.

That strong sympathy with those unjustly persecuted which is ever to be found in English breasts was now thoroughly roused throughout the nation in favour of the Princess, and the formal acknowledgment of her acquittal was hailed with universal rejoicing. The Prince, already feared and disliked, now became despised and detested; satires the most bitter and malicious, charging him with heinous crimes, were freely levelled at him and his friends; whilst ballads in favour of his deserted wife were sung in the streets generally, and in front of Carlton House particularly. Her portraits were exhibited in the shop-windows; her appearance in public was the signal for loud and continued cheering, and even at her first attendance, after her trial, at the royal drawing-room, she was greeted by the courtiers with clapping of hands. The Queen and Princesses received her on this occasion with marked coldness, satisfying themselves with curtseying to her in a frigid, ceremonious manner, but the King was as friendly as usual. When his birthday was celebrated in the following month, she again went to Court, where by some accident she encountered her husband face to face before a vast and brilliant crowd. The scene was dramatic; the courtiers respectfully drew back, leaving these two figures alone and prominent in the great drawing-room of St. James's, in the presence of royalty; for a second the

Prince hesitated, then made a cold, stately bow, which she gracefully returned, after which they exchanged a few words which could not be overheard, and passed on, never again to meet in this world.

A few months after this occurrence, the Princess's mother, the Duchess of Brunswick, whose husband had recently died from wounds received at the battle of Jena, sought a refuge in England, as the forces of Napoleon then occupied Brunswick; she was accordingly welcomed by His Majesty with some show of affection, and permitted to take up her residence with her daughter at Blackheath. The private life of the Princess, which had before been considered indiscreet, now became almost reckless; moods of wretchedness and depression were succeeded by a frivolity and daring that was censured by her enemies and regretted by her friends. At her residence at Blackheath, or at her rooms at Kensington Palace, she still continued to give dinners and suppers, where little ceremony was observed, and where oftentimes discretion and modesty were trenched upon in favour of sarcasm and wit. These entertainments commenced late, and usually lasted till dawn, the hostess being reluctant to rise from the table when surrounded by agreeable society. Amongst her friends were 'Monk' Lewis, Campbell, Walter Scott, the eccentric Lady Caroline Lamb, who followed in the wake of Lord Byron, Viscount Melbourne, a man addicted to pleasure, Lady Oxford, and Mr. Ward, afterwards known as Lord Dudley, and always regarded as a madman.

When Thomas Campbell the poet, described as being 'excellent company when allowed to soar in his own sphere, but totally unfit for the world, and ignorant of its ways as a child,' was introduced to the Princess, he by no means delighted her by reciting verses for which she did not care, but, on a subsequent occasion, he pleased her much better by dancing a Highland reel with her in her drawing-room. Another child of the Muses who was introduced to her was

Lord Byron, then the most remarkable man in society. An acquaintance followed, and the Princess on one occasion told the poet there were two Lord Byrons, one known to the world at large, and another, the real Lord Byron, known to her.

'When I invite him,' she said, 'I say I ask the agreeable lord, not the disagreeable one. He takes my *plaisanterie* all in good part, and I flatter myself I am rather a favourite with this great bard.' How the poet celebrated her husband's traits all generations shall read.

When the royal refugees, Louis XVIII., Madame d'Angoulême, and the French Princes, sought safety in England, the Princess invited them to a breakfast, to which her mother and the Princess Sophia were likewise bidden; but, at a hint from the Prince of Wales, Louis XVIII. and Madame d'Angoulême suddenly found themselves suffering; the one from gout in the knee and toe, the other from a swelled face, and so painful were these ailments on the morning fixed for the breakfast, that they were quite unable to accept the Princess's hospitality.

'So that,' she writes, 'I have not been blest with a sight of these charming creatures. Still, I was reduced to the satisfaction of having forty, including my own family, to this great feast. The sight was not enchanting, as it was loaded with old fograms. My usual resource on this occasion is to show them the great apartments and the rarities they contain. At last (everything, alas! ends) we were obliged to take to another resource, which was walking in the great avenue; and there we walked with all the plebeians and all the mobs. As our conviviality was exhausted, as well as our wit, the military band supplied the sound of our voices. We lounged there till, happily, the clock struck eight, and the party was swept away like magic.'

Her desire of dispensing with all ceremony was occasionally carried too far, as may be judged from the fact that, when she was one day about to visit the British Museum, and three of her gentlemen, Mercer, Craven, and Sir William Gell stood waiting to attend her, 'Now,' she said, turning to them, 'toss up a guinea to know which shall be the happy man to come with me.' Alas! these gentlemen three had not a guinea between them, and she was forced to name which should go with her.

But perhaps her greatest indiscretion was in speaking of her husband in unguarded terms, being surrounded by those whom he had placed in her service, who carried all her words back to him. One of Lord Minto's correspondents writes to him that the Princess came into the drawing-room with a book in her hand, crying, 'Here, my dear, read, read; tell Lord Minto directly that I am in love with his friend Mr. Burke. He has drawn the Prince's character exactly, exactly; read it, read it—"A man without any sense of duty as a prince, without any regard to the dignity of his crown, and without any love to his people; dissolute, false, venal, and destitute of any positive good quality whatever, except a pleasant temper and the manners of a gentleman." Ask Lord Minto if it is not quite like him.' At one of her dinners she spoke to those around her of her unhappy marriage. 'I, you know, was the victim of mammon,' she said; 'the Prince of Wales's debts must be paid, and poor little I's person was the pretence. Parliament would vote supplies for the heir-apparent's marriage; the King would help his little help. A Protestant Princess must be found— they fixed upon the Prince's cousin. To tell you God's truth, I always hated it; but to oblige my father, anything. But the first moment I saw my *futur* and Lady Jersey together I knew how it all was, and I said to myself, "Oh! very well." I took my *parti*—and so it would have been .f—but oh! mine God, I could be the slave of a man I love, but to one whom I loved not, and did not love me— impossible—*c'est autre chose.*'

On another occasion she favoured a friend of hers with some particulars regarding her wedding-night.

'After the play,' writes the author of 'The Memoirs of the Times of George IV.,' 'I was invited to sup with Her Royal Highness; as usual, she talked of her own situation and her previous life. "Judge," said she, "what it was to have a drunken husband on one's wedding-day, and one who passed the greatest part of his bridal-night under the grate, where he fell, and where I left him. If anybody said to me at dis moment, Will you pass your life over again, or be killed? I would choose death, for, you know, a little sooner or later, we must all die; but to live a life of wretchedness twice over—oh, mine God, no!"' The same authority tells of a strange practice of the Princess's. 'After dinner, Her Royal Highness made a wax figure as usual, and gave it an amiable addition of large horns; then took three pins out of her garment, and stuck them through and through, and put the figure to roast and melt at the fire. If it was not too melancholy to have to do with this, I could have died with laughing. The Princess indulges in this amusement whenever there are no strangers at table, and she has a superstitious belief that destroying this effigy of her husband will bring to pass the destruction of his royal person.'

Her mother, the Duchess of Brunswick, set down these traits to the same malady which affected the King; she deplored them to Lord Redesdale, and, tapping her forehead, said, 'But her excuse is, poor thing, that she is not right here.'

In the meantime, the Princess was made aware of her husband's new intrigue with the Marchioness of Hertford; a Venus who, though advanced in years, had not virtue or wisdom sufficient to repel the royal profligate. She had, indeed, at first refused his suit, but opposition had served to increase his passion; and, in order to render himself interesting in her eyes, and show her how his rejected love preyed upon his heart, he strove to reduce his rotund person, and tone down his rubicund complexion by having himself bled for her sweet sake. This was not an infrequent practice of his; and, according to Lord Holland, he had himself operated on several times by various doctors, when 'there was so little necessity for it, that different surgeons were introduced for the purpose, unknown to each other, lest they should object to so unusual a loss of blood.' About this time he had just broken off a connection with the charming Lady Massarene, the daughter of a French gaoler, who became the wife of an Irish peer; and, though His Royal Highness's passion for her was brief, her love for him lasted till her death.

In a connection which, about this time, he strove to establish with another fair woman, the Regent was not attended by that usual success which almost invariably attended him. This new lady who found favour in the royal eyes was Lady Yarmouth, then young and beautiful. The Prince had long sighed for her love, but sighed in vain. It happened that one day, when the first gentleman in Europe had partaken of Lord Yarmouth's hospitality, and the party had broken up, the Prince contrived to lure Lady Yarmouth into an ante-room, where, taking advantage of the opportunity he had long sought, he told her of his passion, and proceeded to kiss her, on which her ladyship was so uncourtly as to scream, a proceeding on her part which quickly brought her husband on the scene, who, in a paroxysm of passion, struck the Prince, and inflicted several injuries on the royal person, some of which caused much subsequent discoloration in the vicinity of his eyes. This treatment caused him for several days to seek the retirement of Carlton House, it being intimated to the public that he suffered from a severe sprain. By degrees, however, the story crept out, and was whispered through the town, hinted at in the press, until finally Peter Pindar celebrated it in verse, under the title of 'A Kick from Yarmouth to Wales;' a publication which ran through several editions, and gained enormous popularity.

The time had now arrived when the Princess of Wales was permanently to lose her chief friend and protector—the King, who, already stricken by blindness, afflicted by the conduct of his eldest son, agitated by political events, and sorely grieved by the death of his favourite daughter, the Princess Amelia, was again deprived of his reason, a condition from which he never wholly recovered. His last appearance in society was on the anniversary of his accession, when the Queen assembled all her children but two at Windsor Castle. The King, looking haggard, old, and helpless from loss of sight, came into the drawing-room leaning on the Queen, when he went round, speaking to all who were present; but in that excited and flurried manner which usually preceded his attacks of madness. This was in the latter part of the year 1810, and in the early months of the new year his mind became gradually worse; at times he had the power of calmly conversing on various subjects, but was beset with certain hallucinations, some of which were painful to those around him. One of these was that his daughter just dead—'his poor Amelia'—was living at Hanover, and was not only perfectly well, but was in the enjoyment of everlasting health and youth; another was that he had an intrigue with the Countess of Pembroke, a lady of spotless reputation, who, in her youth, and in the first years of his reign, had been one of the chief ornaments of the Court; occasionally, he protested that she was his wife, and was wrathful that he was not permitted to see her. Once he said to the Duke of Sussex:

'Is it not a strange thing, Adolphus, that they still refuse to let me go to Lady Pembroke, although everyone knows I am married to her; but, what is worse of all, is that infamous scoundrel Halford was by at the marriage, and has now the effrontery to deny it to my face.'

On the declaration of the physicians that His Majesty was unfit to transact any business of the State, a Regency Bill was once more introduced, constituting the Prince of Wales Regent, under certain restrictions, which were to be removed at the end of the year, in case the King did not recover; these were that he was unable to grant peerages, except for naval or military services, or award, pensions or places for life. The charge of the King and his household were naturally given to the Queen, at which, as the latter conferred considerable political influence on those who possessed it, the Prince was wroth indeed. He expected, he said, to be treated as a gentleman, not as a ruffian, and considered this power given to Her Majesty as a direct insult to himself; an opinion in which his royal brothers of course agreed, and they protested against such a privilege being given to their mother, to the disgust, but not the surprise, of the nation.

During the first year of the Regency, the King's state continued changeable; for days his mind wandered hopelessly, and again he was so well that it was anticipated he would resume the reins of Government before the twelve months had expired. He was so well, indeed, in May, that he was allowed to ride out.

Towards the end of the month his affliction returned, and by the close of the year all hopes of his ultimate recovery were abandoned, and the Prince of Wales was allowed the full powers of a King.

'No Prince,' says Lord Brougham, 'ever ascended the throne with so universal a feeling of distrust and even aversion.' On his way to open Parliament in full state, he seemed nervous and anxious, and was received with dead silence by the crowd which had collected to see the procession; not a hat was taken off, not a cheer greeted him, a circumstance which caused bitter disappointment to one so fond of public approbation. But his displeasure was heightened presently by the behaviour of his daughter, the Princess Charlotte, who, with two of the Royal Princesses, was present in the House of Lords, sitting on the woolsack, near the throne, from which position she spoke to one Peer and nodded to another, both of whom befriended her mother's cause.

'It was remarked,' said Lady Charlotte Campbell, 'that she talked and laughed much, turned her back upon her papa, and had a certain expressive smile which did not displease all the Lords nor all the Ladies there. The Prince, it is said, was much displeased at her manner.'

His unpopularity by no means diminished with time, as may be judged by a letter written by Fremantle to the Marquis of Buckingham in the following year. Speaking of the Regent, he says:

'When he came to the drawing-room on Thursday, he was in his stage-coach, with all the parade of royalty and grandeur, and there were upwards of ten thousand people in Pall Mall, through which he passed, and where he was met by not one single token of applause. It was a dead silence throughout . . . After declaring publicly, right and left, his intention of going to the Lord Mayor, his nerves failed him, and he sent an excuse. I am confident he would have been hissed through the City. The addresses on the assumption of the Regency have failed throughout England, and there is hardly a quarter in which the attempt has not been made to procure them.'

Since the last outbreak of the King's madness, great restrictions were placed on the intercourse between the Princess and her daughter; they met but once a week, but were never allowed to see each other unless in the presence of a third person; even this weekly meeting was, after awhile, prevented by the Princess Charlotte's removal to Windsor on a visit to her royal grandmother. Her continued absence at last became almost unendurable to the Princess of Wales, who, whatever her faults may have been, loved her daughter; she therefore wrote to the Queen, beseeching her to grant her permission to see her child, offering to visit her at Windsor, if she could not attend on her; to which petition Her Gracious Majesty sent back word that Her Royal Highness's studies must not be interrupted.

But, time going by, and their meeting being still prevented, the Princess, fearing a total separation was intended, went to Windsor, selecting Sunday for her visit, as a day on which no excuse for the interruption of studies could be made. When she reached the castle she was cruelly refused permission to see her daughter, on which she requested an interview with the Queen, in order, if possible, to move her to her desires; but, though Her Majesty granted the interview, she refused the Princess's request. The Prince Regent had given strict orders, Her Majesty said, not to allow a meeting between the Princess of Wales and her daughter. The Queen's manners were as ceremonious and cold as ever, and no refreshments were offered to the royal visitor.

At parting, Her Majesty said, as she helped herself to a liberal pinch of snuff, 'I hope you will always preserve the same friendship which you have ever felt for me;' to which the Princess, bowing to the little old woman with profound reverence, answered in most bitter irony, 'Oh, certainly, your Majesty;' and then left the room, almost choked with tears. After this interview, she received an insulting message from one of the Ministers of State, informing her the Prince Regent forbade her going to Windsor again.

Soon after this, however, an unexpected meeting took place between the unhappy mother and her daughter. It chanced that, as the Princess of Wales was out driving one day, she saw her daughter's carriage being driven in another direction; she immediately gave orders to her coachman to follow it, when something like a pursuit took place, but the young Princess's coach, which had entered Hyde Park, was ultimately overtaken near the Serpentine, and both leaned forward from their respective carriages to kiss, and hold some minutes' conversation, being surrounded meanwhile by a crowd of eager sympathizers. About this time, another occurrence took place which caused considerable annoyance to the royal grandmother and the Regent.

The Princess Charlotte had now arrived at an age when it was considered desirable she should be formally presented at Court; arrangements were therefore made for the event, and a day fixed on; it was also arranged by the Regent that his daughter's presentation should be made by the Duchess of York, or some other of the female branches of the royal family, but the young Princess stoutly declared she would be presented by her mother, and by her mother alone. Her illustrious father had by this time come to learn that she had a will of her own, and the matter was allowed to rest. Accordingly, the appointed day having arrived, the Princess of Wales and her daughter were dressed and ready for the ceremony, and were about to set out for St. James's, when, at the last moment, a message was sent from the Regent to his daughter, informing her a presentation by her mother would not be allowed.

'It shall either be my mother or no one,' she spiritedly replied.

The result was that her presentation did not take place.

The restrictions now placed between them became so severe, and so grievous to both, that the Princess of Wales, acting on legal advice, determined to bring her painful situation before Parliament. Before doing so, however, she addressed a touching letter to her husband, in which she said she was at length compelled either to abandon all regard for the two dearest objects she had on earth, her honour and her child, or to throw herself at his feet, who should be the natural protector of both.' She represented that the separation between herself and her daughter could only admit of one construction in the eyes of the world, and that was one fatal to her own reputation. She implored him to reflect on the situation in which she was placed, without the shadow of a charge against her, yet treated, she adds, 'as if I were still more culpable than the perjuries of my *suborned traducers* represented me, and held up to the world as a mother who may not enjoy the society of her own child.'

This letter was forwarded to the Regent under the care of Lords Eldon and Liverpool, but next day was returned unopened; again the Princess had it forwarded, intimating to these noble Lords that, as it contained matter of importance to the State, she relied on their laying it before His Royal Highness; next day, however, it was again sent back unopened.

A third time she forwarded it, expressing her confidence that Lords Eldon and Liverpool would not take upon themselves the responsibility of not communicating the letter to the Prince, and that she should be the only subject in his empire whose petition was not to be permitted to reach the Throne. To this an answer was made, that the contents of her communication had been laid before the Regent, who had no answer to make: upon which she sent her letter to the *Morning Chronicle* for publication, from which journal it was copied into almost every newspaper of the day. The immediate sensation it produced throughout the nation can scarcely be conceived; the Prince's rage was so great that for a time it almost deprived him of reason; whilst the sympathy it evoked from men and women of all classes for the unhappy mother was mingled with the fiercest indignation against her persecutor.

A Privy Council was hastily called together, and of course gave expression to the Regent's wishes; the Lords, who by the way included two Archbishops, in this Council assembled, declared that, having read the Princess's letter, and having also examined the documents regarding her accusation by Lady Douglas, they were of opinion the intercourse between Her Royal Highness and her daughter should continue to be subject to restrictions and regulations. This was but a fresh stab at her reputation, but it was met in a manner little anticipated; the Princess bravely appealed to the nation through Parliament, protesting her innocence, condemning a system that dared to pronounce her guilty, without letting her know on what evidence their verdict was founded, and finally requesting Parliament to enter into a full and strict investigation of the Douglas charges, which would again prove her blameless. A letter to the same purport was sent to the Lord Chancellor, that it might be read in the House of Lords, which Lord Eldon returned to her, advising her for her own safety not to make it public; to which she replied he need have no apprehension for her, as the British constitution, and the laws of England, were her safeguard. Her letter to the Commons was the cause of more than one warm debate. One member, Mr. Whitebread, called attention to the fact, that though the witnesses who bore evidence against the Princess were 'perjured and blasted,' yet Sir John Douglas was then in the service of one of the royal family. Lord Castlereagh stated that the Government had not prosecuted Sir John and Lady Douglas for perjury, because unwilling to place many indelicate accusations before the world; a statement which was received with sceptical and derisive laughter. Another member, Mr. Wortley, said that he had as high feelings for royalty as any man, but proceedings like this contributed to pull them down. He was sorry that the royal family did not take warning in time from what was thought and said concerning them, and that it seemed they were 'the only persons in the country who were wholly regardless of their welfare and respectability.' The Princess of Wales was doubtlessly ill-used, and he would not have the Regent lay the flattering unction to his soul, and think his conduct would bear him harmless through all these transactions. This speech was received with much applause; but after some wrangling, and much bitterness on both sides, the subject was allowed to drop.

The famous publication known as 'The Book,' which contained the whole statements of the Douglas investigation, copies of which had been bought up at vast prices, was now republished and openly sold; this added fresh strength to the popular indignation against the Regent and his friends. Every mark of public sympathy continued to be shown to the Princess; addresses were poured in on her from numerous public bodies, congratulating her on 'having escaped a conspiracy against her life and honour,' in which the city of London took the lead, the borough of Southwark, and the city of Westminster, the county of Middlesex, the towns of Bath, Bristol, Rochester, Sheffield, Berwick-on-Tweed, and Dublin following suit. When the address was carried by the Common Council, one of its members, Sir William Curtis, said publicly that the Princess 'had been grossly, infamously, and abominably treated—her innocence was undoubted, her persecution had been shameful;' not satisfied with this honest assertion, he, after the Princess's answer to the address, took that opportunity to state that he believed her Royal Highness 'had been traduced most wickedly and most abominably.'

The mob, of course, took up the injured woman's cause, and demonstrated its feelings in its own way. This took the shape of an effigy dressed in white, supposed to represent Lady Douglas, which held in its hand a parasol, on which were written, in letters so large that those who ran might read, the words *Conspiracy and Perjury*, whilst on her back was the inscription, *Diabolical Perjury*. This effigy, attended by an indescribably vast concourse of people, was exhibited in front of Carlton House, that His Royal Highness might have the benefit of the sight, and after being carried through the town, preceded by a bell-ringer announcing the execution at the stake of a certain lady at eight o'clock in the evening at Blackheath, the effigy was burnt amidst tumultuous shouts and great signs of rejoicing.

KING GEORGE IV.

CHAPTER XV.

The Reign of the Regent—A Levée at Carlton House—Difficulties of his Ministers—Visit of the Foreign Sovereigns to London—The Princess and the Emperor of Russia—At the Opera—The Prince of Orange and the Princess Charlotte—Anxiety of the Regent to get her out of the Kingdom—The Grand Duchess of Oldenburg's Opinion of the Regent—The Princess becomes Rebellious—She breaks off her Marriage—Wrath of the Regent—The Princess's Flight—A Royal Captive.

WHEN time confirmed the opinion of the physicians regarding His Majesty, and his recovery became utterly hopeless, the Regent, holding the full powers of State, was regarded as a King in all but name, whose favour was steadily courted, and whose displeasure was regarded as the greatest misfortune. In order, therefore, that the zealous courtiers might gain the one and avoid the other, they gradually fell off in their attendance on the Princess, who at last found herself reduced to the society of a few faithful friends. Meanwhile the Prince gave entertainments, famed for their costly magnificence and brilliancy, which were found far more acceptable than the dinners or suppers at Blackheath and Kensington Palace.

Richard Bush, a minister of the United States, gives an account of a levée which somewhat astonished his Republican soul. His conveyance having slowly steered its way through an immense crush of coaches and vehicles, he at length gained the great hall of Carlton House, which was lined with the Yeomen of the Guard, having velvet hats adorned with wreaths upon their heads, halberds in their hands, and rosettes ornamenting their shoes, a great stream of courtiers, in handsome and many-coloured costumes, was pushing its way through the spacious apartments, whilst from beyond the open columns of the portico came the mellifluent music of bands. In one of the rooms, awaiting the royal presence, were the Cabinet Ministers, with bags and swords, the diplomatic corps, the Lord Steward with his badge of office; the Lord Chamberlain with his; the Lord Chancellor in his black silk gown and wig; the Bishops and Church dignitaries, with whom the tainted atmosphere of Carlton House by no means disagreed, likewise in wigs; the ambassadors in their national costumes, and many Knights of the Garter. When, presently, the Regent came from his closet, doors hitherto shut were thrown wide open, and revealed a vast assembly of brilliant courtiers, who had come to pay their homage at the shrine of royalty, all of whom were honoured by a word, look, or smile from the Prince.

The Regent was never better pleased than when he was the observed of all observers, holding drawing-rooms, giving fêtes, or presiding at some gorgeous ceremonial; so far as the business of the State was concerned, he was utterly useless, as his conduct frequently perplexed and occasionally disgusted his Ministers. An example of this was given during the first year of his Regency.

At a dance given at Oatlands Park, whilst skipping about in a Highland fling, the Prince wrenched his ankle. 'This took place,' says a correspondent of the Duke of Buckingham's, 'ten days ago, since which he has never been out of his bed. He complained of violent pain and spasmodic affection, for which he prescribed for himself, and took a hundred drops of laudanum every three hours. When Farquhar and the other medical men came down, they saw him under the influence of this laudanum, so enervated and hurt that they immediately prescribed the strongest dose of castor-oil; but he still perseveres in his laudanum, which he says relieves him from pain, and lays constantly on his stomach in bed. He will sign nothing, and converse with no one on business, and you may imagine, therefore, the distress and difficulty in which the Ministers are placed. The Duke of Cumberland is going about saying it is all a sham, and that he could get up and would be perfectly well if he pleased.'

In June, 1814, the Emperor of Russia and the King of Prussia, with his brother, his sons, and various minor Princes, visited London; when the Regent had another opportunity of giving some of those gorgeous fêtes which delighted his royal soul. On this occasion it had been announced that Her Majesty would hold two drawing-rooms in honour of her illustrious guests, at which the young Princess Charlotte would be presented; the reason for holding two drawing-rooms, it was freely whispered, was in order to allow the Princess to appear at one when her husband would not be present, he in turn attending the other when she would not be there. The Princess, accordingly, in great glee, prepared for the occasion, but her hopes and intentions were destined to meet with bitter disappointment once more, when she received a message from Her Gracious Majesty that it was impossible to receive her, as she had a communication from the Regent, in which he declared he considered his own presence at Court on both occasions indispensable, and 'his fixed and unalterable determination not to meet the Princess of Wales upon any occasion, either public or private.' To this cruel treatment, intended by her husband to not only humiliate her in the eyes of the nation, but in those of the illustrious sovereigns about to visit England, she was determined not to submit. She, therefore, decided on going boldly forward to claim the right of appearing at the drawing-room due to her station, but was unfortunately dissuaded from this resolution by one of her most zealous friends and advisers, Mr. Whitebread. At his suggestion, she wrote to the Queen in a submissive tone, asking the cause of this fresh slight put upon her. When another of her friends, Creevey, heard of this counsel of Whitebread's, he said to him, 'You have cut her throat.' Mr., afterward Lord Brougham, was also of opinion that his advice was wrong; but it was now too late to retrieve the step already taken, and the only thing left for her was to pen a letter to the Regent. He might refuse to read it, she said, but the world would know she had written it; she had been declared innocent, and now she would not submit to be declared guilty. 'Of all His Majesty's subjects,' she concluded, 'I alone am prevented by your Royal Highness from appearing in my place, to partake of the general joy; and am deprived of the indulgence in those feelings of pride and affection permitted to every mother but me.'

But this was not the only insult which this occasion was to bring her; before his arrival in England, the Emperor of Russia received a message from the Regent, formally delivered by Sir Thomas Tyrwhitt, requesting His Majesty to take no notice of the Princess of Wales. When their Majesties arrived in town, she despatched her Chamberlain to bid them welcome to England, a compliment which they acknowledged by sending their respective Chamberlains to wait on her. The King of Prussia—in whose cause her father had fought, and her brother lost his life—sent her his regards, but avowing that, under the circumstances, he dared not come himself; this line of conduct was followed by all the foreign Princes who arrived, and even by a nephew of hers, a 'little vile Prince of Wurtemburg.'

Yet her anxiety that His Imperial Majesty of Russia, whom Napoleon in the day of his power was wont to style a *petit maître*, would visit her was painful. 'My ears are very ugly,' she said, striving to laugh, whilst yet the tears stood in her eyes, 'but I would give them both to persuade the Emperor to come to me to a ball, a supper, or any entertainment that he would choose.' She waited and hoped until her patience was almost exhausted and her hopes dead, but the great man never came. On one occasion she received a private message from a friend that the Emperor intended visiting her, when in great delight she dressed for the occasion and sat patiently with her ladies for four hours expecting him every minute; but, alas! was again doomed to disappointment. Another day her daughter sent her word secretly that it was positively the Emperor's intention to visit her, and that he had already sent to intimate his intentions of so doing to the Regent, who had not since then spoken to him. Again her hopes were in the ascendant, and no doubt she would have had the honour she so desired, but that, as the Emperor was about leaving his apartments to call on her, one of the Regent's Ministers arrived, and besought him in so forcible a manner not to put his intentions into execution, that His Imperial Majesty yielded to his entreaties. Still the Princess was destined to see their Majesties before they left England, if not to meet them.

Lady Charlotte Campbell's graphic pen describes the occasion. After dinner 'there came a note from Mr. Whitebread, advising at what hour she should go to the opera, and telling her that the Emperor was to be at eleven o'clock at the Institution, which was to be lighted up for him to see the pictures. All this advice tormented the Princess, and I do not wonder that she sometimes loses patience. No child was ever more thwarted and controlled than she is—and yet she often contrives to do herself mischief in spite of all the care that is taken of her. When we arrived at the opera, to the Princess's and all her attendants' infinite surprise, we saw the Regent placed between the Emperor and the King of Prussia, and all the minor Princes in a box to the right. "God save the King" was performing when the Princess entered, and consequently she did not sit down. I was behind, so of course I could not see the house very distinctly, but I saw the Regent was at that time standing and applauding the Grassinis. As soon as the air was over the whole pit turned round to the Princess's box and applauded her. We who were in attendance on Her Royal Highness entreated her to rise and make a curtsey, but she sat immovable, and at last, turning round, she said :

'" My dear, Punch's wife is nobody when Punch is present."

' We all laughed, but still thought her wrong not to acknowledge the compliment paid her ; but she was right, as the sequel will prove.

'" We shall be hissed," said Sir William Gell.

'" No, no," again replied the Princess, with infinite good-humour. "I know my business better than to take the morsel out of my husband's mouth ; I am not to seem to know that the applause is meant for me until they call my name."

' The Prince seemed to verify her words, for he got up and bowed to the audience. This was construed into a bow to the Princess, most unfortunately ; I say most unfortunately, because she has been blamed for not returning it ; but I, who was a witness to the circumstance, know the Princess acted just as she ought to have done. The fact was, the Prince took the applause to himself; and his friends, or rather his toadies (for they do not deserve the name of friends), to save him from the imputation of this ridiculous vanity, chose to say that he did the most beautiful and elegant thing in the world, and bowed to his wife.

'When the opera was finished, the Prince and his supporters were applauded, but not enthusiastically ; and scarcely had His Royal Highness left the box, when the people called for the Princess, and gave her a very warm applause. She then went forward and made three curtseys, and hastily withdrew. I believe she acted perfectly right throughout the evening—but everyone tells a different story, and thinks differently. How trivial all this seems, how much beneath the dignity of rational beings! When the coachman attempted to drive home through Charles Street, the crowd of carriages was so immense it was impossible to pass down, that street, and with difficulty the Princess's carriage backed, and we returned past Carlton House, where the mob surrounded her carriage, and having once found out it was her Royal Highness, they applauded and huzzaed until we who were with her were completely stunned. The mob opened the carriage-doors, and some of them insisted on shaking hands with her, and asked if they should burn Carlton House.

'"No, my good people," she said; "be quite quiet—let me pass, and go home to your beds."

'They would not, however, leave off following her carriage for some way, and cried out:

'"Long live the Princess of Wales! long live the innocent," etc., etc.

'She was pleased at this demonstration of feeling in hei favour, and I never saw her look so well, or behave with so much dignity; yet I hear all this has been misconstrued and various lies told.'

A couple of days after this she was sent word by the box-keeper at Covent Garden, that no box could be kept for her at that theatre; and on the occasion of a common night at Drury Lane, she received word to the same effect from the manager of that play-house, both gentlemen having of course received instructions to this effect from the Court. All these indignities, petty and galling, inflicted by the first gentleman in Europe on his wife, received public comment, and were bitterly resented by the mob. As he drove through the streets, accompanied by his illustrious visitors, he was hissed, hooted, and groaned at; and on the occasion of his visit to the great dinner given by the Lord Mayor to the foreign monarchs, the immense crowd which lined the way from Temple Bar to the Guildhall not only groaned and hissed, but shouted out:

'Where's your wife? where's your wife?'

At which delicate inquiry the Prince grew livid with rage, and swore a great oath, which, strange to say, he kept, that he would never again honour a civic banquet with his presence.

The Princess of Wales and her daughter were greeted, whenever they drove abroad, in a far different style; instead of hisses, they got cheers and words of rough but honest sympathy. To the former was cried out, 'God bless you, we will make the Prince love you before we have done with him,' 'You will soon overcome your enemies;' and to the latter, 'God bless you, but never forsake your mother.' These tokens of popular esteem used to bring tears into the eyes of the outraged wife, who was now weak and nervous from the long struggle for right and justice which she had had to sustain.

Amongst the minor Princes who were in London during the visit of His Imperial Majesty and the King of Prussia, were two suitors for the hand of Princess Charlotte. She was at this time in her eighteenth year, and has been described as above the middle height, 'with all the fulness of a person of five-and-twenty, extremely spread for her age, her bosom full but finely shaped, her shoulders large, and her whole person voluptuous; neither graceful nor elegant, yet having a peculiar air *et tous les préstiges de la royauté et du pouvoir.*' Though she had been presented at Court, she was not permitted to join in any of the festivities that filled the town with the fame of their magnificence, but one, at Carlton House; as it was the Regent's wish to treat her as a child as long as possible, and keep her out of the sight of the public, who invariably received her with every mark of affection and enthusiasm; a fact proving such a marked contrast to the feelings with which he was greeted, that his vanity was sorely hurt. She had now a residence in town appropriated to her, a dull old building, quiet as a convent, known as Warwick House, which stood opposite Carlton House, from which it was merely divided by a road. It was arranged that she was to live occasionally at Windsor, where her royal dragon of a grandmother still kept watch over her. No life could be more dull than that of the young Princess, who was now seldom permitted to see her mother, forbidden the society of friends of her own age, and continually guarded night and day by the ladies whom the Prince had appointed to her household. At the fête at Carlton House, at which she was permitted to be present, her cousin, the Duke of Gloucester, son of the late Duke who had married the Countess Waldegrave, was bidden. She had, she confessed, 'found him delightful'; and the Duke, who was generally known by no other style than 'Silly Billy,' was wise enough to profit by her regard and elevate himself to the rank of a suitor. During the fête he sat down beside her and talked to her, which much displeased the Regent, who was walking up and down the room with Lady Liverpool, whom he at last sent to request the Princess that she would change places with Lady Bathurst, who sat on the other side of her. This the Princess would not do, but, with great spirit, stood up and walked into the next room.

'Silly Billy' was much offended, but the Princess subsequently apologized, when he confidentially informed her she might consider him devoted to her, and ready to come forward whenever she cast her eyes on him.

A few days later, it being the Regent's birthday, the Queen presented new colours to the Cadet Battalion, at Sandhurst Military College; when the Princess Charlotte was present, as well as all the royal family, the Bishop of Salisbury, the Ministers and their wives. The Regent did not condescend to speak to, or in any way notice his daughter, giving it as an excuse that 'he could not bear to see those damned ladies' that accompanied her, meaning the Duchess of Leeds and Miss Knight, who behaved with kindness to the almost friendless Princess. ,'He looked,' says the latter, 'as if he wished to annihilate us.' The royal family dined in the house, the rest of the company under tents in the garden, and in the evening there was a little dance of five or six couples, promoted by the Duke of Clarence. The day had been remarkably hot, and the evening was a beautiful moonlight. When the Queen was about to depart, the Prince Regent was not to be found, and we afterwards learned that he, with the Duke of York, Prince of Orange, and many others, were under the table. The Duke of York hurt his head very seriously against a wine cellaret; in short, it was a sad business.'

Shortly before the visit of the foreign sovereigns, the Prince of Orange had arrived in town, and taken lodgings over a tailor's shop; his visits to Carlton House were frequent, and it soon became whispered that he was a suitor for the hand of the Princess Charlotte. This princeling was a shallow, frivolous young man, 'particularly plain and sickly in his look, his figure very slender, and his manner rather hearty and boyish.' The Regent, partly from political reasons, but principally because he wished to get his daughter out of his way, was highly favourable to the marriage. He had no affection for her, and had long dreaded the stimulus which her public appearance gave to the almost universal sympathy felt for her mother; moreover, he had carefully avoided everything which could look like a recognition of her as heiress presumptive to the Crown, hoping that death or divorce might rid him of his wife, and allow him to marry again, when he might have a son, who would, of course, exclude the succession of the daughter of his abhorred spouse.

The Queen was likewise anxious to get her out of the country, having a deadly fear of her growing popularity, and had eagerly seconded the Regent in his plans for her seclusion, knowing that if the Princess assumed her rightful place, the cold austerity and somewhat ridiculous etiquette dear to the German heart of Her Majesty must fall into disuse. The Princess's marriage with His Highness of Orange would, it was believed, necessitate her leaving the kingdom, and the Regent therefore resolved that their union should take place; he had no doubt that she would obey his royal will, and the means he adopted of gaining her consent were singularly free from subtlety. She was invited to dine at Carlton House, to meet the man selected as her future husband.

Previous to the dinner the Regent took them into a room, when they walked up and down together for some time; after which he drew her aside, and abruptly said, 'Well, it will not do, I suppose?' to which she answered, 'I do not say that. I like his manner very well, as much as I have seen of it.' The Regent could not conceal his joy at this, and immediately joined their hands together. But the course of their royal love did not run quite so smoothly as the Regent desired: it happened next morning that the Prince of Wales and his son-in-law elect called to visit the Princess at Warwick House, and whilst the Regent was talking to Miss Knight, they suddenly heard Her Royal Highness break into a violent fit of sobs and hysterical tears; at which the royal parent looked very much frightened, and rushed into the next room to find His Highness of Orange looking much disturbed and his daughter in great distress. 'What! is he taking his leave?' said the Regent, to which she answered with a sigh, 'Not yet.'

The cause of the disturbance was that the Prince of

Orange told her that when they were married she should reside in Holland part of each year, and even, when necessary, follow him to the army; that he wished her to go to Berlin and travel in Germany, and that she could invite over what friends she liked. He thought it better to tell her all this, and be open and fair; though the Regent wished him not to mention it. She had not before suspected that this marriage was pushed forward to get rid of her, but now she began to suspect the fact, and to resent it; and, moreover, to dread the idea of leaving her mother in the critical position in which she was then placed; however, she then made no effort to break off the intended marriage, and, the Regent considering it as settled, the Prince of Orange left England.

The subject was allowed to drop for a few months, during which time the Grand-Duchess of Oldenburg, sister to the Emperor of Russia, arrived in town. This lady was a widow and an *intriguante*, who carried a certain agreeable Prince Gagarin in her train. She was graciously received by Her Sacred Majesty and the Court, and the Princess Charlotte was charmed with her when they met. In the course of a visit which the young Princess paid her, the Duchess, among other things, complained sorely of 'the assiduities of the Duke of Clarence, of his vulgar familiarity, and of his want of delicacy;' she also informed the Princess that her father was '*un voluptueux*'; and in return Her Royal Highness informed her that many persons had supposed she was to marry the Regent if he could have found cause for a divorce; to which the Grand-Duchess replied, that though she would have done anything to oblige her brother the Emperor, now that she had seen the Prince, she could never think of marrying him.

It was supposed that the Duchess was not favourable to the Orange alliance, and that her views concerning it but served to make the Princess more discontented than she had yet been with her future lot. Soon a formal petition was sent for her hand from the Sovereign of the Netherlands, on behalf of his son, the Prince of Orange, and a marriage contract was speedily drawn up by the Ministers, at the urgent request of the Regent. If she had before suspected, she was now convinced that her marriage was but a pretext for exiling her.

'I have now no manner of doubt,' she wrote to a friend, 'that it is decidedly *an object and wish of more than one* to get rid of me, if possible, in this way. You are far too sensible not to know that this marriage is only *de convenance*, and that it is as much brought about by force as anything, and by deceit and hurry. I am much more *triste* at it than I have ever chosen to write—can you be surprised?—a twenty-four hours' acquaintance, too, really, and where, and how?'

She had been forbidden to communicate the news to her mother, but she managed to write and tell her, and, when she was allowed to see her, spoke of her personal feelings towards her future husband. According to Lady Charlotte Campbell, she said to her mother that she was determined not to marry him; that 'his being approved of by the royal family was quite sufficient to make him disapproved of by her; for that she would marry a man who would be at her devotion, not at theirs.'

'Marry I will,' she said to the Princess of Wales, 'and that directly, in order to enjoy my liberty; but not the Prince of Orange. I think him so ugly that I am sometimes obliged to turn my head away in disgust when he is speaking to me.'

'But, my dear,' replied her mother, 'whoever you marry will become a King, and you will give him a power over you.'

'A King! Pho, pho! never! He will only be my first subject—never my King.'

The seclusion and coercion which her father intended should keep her in a childish state, and render her submissive to his will, had the unforeseen effect of ripening her faculties, sharpening her observation, and strengthening her self-dependence; and these qualities now coming to her aid, she declared she would never consent to leave the nation, unless by an Act of Parliament, and that her marriage should be broken off. The Regent was furious at having his desires balked, but was powerless in the face of the country to compel obedience to his wishes. Knowing contradiction would be useless, he resolved to try strategy, and secretly sent for the Prince of Orange, who quickly arrived in England, and duly presented himself at Warwick House, under the feigned name of Captain St. George. The Princess, being unwell, and not yet up, sent one of her ladies to see the unknown captain, and was surprised to find His Highness of Orange.

After a while, the Princess consented to see him, said she had no complaint to make against him, but that she would not leave the kingdom. She had asked to see the marriage contract, as she had heard it made no provision for a house or settlement for her in England; which she considered was tantamount to an agreement that she was to reside abroad; but her request had the effect of sending the Regent into a fresh rage. He declared he had no intention of banishing her from the kingdom, but he, who was so well versed in the duties of wives to their husbands, informed her every woman should follow her husband. She had no business, he said, to see her contract, but he told her it contained a settlement of £50,000 on her, that one clause stated her eldest son was to be the future King of England, that he would be taken from her at the age of four, in order that he might be educated in this country, and that her second son should be King of Holland. She determined not to be so easily disposed of, and, after receiving this message quietly, turned to read Burnet regarding the provisions made by the

Peers to prevent Queen Mary from being taken out of England by Philip of Spain, and then addressed a letter to her uncle, the Duke of York, on the subject. He came next day to expostulate with his niece, who declined the honour of seeing His Royal Highness. He then sent her word by one of her ladies that she laboured under a great mistake in considering herself heir-apparent, whereas she could hardly be considered heir-presumptive.

The Prince of Orange wrote to inform his father of the Princess's determination not to leave the kingdom; and that wise man, who was loath to let such an alliance slip, agreed to her demands, that she should not leave the country without the joint consent of the Regent and herself, which limited her power to go abroad and left her power to remain in England uncontrolled. The Regent in vain endeavoured to prevail on her to retract these stipulations, on the plea of giving offence to the Orange family, but she remained firm. He was then anxious the marriage should take place at once, and the Queen bought the wedding garments; these included but one Court dress, which her economical Majesty considered sufficient, 'as hoop-petticoats were not worn in Holland.'

About this time the foreign sovereigns visited England, and in their train came a youthful Prince, who was not long in gaining the Princess's notice: this was Leopold, third son of the Prince of Coburg, who was in the service of the Russian Emperor, and who, during his visit, lodged over a grocery shop in High Street, Marylebone Road. This Prince was gifted by nature with good looks, and was pronounced to be the possessor of an elegant form. He had boldly introduced himself to the Princess Charlotte by bringing her a letter from some German cousin a hundred times removed, of whose existence she had probably never heard before. This incident led her to the knowledge that the Prince's manners were agreeable, and she sought to improve his acquaintance; but, alas! as she was not permitted to be present at any of the fêtes, little opportunity for this offered itself; however, rather than run the risk of never meeting him again, she asked him to tea, to partake of which refreshing beverage the wily youth frequently presented himself at Warwick House. By the time he took his departure he had contrived to leave a very favourable impression on her mind.

The Prince of Orange was, of course, in town during the visit of the illustrious sovereigns, but did not seem to prosper in the good graces of his bride-elect: the more she saw of him the less she liked him, and the more she felt convinced that a man with such little depths of thought or feeling was not calculated to be a guide for her in the stormy path which she would probably have to tread. This fact, however, did not seem to disturb him; he amused himself vastly by attending balls, races and fêtes, nor was his enjoyment seemingly lessened by the fact that she was not present at these entertainments to amuse herself likewise; occasionally, too, he drank more than was at all good for him, in which condition he presented himself before her, and behaved in a manner which may be described as rowdy. One day, the Princess informed him that one of her reasons for wishing to remain in England was on account of her mother; that on having a house of her own, it must be opened equally to both her parents; and that she, as their daughter, must ignore all difference between them. His Orange Highness, who feared the Regent, demurred, and said the motives urged by her for stopping in England were to him arguments for getting away from disagreeable complications, and that if she refused to go abroad with him, their respective duties were irreconcilable and their marriage impossible.

After this, some common-place disagreement ensued: the Princess asked him to go with her to the riding-house, he refused; she persisted, and reproached him for his incivility, when he, in a fit of anger, left her, but not before she told him she would never consent to become his wife. She followed up this statement by a letter, in which she said she was fully convinced that her interest was materially connected with that of her mother, and that her residence out of the country would be equally prejudicial to her interest and that of the Princess of Wales. 'After what has passed upon this subject this morning between us,' she continued, 'I must consider our engagement from this moment to be totally and for ever at an end.' He heeded her letter but little, and at a ball which he attended at Hertford House on the evening of its reception, he spoke of her tantrums, but looked surprised when he was told they were no laughing matter. He took two days to consider the subject before replying; and he concluded the note he then wrote her by 'hoping you will never repent of this step'; she only laughed at his letter for the specimens of bad English which it contained.

Before leaving, the Emperor of Russia paid the Princess several visits, waxed eloquent over the virtues and qualities of his Orange Highness, and strongly advocated her marrying him, which from political motives would have been agreeable to His Imperial Majesty; but these entreaties having no effect, he had a private interview with her just before his departure, when he used all his endeavours to change her mind, and prevail on her to see the Prince of Orange, who was then waiting for the purpose in her house, without her knowledge; but this she stoutly refused, and declared over and over again she would have nothing to say to him. At this time she was suffering severely from a hurt she had received in her knee, which caused her pain by day, and restlessness by night, and this, with the mental agitation she had undergone concerning her marriage, made her ill. Three doctors who attended her recommended her to the sea-side, but her affectionate father, who now refused to see or speak to her, would not consent to her leaving town. 'I am grown thin, sleep ill, and eat but little,' she writes to one of her friends, at this time. 'Dr. Baily says my complaints are all nervous, and that bathing and sailing will brace me; but I say, oh no; no good can be done whilst the mind and soul are on the rack constantly, and the spirits forced and screwed up to a certain pitch. I always think six months got over of this dreadful life I lead, six months gained; but when the time comes for moving from place to place, I do it with reluctance, from never knowing my lot, or what next may befall me.'

The Regent, having had his plans thwarted and his royal will set aside by one whom he had treated as a child, strove to revenge himself on her with all the pettiness of his vindictive nature. The Bishop of Salisbury was sent to her with threats, that if she did not hold out a hope of marrying the Prince of Orange, certain arrangements would be made regarding her by no means agreeable to her inclinations. She replied she could give no such hope: she was then sent for to Carlton House, but was too ill to go, and despatched Miss Knight with an excuse. This lady found the Regent 'very cold, very bitter, very silent.' Next evening, accompanied by his Grace of Salisbury, the Prince called on his daughter, still looking black with anger, and remained shut up with her for three quarters of an hour alone; then his spiritual lordship was called in, and the conference was continued for some time longer; after which the door opened, and the Princess came out, trembling, agitated, and in the greatest agony. . Her father had revealed to her his plans for her future; all her ladies and members of the household were to be instantly dismissed, and new companions selected by the Prince were already in the house, who were to guard and watch her in the future. She was to leave Warwick House that night, and after five days' confinement in Carlton House, she was to be taken to Cranbourn Lodge, in the midst of Windsor Forest, where she was to be allowed to see no one but the Queen once a week.

After telling this to Miss Knight, she fell on her knees and cried out in great agitation, 'God Almighty grant me patience!' Miss Knight was then sent for by the Prince, who dismissed her, saying, in a surly tone by way of apology, that he had a right to make any changes he pleased; that he was sorry to put a lady to inconvenience, but that he wanted her room that night for the ladies who were to attend the Princess; that if she had nowhere to go, there was a room at Carlton House which she might have for a night or two; to which she replied with some spirit, that her father having served His Majesty for fifty years, and sacrificed his health and fortune in that service, it would be very strange if she could not put herself to the temporary inconvenience of a few hours. When she left his august presence, she found that the Princess, overcome with distress and perplexity, had rushed out of the house before anyone could stop her, and had gone to her mother.

The fact was, that when Miss Knight left her, the Princess had put on her bonnet, slipped out of the house, stepped into the first hackney-coach she could find, and putting a guinea into the driver's hand, desired to be taken to Connaught House, where her mother then resided. Arrived here, she found the Princess of Wales had gone to Blackheath, when she sent for her immediately, as also for her friend Miss Mercer; then, flinging herself down on a couch, she cried out in a passionate burst of tears, 'I would rather earn my own bread and live on five shillings a week than lead the life I do.' Meanwhile the Princess of Wales, accompanied by Lady Charlotte Lindsay, arrived in town in great haste, and drove at once to the House of Parliament, where she asked to see Mr. Whitebread; he was not present, and she then inquired for Earl Grey, who was likewise absent; she then drove home and sent for Mr. Brougham.

The Princess did not receive her daughter with the sympathy and affection which the latter had expected; for Her Royal Highness was at that time meditating a journey abroad, and feared that any annoyance to the Regent might prevent him from granting her desires; the Princess Charlotte felt this bitterly, and from that time never regarded her with the same feelings as before. When Mr. Brougham arrived, the young Princess rushed forward, and, taking him by both hands, told him of the treatment with which her father threatened her, and of the proposed marriage, the thought of which had now grown abhorrent. He told her that, without her consent, it could not take place; to which she replied, 'They may wear me out by ill-treatment, and may represent that I have changed my mind and consented.' Mr. Brougham sent for the Duke of Sussex, for whom of all her uncles the Princess cared most, and he arrived presently.

The Regent had in the meantime sent for his Ministers, and informed them of his daughter's flight, carefully concealing from them the part which he had acted; and after a short council, Lord Chancellor Eldon, the Bishop of Salisbury, Lord Ellenborough, Leach, and finally the Duke of York, were despatched to convey her to Carlton House. They arrived one after another in hackney-coaches, and all of them but Lord Eldon were shown into the drawing-room downstairs, his lordship being, at the request of the Princess Charlotte, who detested him, allowed to remain in his hackney-coach. In an upper drawing-room the two Princesses and their friends held council; the mother besought her daughter to return to Carlton House, but the Princess would not consent, she sobbed and cried bitterly, and refused to return. Mr. Brougham then assured her that the Regent would have a *habeas corpus* issued to force her away, which indeed he had already done; at which she became still more affected. 'I have told many a client,' writes Lord Brougham, 'he was going to be convicted, but

I never saw anything like her stupefaction: for a quarter of an hour she was lost.'

At last she wrote to her father, offering to return if she might retain one of her ladies, Miss Knight, and her maid. The Bishop undertook to deliver this communication, and presently returned with word that nothing but unconditional surrender would satisfy the Regent. She then appealed to Mr. Brougham for advice, to which he replied, 'Return to Warwick House or Carlton House, and on no account pass a night out of your own house.'

'She was extremely affected, and cried,' he writes, in his interesting 'Life and Times,' 'asking if I too refused to stand by her; I said quite the contrary, and that as to the marriage I gave no opinion, except that she must follow her own inclination entirely, but that her returning home was absolutely necessary; and in this all the rest fully agreed— her mother, the Duke of Sussex, Miss Mercer, and Lady Charlotte Lindsay, for whom she had a great respect and regard. I said that, however painful it was for me, the necessity was so clear and so strong that I had not the least hesitation in advising it. She again and again begged me to consider her situation, and to think whether, looking to that, it was absolutely necessary she should return. The day now began to dawn, and I took her to the window. The election of Cochrane was to take place that day. I said, "Look there, madam; in a few hours all the streets and the park, now empty, will be crowded with tens of thousands. I have only to take you to that window, and show you to the multitude, and tell them your grievances, and they will all rise in your behalf."

'"And why should they not?"' I think she said, or some such words.

'"The commotion," I answered, "will be excessive; Carlton House will be attacked—perhaps pulled down; the soldiers will be ordered out, blood will be shed, and if your Royal Highness were to live a hundred years, it never would be forgotten that your running away from your father's house was the cause of the mischief; and, you may depend upon it, such is the English people's horror of bloodshed, you never would get over it."

'She at once felt the truth of my assertion, and consented to see her uncle Frederick (Duke of York) below stairs, and return with him. But she required one of the royal carriages should be sent for, which came with her governess; and they, with the Duke of York, went home about five o'clock.

'Before she went, however, she desired me to make a minute of her declaration that she was resolved not to marry the Prince of Orange, and that, if ever there should be an announcement of such a match, it must be understood to be without her consent and against her will. She added, "I desire Augustus (Duke of Sussex) and Mr. Brougham would particularly take notice of this." When I had made the note, it was read distinctly and signed by all present, she signing first, and six copies were made and signed, and one given to each person present. Her positive injunction was that, if ever we heard the match announced as being to proceed, we should make her declaration in the note public.'

When she arrived at Carlton House, she was obliged to remain for half an hour in the coach-yard while it was debated how she should be received. Next day Miss Knight called, but was not admitted beyond the gate of Carlton House, and in a few days after she was removed to Cranbourn Lodge. Here, during the first week of her captivity, she managed to steal a piece of paper, and with a pencil wrote a note, which was secretly conveyed to Miss Knight, to be forwarded by her to the Duke of Sussex. 'His Royal Highness,' wrote that lady, 'read it to me, and it contained a melancholy description of the manner in which she was confined and watched night and day.'

Four days after the Princess's flight, the *Morning Chronicle* published a detailed account of the matter, and of the restrictions with which she had been threatened, and great was the public wrath once more stirred up against the Regent; the press teemed with comments by no means favourable on his conduct, lampoons swarmed, and his treatment of his daughter became the universal topic.

The Duke of Sussex wrote to the Prime Minister, asking permission to see his niece, and received in return a brief reply: 'The Regent has read the letter, and has no commands.' After this he took an early opportunity of asking Lord Liverpool, in the House of Lords, several pertinent questions. He wished to be informed whether the Princess Charlotte 'is, since her residence at Carlton House, in that state of liberty which persons considered not as in confinement ought to be in? whether she has had the liberty of that communication in writing and by letter—of receiving and sending letters—and the use of pens, ink, and paper that she had whilst at Warwick House? whether she was not recommended, as proper for her health, the use of the sea-bath? and whether, having arrived at the age of eighteen years and a half—past the period when Parliament has frequently recognised the capacity of persons of the royal family to assume the government of the country without assistance —whether there is any intention of providing an establishment suitable for Her Royal Highness, and proper for her to live and appear according to her due rank in that society over which it will be her lot one day to reign?' After an awkward pause Lord Liverpool replied at some length, that 'the Prince Regent had his daughter's benefit, interest, and advantage in view in his conduct towards her.'

The Prince was so indignant at these questions asked by the Duke of Sussex, that he never forgave him. He assembled all his family, and told them they must choose between him and the Duke; all of them declared in favour of the Regent, except the Duke of Gloucester, who stoutly refused to give up the friendship of the Duke of Sussex. This latter Duke became so alarmed at these proceedings that he found himself suddenly attacked by asthma, which was so severe as to prevent him taking any further steps in his niece's behalf, and she was therefore abandoned to her fate.

The Regent, however, was somewhat in fear of the public storm, and the Princess was sent to Weymouth under a strong guard of ladies, whose watch never relaxed; after this visit she was conducted back again to the dreary seclusion of Cranbourn Lodge, where she was kept till her subsequent marriage. Her Majesty all this while was guiltless of all friendly interference on behalf of her granddaughter; and this the public resented. On her going to St. James's in a sedan-chair to hold a drawing-room, a great crowd gathered round her, and, with menacing looks, demanded, 'What have you done with the Princess?' 'Where's your granddaughter?' Then followed a sharp shower of hisses, and, according to Lord Grey, 'there was no form of reproach that did not assail her ears.'

CHAPTER XVI.

The Princess of Wales determines to leave England—The Opinion of her Friends—The Regent rejoices—Her Departure—The Princess Charlotte's Marriage—Prince Leopold and the Mob—The Marriage Ceremony—Brief Illness and Death—Sorrow of the Nation—Indignation against the Queen and Prince—Marriages of the Royal Dukes—Death of the Queen—The Last Days of the King—His Death.

THE Princess of Wales, worn out by humiliations, petty persecutions, and trials, resolved to leave England and travel on the Continent for some time. This plan was opposed by most of her friends, and especially by Mr. Brougham, who told her that as long as she stayed in this country he would answer that no plot could succeed against her, but living abroad she would be surrounded by spies and tools of her enemies, ready to swear or invent as they were directed. 'In England,' he wrote to her, 'spies and false witnesses can do nothing; abroad everything may be apprehended from them. Depend upon it, madame, there are many persons who now begin to see a chance of divorcing you from the prince.'

But the Princess would not listen to his advice; she was exhausted by constant agitation and fears, and weary of a country in which she never had one day's happiness; she, therefore, drew up a letter to Lord Liverpool, informing him of her desire to go abroad, and inquiring if there would be any opposition on the part of the Ministry to her fulfilling her intentions; to which his Lordship, by order of the Regent, declared there was none. This unusual accession to her request, together with the promptness and civility of the answer, should have been sufficient to make her suspicious of the wisdom of her scheme. Whether it had this effect or not, she at once prepared for her journey, and wished to make over her house at Blackheath to her daughter. When this desire was made known to the Regent, he caused her to be informed that the Princess Charlotte would never be permitted to reside in a house which had once been occupied by the Princess of Wales.

Before leaving England, the Government made her a grant of £50,000 a year, which was a boon to one who had frequently been in debt and in many pecuniary difficulties, to redeem herself from which she had been obliged to sell her plate, and occasionally some of her jewels. 'I have found a pair of old earrings,' she once wrote to a friend of hers, 'which the devil of a Queen once gifted me with. I truly believed that the sapphires *ar fals* as her *heart* and soul is, but the diamonds are good, and £50 or £80 would be very acceptable for them indeed.' Though she had made up her mind to leave England, yet she was not without apprehending the danger she was about to risk; and, before starting, wrote to Canning that if any machinations were going on against her, were it only a whisper, she would quickly return and defend her innocence. This letter was shown to the Regent, who, to throw her off her guard, falsely declared no such thing was intended. His royal soul was now almost overpowered with joy at the prospect of getting rid of his wife; and, in order to celebrate her departure, he entertained some choice spirits at dinner, after which, being probably drunk at the time, he gave the toast, 'To the Princess of Wales, damnation, and may she never return to England.'

The Princess, being prepared for her journey, went to Worthing, where she was to embark, and where she was permitted to have a brief interview with her daughter, whom she was destined never again to see in this world. Her spirits, on the eve of this journey, to which she had looked forward with much expectation, became miserably depressed and gloomy, and she would sit for hours at night on the beach looking out at sea, silent and thoughtful, as if filled with melancholy presentiments.

'Ah, well,' she said once, starting from one of these reveries, 'grief is unavailing when fate compels me.'

Her suite consisted of Lady Charlotte Lindsay, Lady Elizabeth Forbes, Sir William Gell, Dr. (afterwards Sir Henry) Holland, and Mr. St. Leger, besides their attendants. On the morning of August 9, 1814, she drove to the Worthing beach, dressed in 'a dark cloth pelisse, with large gold clasps, and a cap of velvet and green satin, of the Prussian hussar costume, with a green feather.' It had been her intention to embark from here, but so great was the crowd, which increased every moment, that she withdrew as quickly as possible to South Lancing, about two miles further off, where a boat destined to convey her to the frigate in which she was to sail proceeded to meet her. Her purpose, however, was noticed, and she was followed the whole way by an enormous crowd in carriages and on foot, which was anxious to show her its sympathy and respect.

The departure of this much-injured woman, who may be said to have been driven from the country by the relentless persecution of one whose duty it was to protect her, was not without a touch of pathos. Tears stood in her eyes as she got into the barge amidst the respectful silence of the vast throng; she could not venture to speak, but, turning round to the people, she kissed her hands to them in route farewell; immediately every man uncovered, and the women waved their handkerchiefs, while the Princess was so overcome that she fainted.

Shortly after her mother's departure, the Princess Charlotte was removed to Warwick House, the entrance to which by the road was secured by iron bars on the inside, so that all who entered or left this prison were obliged to pass through the courtyard of Carlton House. Moreover, the Regent gave a list of those whom she was permitted to see; and to show the public that she was not quite such a prisoner as vile rumour hinted, she was allowed to go to the opera or play once a week, guarded by her ladies, on the understanding that she left the theatre before the performance concluded, and that she in no way courted popularity. But the nation was not forgetful of her existence, and it became plain to her royal father that he could not much longer keep her in durance vile; he was, therefore, resolved to get her married as soon as possible, as otherwise the Opposition might clamour for her being treated as heir-apparent to the throne, which he was most anxious to avoid. So determined, indeed, was he that no honours should be paid her, that on one of her birthdays, when the good citizens prepared to illuminate at night, he sent word to have such proceedings stopped, and the anniversary was passed over in silence.

Having made up his mind to get her married as soon as possible, the Regent bethought himself of Prince Leopold, who had, before leaving England with the Russian Emperor, offered himself to the Prince as a suitor for his daughter's hand, and been promptly rejected. He was now sent for, and the Princess was summoned to accompany the Queen to Brighton, where, to her surprise and joy, His Serene Highness was presented to her as the man selected for her future husband. Prince Leopold enjoyed the not too extravagant income of two hundred a year, which those who spoke irreverent things of royalty said was just sufficient to buy him two coats and a dozen shirts; but he was now about being raised to a position in which he could afford to buy himself a complete wardrobe. The sum of £60,000 a year was settled on the young couple, out of which the Princess was to have the sole and separate use of £10,000; they were also granted the round sum of £60,000 to purchase an outfit, £10,000 of which was to be laid out on clothes, and an equal sum on jewels.

When His Serene Highness of Coburg came to London as the accepted suitor of Princess Charlotte, he forsook his old lodgings over the grocery shop in High Street, and hired a bedroom at Jacquin's Hotel in Bond Street, which, at the Regent's request, he subsequently quitted for Clarence House, where all the necessaries of life were supplied to His Serene Highness from Carlton House.

The wedding was fixed for May 2, 1816. Such an event caused much interest, curiosity and excitement; and the eagerness of the people was so great to see the young foreigner who was about to become the husband of one whom they regarded as their future Queen, that crowds assembled round Clarence House the whole of the forenoon of the wedding-day. Between them and the Prince an understanding was soon established. As soon as a sufficiently large number had gathered, they clapped hands, on which signal the Prince of Coburg, habited in a blue coat, buff waistcoat, and grey pantaloons, came forward on the balcony and bowed repeatedly like a mechanical toy. The crowd then went its way, busy with many conjectures and comments, and in another quarter of an hour a fresh concourse of people had collected and the same performance was gone through. 'His ready and cheerful exhibition of himself,' says one of the newspapers of the day, 'seemed to diffuse the highest satisfaction among the spectators, and excited, long before the close of the day, a cordial familiarity.'

On the evening of May 2, the Queen, the Regent, and Prince Leopold gave dinner-parties at their respective residences, after which all assembled at Carlton House, in one of the apartments of which, known as the Great Crimson Room, the marriage service was to take place. Here in due time gathered the Queen, looking now somewhat shrunken, old, and careworn, but as rigidly ceremonious as ever, accompanied by the Princesses, blonde and buxom, and the Regent, whose corpulency was rapidly increasing to unbecoming dimensions, and whose face had a deep rich hue, not altogether attained by exposure to weather. The Royal Dukes were likewise present, as were two Archbishops and an equal number of Bishops, and many Peers and Peeresses, and Ministers of high estate. The apartment was lit up with an exceeding great number of wax-lights, and the whole scene was brilliant to behold.

The Regent, with hearty good-will, gave the bride away to her future lord and master, who rejoiced to take her, and the Archbishop of Canterbury performed the ceremony ; at the conclusion of which, at twenty minutes past nine of the clock, the guns in the Tower of St. James's announced to the eager crowds that had gathered in the streets that these two had been made one till death did them part. Illuminations and many demonstrations of joy followed. The bride and bridegroom then retired to change their dresses, after which Her Royal Highness, without waiting to receive the congratulations of the illustrious company, quietly slipped down the private stairs from the state apartments to the ground-floor, and entered the carriage waiting for her in the garden, when she and her new-made husband drove to Oatlands to spend the honeymoon. They afterwards took a house in Park Lane, and finally bought Claremont, where most of the Princess's brief but happy married life was spent.

The existence she now led was as blissful as could be, and simple. Prince Leopold proved wise, cautious, and affectionate ; and she, whose days had heretofore been spent in misery and restraint, became one of the happiest subjects in the kingdom.

'We lead a very quiet and retired life here,' she writes from Claremont, a few months after her marriage, 'but a very, very happy one!' Unfortunately these halcyon days were destined to be of short duration. Early in November of the year following her marriage, the nation looked forward to her accouchement with keen interest, and it was hoped that the birth of an heir would increase her store of gladness. On the fourth of this month the great officers of state were summoned that they might be present at the expected event; and Sir Richard Croft, a fashionable but not very skilful accoucheur, and Mrs. Griffiths, a lady who had never been a mother, but who, through interest, was now appointed nurse, were sent for likewise. At so momentous a time as this to the Princess, it was strange and sad that she was completely deserted by her family, and that not a matron was to be found in her household. The Regent was spending his days in the company of the Marchioness of Hertford, at Ragley Hall in Suffolk, whilst the Queen and the Princesses were at Bath. According to Huish, Her Majesty had offered to remain in town for this critical occasion; but 'the offer was indginantly rejected by the Princess Charlotte, who declared she would not have any of her enemies about her.'

The Princess's labour commenced on the night of November 4, and lasted forty-eight hours, during which Sir Richard Croft did not think well of sending for a second medical man until fatal symptoms appeared. Sir Richard, indeed, was tenacious of his professional dignity, and had said to Baron Stockmar, a member of the household, who had ventured to give it as his opinion that the Princess was sinking, 'Are you or I, sir, in authority here?' At nine o'clock on the evening of the 5th she was delivered of a still-born child, and five hours afterwards died in her husband's arms, November 6, 1817.

The sudden and melancholy shock of her death was felt throughout the length and breadth of the country, and was regarded as one of the most disastrous events that had ever befallen the nation. With hope and confidence the people had looked forward to her reign over them, and their grief and disappointment at her death were bitter and deep. A universal mourning was at once adopted by all classes; theatres, operas, and all places of amusement voluntarily closed; marriages and private entertainments were postponed; business was deferred; the churches were hung with black; and signs of earnest sorrow were visible throughout the land.

When the news reached the Regent, he hastened to town, and declared himself so ill from grief that he wished to have his favourite operation of bleeding performed. He then went to Windsor, where the Queen had returned, then journeyed back again to town, and after a few days his sorrow was sufficiently abated to permit him to visit the Pagoda at Brighton, where, according to the press, 'he had resolved to indulge his melancholy for a short time.' He became so much better, surrounded by a society that had always fresh charms for his soul, that the *Morning Chronicle* was enabled to inform its readers 'all apprehensions relative to his health had subsided;' he did not, however, return to town until after the funeral. Intelligence of the sad event was conveyed to the Princess of Wales by Prince Leopold's equerry, for even on such an occasion as this the Regent had resolved to ignore the existence of his wife; the unhappy woman fainted when the news was broken to her.

'She is gone before,' she said, 'and I trust we shall soon meet in a better world than the present one.'

When the first outburst of national grief had subsided, the most violent indignation was felt against the Queen and the Regent. The cruelties practised by the latter on his daughter but a few months ago were remembered, and the fact that no male or female member of the royal family was present during the Princess's illness was commented on with scathing severity. It was asserted on excellent authority that, humanly speaking, her life could have been saved, or, in other words, that she died through wilful neglect. The share of public odium which fell on Sir Richard Croft was so great, and made such an impression on a mind more sensitive than those of his superiors, that he soon afterwards committed suicide. Strange to say, this incident, instead of disarming public censure, but served to excite amongst the people some wild and terrible suspicions which had gradually been gaining ground, that the Princess had been unfairly dealt with; and Sir Richard's death by his own hands was regarded as the result of remorse. It was likewise noted that Mrs. Griffiths, the nurse, whose name had been previously mixed up with Sir Richard's in an unpleasant manner, and who was never a suitable person for the responsible post she held towards the Princess, mysteriously disappeared. These dark surmises gained such ground that the press and public demanded a searching inquiry into the circumstances of Her Royal Highness's illness.

'The cry for an investigation of the circumstances attending the mortal accouchement of the late Princess Charlotte,' says the *Morning Chronicle*, 'becomes day by day more audible. It is the topic of every assembly, and we lament to see it inflamed by the writings of medical men. We have numerous letters on the subject, which we have suppressed from a conviction of the inutility of such a retrospect.'

When Huish was compiling the Memoirs of George IV., he tells us he repeatedly visited Esher, the town near Claremont House, for the purpose of obtaining information regarding the Princess Charlotte. He says, 'There was scarcely an inhabitant of the town who did not shake the head, with all the expression of suspicion, whenever the Princess's death was mentioned; and,' adds this historian, there is a corroding belief yet existing in many minds that there is some mystery still to be revealed, and that the fairest flower of Brunswick's royal line would, in other hands, have lived to perpetuate their destiny, and to be a blessing to the country of her birth.' No investigation regarding the Princess's illness was ever made.

This public grief, according to Earl Grey, was 'annoying to the Prince,' but he was powerless to set it aside. The abuse heaped on him by the press was only equalled by that preached in the pulpit, which was dealt out to him without stint by such unworldly men as had no aspirations towards lawn sleeves. Indeed, one celebrated preacher at Cheltenham went so far as to dwell on a verse in Jeremiah, which says, 'He shall not reign, nor any of his seed,' words which were applied to the Regent, of whom it was devoutly hoped they might prove prophetic. Never, perhaps, was the unpopularity of any King or Prince so great; he was loathed by the nation, and censured for his extravagance at a time when the country was depressed, bread scarce, taxes high, and the public ready for an outbreak at any favourable moment. The people occasionally gave vent to their feelings by writing on the walls of Carlton House, 'Bread, or the Regent's Head'; and on one occasion they left a loaf steeped in blood on the parapet in front of the building.

The spirit of disloyalty went a step further, and, on his return from opening Parliament in 1817, he was fired at from the crowd that had gathered to sullenly watch his progress. The bullet broke one of the windows of his carriage, but did no further injury. The Government promptly offered the reward of £1,000 for the discovery of the intended assassin; but, though there must have been numbers who witnessed the act, it speaks for the general feelings of the people that no one was found willing to hand over to justice the man who sought to rid them of a ruler they detested.

By the death of the Princess Charlotte, the Duke of York became heir-apparent to the throne; but he having no issue, there was a prospect of his royal brothers succeeding in due course; and so they resolved to settle and marry. Accordingly the three Royal Dukes of Clarence, Kent, and Cambridge rushed over in hot speed to Germany, and made a descent on various Courts to select their respective wives. They evidently fell in love at first sight with the ladies destined to become their spouses, for their choice was made in remarkably quick time, and the nation was called on to provide them with additional incomes in order to maintain establishments suitable to their new position as the husbands of Serene Princesses, scandalously stigmatized by the press as 'German paupers, one more ugly than another.'

Not many months had elapsed after the death of the Princess Charlotte when it was announced that the Queen was dying—an event which was regarded neither by her own family nor by the nation at large as a calamity. During her most serious illness the Regent enjoyed himself as usual, and not many weeks before her death he entertained the foreign ambassadors at his Court at dinner, after which, being in a merry mood, he diverted the ministerial gravity by singing them some jovial songs. Her Majesty had been suffering for about ten months from spasmodic attacks and dropsy, and finally, mortification setting in, her imminent danger became obvious to all but herself. It was well known that Her Majesty possessed a goodly share of personal property, and it was also a recognised fact that, notwithstanding their frequent quarrels, the Prince of Wales was her favourite child. The Prince was well aware of this, and took pains to ascertain that she had made no will. He therefore caused her to be informed 'that if Her Majesty had any affairs to settle, it would be advisable to do so whilst she had health and spirits to bear the fatigue.' The poor Queen was startled, but she took the hint, and made a will in which she never mentioned his name. Her personal property was, after her death, sworn to as being under £140,000; the greater part of which lay in the jewels for which she had always had a passion. Those given her by the King on her marriage, valued at £50,000, and paid for by the nation, she bequeathed to the crown of Hanover as an heirloom; the magnificent jewels presented her by the Nabob of Arcot, together with those which she had bought from time to time and had received as presents, she ordered to be sold, and to have the proceeds thereof divided amongst four of her daughters—the remaining daughter, the Queen of Wurtemburg, with whom Her Majesty had had a misunderstanding, was not to derive any advantage from the sale. The diamonds were valued at almost a million. The remainder of her property was likewise divided between these four daughters, no mention being made of her sons, or those who had served her, with the exception of one German woman, Madame Beckendorff, to whom she left her wardrobe, said to be the finest in Europe. There was another item in this royal will which caused much amusement at the time. Her Majesty had made a careful list of such articles of faded finery as she had brought with her when she came as a bride to England, and for which, by the way, the country had handsomely paid; these, consisting of some dresses now a trifle musty and tarnished, and tawdry trinkets, she desired should be sent back to the senior branch of her illustrious house of Mecklenburgh Strelitz.

On November 17, 1818, the Queen expired whilst sitting in an easy-chair, the Regent, the Duke of York, and two of the Princesses being present. The other members of the royal family were conspicuous by their absence, a fact which the *Times* commented on in the article announcing the royal demise. 'Were it safe to found a judgment,' says this leader, 'on the recent dispersion of the Princes of the blood royal, and of some of the Princesses, we might, however reluctantly, conclude that Her Majesty had not altogether succeeded in attaching to her the hearts of her children. The Duke of Cumberland is out of the question. The inflexible, though well-meant, determination of the Queen to stigmatize her niece, by shutting the doors of the royal palace against her, may excuse strong feelings of estrangement or resentment, on the part of the Duchess and of her husband; but that the Dukes of Clarence, Kent, and Cambridge at the same time should have quitted, as if by signal, their parent's death-bed, is a circumstance which in lower life would have at least astonished the community. The departure of the Princess Elizabeth,* the Queen's favourite daughter, who married and took leave of her in the midst of that illness which it was pronounced would shortly bring her to the grave, may perhaps have been owing to the injunction of Her Majesty. The Duke of Gloucester stands in a more remote degree of relationship: Prince Leopold more distant still; but they all quitted the scene of suffering at a period when its fatal termination could not be doubted.' Notwithstanding the insupportable grief of the royal family, the building of the Pavilion at Brighton was not discontinued for a day; and strange is it to read in the *Morning Chronicle* of November 24, the announcement that ' His Royal Highness the Duke of Clarence will give a

---

* The Princess Elizabeth married His Serene Highness of Hesse Homburg, popularly styled 'Hesse Humbug,' who was described by Fremantle as 'a monster of a man—a vulgar-looking German corporal, whose breath and hide is a compound between tobacco and garlic. He has about £300 per annum.' Another correspondent of the Marquis of Buckingham's, describing His Serene Highness, says, ' An uglier hound, with a snout buried in hair, I never saw.'

splendid ball next Thursday, at which the nobility, the officers down to the rank of lieutenant, and many persons high in civil affairs, will be present.'

Her Majesty was buried at Windsor on the second of the following month with great state, when the Prince Regent acted as chief mourner. He evidently regarded the occasion as one on which he might indulge in one of those theatrical displays so dear to his royal soul, and went attired in a black cloak, long, and of 'a great amplitude of folds,' on the left breast of which was a star of brilliants, and round the neck were four collars of knighthood, whose colours finely contrasted with the weeds of woe, and glittered with excellent effect. It was night before the procession, surrounded by Lancers and Guards, reached St. George's Chapel, and torches were lit and borne by the military. 'These,' says Mr. Bush, 'gleaming upon the soldiers' helmets, and partially disclosing now the hearse, then the long, solemn procession, winding its slow way with its trappings of death, presented a spectacle for the pencil of the muse.'

After the death of Her Majesty it was suggested by the Regent to place 'the care of the King's sacred person in the Duke of York.' This guardianship consisted in two brief visits to the King weekly, for which it was proposed His Royal Highness should receive £10,000 a year. The Duke, notwithstanding his pay as Commander of the Forces, and as Colonel of the Grenadier Guards, with other posts, whose salaries amounted in all to £36,000, was in debt to the extent of £200,000, and was, in fact, at this time insolvent. His property was assigned under bills of sale to fictitious creditors, in order that he might the better defraud the tradespeople and others who had been so foolish as to trust to his royal honour; but so little respect had these dupes for him, that at the order of one of them his horses and carriage were seized in the public street, whilst the Royal Duke was using them. It may be added here that at his death the Duke's creditors received the sum of one shilling in the pound, by way of payment of his debts. One cannot wonder at Lord Minto's opinion that 'if anything can make a democracy in England it will be the Royal Family.'

In consequence of his need, he therefore grasped at this enormous salary, to be filched from the public pocket for his benefit. The announcement of awarding him this sum for such a duty caused wide indignation. His late nefarious transactions in connection with Mrs. Clarke were again brought forward, and so stormy were the debates in Parliament on this question of the allowance, that he from very shame determined to forego the salary, but when he communicated this resolve to the Regent, that royal man became furious.

'So, sir,' he said with a sneer, 'you would be popular at our expense!' The Duke then changed his mind, and the sum was granted by Parliament; but he did not receive it for more than two years, when his royal father died.

To the public at large His Majesty had long ceased to exist: for years his lucid intervals had been rare, but his fits of frenzy had fortunately been rarer yet. Totally blind and deaf, almost deserted by his wife in the last years of her life, and by his children, worn and stooped, his white hair hanging on his shoulders, his silver beard sweeping his chest, he wandered purposelessly from room to room, in the suite of apartments allotted to him in his royal palace at Windsor, a desolate and melancholy figure. Waterloo had been lost and won; the idol of France and fear of Europe had fallen from his high estate; the Bourbons once more sat on their hereditary throne; the Princess Charlotte had wedded and died; the Royal Princesses had been given in marriage; the Princes had taken to themselves wives; the Queen and the Duke of Kent had passed away, and yet of all these events the King had remained wholly conscious—to him all the world was a blank.

On one occasion, during one of his lucid intervals, he received a visit from the Queen, an unusual thing on her part. Her Majesty found him singing a hymn in a quavering mournful voice, whilst he accompanied himself on the harpsichord, a favourite instrument of his. When he had ceased, he hesitated for a moment, and went slowly down on his knees, when he prayed for Her Majesty, then for his family, and the nation, concluding with a touching petition for himself, that it might please God to avert his heavy calamity from him, but if not, to give him resignation to submit; after which he burst into tears, and his brief gleam of reason vanished, leaving him once more in mental darkness. At times he would hold imaginary conversations with statesmen long since dead and gone; and on other occasions he lost all sense of his own identity, and believed himself dead.

'I must have a new suit of clothes,' he would say, 'and I will have them black, in memory of George the Third; he was a good man.'

One of his daughters, the Princess Elizabeth, speaking of him in her correspondence, says: 'He considers himself no longer an inhabitant of this world, and often, when he has played one of his favourite tunes, observes that he was very fond of it when he was in the world. He speaks of the Queen and all his family, and hopes they are doing well now, for he loved them very much when he was with them.'

Towards the middle of January, 1820, it became evident to his doctors that his life was not destined to be of much longer duration, and his family were prepared for news of his expected demise. He lingered, however, till the 29th of the month, when the solemn toll of the great bell of St. Paul's announced to his subjects that their Sovereign was no more. He died calmly, but without recovering his reason during his last hours—the only one of his sons present at the dread moment being the Duke of York. He had reigned over sixty years, and had entered into his eighty-second year.

CHAPTER XVII.

Schemes for a Royal Divorce—The Princess Abroad—The Milan Commission—The New Queen—Her Journey to London—The Trial begins—Lord John Russell's Hint to His Majesty—Italian Witnesses going to Westminster—Accusations against the Queen—Bergami in the Tent—Result of the Trial and General Rejoicings—Public Feeling against the King—Pamphlets and Ballads—The Broadfaced Naval Gentleman.

ALL this while the one predominant thought which seized and held forcible possession of the Regent's brain, was how he should rid himself of the spouse who was not of his bosom. But four months after her departure from England, Brougham, in writing to Earl Grey, says, 'Certain it is that some movements towards a divorce have been in discussion at least at Carlton House;' but the hour for the execution of this treasured scheme was not yet at hand, and meanwhile the royal man bided his time and plotted his plots.

On leaving England the Princess had gone to Brunswick, where, after tarrying for some time at her brother's Court, and relieving her purse of a considerable sum for his benefit, she betook herself to Germany, and from thence to Italy, the land she had selected as that of her future residence. From time to time during her absence abroad, rumours reached England of acquaintances she had made unworthy of her notice as a British Princess; of her characteristic familiarity with strangers; of her love of gaiety; and of her general carelessness of behaviour. Repudiated by her husband, separated from her child—at first by royal command, and then by death—bereft of friends, homeless and a wanderer, she grew reckless, and her indiscretions were construed by the spies who surrounded her into serious crimes.

'From the first moment she quitted British ground,' as the *Times* subsequently stated, 'she was dogged and tracked by a band of lurking villains who were set to spy out all her actions, with the certainty that, if they could either find or impute crime, they would also find ready and grateful auditors.' At Geneva it was said the Princess had appeared at a ball, likewise honoured by Marie Louise, the ex-Empress of France, dressed in the costume of Venus, which admitted a view of her back-bone to a considerable extent; at Naples she graced an entertainment, given by Murat, as the Genius of History, in a dress which, even in a warm climate, was not considered a burden to the shoulders; whilst at Athens she witnessed the Dervishes dancing. Such acts as these were quickly reported in England with due exaggeration, and she mischievously enjoyed raising the storm which, subsequently, almost overwhelmed her.

Once, when at Como, she entertained a guest whom she had strong reasons to suspect was one of her husband's spies, and she immediately entered into a light and frivolous conversation with him, and behaved with much familiarity; on which one of her suite privately warned her that her every word and action would be reported to the Prince.

'I know it,' she replied, 'and therefore I speak and act as you see. The wasp leaves his sting in the wound, so do I. The Regent will hear it? I hope he will; I love to mortify him.' For this reason she courted the dangers that were almost her ruin.

Before she had been long abroad, her suite left her, disgusted, her enemies said, by her conduct; but such was not the case. Mr. St. Leger was obliged to return to England, as his health could not bear the fatigue of travelling; Lady Charlotte Lindsay left for the purpose of visiting her relatives, and subsequently rejoined her at Naples with her brother, Lord North; Sir William Gell, according to his subsequent evidence, took his departure because he disliked travelling in winter, and joined her when she returned from her tour in Palestine; whilst Mr. Keppel Craven was obliged to return to his family, in order to regulate some business. This suite was replaced by Italians; but, before most of her friends went their various ways, an actor had stepped on the scene, destined to play an important part in the tragedy of the Princess's life. At Milan a courier had been dismissed for misconduct, when the Marquis Ghisiliari recommended in his place an Italian of good family named Bartolomeo Bergami. This individual, from being a courier, was gradually raised to be chamberlain, and his name soon became scandalously connected with that of the Princess in the mouths of her enemies.

But, notwithstanding the rumours which had been carried to England concerning her, no condemnatory step was taken until the death of the Princess Charlotte. A few months after that sad event, a secret Commission, consisting of a Chancery barrister named Leach, subsequently elevated to the post of Vice-Chancellor, Mr. Cooke, also a barrister, Mr. Powell, Colonel Brown, and Lord Stewart, were sent to Milan, near where the Princess was then residing. Salaries were, of course, attached to the respective offices of these gentlemen, who had the power of rewarding in the handsomest manner such witnesses as bore testimony to their desires; so that the Commission, it was subsequently stated by Sir Roland Ferguson in the House of Commons, cost the country between thirty and forty thousand pounds. When the Princess became aware that this secret tribunal was sitting, she wrote a letter remonstrating with her husband,

and demanding to know its object, to which no attention was paid.

The Commission examined several witnesses, many of whom were discharged servants of the Princess, with whom ready terms could be made; where such failed, threats were used, and the result was that these gentlemen returned from whence they had come with evidence which they believed sufficient to blast the Princess's character in the eyes of all men. She would have returned to England at once, but her chief adviser, Mr. Brougham, urged her to remain abroad, a counsel to which she submitted. No important step was taken by the Regent towards the end he desired until the King's death, when the new monarch announced to his Ministers that he must have a divorce. They were, however, not quite so ready to comply with his wishes as he had hoped, a fact that made the monarch exceedingly wrathful.

'His Majesty is most firmly bent upon a divorce,' writes Mr. Bankes to Lord Colchester; 'but, as those who must carry his project into effect very naturally cast about and calculate their means, his Ministers report to him unanimously that it is *not feasible*, and neither can nor ought to be attempted. He perseveres. He insists most obstinately. The Ministers *positively refuse.* He threatens to dismiss them all, to which they reply that they are ready and willing to retire from his service.'

Lord Castlereagh, in writing to Lord Stewart, confirms this statement; the Ministers received from the King, his Lordship states, 'a written minute with a distinct intimation that, if they were not prepared to advise His Majesty to proceed by way of divorce, his determination was taken, namely, to change his Government; and, if he could not form a Government which would relieve him *to that extent*, His Majesty's intention was to retire to Hanover.'

His Ministers, even when threatened with so stupendous

a loss as the absence of His Majesty's sacred person from a nation that abhorred him, hesitated in condemning a powerless and persecuted woman; they were willing, however, to temporise, and consented to have her name omitted from the Liturgy of the English Church service, and to deny her the honour of coronation. With this the King was obliged to be satisfied for the present. The omission of her name was an insult which the new Queen felt deeply—not that it entailed her any spiritual loss, if the effects of the nation's prayers for the members of the royal family might be judged by their conduct, but because it was a grievous insult to her dignity. She therefore wrote at once to the Premier in a note that betrayed far more spirit than knowledge of English—

'The Queen of this relams wishes to be informed, through the medium of Lord Liverpool, First Minister to the King of this relams, for which reason or motife the Queen name has been left out of the general Prayer-Books in England, and especially to prevent all her subjects to pay her such respect which is due to the Queen. It is equally a great omittance towards the King that his consort Queen should be obliged to soummit to such great neglect, or rather araisin from a perfect ignorance of the Archbishops of the real existence of the Queen Caroline of England.'

To this communication she received no reply. Earl Grosvenor afterwards remarked that, 'feeling as he did the evils which the erasure of the Queen's name from the Liturgy was likely to entail upon the nation, as well as its repugnance to law and justice, he would, had he been Archbishop of Canterbury, have thrown the Prayer-Book in the King's face sooner than have consented to it.'

She now resolved to return to England, and for this purpose passed rapidly through France. This movement had not been expected by the King, who believed and desired she would never return. Lord Hutchinson was therefore hastily despatched to meet her, and make her certain offers. Her income had ceased, Parliament having only granted it to her as Princess of Wales, and she was depending in a great measure on the present Government, who were the King's tools, and her avowed enemies. Lord Hutchinson was therefore commissioned to offer her a bribe of £50,000 for life, on condition that she would not assume the title of Queen of England, or any title attached to the royal family of England, and that she should not reside in or visit any part of the United Kingdom. Fearing she might refuse this offer, Lord Liverpool begged to inform her confidentially that 'the decision was taken to proceed against her as soon as she sets her foot on the British shores.'

This proposal she at once rejected with scorn; her spirit, she said, was yet strong, and she would go to England and demand justice of the nation. She then dismissed her foreign attendants and set out for Calais. During her absence her popularity had not flagged, and the spirit she displayed in bearding the royal lion in his den went far towards increasing it, whilst even her enemies admitted that such an act was not like that of a guilty woman.

Arrived at Dover, she was received by a royal salute, as no orders to the contrary had been received by the garrison; already vast numbers had collected to receive her, and she, being impatient to land, got into an open boat and was rowed to shore. The instant she landed she was received by a shout of welcome, that was renewed again and again with ever-increasing force. The horses were taken from the carriage which was to convey her to the York Hotel, and she was drawn through the streets by a right eager crowd, preceded by a band playing a triumphal march; whilst two large flags, bearing the inscription, 'God save Queen Caroline,' waved at either side of the carriage. A guard of honour was placed at the door of the hotel, but as its presence did not seem to please the people, the Queen sent word to thank the commandant and to decline the guard, as her reliance was placed on the first principles and cordial attachment of the people; the military then played 'God save the King' and retired.

A few hours after her landing, a deputation presented her with a congratulatory address, the first of hundreds which were to follow; and after a short rest, she got into her carriage, which was once more drawn by the people outside the town; the horses were then put in, and she proceeded to Canterbury. It was almost dark when she reached that city, where she was met by a procession bearing over a hundred flambeaux, whilst again the horses were removed from the carriage, and she was drawn by an excited crowd to the Fountain Hotel. But this was not all; at the inn, the gallant mayor and his aldermen brave were waiting to receive Her Majesty, and to offer her, in fine ponderous phrases, their pompous congratulations. In the morning the scene of the previous evening was renewed; the streets, windows, and balconies were lined with people; the mob drew the carriage; the church bells rang, cheers filled the air, and everywhere were signs of rejoicing.

Her journey to town was indeed one continued triumph, which reached its climax as she approached London. At Dartford, a number of horsemen came to meet, and greet, and accompany her on her way, whilst at Shooter's Hill, hundreds of vehicles of all descriptions joined the procession, which now increased every moment. At Blackheath all kinds and conditions of men and women were awaiting her arrival; they received her with deafening cheers, and followed in her wake to town. Here all business was suspended; dense crowds filled the thoroughfares through which she passed; handkerchiefs were shaken, hats tossed in the air, bands played, banners waved, and cheers greeted her everywhere. The procession now extended for miles, and was headed by a goodly cavalcade, which bent its mischievous way up Pall Mall, so as to pass His Majesty's royal residence, Carlton House. As it approached the palace, the cheers gained fresh strength, and loud were the repeated huzzas announcing the Queen's arrival, which were as gall and wormwood to the kingly soul of the royal monarch within, whose wrath was passing great. The merry crowd swept on in triumph to South Audley Street, the residence of Alderman Wood, the Queen's friend, where she was obliged to stay for some days, as no house had been prepared for her reception. When she had entered the mansion, the crowd blocked the street from end to end, and showed no disposition to disperse until she appeared at the balcony, and acknowledged the loyal feelings of her subjects by many smiles and curtsies.

On that same day, June 6, 1820, His Majesty sent a message to the House of Lords, stating he considered it necessary. in consequence of the arrival of the Queen, to communicate certain papers respecting her conduct since her departure from the kingdom. He added that he had the fullest confidence Parliament would adopt that course of proceeding which the justice of the case and the dignity of His Majesty's crown required. This message was delivered by Lord Castlereagh to the House of Lords, and by Lord Liverpool to the Commons; and each of these gentlemen laid before him on the tables of the respective Houses a green bag, supposed to contain the papers relative to the Milan Commission.

Next day Mr. Brougham delivered a message from Her Majesty, in which she informed her faithful Commons she had been induced to return to England in consequence of measures pursued against her honour and peace by secret agents abroad, whose conduct was sanctioned by the Government at home. It was fourteen years, she reminded them, since the first cruel investigation was made into her conduct, from which fiery ordeal she had come forth scathless. She now desired an open investigation, in which she might see both the charges and the witnesses against her, a privilege not denied to the meanest subject in the realm. She loudly protested, in the face of the Sovereign, the Parliament, and the country, against a secret tribunal to examine documents privately prepared by her adversaries, a proceeding unknown to the law of the land, and a flagrant violation of all the principles of justice. . From this, the only danger she had any reason to fear, she appealed to the House of Commons to protect her. These preliminaries over, the fight commenced.

On the following day Lord Liverpool moved that a select committee of fifteen Lords be chosen to examine the papers relative to the Queen. The chairman of the committee was Dr. Manners Sutton, Archbishop of Canterbury. Having taken this step, the Ministry were anxious to ascertain how far they would be supported by their friends. The result of this inquiry was that a large portion of the community were strongly adverse to the proceedings; and some members of the House of Commons who declared themselves friends alike of the King and Queen, suggested that an amicable arrangement of the unhappy business might be concluded. To this the Queen was not adverse, and the Duke of Wellington and Lord Castlereagh, on the part of the King, and Mr. Brougham and Mr. Denman, on the part of Her Majesty, were selected as men best fitted for the management of the negotiations. These, however, proved unsatisfactory. The case, therefore, went on, and the report of the committee selected to examine 'certain papers connected with Her Majesty's conduct,' gave it as their judgment that those 'documents contained allegations charging her with an adulterous connection with a foreigner, originally in her service in a menial capacity; and attributing to Her Majesty a continued course of conduct highly unbecoming Her Majesty's rank and station, and of the most licentious character.'

The day after this report was made, Lord Dacre presented a petition from the Queen, stating that she was ready to defend herself from these gross charges, and praying that she might be heard through her counsel; this was refused, the excuse being given that such a proceeding was irregular. Lord Liverpool then introduced the Bill known as 'An Act to deprive Her Majesty, Caroline Amelia Elizabeth, of the title, prerogatives, rights, privileges, and exemptions of Queen-Consort of the realm, and to dissolve the marriage between His Majesty and the said Caroline Amelia Elizabeth.' This Bill charged her with carrying on 'a licentious, disgraceful, and adulterous intercourse' with Bartolomeo Bergami. When Her Majesty was served with a copy by Sir Thomas Tyrwhitt, she received it with an emotion which she in vain sought to conceal. Had the prosecution commenced a quarter of a century earlier, she remarked, it might have suited her husband's purpose better. 'But,' she added, 'as we shall not meet in this world, I hope we shall in the next, where justice will be rendered me.'

This Bill, the first of its kind introduced since the days of Henry VIII., was regarded as a vile proceeding, which might serve as a dangerous precedent. As Lord John Russell begged to remind His Majesty, in a letter to that gracious personage, which pointed a moral, 'in uncrowning a head without necessity, we see much to alarm us in the example, nothing to console us in the immediate benefit; not,' says his Lordship, remembering that he addressed a monarch, the first of whose line were a century before as strangers in a strange land, 'not that we do not recognise the right of Parliament to alter the succession to the Crown; none respect more than we do the Act of Settlement which took away the Crown from its hereditary successors, and gave it to the House of Brunswick.' Then follows a hint that

Parliament might be called on to regulate the succession once more. The *Times* powerfully stigmatized the Bill, and spoke of the desired divorce as 'an infamous object sought through illegal means'; it pointed out that, instead of the divorce following the proof of adultery, the charge was made and the divorce sought for in the same Bill. 'It would be little less remarkable,' it added, 'if the divorce were passed first and the adultery were proved afterwards.'

The Queen, through Lord Dacre, petitioned the House of Lords against the Bill; the only alleged foundation for it, she urged, was the report of the secret committee, proceeding solely on papers submitted to them, and before whom no single witness had been examined. She pointed out that her counsel had been refused a hearing at the bar, at a stage of the investigation when it was most natural they should be heard, and that a list of the witnesses, whose names were known to her accusers, was refused her; she therefore protested against the whole proceedings, and once more prayed that her counsel might be admitted to state her claims at the bar of the House of Lords. Her counsel, Brougham and Denman, were then, when refusal was no longer possible, admitted, and Brougham asked for a delay of two months previous to further proceedings, in order to enable the Queen to summon her witnesses for the defence; this was finally allowed.

During this cessation of hostilities, Her Majesty addressed a long and stirring letter to her husband, setting forth her violent wrongs and protesting her innocence.

'When to calumniate, revile, and betray me became the sure path to honour and riches, it would have been strange indeed if calumniators, revilers, and traitors had not abounded.' She said, 'Your Court became much less a scene of polished manners and refined intercourse than that of low intrigue and scurrility. Spies, bacchanalian tale-bearers, and foul conspirators swarmed in those places which had before been the resort of sobriety, virtue, and honour.' Speaking of the Bill, she continues, 'I must either protest against this mode of trial, or, by tacitly consenting to it, suffer my honour to be sacrificed. No innocence can secure the accused if the judges and the jurors be chosen by the accuser; and if I were tacitly to submit to a tribunal of this description I should be instrumental in my own dishonour.' She finally concludes: 'You wrested from me my child, and with her my only comfort and consolation. You sent me sorrowing through the world, and even in my sorrows pursued me with unrelenting persecution. Having left me nothing but my innocence, you would now by a mockery of justice deprive me even of the reputation of possessing that. The poisoned bowl and the poignard are means more manly than perjured witnesses and partial tribunals; and they are less cruel, inasmuch as life is less valuable than honour. If my life would have satisfied your Majesty, you should have had it on the sole condition of giving me a place in the same tomb with my child; but, since you would send me dishonoured to the grave, I will resist the attempt with all the means that it shall please God to give me.'

This letter, from which these extracts are taken, being inserted in many of the daily papers, published as a pamphlet, freely circulated, and posted on almost every wall in the metropolis, served in no small measure to rouse up the bitterest feelings against the King and his Ministers. The whole nation from end to end was dangerously excited against the measures about to be taken, and the sympathy felt for the Queen was almost universal. Public meetings were held in almost every parish and county in England, when votes of confidence in her innocence were passed, and hopes that she might escape from the toils of her enemies were expressed; whilst the corporations of all the principal cities and towns in England, headed by the Common Council of London, presented her with addresses. These deputations were generally followed by enormous crowds, which usually shaped themselves into processions, with bands and banners; so that from the day of her landing until weeks after the termination of the trial, London was kept at a fever-pitch of excitement. Nor was the object of the general enthusiasm at all averse to it.

'I have derived,' she said, in reply to one of these presentations, 'unspeakable consolations from the zealous and constant attachment of this warm-hearted, just, and generous people, to live at home with, and to cherish whom will be the chief happiness of the remainder of my days.'

Meanwhile, preparations for the great trial were being rapidly made, and the Italians selected to bear evidence against the Queen—who, it was generally understood, were to be liberally rewarded—were summoned to England. Arriving at Dover, they were treated roughly by a large crowd, who had gathered to give them a warm reception; and, but for the protection of the military, it is doubtful if they would ever have seen London town. When there, however, they were scarcely less open to danger; and the Ministry, after having moved them from one residence to another, finally shipped them off to Holland, until such time as their presence was necessary in the House of Lords. When that period arrived, they were conveyed at night from the docks in an open boat, rowed with muffled oars, and lodged at Cotton Garden, close to Westminster. The Queen announced her intention of being present in the House of Lords every day during her trial.

After a short residence at South Audley Street, a house was procured for her in Portman Street, from where she moved to Brandenburgh House, near Hammersmith, where volunteer sentinels kept nightly watch over her safety. But Brandenburgh House being considered too inconvenient a residence for her during the trial, she gratefully accepted an offer made her of a house in St. James's Square by the widow of Sir Philip Francis. Driving from this residence every day to Westminster, she was obliged to pass Carlton House, at which point of her journey the cheers of the crowd, who invariably accompanied her, were pitched in a higher and more defiant key.

On August 17 this trial, which will be for ever memorable in the history of this country, commenced. The Queen, accompanied by her faithful friend, Lady Anne Hamilton, drove to the House of Lords in a new state carriage drawn by six bay horses, and preceded by her chamberlain and Alderman Wood in a carriage drawn by four horses; vast crowds lined every inch of her route, and she was received by the heartiest acclamations. Never, indeed, had the public been so demonstrative; loud cries of 'The Queen! the Queen!—long live Queen Caroline!' were shouted, and taken up by the throng, long before her carriage came in view; whilst the house-tops were crowded, as well as the windows and balconies, by those anxious to catch sight of her. Her Majesty, according to an eloquent description in the daily papers, was dressed in black, 'with a rich white lace veil, which flowed gracefully over her shoulders, and hung like an antique vestment over her dress.'

Preparations had already been made at Westminster to withstand the expected crush, or any rebellious outbreak of the multitude; the whole area in front of the House of Lords was enclosed by double rows of strong timber fences; within this a large body of constables were placed, under the orders of such dignitaries as the high bailiff and the high constable, all being in attendance before seven o'clock in the morning. A body of the Foot Guards were posted at the King's Bench Office and the Record Office; gunboats were stationed at the river side of Westminster Hall; a troop of Life Guards formed a line in front of the principal gate; a detachment of Foot Guards were posted under the piazza of the House of Lords; a body of the Surrey Mounted Patrol paraded Parliament Street, Whitehall, and Charing Cross; whilst another detachment of the Life Guards rode through Abingdon Street. It seemed, indeed, as if a battle were about being fought instead of a cause being tried.

Arrived at the House of Lords, the Queen was received with military honours, and conducted by Sir Thomas Tyrwhitt and Mr. Brougham to the place assigned her near her counsel, where a throne-like chair and cushion were fixed for her. At her entrance into the House, the Peers rose to their feet and bowed, and she acknowledged the courtesy with dignity and grace. The first days of the trial bore but little interest, with the exception of that aroused by a speech of Brougham's, in which he referred to the Queen's generosity, which induced her to refrain from all recrimination, and mentioned the unusual circumstance of the defendant in a divorce case being prevented from exposing the guilt of the accuser. The trial could have but one aspect in the eyes of the people, he remarked, and they will naturally say, 'Here is a man who wishes to get rid of his wife; he talks of the honour and safety of the country, yet its dearest interest, its peace, its morals, and its happiness, are to be satisfied to gratify his desires.'

After the King's Attorney-General had opened the case for the plaintiff, those who were to bear witness against the Queen were called, the first of whom was Theodore Majoccni, formerly in Her Majesty's service. He had no sooner appeared than Her Majesty, overcome for the moment, exclaimed, 'Oh, traitor!' and at once retired to the apartment allotted to her use; nor did she again appear in the House of Lords during that day. Majocchi was the principal witness, and the sum and substance of his evidence was that a tent had been erected on the deck of a vessel in which the Queen sailed, that she slept in the tent, and that Bergami slept there also; furthermore, that

Bergami attended her when in her bath. This evidence was regarded as damning by her enemies, and even her friends grew fearful of the result. It was the best card the prosecutors had to play, and the King's Solicitor-General, Copley, made the most of it by purposely protracting his examination until such time as he hoped its effects had sunk so deeply into the public mind that they could not be dispelled by any subsequent contradiction.

When Copley had finished, Majocchi was subjected by Brougham to a most searching and rigorous cross-examination, which had the effect of tearing his evidence to shreds, and utterly demolishing him. It was shown that though Bergami rested beneath the same tent with the Queen, the tent was open on all sides, as was rendered necessary by the heat of the climate; that sailors passed to and fro continually; that the light of a tropical sky rendered it possible to see all that passed within the tent at any hour; and that whilst in the bath she invariably wore a bathing costume. A cloud of witnesses followed, and a very dark cloud they were. One of these, Rastelli, was another servant of the Queen's, whom she had discharged for robbery. So palpable were the lies uttered by this rogue, that those who had summoned him became heartily ashamed of him, and sent him quietly away before his re-examination could take place. Another of them, Louisa Demont, had formerly passed herself off as the Countess Colombier. This distinguished lady had also been dismissed from the Queen's service, and in her cross-examination admitted she 'had not spoken true,' whilst at the same time a light was thrown on the motives which had induced her to favour this country with her presence. She had received a mysterious letter without a signature, proposing that she should set off for London under the pretence of being a governess, and promising that in return for her compliance she would be rewarded with ' high protection and a brilliant fortune in a short time': she was also informed that she might draw on a certain bank for whatever amount she pleased. As Brougham reminded the Lords, the witnesses which the Crown had ventured to call were every-one of them irreparably damaged in their credit: their testimony he characterized as 'inadequate to prove a debt, impotent to deprive of a civil right, ridiculous to convict of the lowest offence, scandalous if brought forward to support a charge of the highest nature which the law knows, monstrous to ruin the honour, to blast the name of an English Queen.'

The witnesses who were brought forward in favour of Her Majesty included Lords Guilford, Glenberrie, and Llandaff, Lady Charlotte Lindsay, Sir William Gell, and Sir J. P. Beresford, all of whom had been in her company abroad, and who had failed to see any improprieties in her conduct. The case for the Crown closed on September 7, and the House adjourned till October 3, when Brougham defended his royal client in a speech remarkable for its power and eloquence, which delighted, and even surprised, the most sanguine of his friends. But if it astonished his friends, it appalled his adversaries by its boldness. 'He declared,' says Rush, 'that nothing should check him in fulfilling his duty, and that he would recriminate upon the King if necessary. He said that an English advocate could look to nothing but the rights of his client; and that even should the country itself suffer, his feelings as a patriot must give way to his professional obligations.' His speech made a strong impression on his hearers, and this was increased by Denman's forcible words which followed. The debates which ensued were stormy. Earl Grey declared if the Bill passed it would prove the most disastrous step the House had ever taken: he charged the servants of the Crown with the grossest neglect of duty, in the first instance in listening only to *ex parte* evidence, and giving a willing credence to the most exaggerated and unfounded calumnies : whilst Lord Grosvenor said, that sooner than remain one of His Majesty's Administration, he would, 'under such circumstances as the present, have trampled upon the seals of office.'

But the Lords temporal were not more divided amongst themselves than the Lords spiritual. The Archbishop of York, and some minor luminaries of the Church, refused to recognise a divorce; but his Grace of Canterbury proving himself to be a man of principles, ingeniously contrived to shift when necessary, and informing such of their Lordships as might entertain any foolish conscientious scruples about parting those whom God had joined together, that divorces were consistent with his Master's word : nay, 'he must tell their Lordships that they were directly and expressly declared to be lawful by our Saviour Himself.' On hearing which, the Right Reverend Father in God, the Bishop of London, jumped on his ecclesiastical feet, and gave his testimony that 'divorces were authorized by our Saviour': he furthermore added, for the benefit of his unenlightened and uncourtly brethren, the information, equally religious and true, that 'the King could do no wrong ; he could not commit a fault, far less a crime.' Strange to say, there were those among his hearers who laboured in such gross and heretical darkness as not to believe the words of this spiritual teacher ; and the height of profanity was reached next day when an epigram, which ran as follows, gained circulation, relative to his wise speech—

> 'Not commit any folly nor do any wrong,
> May be said or be sung as a very good song ;
> But what, don't *you* own then, in this maxim so starch,
> He can add to a Bishop the prefix of Arch'—

whilst the daily papers reminded the Archbishop of Canterbury of Wolsey's fate, and thought that in a little while he might find the famous lines, 'Had I but serv'd my God with half the zeal I served my King, he would not in mine age have left me naked to mine enemies,' applicable to his own case.

When the votes were taken against one clause of the Bill, the majority against the Queen was twenty-eight; and she at once signed a protest against the proceedings. Her Majesty, this document said, 'now most deliberately, and before God, asserts that she is wholly innocent of the crime laid to her charge.' When the House divided on the question, 'That the Bill be now read a third time,' there were one hundred and eight contents and ninety-nine not contents, which left the Crown a majority of nine, the exact number of Peers who were members of the Cabinet. Lord Liverpool, after a short deliberation, then rose and said he could not be ignorant of the state of public feeling regarding the measure, and that the Crown had come to the conclusion of not proceeding further with it.

The Queen was in her apartment in the House of Lords when news was brought her that the Bill had been abandoned. She received the intelligence in silence, and with perfect composure, not perhaps knowing how it would affect her, but on reaching her carriage burst into a tempest of tears. Though nominally the Crown had gained the day, yet it was felt that in reality Her Majesty had triumphed, and the rejection of the Bill was regarded, as the famous Lord Erskine said, as 'the victory of right and justice over wrong and malignity.'

During the great trial the people had continued in a state of excitement bordering on revolt; and this feeling was largely and dangerously shared in by the military. One regiment of cavalry vowed they 'would fight up to their knees in blood for the Queen'; whilst Lord Brougham tells us, in his 'Life and Times,' that during the examination of Majocchi, when the evidence seemed most unfavourable to Her Majesty, the Guards, in their undress trousers and foraging-caps, came to a house where her friends were and called out, 'Never mind; it may be going badly, but, better or worse, we are all with you;' for which language they were ordered out of London, but mutinied at Kingston. On another occasion the military stationed at the mews at Charing Cross, who had betrayed symptons of discontent at the crowded state of their barrack, were invited by the mob to come out and join them in a demonstration for the Queen; heaven only knows what might have happened, but that Lord Sidmouth, who chanced to be riding by, seeing the imminent danger, galloped to the Horse Guards at full speed, and called out a troop of the 2nd Life Guards to quell this revolutionary spirit. It was indeed believed by many that, if the Duke of Kent, the most popular member of his family, were living, a revolution would have broken out in his favour, and the country have been steeped in the horrors of civil warfare.

This fact was fully recognised at the time, as there is abundance of evidence in the public press and private correspondence of the period to show. Even the Attorney-General, as the Right Hon. Thomas Grenville writes to the Marquis of Buckingham, 'in his speech yesterday in the House of Commons, used the expression "that there was no doubt that a revolution was in contemplation."'

The storm of public abuse which burst over the King's head was daily added to by publications the most keenly satirical, personal, and abusive, all of which His Majesty, who lived in strict seclusion during this time, thought well to overlook.

Denman, the Queen's counsel, in his famous speech, which had followed Brougham's, had compared His Gracious Majesty to Nero, and the *Times* had followed suit by contrasting him with Henry VIII., to the favour of the latter; upon which hints, the general press ransacked history for the most infamous characters it contained, and placed them on a parallel with the Sovereign Lord and King. Pamphlets, scurrilous poems, and ridiculous caricatures were issued almost hourly, and many of them are yet preserved in our national library. Amongst the most popular of these publications were, 'A Peep at the Divan,' 'Nero Vanquished,' 'The Degraded Son,' reciting, in a brief manner, his infamous career from his youth up until now, 'Caroline and the Italian Ragamuffins,' 'The Bag of Lies,' 'John Bull Peppering the Italian Rascals,' 'Gorgeous Whelp' (Guelph), and 'The Acts of Adonis the Great,' 'Sultan Sham and his Seven Wives.' 'Gorgeous Whelp' was a poem, sung to the air of 'Robin Adair,' and ran as follows:

> 'I am but just threescore,
> > Gorgeous Whelp.
> My wife! ah, there's the bore,
> Haunts me on sea and shore!
> > Gorgeous Whelp.
>
> 'She haunts me up and down,
> > Gorgeous Whelp;
> She wants to crack my crown;
> I'll go to Colonel Brown.
> > Gorgeous Whelp.'

This strain was continued through many verses.

Caroline and the Italian Ragamuffins' enjoyed wide celebrity, and was boldly sung in the public streets to large crowds; whilst another satire, 'The Acts of Adonis the Great,' was written in Scriptural style, and, as an instance of the liberty allowed the press, may be quoted:

'And it came to pass, in the reign of Guelpho, King of Bull, there was much murmuring throughout all the land.

'For the King's son Gorge, which, being interpreted in the Bullish, signifieth *Great Eater and Drinker*, had done evil in the sight of the law, and had committed drunkenness and debauchery in high and low places.

'Moreover, he had dwelt with concubines and evil counsellors, and had filled the land with abominations and uncleanness, and had wasted the treasure of the children of Bull in debauchery, and the tradesmen of Bull wept, and put on sackcloth and ashes; for he was deep in their debt, and they mourned that they could not recover it.

'And they cried out, with loud voices, "Oh, Gorge, thou son of Guelpho, pay thy people."

'And the King's son was troubled at the words of the children of Bull, and he smote his whiskers, and cursed them.

'And he took unto wife Enilorac, the daughter of Brun.

'But the concubines and evil counsellors were wroth that he had taken her to wife, seeing that he would no longer give unto them riches and much treasure.

'And they conspired together to fill his heart with lies, and they tempted him, and mocked his wife Enilorac.

'And they made him drunk with wine; and he mocked her also.

'And there was murmuring all over the land, and the people hated Gorge, because he had dared to mock Enilorac his wife.

'And Gorge was drunk with wine every day, from the rising of the sun to the going down of the same, and his face was bloated with drink, and the tip of his nose was of a blue colour.

'Now King Guelpho waxed old, and his sight departed from him, and his senses fled, and he was like a new-born infant.

'And the nobles of the land and the captains of the hosts and all the wise men gathered themselves together, and they mourned because of the exceeding weakness of the King.

'And they said unto each other, "It is fitting we should have another ruler, seeing the King can no longer govern his people," and they appointed Gorge his son to reign over them.

'And they called him Re-gent, which, in the Bullish language, signifieth, "No longer blackguard," and all the people prayed he might alter his ways, and do that which was right.

'And he was two score and eighteen years old when he filled the seat of his father, and he wore a wig of many curls.

'And Queen Snuffy, his mother, died, and she was buried in the sepulchre of the Princes of Bull.

'And she bequeathed unto her loving son Gorge a huge vessel of Strasburg, and tears came into his eyes.

'And the people put on black garments, and the tobacconists mourned over all the land, and there was a fall in the price of snuff of one silver sixpence in the pound.

'And Enilorac, his wife, said unto her counsellors, "Wherefore should I tarry longer in the land, seeing my husband setteth an evil example and debaucheth the morals of the people? Verily I say unto ye, I will leave this land, and travel to some far country, for my husband protecteth me not, neither endeavoureth he to do good unto me."

'And she departed out of the land, saying, "My husband Gorge disregardeth his marriage vow, neither careth he for my welfare."'

Perhaps the height of irony was reached when addresses were proposed to be offered to His Majesty, to congratulate him on 'the happy escape of his illustrious consort from the snares of her enemies;' and the depth of ridicule sounded by the following advertisement:

'STRAYED AND MISSING.

'An infirm elderly gentleman in a Public Office lately left his home, just after dreadfully ill-using his wife about half-a-crown, and trying to beat her. He had long complained a great deal of his forehead, and lately had a leech put upon him. He was last seen walking swiftly towards the Horns without a crown to his hat, accompanied by some evil-disposed persons, who tied a great green bag to his tail full of crackers, which he mistook for sweetmeats, and burnt himself dreadfully. Every person he met in this deplorable condition tried to persuade him to go back, but in vain. He is very deaf and very obstinate, and cannot bear to be looked at or spoken to. It is supposed he has been carried off by some artful female. He may be easily known by his manners. He fancies himself the politest man in Europe, because he knows how to bow and to offer a pinch of snuff; and he thinks himself the greatest man in Europe, because people have humoured him and let him have his own way. He is so fond of tailoring that he lately began a suit that will take him his life to complete. He delights in playing at soldiers, supposes himself a cavalry officer, and makes speeches that others write for him in a field-marshal's uniform. Sometimes he fancies himself "Glorious Apollo." His concerns are very much deranged. Not long ago he imported a vast quantity of Italian images at enormous prices upon credit; since then things have gone all against him, and he has been in a very desponding state. It is of the utmost consequence to himself that he should be at his post, or he may lose his place, one of his predecessors some time ago having been cashiered for his misconduct. If this should meet his eye, it is earnestly requested that he should return to his duty.'

Nor was it at the King alone that these poison-tipped arrows were driven. One, at least, of his royal brothers came in for a share of them; this was the Duke of Clarence, afterwards known as His Sacred Majesty William IV. He had once been the most friendly member of his family towards the Queen, but had in her days of danger not only forsaken, but grossly calumniated her.

Rush narrates that Denman, when making his famous speech, turned to where this Royal Duke sat, and, fixing his eyes on him, called out, 'Come forth, thou slanderer!' When, according to the *Morning Chronicle*, the Lords gave their votes on the Queen's Bill, they generally 'preserved decorum on whichever side they determined; but the Duke of Clarence, a Prince of the blood royal, brother-in-law and cousin-german to the accused, distinguished himself from all others by the vehemence of his manner.' Shortly after the trial, Turner, of Aldersgate Street, published a pamphlet which commenced—

'ABSCONDED.

'The Slanderer, a broad-faced, naval gentleman, about fifty-five years of age, accustomed to slander, and late an inhabitant of the river Jordan. He was last seen in the gallery of a place of public entertainment; and has lately been particularly anxious to disseminate lies and other improprieties, in the hope of obtaining a crown which had been slily offered him,' etc.

But the whole of this pamphlet will not bear republication.

CHAPTER XVIII.

The Queen's Thanksgiving—The Coronation and the King's Vanity—Exclusion of Her Majesty and its Effects—Her Death and Remarkable Funeral—Riots and Bloodshed—The King with his Irish Subjects—O'Connell and the Modern Cæsar—The King's Seclusion—His Eccentric Life at Windsor—The Marchioness of Conyngham and her Despotic Rule—The King's Last Days—His Love of Mimicry—His Hallucinations and Death.

THE people were satisfied with the victory which the Queen had gained, and rejoiced over it exceedingly; for three successive nights London was illuminated, and presented a blaze of light from end to end. 'A town relieved from a twelve-month's siege,' says the *Morning Chronicle*, 'could not have displayed more tumultuous gladness.' Bands patrolled the streets; bonfires blazed in the squares; the effigies of those who had borne false witness against the Queen were paraded through the town, and hung high upon a mimic gallows; the windows of houses which exhibited no lights were ruthlessly smashed; the residences of Lords Castlereagh and Liverpool were guarded by the military; and great was the general excitement.

Amongst the first to call on Her Majesty and offer her their congratulations were Prince Leopold and the Duke of Sussex; the latter had been summoned to the House of Peers by the Lord Chancellor for the second reading of the Bill, but had stoutly refused compliance. Their example was quickly followed by numbers of the nobility; many old friends flocked round her, and addresses poured in on her by the hundred. Her triumph had such effect that the Funds rapidly rose, 'and have,' says the *Times*, 'continued rising since the receipt of intelligence in the City that this Bill, this nightmare on the national credit and tranquillity, had vanished into the regions of utter darkness whence it originated.' Immediately after her trial she applied to the Premier to be furnished with a suitable residence and provision; to which Lord Liverpool replied, the King had no intention of permitting her to reside in any of the royal palaces, but the allowance she had enjoyed would be continued to her. A subscription was then set on foot for the purpose of building her a palace 'at once befitting the dignity of the Queen, the gift of the people, and their sympathy in her sufferings from the first moment of her landing on the English shore.' Large subscriptions were received, and, had she lived, the palace would no doubt have been erected.

She now determined to proceed to St. Paul's in state, there to return public thanks for her recent delivery from the hands of her enemies. When intimation of this was given by the Lord Mayor to the Dean and Chapter of the cathedral, they were by no means ready to lend their aid towards carrying out the necessary arrangements, having already received due instructions from high quarters. Lord Sidmouth, in a letter to the Dean, Dr. Van Mildred, Bishop of Llandaff—a mild and paternal shepherd, who had expressed himself in favour of the royal divorce, and had been obliged to take refuge from a flock that had ousted him from his parish of Ewelme—regretted 'it was wholly out of the power of the Government to prevent Her Majesty's intention of attending divine service at St. Paul's Cathedral from being carried into effect.'

It was arranged by the ruling powers that no special service should be held; that the doors of the church should be thrown open to the public as upon ordinary occasions; and, moreover, that the Lord Mayor and Corporation would be held responsible for any injury the cathedral might sustain. On November 30, the Queen came in such state as she could summon, and was attended by a voluntary guard of honour, consisting of fifty horsemen and an immense number of people. She was received at Temple Bar by the Lord Mayor, sheriffs, sword-bearer, and many members of the Corporation, who conducted her to the City. The church was crowded to excess, but it was noted that two seats were vacant, the Bishop's throne and the Dean's seat, both of these good men having written to the Lord Mayor prohibiting them from being used. All that the Dean and Chapter could do to lessen the effect of the service was carefully done. In the Litany no mention was made of the Queen's name, and in the general 'thanking,' Mr. Hayes, one of the minor canons, who was the officiating clergyman, omitted the particular thanksgiving which it had been customary to offer up at the request of any individual, and which the Queen had desired might be offered on her behalf.

When the service was over, Her Majesty and the procession returned in the same manner as they had come, and, notwithstanding the great and excited crowds which surged through the thoroughfares, no injury was done. Even the saintly Bishop of Llandaff afore-mentioned admitted that 'this strange exhibition had gone off with less disgrace to the country than might have been expected; although, after all,' added his spiritual Lordship, 'it had been a mockery of religious solemnity at which every serious Christian must shudder.'

Her Majesty was destined to appear at but one more public celebration, and then the curtain descended upon the troubled drama of her life for evermore. This was at the coronation of the King, fixed for July 19, 1821, a pageant celebrated with much pomp and state, and all that theatrical effect so dear to His Majesty. For days and nights he held grave council with his friends and flatterers as to the dresses, colours, and combinations which were to make up this fine show, in which he was to be the observed of all observers, and which cost the nation the sum of £250,000. His Sacred Majesty intended to surround himself with such royal magnificence as would dazzle the eyes of his subjects, and no expense was therefore spared. His own robes, which were to be worn but a few short hours, cost his subjects the extravagant sum of £25,000, and so charmed was his royal soul by their splendour, that he had one of his servants dressed up in them, and ordered him to parade up and down the apartments, whilst His Majesty lay back in his chair lost in rapture and admiration at their effect. The King afterwards had his picture taken in these robes, and so proud and delighted was he with the presentment of his magnificence, that he sent copies of it to all the Courts and British embassies in Europe.

The Queen had addressed a letter to her royal spouse, praying that she, his lawful wife, might also be crowned, to which prayer a brief answer was returned by Lord Liverpool, informing her she 'could form no part in the ceremonial.' Not intimidated by this reply, she petitioned the Secretary of State for the Home Department to the same effect, when she was informed she had 'neither claim nor right to the ceremonial.' However, Her Majesty was not yet willing to give up the point, and she announced her intention of being present at the coronation as one of the audience, if she could not be one of the actors, and demanded of Lord Sidmouth that a suitable place might be provided for her. His Lordship, in return, informed her His Majesty would not allow her to be present. She was, however, determined that she would, and, notwithstanding that her legal advisers begged of her to abandon the resolution, she, accompanied by Lady Anne Hamilton, Lord Hood, her present Chamberlain, and Lady Hood, drove to Westminster in a carriage drawn by six horses.

The people, faithful to her to the last, hailed her as usual with cheers, and accompanied her to the Abbey; the cries of 'The Queen, the Queen!' were heard within the sacred walls, and the doors were immediately bolted on the inside. Never was there such a remarkable scene. Already a dense and motley crowd had collected in the vicinity, to witness as much of the royal pomp as might be vouchsafed to their hungering eyes. Men pushed their way with good-humoured violence, women struggled and shrieked, curses and laughter fell on the ear, and above the loud din could be heard the voice of authority, speaking through the lips of Mr. Townshend, the Bow Street officer, a little man in a flaxen wig and a broad-brimmed hat, crying aloud, 'Gentlemen and ladies, take care of your pockets, for you are surrounded by thieves.' Alas! this warning had fallen too late on the ears of one who had travelled a far way, a Welsh gentleman, who replied to the Bow Street officer:

'Mr. Townshend, Mr. Townshend, I have been robbed of my gold watch and purse containing all my money. What am I to do to get home? I have come two hundred miles to see this sight, and, instead of receiving satisfaction or hospitality, I am robbed by those cut-throats called the swell-mob.'

The crowd evinced no sympathy for this sorrowing gentleman, whom it merely laughed at, and to whom it replied in an odd manner by singing 'Home, sweet Home,' mingled with cries of 'Get back to your goats, my good fellow.' On his remonstrating with his mocking, yelling enemies, now dancing round him in derision, his hat was beaten over his eyes, his neckcloth dragged from his neck and the clothes from his body; for the London rough was then, as now, a terrible and unholy specimen of humanity.

The crowd now followed the Queen to the principal entrance of the Abbey, where she presented herself for admission. The officer on guard demanded her ticket, when she replied that as Queen of England she needed none; on which he expressed his regret, but said he must obey his orders and admit none but those who held tickets. Deeply humiliated, Her Majesty turned away and, attended by her little band of friends, went to the other doors, where she repeated her demand for admission and was again repulsed; as a final insult, a file of soldiers were formed across the platform to prevent her proceeding farther. With a broken heart she left the scene, and in less than a month from that time death had ended all her troubles.

The continued excitement under which she had laboured for months brought on a disease from which she knew there was no recovery. 'I know I shall die,' she said quietly, 'and I don't regret it.' Though she had but little to leave, she made her will, caused her diary, which had been kept for years, and which contained many strange pages, to be burned in her presence, and spoke forgivingly of her enemies. Her death took place on the 7th of August, 1821. 'I desire,' she said in her will, 'that the inscription on my coffin be, "Here lies Caroline of Brunswick, the injured Queen of England.'

Lord Sidmouth hurried to Holyhead to communicate the intelligence of her demise to the King, who had a little while before started to visit his Irish subjects. Five days after that on which she died His Majesty landed in Ireland, and the spot on which his royal foot was first set is unto this day marked by a monument erected by his most grateful Hibernian subjects.

His Majesty's passage to Dublin was, according to the Duke of Buckingham's 'Memoirs of the Court of George IV.,' 'occupied in eating goose-pie and drinking whisky, of which His Majesty partook most abundantly, singing many joyous songs, and being in a state, on his arrival, to double in sight even the numbers of his gracious subjects assembled on the pier to receive him. The fact was that they were in the last stage of intoxication.'

Hours before he landed a vast crowd had collected on the shore, all eager to catch a glimpse of the burly-figured, mutton-chop-whiskered, rubicund-complexioned, elderly gentleman, daintily attired in a blue frock-coat and pantaloons, with Hessian boots and a little foraging-cap bedizened with gold lace stuck jauntily on his head. In their excess of enthusiastic loyalty and at the rare sight of royalty, some of the people shed tears, and all of them cheered him to the echo.

The pious and portly monarch extended a hand somewhat unsteady, cased in a white silk glove, over them, and prayed, in rather husky tones, that God would bless them ; for which they filled the air with the sound of loud acclamations, and in return His Majesty removed the little foraging-cap from his kingly brow again and again. He then drove to the Viceregal Lodge, where he made the crowd which had followed him a very remarkable speech, to which they listened with great respect and much amazement.

He was obliged (invariably pronounced 'obligeed' by the royal lips) to them for their reception ; 'particular circumstances' (he said, alluding to the Queen's death) 'have occurred, known to you all, of which it is better at present, he added in confidence, 'not to speak ; upon these subjects I leave it to your delicate and generous hearts to appreciate my feelings.' In the next sentence he, with characteristic delicacy, assured them this was the happiest day of his life, and imparted to them the astonishing information that his heart had always been Irish ; 'from the day it first beat,' he said, 'I have loved Ireland.'

But neither this assurance nor what followed was too strong for his hearers, who loved to be flattered as well as to flatter. Rank, station, and honour His Majesty held as nothingness and vanity; but to live in the hearts of his Irish subjects was to him the most exalted happiness. He would give a proof of his affection to them that day by drinking their health in a bumper of Irish whisky, and he hoped they would do the same unto him. His Majesty, it may be added, forgot to give the barefooted and ragged crowd who had tramped after him nine miles to the Vice-regal Lodge the means of following his royal advice; but waving his tinsel-adorned cap to them once more, he disappeared within the Lodge.

Meanwhile the Government, acting under special instructions from the King, made speedy preparations for the Queen's funeral. She had desired to be buried in Brunswick; and August 14 was the day fixed for the *cortège* to start for Harwich. Lady Hood addressed a letter to the Premier, asking that some delay might be made, as the ladies who were to accompany the Queen's remains had not time to prepare. To which a brief answer was made, that if the ladies were not ready, they might stay behind, and, when convenient to themselves, might join the procession on its route. Common courtesy had not been paid the Queen during her life, and common respect was denied to her remains. Her Majesty's friends were refused information as to the route by which the funeral would proceed.

The most direct way lay through the City, and the Lord Mayor and Corporation made ready to receive the royal remains at Temple Bar and accompany them to Whitechapel. The Government, however, privately determined that the procession should not pass through the City, and that the people should not be permitted the opportunity which would be afforded them, if the body were allowed to pass through the principal streets, of paying their last tributes of sympathy and respect to one whose life had known persecution and sorrow. They kept their peace, however, until the morning of the 14th. On that day, when Sir George Naylor, who was instructed by the Government to see their directions carried out, arrived at the Queen's residence, and entered the apartment where the royal body lay, he was met by the few intimate friends of the Queen, headed by Dr. Lushington, who censured the steps taken by those in authority.

'I enter my solemn protest,' said the doctor stoutly, 'in right of the legal power which is vested in me by her late Majesty as executor. I command that the body be not removed till the arrangements suitable to the rank and dignity of the deceased are made.'

His words might as well have been addressed to empty air. The remains were at once removed, and the procession —bereft of all signs of state and dignity, save for the attendance of a squadron of cavalry, whose presence was intended to quell all popular demonstrations—set out, followed by her late Majesty's legal advisers, physicians, and few friends, most of whom drove in their private carriages. The sky was overcast, the day gloomy, and torrents of rain fell unceasingly; yet the road was thickly lined with people, who, having heard of the intention of conveying the body through the byways and the outskirts of the City, showed by their excited and threatening manner that, in spite of all opposition, they were determined to have the Queen's remains spared this last insult, and have them carried through the streets of London.

All went well until the procession reached Kensington Church, when an attempt was made by those in authority to turn the *cortége* up Church Street into the Bayswater Road, in order to avoid the City, when a hoarse cry went up from the assembled thousands, mingled with groans and hisses; but this indication of the people's feelings not having the desired effect, they pressed forward, quickly dug up the road, and, in an incredibly short space, barricaded it so effectually that progress was impossible. Sir Richard Baker and a company of Life Guards were now sent for, but, their services being of no use, orders were given that the direct road to London should be taken. The people celebrated this victory with ringing cheers; and once more this strange, but far from solemn, procession wended its unseemly way.

However, the Government were as determined as the crowd that their will should not be thwarted; and orders were at once sent to Sir Richard Baker and the commander of the Life Guards that the remains of this most sad and uncrowned Queen should be taken through Hyde Park into the Edgware Road, and so avoid the City. When the procession, therefore, arrived at Hyde Park Corner, another scene was enacted. The crowd, whose numbers were now much increased, seeing the intention of those in authority, firmly held the gates, crying out, in a voice of thunder, 'The City! the City!' Deaf to this appeal, an attempt was made to cross the Park; but the resistance of the populace proved too strong, and an effort was then made to proceed down Park Lane. This was likewise defeated; but, whilst the attempt was being made, and the attention of the people directed to this spot, part of the procession forced its way into the Park, and its entrance was quickly followed by the soldiery, who closed the gates on the people. The royal remains were now quickly trotted across the Park, followed by the disorganized cavalry; but, before they could reach Cumberland Gate, the crowd had rushed round the walls, and were ready to meet them. The people were now furious in their excitement, and resolved to have their desires carried out at any sacrifice. Packed closely together, they made all further progress impossible. A halt was therefore made; but as no signs of turning back were given, the exasperated crowd pulled down a great part of the Park wall, and commenced to fling stones at the soldiers and officers; in return a volley was fired, which had the effect of killing two men and wounding many. Frightened and subdued for the moment, the crowd gave way, and the Queen's remains were galloped towards the Edgware Road. Meanwhile the people, always mighty when united, had recovered their first surprise, and now, more enraged than before, barricaded the road in such a manner that it was impossible for the procession to proceed without the aid of artillery.

Sir Richard Baker, fearing more bloodshed, and the probable destruction of many lives, yielded to the wishes of the people, and, after the royal remains had been for seven hours exposed to the uttermost humiliation, and driven, now here, now there, through a pitiless storm of wind and rain, they were at last forced down Drury Lane into the Strand. For the consideration and humanity which Sir Richard Baker showed in not following out the blindly obstinate wishes of the Government, and refusing to risk the lives of soldiers and civilians, he lost his office of chief magistrate, by the King's desire.

At Temple Bar the funeral was met by the Lord Mayor, who, in virtue of his office as City King, forbade the Life Guards to cross the barrier marking the boundary of his kingdom. He and his Corporation attended the remains as far as Whitechapel, from whence they were taken to Colchester, and allowed to rest the night at St. Peter's Church. The plate bearing the inscription, 'Here lies Caroline of Brunswick, the injured Queen of England,' was at dead of night affixed to the coffin, but was ruthlessly wrenched off next morning, and replaced by another, on which her name and date of her death were merely inscribed.

Arrived at Harwich, the coffin was conveyed with little ceremony to the frigate *Glasgow*, followed still by a few faithful friends—Lord and Lady Hood, Lady Anne Hamilton, Count Vassali, and Dr. and Mrs. Lushington. On

August 24 the remains reached Brunswick, where they were placed between those of the deceased's father and her brother, in the vaults beneath the church of St. Blaise; and here at last this most unhappy woman was allowed to rest in peace.

The King returned to London, on September 15, from his visit to the Emerald Isle, where he had eaten many heavy dinners, drunk more bumpers of whisky punch than was good for him, and made many flowery and foolish speeches. On departing, he once more blessed his loyal Irish subjects, and told them, with a voice which emotion and a too liberal libation of whisky had helped to make unsteady, that he 'felt depressed with sincere sorrow' at leaving them; he had 'never felt sensations of more delight,' strange to say, than when he arrived, and now he could not 'expect to feel any superior, nor many equal, till,' says he, 'I have the happiness of seeing you again.' Alas! Providence spared the Irish people the pleasure of seeing him once more.

When he was about to embark, Daniel O'Connell, followed by a deputation of ten gentlemen, arrived, and, going down on their loyal knees on the pier, presented this modern Cæsar, in hessians and a little foraging-cap, with a laurel crown. The King graciously raised up Daniel, shook hands with him, and paid him a compliment. Some time after, when the Liberator attended one of His Majesty's levées, royalty ungraciously turned its broad back on him, and took no notice of him, beyond muttering to its next neighbour, 'Damn the fellow! what does he come here for?'

Shortly after his return from Ireland, His Majesty visited his faithful Hanoverian subjects, and finally permitted the light of his countenance to shine in brief splendour upon the Scotch, who had remained long the enemies of the house of Guelph. These visits seemed to have exhausted his love for display; when he returned from the 'land o' cakes,' he was seen by his subjects but three times in public; once when he prorogued Parliament, and twice when he visited the theatres.

During the last six years of his life, the world saw him not. Even his beloved Brighton, the scene of his lavish expenditure and Oriental voluptuousness, was forsaken for the seclusion of Windsor. Here he indulged his taste for building by erecting the Chinese and fishing temples; and occasionally diverted his elegant leisure by fishing in, and sailing on, the Virginia Water. This self-sought retirement was, however, brightened by the presence of the Marchioness of Conyngham, a woman of great attraction and easy virtue, who exercised a sway over this ruler of three kingdoms which lasted tell his death. She had indeed cheered his stay in Ireland by her presence, the royal yacht having been sent to Holyhead to convey her to Dublin.

'I never in my life,' writes Fremantle to the Marquis of Buckingham, 'heard anything to equal the King's infatuation and conduct towards Lady Conyngham. She lived exclusively with him during the whole time he was in Ireland at the Phœnix Park. When he went to Slane, she received him dressed out as for a drawing-room. He saluted her, and they then retired alone to her apartments.'

With the beauty of an angel, the Marchioness possessed the wisdom of the serpent, and moulded the mighty Sovereign in all things to her will. At her desire, Ministers rose and fell; shepherds, with a salary of some thousands per annum, were appointed to govern their spiritual flocks; favourites were raised to high places, and enemies humbled to the dust. Nor did her Ladyship forget what was due to herself and her family. Her nominal Lord, by virtue of his position as her husband, was created a Marquis; likewise a Lieutenant-General in the army; likewise a Judge of the Marshalsea Court, and of the court of the King's palace;

likewise Lord Steward of the King's household and Constable and Lieutenant of Windsor Castle; whilst her eldest son, Lord Mount-Charles, was appointed Master of the Robes to the King, salary £4,000, and Groom of the Bedchamber, salary £500. She herself is said to have received half a million of money from her royal slave, besides jewels of exceeding great value, one of which was a large sapphire, an heirloom of the Stuarts, presented by Cardinal York to George III. When Regent, the King had given this to his daughter, but at her death had asked it from Prince Leopold, making the excuse that it was one of the Crown jewels. At the King's death it was with some difficulty obtained from the Marchioness, whose attractive person it had long adorned.

'The King,' writes Charles Greville, Clerk of the Privy Council, 'continues to heap all kinds of presents upon Lady Conyngham, and she lives at his expense; they do not possess a servant; even Lord Conyngham's *valet de chambre* is not properly their servant. They all have situations in the King's household, from which they receive their pay, while they continue in the service of the Conynghams. They dine every day while in London at St. James's, and, when they give a dinner, it is cooked at St. James's and brought up to Hamilton Place in hackney-coaches, and in machines made expressly for the purpose; there is merely a fire lit in their kitchen for such things as must be heated on the spot. A more despicable scene cannot be exhibited than that which the interior of our Court presents—every base, low, and unmanly propensity, with selfishness, avarice, and a life of petty intrigue and mystery.' The same authority tells us that, during the King's last illness, 'waggons were loaded every night and sent away from the Castle, but what their contents were, was not known.'

Watchful and jealous of the position she held, avaricious and far-seeing, it became her policy to exclude the outer world as far as possible from his sybaritic Majesty, and keep him bound in the chains of her evil fascinations, within that charmed circle over which she held absolute sway. She carried out her project with such skill, that in a short time the royal voluptuary completely immured himself within the walls of Windsor Castle, and his people knew him but by name. So strict a watch did she keep over him that, according to Lord Colchester's diary, dated March, 1820, 'The Chancellor told Sir T. Tyrwhitt that, since Lady Conyngham was at Windsor, he had never been suffered to enter those gates, except once that he was sent for when Lady Conyngham was absent.'

From want of exercise and too free an indulgence in cherry-brandy, the kingly form—once padded, pinched, decked in silks, satins, tawdry tinsels, and French paste, until its beauty dazzled humanity—became unwieldy; and the royal countenance, once bewigged and bepowdered so beautifully that its mere glance was rapture, its smile intoxication, now grew terribly bloated. Therefore, his vain but sacred Majesty, who feared ridicule more than aught else in life, grew sorely sensitive to the gaze of all eyes, and shunned them as much as possible, because, as the Duke of Wellington told Charles Greville, 'he is afraid of the jokes that may be cut on his person.' When he fished in the Virginia Water, or visited the gimcrack temples he had erected, the only person allowed to accompany him was his beloved Marchioness; and when he honoured the menagerie at the lodge with his presence, strict orders were given that no one was to be admitted. When he went out in his pony-chaise, if any persons were seen on the road in the park, the ponies' heads were turned sharply round, and His Majesty drove in a contrary direction, to escape even the casual glances of his subjects. The Reverend George Croly tells us that the Monarch seldom rode in the long walk from the Castle, because he feared to meet the Windsor people on his way to Frogmore. 'His most private way,' he continues, 'was through a small gate in the Park wall, opposite another small gate in the walls of the grounds at Frogmore, at the Datchet side. He there crossed the road in a moment, and had rides so arranged between Frogmore and Virginia Water that he had between twenty and thirty miles of neatly-planted avenues, from which the public were wholly excluded. At certain points of these rides which open towards the public thoroughfares of the Park, there were always servants stationed on these occasions to prevent the intrusion of strangers upon the King's privacy.'

The irreverent gaze of workmen continually employed in making repairs and alterations at Windsor soon became more than he could brook, and sent him into towering passions. One day, when Captain Gronow called at the royal residence on Sir Benjamin Bloomfield, they were suddenly surprised by the entrance of His Majesty, who, in a royal rage, without any ceremony, shouted out, 'I will not allow those maid-servants to look at me when I go in and out; and if I find they do so again I will have them discharged.' 'I could hardly believe my ears,' says the captain, 'that a man born to the highest rank could take umbrage at such pardonable curiosity. But while riding in Hyde Park the next day, I was joined by General Baylie, who told me that the King constantly complained of the servants staring at him, and that strict orders had been given to discharge anyone caught repeating the offence.'

The older he grew, the more eccentric His Majesty became, and the more extraordinary his mode of life. The suite of rooms he inhabited he caused to be artificially heated until they were overpowering to all who entered them. About seven in the morning the window-curtains of his bedroom were opened, yet he, during the last years of his life, never rose till six o'clock in the evening, though being at the same time perfectly well in health. Here, lying in bed, he breakfasted, and during the day he drank many glasses of his favourite cherry-brandy, read such letters as were delivered to him, received such visitors as were permitted him; the Marchioness and her noble family being regularly amongst the number. He delighted to keep those who came to see him on business of State waiting for hours in an antechamber, whilst he 'cut his coarse jokes with all the coarse merriment which is his characteristic' with the pages and menials around him; or listened to all the gossip and scandal which his surgeon, O'Reilly, could tell him, His Majesty being 'the greatest master of gossip in the world,' whose 'curiosity about everybody's affairs is insatiable.' When the surgeon had duly discharged his budget and turned his back, his royal master confided his opinion to the pages that O'Reilly was 'the damndist liar in the world.'

At six o'clock this King, by the grace of God, rose, and allowed himself to be dressed; then visited his beloved Marchioness in her apartments for an hour, after which he dined, principally on vegetables and pastry, of which he was excessively fond.

'His conduct,' says Captain Gronow, 'from being that of a sensual, greedy old man, became that of a spoilt child; and the way he spent his time was frivolous in the extreme. He was very fond of punch, made from a recipe by his *maître d'hôtel*, Mr. Maddison, and which he drank after dinner; this was the only time he was agreeable, and on these occasions he would sing songs, relate anecdotes of his youth, and play on the violoncello; afterwards going to bed in "a comfortable state." But, though he retired in this condition, his sleep was short and restless; he rang the bell forty times during the night, and tossed about wearily until morning, when the same daily programme was gone through. The Duke of Wellington told Mr. Raikes that, when the King sent for him to form a new Administration, in 1828, he found His Majesty 'dressed,' said the Duke, ' in a dirty silk jacket and a turban night-cap, one as greasy as the other; for, notwithstanding his coquetry about dress in public, he was extremely slovenly and dirty in private. The first words he said to me were, " Arthur, the Cabinet is defunct ": and then he began to describe the manner in which the late Ministers had taken leave of him in giving in their resignations. This was accompanied by the most ludicrous mimicry of the voice and manner of each individual, so strikingly like, that it was quite impossible to refrain from fits of laughter.'

Mimicry was indeed a thing in which he excelled, and which afforded him vast amusement. By the exercise of this talent he gained considerable applause when he, lying in bed, gave some capital imitations of his stud-groom, Jack Radford, for the benefit of his *valet de chambre* and his pages. His hallucinations were also remarkable, but took a more amusing turn than those of his late father. When he had dined, and had become garrulous, he was wont to tell those around him, including the Duke of Wellington, of the Battle of Waterloo. He had so often dressed himself in the uniform of a field-marshal, that at last he came to believe himself a man of right valiant deeds, and spoke of the manner in which he had charged the French with the Household Brigade. On one occasion he told the Iron Duke that he, the King, had 'completely bowled over the French cavalry commanded by Marshal Ney.' The Duke listened to him with the patience due to royalty, and, when he had finished his foolish speech, replied :

'I have heard you, sir, say so before; but I did not witness this marvellous charge. You must know that the French cavalry are the best in Europe.'

The idea of having, by his great achievements in this famous battle-field, overthrown Napo'eon, and given peace to Europe, was one which had haunted him for years,

Sheridan, who had once heard him make this boast, said, when he had quitted his presence, 'That is well enough, but what he particularly piques himself upon is the last productive harvest.' On another occasion the King said he remembered old Lord Chesterfield, the polite letter-writer. The famous Earl, His Majesty declared, had said to him, '"Sir, you are the fourth Prince of Wales I have known, and I must give your Royal Highness one piece of advice —stick to your father; as long as you adhere to your father, you will be a great and a happy man, but, if you separate yourself from him, you will be nothing, and an unhappy one;" and, by God,' added the King, 'I never forgot that advice, and acted upon it all my life.'

'We all,' said the Duke of Wellington, who told the story, 'looked at one another with astonishment.'

No wonder they looked at each other, remembering the shameful conduct of the King to his father, and their disgraceful quarrels. But His Majesty went still further with his delusions, and told his friends that the late King—who had feared and detested his eldest born, and had thanked God that of all his sons his heir alone was a coward—said to him, 'Of all the men I have ever known, you are the one on whom I have the greatest dependence; and you are the most perfect gentleman.'

Towards the last years of his life, he was threatened with loss of sight.

'He is in a great fright,' writes Charles Greville, 'with his father's fate before him, that he will become blind and mad too; he is already a little of both.'

It was also reported that he suffered from gout in the knee, but Fremantle, now made treasurer to His Majesty's household, writes to a friend:

'I rather suspect it is more in the mind, the disease, than in the knee.'

So his useless, burdensome life, voluptuous and petty,

magnificent and mean to the last, passed on, and in May, 1830, prayers were offered to heaven in the churches all over the land that God in His wisdom and justice might spare this august Monarch to his people; it being quite well understood at the same time that his life could not possibly last many months. He suffered from gout, affection of the heart, and dropsy, but he had no apprehensions of his own death, nor even of his immediate danger, and his physicians, being thorough courtiers, up to this time withheld from shocking his royal nerves by insinuating that anything so natural as death could approach him. In these his last days he was friendless, and would have been alone save for his paid sycophants. All his life he had posed as a fine gentleman, and had found many to believe him such; he had dressed himself in gaudy stuffs, had worn five thousand steel beads on his hat, and had invented a new buckle for his shoes; his bows outrivalled those of his French dancing-master, his smiles were pronounced irresistible, his deportment grace itself; but behind this outward show all was false; the puppet, perfect in its dress and movements, was stuffed with bran, and there was no trace of heart, honour, or manhood to be found in its composition. He lied to and deceived men; he flattered and ruined women; was insincere to his friends; cajoled and cheated his creditors; hated and imposed on his Ministers; and burdened his people in the days of commercial depression by boundless extravagance. With prize-fighters,[2] jockeys, tailors, and money-lenders he was familiar; but the petty German pride he inherited never permitted him to be friendly with his aristocracy. Such he had been through life, and, now that his last days had come, none were found to regret his inevitable death.

On the night of June 25, 1830, having paid his accustomary visit to the Marchioness, he retired to bed, without feeling any symptoms of illness, but at two o'clock he suddenly awoke in great agitation, and called out for assistance. Sir Wathen Waller was soon by his bedside, and raised him up.

'They have deceived me,' he whispered fearfully, his bloated face wild from terror, his whole frame quivering; then came the terrible cry, 'O God, I am dying!' and with one short gasp he fell back dead.

An immense and costly wardrobe, which he left behind, is said to have been sufficiently various and splendid for Drury Lane Theatre. It contained uniforms of every sort, the costumes of all the orders in Europe, magnificent furs, pelisses, hunting coats, and breeches without number. 'His profusion,' says Greville, 'in these articles was unbounded, because he never paid for them, and his memory was so accurate that one of his pages told me he recollected every article of dress, no matter how old, and that they were always liable to be called on to produce some particular coat or other article of apparel of years gone by.' He had long enjoyed, and was proud of, the distinction of being the best-wigged prince in Christendom and the best-dressed man in Europe; but the attainment of such honours was costly—to the nation.

'Incredible as it may appear,' writes Mr. Raikes, 'I have been told by those about him, and by Bachelor, who entered his service as *valet de chambre*, that a plain coat, from its repeated alterations, would often cost £300 before it met his approbation. This, of course, included the several journeys of the master and his men backwards and forwards to Windsor, as they almost lived on the road.'

His effects included the finest collection of snuff-boxes in England; he seemed to have had a passion for them, and in the early days of the Regency he had called on the Government to pay the sum of £22,500 for these articles, which he had presented to foreign ministers during the previous thirty months. His belongings also contained three hundred whips, canes of all shapes and sizes, a vast number of wigs, five hundred pocket-books of different dates, and in every one of them money; gold was also found scattered through all his boxes, the whole sum of which amounted to £10,000. There were other things, too, in the strange collection which told a sad tale of the useless, profligate, flippant life of the owner; among them a vast quantity of women's hair, of all colours and lengths, some locks having the powder and pomatum yet sticking to them; also a heap of women's gloves, *gages d'amour*, with the perspiration still marked on the fingers; a quantity of trinkets, many of which were discovered to be mere showy, useless trash, for the most valuable had been already secured by Lady Conyngham, those in her possession being estimated to be worth £80,000; and, finally, notes and letters in abundance.

The King was dead, but there was no sign of mourning in the royal household, nor did the nation mourn. His next brother, the Duke of York, having also passed away, His Royal Highness of Clarence was proclaimed King, and the world went on its way as usual; then came the day appointed for the committal of his late Majesty into kindred dust.

'The funeral of George IV.,' says Huish, 'was a positive jubilee. Crowds hastened to witness the pageantry of the spectacle; but not on a single countenance was observed an expression of grief. The Park was thronged with joyous parties, and shouts of revelry and mirth were interrupted only by the firing of the minute-gun, of the rolling of the carriages conveying the *mourners* to the ceremony. Under one tree was heard the glee of "When Arthur first at Court began," and at another, "A merry King, and a merry King, and a right merry King was he"; whilst in the streets of the town, in the immediate vicinity of the Castle—where lay, in all the magnificence of royalty, and all the littleness and insignificance of humanity, the putrefying remains of England's Sovereign defunct—a kind of fair was held, where the life and portrait of the late King of blessed memory were to be had for one penny; and the amours of the Marchioness of Conyngham, as a necessary appendix, for a penny also. It was intended to be a holy-day, but it was a genuine *bona-fide* holiday.'

The evidence of Charles Greville, who was also present, may be added:

'The ceremony,' he writes, 'was very well managed, and a fine sight, the military part particularly, and the Guards were magnificent. The attendance was not very numerous, and, when they had all got together in St. George's Hall, a gayer company I never beheld; they were all as merry as grigs. The King was chief mourner, and to my astonishment, as he entered the chapel directly behind the body, in a situation in which he should have been apparently, if not really, absorbed in the melancholy duty he was performing, he darted up to Strathallan, who was ranged on one side below the Dean's stall, shook him heartily by the hand, and then went on nodding to the right and left.'

So passed away a King who, by the many vices of his character, earned the detestation of his people.

'He was, indeed,' said the Duke of Wellington, 'the most extraordinary compound of talent, wit, buffoonery, obstinacy, and good feeling that I ever saw in any character in my life;' while Greville, who also knew him, writes : ' The littleness of his character prevents his displaying the dangerous faults that belong to great minds, but with vices and weaknesses of the lowest and most contemptible order, it would be difficult to find a disposition more abundantly furnished . . . a more contemptible, cowardly, selfish, unfeeling dog does not exist

than this King on whom such flattery is constantly lavished.'
Praed has written his epitaph in graphic lines :

> 'A noble, nasty course he ran,
> Superbly filthy and fastidious ;
> He was the world's first gentleman,
> And made the appellation hideous.'

THE END.

www.ingramcontent.com/pod-product-compliance
Lightning Source LLC
Chambersburg PA
CBHW020538300426
44111CB00008B/712